VAX-BASIC
with
Structured
Problem Solving

Second Edition

DAVID G. WEINMAN

HOLLINS COLLEGE

BARBARA L. KURSHAN

JANUS LEARNING CENTER

Prentice Hall, Englewood Cliffs, NJ 07632

Library of Congress Cataloging-in-Publication Data

WEINMAN, DAVID G.
    VAX-BASIC with structured problem solving.

    Rev. ed. of: VAX-BASIC. c1983.
    Includes index.
    1. VAX-11 (Computer)—Programming.   2. BASIC
(Computer program language)   I. Kurshan, Barbara L.
II. Weinman, David G.   VAX-BASIC.   III. Title.
QA76.8.V37W44 1987   005.265   87-25737
ISBN 0-13-940990-4

**Editorial / production supervision and
    interior design: Ellen B. Greenberg
Cover designer: Lundgren Graphics, Ltd.
Manufacturing buyer: Cindy Grant**

Printed in the United States of America
10 9 8 7 6 5 4 3 2 1

ISBN 0-13-940990-4   025

Prentice-Hall International (UK) Limited, *London*
Prentice-Hall of Australia Pty. Limited, *Sydney*
Prentice-Hall Canada Inc., *Toronto*
Prentice-Hall Hispanoamericana, S.A., *Mexico*
Prentice-Hall of India Private Limited, *New Delhi*
Prentice-Hall of Japan, Inc., *Tokyo*
Simon & Schuster Asia Pte. Ltd., *Singapore*
Editora Prentice-Hall do Brasil, Ltda., *Rio de Janeiro*

**To Ellen and Richard and our children
for their understanding**

Contents

APPENDICES 299

Preface to the
Second Edition

This text is designed as an introduction to computer programming using VAX-II BASIC. The book could also be used in a course for some subjects which require programming as a tool. No familiarity with computers is assumed, and there are no prerequisites beyond high school algebra. The majority of the material can be covered in a one semester course.

The emphasis is entirely on writing usable programs. We do stress thinking before attempting to write a program, but do not follow any rigid set of rules for writing programs only the generally accepted rules of structured programming. In particular, we do not use flowcharts or pseudo-code, but these can be added easily if the instructor wants to do so.

We also emphasize writing well-structured programs. Roughly, a program is well-structured if a reader can easily see what the program is doing and how it accomplishes its purpose. We follow several commonly accepted conventions that make programs easy to read.

The sequence of topics in the book is approximately in the order we follow in our elementary programming course. We strive to cover program control early in the course, and we are convinced that the IF statements (Chapter 4) should be covered before FOR/NEXT loops (Chapter 5).

Chapter 6 on program control introduces WHILE and UNTIL loops and subroutines, which are a very important part of structured programming. We strongly recommend following the book through Chapter 6 (new), but after that, topics can be chosen in almost any order desired.

The major changes in the second edition of this book are:

1. An expanded treatment of files. Chapter 8 (all new) introduces terminal format files, the simplest files in VAX-BASIC. Chapter 11 treats sequential files and

gives a brief introduction to relative files. Chapter 12 is entirely new; it discusses indexed files which allow very easy access to the data stored in them.

2. More discussion of structure in programs, particularly in the expanded discussion of WHILE and UNTIL loops, but also spread throughout the book.

3. More extensive discussion of error handling, primarily in relation to files.

4. The old Chapter 7, Advanced Print Commands, has been dispersed into other chapters to allow an earlier introduction to the printing of well formatted output.

5. Some new features in VAX-BASIC Version 3.0, such as the MAX, MIN, and MOD functions, the OPTION ANGLE = DEGREES statement, and subscript bounds set by the programmer.

Several new features in VAX-BASIC Version 3.0 have not been included because they are beyond the scope of this book. In particular, we have stayed with the older ON ERROR statement instead of introducing the new and more versatile (but also more complicated) WHEN_ERROR statement.

The draft for the book was stored on our VAX computer and printed using the editor and RUNOFF formatter. The table of contents and index were generated on the VAX using the RUNOFF index utility.

We hope you find this book useful. If you have any comments, favorable or otherwise, about the book, please write to us.

Barbara Kurshan   David Weinman

Computer Science   Statistics

Janus Learning Center Hollins College

Acknowledgments

First, we would like to extend a big "Thank you" to everyone who used the first edition of the book. If not for you, there would not be a second edition.

Special thanks to Walter Neilsen-Steinhardt of Digital Equipment Corporation and Professor Roland Sussex of the University of Melbourne, Australia, for providing detailed criticisms of the first edition. Both were exceedingly helpful and had a great impact on the shaping of the second edition.

We are grateful to the reviewers of both editions for their many helpful comments, most of which were incorporated into the book. A special thanks to William Radulovich of NOVA University, Alicia M. Kime of Alderson-Broaddus College, Keith B. Olson of the Montana College of Mineral Science and Technology, Karen M. Wilson of the University of Hawaii, and Richard A. Dilling of Grace College.

Thanks to all the many students who have taught us much about teaching programming, and the slightly smaller number who assisted in the production of the book. Particular thanks to Lisa Gray who supplied the answers to nearly all the programming exercises, proofread, and offered many helpful suggestions.

We are especially grateful to Barbara McClarrin for supervising the entire production process of the first edition at Hollins College and to Melody Blankenship for performing similar duties for the second edition, including proofreading, indexing, checking programs, and loading the manuscript onto diskettes that were sent to the publisher.

Special thanks go to Caren Diefenderfer, Susan Smith, Scott Stuart, and Ellen Witt, who taught from the notes for the text and made several valuable suggestions.

Introduction

A. WHAT IS A COMPUTER?

We will not give a full answer to the question, since this is not a book in computer architecture. Our working definition is: A computer is an electronic device that can store and manipulate data according to a stored set of instructions, and uses the instructions to operate on the data.

Most of our data will be numbers but data can also be words, or more generally strings of printable characters. We can instruct a computer to store 10,000 numbers and calculate their sum, or we can store 5,000 names in the computer and instruct the computer to sort them into alphabetical order. The computer is ideally suited to tasks like these because it can store vast amounts of data and it operates with incredible speed.

The VAX is a digital computer; it stores data as binary digits, or bits. We usually call the binary digits 0 and 1, but in the computer bits are represented by current flowing in one of two possible directions. Instructions are also stored in the computer as a series of bits. Fortunately, you do not have to know this "bit language" to use the computer. You can use a language closer to your own English, the BASIC programming language.

B. WHAT IS BASIC?

The name BASIC stands for Beginners All-Purpose Symbolic Instruction Code. BASIC was first developed at Dartmouth in the middle 1960's. Like most living languages, the original BASIC spawned a large number of dialects, or innovations. You may hear names such as TRUE BASIC, CALL BASIC, MICRO-SOFT BASIC, DARTMOUTH BASIC, BASIC PLUS, and a host of others.

The BASIC version used in this book is VAX-11 BASIC, which we generally shorten to VAX-BASIC. (To be even more specific, we are using VAX-11 BASIC, Version 3.0.) VAX-BASIC was developed by Digital Equipment Corporation (DEC) for use on its VAX computers. VAX-BASIC is certainly one of the most powerful versions of BASIC; it contains many features not found in other versions. Yet, as the name BASIC implies, it is an easy language for beginners to learn.

VAX-11 BASIC is virtually identical to BASIC-PLUS-2, which runs on the PDP-11 family of computers built by DEC. All the example programs in the first edition have been run unchanged in BASIC-PLUS-2. There are many other versions of BASIC that are very similar to VAX-BASIC.

To know everything in the VAX-BASIC language you would have to know over 300 keywords (listed in Appendix A). However you can start writing programs after learning only 4 keywords, and you can write meaningful programs if you know fewer than 20 keywords. This entire text discusses only about 80 keywords; it is an introductory text. (Even VAX-BASIC does not use all the keywords; some are merely reserved for possible future use.)

Since all BASIC languages have much in common, you *can* use this book to learn about any version of BASIC. If you are using some other version of BASIC, you should have at least: a reference manual for the version of BASIC you are using; the patience to flip back and forth between that manual and this text; and the courage to experiment to find out what works.

C. WHAT IS A PROGRAM?

Recall we said that a computer operates "according to a stored set of instructions". That's what a program is; a stored set of instructions. When you write a program, you are storing instructions in the computer. The rest of this book is devoted to writing programs.

Does the computer understand (in any sense) what you put in it? No! The computer is a machine. It cannot know or understand anything. How than can it use your instructions? There is a "super-program" in the computer that translates your program into instructions that the machine can carry out. This program is called the VAX-11 BASIC compiler. Roughly, you can think of compiler as meaning translator. Your computer probably contains several compilers for other languages such as FORTRAN, COBOL, and PASCAL.

Because the computer is a machine, and without intelligence, you have to be very specific when you give instructions to a computer. People can speak very imprecisely and still be understood (sometimes) because the listener is an intelligent being. You will discover that the computer does exactly what you tell it to do, and this will sometimes be dismaying. Don't be disturbed when the computer takes you literally; it can't help it. You, intelligent as you are, can help it. Learn to be precise when situations call for precision.

A final word of encouragement; do experiment with the computer. If this book or your instructor tells you one way to do a problem, and you think of another way that might work, try it. Or if you think, "I wonder what the computer will do if I _____", try it. You can learn a lot by experimenting, and the computer is non-judgmental if your experiment doesn't work or takes an extensive amount of time to perfect.

VAX-BASIC
with
Structured
Problem Solving

Second Edition

Getting Started in VAX-BASIC

1

To learn any computer language, you need to be able to get onto the computer. That is called *logging on* or *logging in*.

1.1 LOGGING IN

Before you try to log onto the computer, someone in authority must give you a USERNAME and a password. To log on:

1. Turn the terminal on and wait a moment for the screen to warm up. [We assume that you are using a cathode ray tube (CRT) terminal—that is, a terminal with a TV-like screen.]
2. Press the RETURN key. (We usually abbreviate this to ⟨RET⟩.)
3. The computer should type

   Username:

   Type in your username and ⟨RET⟩.
4. The computer should type

   Password:

1

Type in your password and ⟨RET⟩. As you type your password, it will *not* show up on the screen. This is to keep your password secret so that others cannot use your account.

The computer should now type a message, such as WELCOME TO VAX-VMS, and a dollar sign ($) at the left margin. The $, called a *prompt,* is the VAX's way of telling you it is ready for you to give it a command. If you get instead a message such as "Unauthorized Password," start over at step 2 by pressing ⟨RET⟩.

When you have the $ at the left margin, you may use any command in the Digital Command Language (DCL). This language is as rich as BASIC, but we will use only a few of its commands, and these will relate to getting on or off the machine and using the VAX-BASIC language.

To get the BASIC language facility, type BASIC (or BAS) and ⟨RET⟩ after the $. The log-in and getting into BASIC should look like the following (assuming you type in caps):

```
Username: DJONES  <RET>      (<RET> will not show on the screen.)
Password:          <RET>     (Your password will not show.)

              Message from the VAX-VMS System

$ BAS <RET>

VAX BASIC Version xxx

Ready
```

The word "Ready" from BASIC is a prompt, like the $ from DCL. It signals that BASIC is ready for you to type in commands or programs.

1.2 THE PRINT STATEMENT

The PRINT statement is indispensable in BASIC. It is the only means BASIC has of writing results, calculated by a BASIC program, on your terminal screen. Nearly every program you write will contain at least one PRINT statement.

You can cause the computer to print any characters you wish by typing PRINT followed by those characters inside double quotes. For example,

```
PRINT "HELLO" <RET>
```

will cause the computer to print

```
HELLO
```

The item inside the quotes is called a *literal string*. BASIC literally copies the item. A PRINT statement used this way is called an *immediate mode* statement because the computer executes, or carries out, the statement immediately. We will discuss statements in *program mode* in the next chapter.

The BASIC PRINT statement is sometimes called a "calculating" PRINT statement, because numerical calculations can be contained in the PRINT statement. For example,

```
PRINT 6 + (12 + 9) / 7 <RET>
```

will cause the computer to print

```
9
```

However, if you type

```
PRINT "6 + (12 + 9) / 7" <RET>
```

the computer will type

```
6 + (12 + 9) / 7
```

BASIC does not try to translate or calculate anything you have enclosed in quotes.

You probably know that the asterisk (*) is used to signify multiplication. Symbols for the other arithmetic operations should be familiar to you: + for addition; − for subtraction; and / for division. It is a common error to forget the multiplication sign, since it is often omitted in algebra. Most people would know what 6(12 + 9) / 7 means, but the computer requires the asterisk: 6 * (12 + 9) / 7.

The Comma

If you want more than one piece of information printed on one line, separate the items to be printed by a comma. The command

```
PRINT "The answer is", 9*5 - 6*4 <RET>
```

causes the computer to print

```
The answer is 21
```

The command

```
PRINT "Area =", 6*5 <RET>
```

will result in

```
Area =        30
```

Notice the spaces between the equals sign and the number 30. BASIC partitions a line into *print fields* of 14 columns. Thus, the fields begin in columns 1, 15, 29, 43, and so on. When a comma is used in a PRINT statement, the item after the comma is printed starting at the beginning of the next field. Thus the 30 above is printed starting at column 15. The 3 actually appears in column 16 because BASIC prints a leading space before a positive number.

The number of fields in a line depends on the characteristics of the terminal being used. In some terminals the line length is fixed, while in others the line length can be set. Some common line lengths are 70, 72, and 80 columns. With 70 columns, there would be exactly 5 fields of 14 columns each. With 80 columns, there would be 5 fields of 14 columns plus a partial field with 10 columns. The remaining 4 columns of this last field would begin on the second line.

To illustrate, type

```
PRINT 1, 2, 3, 4, 5,"12345678901234" <RET>
```

With 70 columns per line the computer will type

```
1               2               3               4               5
12345678901234
```

However, with 80 columns the computer will type

```
1               2               3               4               5               1234567890
1234
```

With 70 columns per line, the comma causes numbers to be lined up in columns. For example,

```
PRINT 1, 2, 3, 4, 5, 6, 7, 8, 9, 10 <RET>
```

would result in

```
1               2               3               4               5
6               7               8               9               10
```

Notice that the comma in a PRINT statement affects the item *after* the comma. It has no effect on items before the comma. Roughly, the comma tells the computer to start printing the item after the comma at the beginning of the next available field.

The Semicolon

Often it is desirable to have items printed closer together than the comma allows. A semicolon (;) in a PRINT statement tells the computer to start printing the item after the ; in the next available column. For example,

```
PRINT "The area is"; 6*8 <RET>
```

causes the computer to type

```
The area is  48
```

Notice the space between "is" and 48. This occurs because BASIC leaves space for a plus or minus sign on numbers. However, BASIC also follows the usual convention of not printing a plus sign.

When a number is negative and follows some text in a PRINT statement, it is necessary to include a space after the text but before the last quote. Note the following examples.

```
PRINT "The answer is";7-12
```

results in

```
The answer is-5
```

but

```
PRINT "The answer is ";7-12
```

results in

```
The answer is -5
```

We obviously prefer the latter form.

VAX-BASIC also leaves a space *after* a number in a PRINT statement. For example,

```
PRINT 6 * 5; "is the answer." <RET>
```

causes the computer to type

```
30 is the answer.
```

You must have at least one space immediately following the word PRINT. Spaces inside quotes will be copied exactly as you placed them. Otherwise, BASIC ignores spaces in PRINT statements. BASIC considers the following statements to be identical:

```
PRINT 6 * 5 ; "is the answer"
PRINT 6*5;"is the answer"
PRINT    6 * 5 ;  "is the answer"
```

We will follow the form of the first example in this book. *Use spaces to make the statement more readable.*

The BASIC PRINT statement has other options available which allow the programmer to specify precisely the position and form of printed items. In particular, the TAB function and PRINT USING will be discussed in Chapter 5.

EXERCISES

1. An employee works 37.5 hours one week at a pay rate of $6.50 per hour. Write a PRINT statement that causes the computer to type

```
Weekly gross pay is  (the appropriate number)
```

2. Write a PRINT statement that causes the computer to type the first five letters of the alphabet:
   a. Spaced 14 columns apart.
   b. With no spaces between them, using semicolons.
   c. With no spaces between them, without using semicolons.

1.3 MISTAKES

If you make a mistake in typing, press the DELETE key to delete the last character you typed. You can press the key several times to delete several characters. On CRTs the effect of the DELETE key is very clean; the characters actually disappear. With some machines that print on paper (hardcopy terminals), erasing is not possible, but the machine prints a backslash (\) and types the character that will be erased each time you press DELETE. On some terminals, the DELETE key is called the RUB-OUT key. Check your terminal's delete procedure if there is not a DELETE key.

Two very common mistakes involve confusing the letter O with the number 0, and the number 1 with the lowercase letter l or the capital letter I. The O, 0 confusion occurs more often because the symbols are so close together on the keyboard. Remember, the computer does not know your intent, so make sure you use the correct one for your application.

1.4 GETTING OUT

Getting out really means two things: getting out of BASIC and getting off the computer. To get out of BASIC, type

```
EXIT <RET>
```

The computer should then type a $, signifying that you are at the DCL level. Type

```
LOG <RET>
```

to get off the computer. The computer will then type a brief message, such as

`DJONES logged off at 23-JUL-1987  12:23:48.60`

Finally, turn off the terminal.

Review Questions

1. Write a PRINT statement that causes the computer to type each of the following:
   a. 3 + 5.
   b. The last three letters of the alphabet.
   c. The product of 62 and 3 preceded by the message "The product is".
   d. The first ten digits with comma spacing and then with semicolon spacing.
2. Match up the purpose with the key or activity associated with VAX-BASIC.

   _____ 1. Comma   a. The command to get into BASIC

   _____ 2. BAS   b. Wide spacing with 14-column

   _____ 3. DELETE key   print field

   _____ 4. Semicolon   c. Used to erase a character on

   _____ 5. EXIT   the screen

                                           d. Command to exit BASIC to DCL

                                           e. Used for closer printing

SUMMARY OF CHAPTER 1

CONCEPTS, STATEMENTS, AND COMMANDS
INTRODUCED IN THIS CHAPTER

Concepts	Related Statements and Commands
1. Logging on and off	LOG
2. Entering BASIC	BASIC
3. Correcting a mistake	
4. Printing numbers and strings	PRINT
5. Leaving BASIC	EXIT

Writing a Program

2

Writing programs consists of two parts, a problem-solving phase and an implementation phase. Problem solving requires you to define the problem, then analyze it and develop an algorithm for its solution. An *algorithm* is a step-by-step procedure for solving a problem in a certain (finite) number of steps. Once an algorithm is developed it must be tested to see if it works.

The implementation phase requires you to write a program from the algorithm. A *computer program* is a set of instructions to the computer written in a programming language the machine understands. The program is typed into the computer and run. Program errors or *bugs* are corrected during the testing phase, and then the program is ready to be used. This text will help you understand the VAX-BASIC programming language for implementing algorithms.

2.1 PROGRAM FORMAT

When you enter BASIC, the computer sets aside a certain amount of temporary storage, called your *workspace*, for programs you write. When you leave BASIC, programs in your workspace disappear. We present here some very short programs. In the next section we will discuss, among other things, how to run programs and save them in permanent storage.

When you enter BASIC to write programs, enter with the DCL command

```
$ BASIC / SYNTAX
```

8

This causes VAX-BASIC to check the syntax of each program line you write as soon as you press the RETURN key at the end of the line. Without the SYNTAX qualifier, BASIC will not check syntax until you have written a complete program and attempt to run it.

The END Statement

A program is usually several lines of program statements. So far the only program statement we have discussed is the PRINT statement. Another statement which should be included in every BASIC program is the END statement, which tells the computer the end of the program has been reached.

Line Numbers

A fairly trivial program using the PRINT and END statements is:

```
10 PRINT "1 + 2 + 3 + 4 + 5 ="; 1 + 2 + 3 + 4 + 5
20 END
```

When these lines are typed into the computer, nothing seems to happen. Actually, the computer has taken the lines as you typed them and stored them. The numbers 10 and 20 are *line numbers*. Every line in a BASIC program can have a line number, which must be a positive integer from 1 to 32767.

VAX-BASIC allows programs without any line numbers. Such programs cannot be written in the BASIC environment but require the use of an editor. Even programs containing line numbers do not require a number on *every* line. For now we will use a line number on every line. Later on you will see which lines do not need line numbers in VAX-BASIC.

The line numbers serve two major purposes. First, they signal the computer that the line is part of a program and is *not* to be executed immediately. Second, they determine the order in which the computer executes the lines. The latter point is important; the program above could be written

```
20 END
10 PRINT "1 + 2 + 3 + 4 + 5 ="; 1 + 2 + 3 + 4 + 5
```

The computer will not be confused; it knows line 10 comes before line 20.

2.2 BASIC COMMANDS

The BASIC language has two parts, program statements and commands. PRINT and END are program statements; EXIT is the only command we have discussed so far. All the other commands tell BASIC to do something concerning a program. These commands are not parts of programs, so they should not have line numbers.

The RUN Command

Once a program is written (and stored in the computer), there must be a way to make it run. This is the function of the RUN command. Notice that we call RUN a *command,* not a statement; it is not part of a program and therefore does not have a line number. It tells the computer what we want done with a program and is always in immediate mode.

To run any program currently stored, simply type

```
RUN<RET>
```

(We will stop writing ⟨RET⟩ at the end of each line you type. Don't forget to press RETURN, though.) For example,

```
10 PRINT "The volume of a 4-foot cube is"; 4 * 4 * 4
20 END

RUN
```

causes the computer to type

```
NONAME (The current date and time)

The volume of a 4-foot cube is 64
Ready
```

The line beginning NONAME is called a *header.* NONAME simply means the program does not have a name; if it does have a name, that name is typed in place of NONAME. "Ready" is a signal from BASIC that it is finished doing what you requested (RUNning the program).

If you do not want the header typed when the program runs, you can use the command RUNNH (which stands for RUN, No Header) in place of RUN.

Do not number lines consecutively, such as 1, 2, 3, 4, and so on. Instead, use multiples of 5 or 10. Then if you need to insert a line between lines 10 and 20, you can simply write 15 and the proper statement. For example, suppose the previous program has already been written and run and you decide that you want the surface area of the 4-foot cube calculated, too. Just type

```
15 PRINT "Surface area = "; 6 * 4 * 4

RUN
```

The computer will then type

```
NONAME        (date and time)

The volume of a 4-foot cube is 64
Surface area = 96
Ready
```

Other Commands

Besides RUN, BASIC contains several other important commands to use while writing, testing, and executing BASIC programs. The accompanying chart includes the most important commands and their results.

Command	Result	Example
LIST	The computer types all the lines of the program in your workspace.	LIST
LISTNH	The computer types all the lines of the program, with no header.	LISTNH
LIST N	The computer types line N, where N is a line number in the program.	LIST 30
LIST N1, N2	The computer types lines N1 and N2.	LIST 40, 50
LIST N1-N2	The computer types all lines from line N1 through line N2.	LIST 10-50
SAVE	The computer places a copy of the program in your workspace on the computer's disk. The disk copy will remain there after you log off. If you have not named the program, it is saved as NONAME.BAS. A message is returned after the SAVE command which tells you the file has been written to disk.	SAVE
SAVE NAME	Same as above, but the saved program name is the name specified after SAVE.	SAVE CUBE
OLD NAME	The computer copies a saved program from memory into your workspace.	OLD CUBE
NEW NAME	The computer erases anything written in your workspace and gives the next program you write the specified name.	NEW SQUARE
UNSAVE	The computer erases a saved program from the computer's disk but does not erase anything in your workspace.	UNSAVE CUBE
DELETE N	The computer removes line N from the program in your workspace. (Do not confuse this with the DELETE key.)	DELETE 30
DEL N1, N2	The computer removes lines N1 and N2 from the program in your workspace.	DEL 30, 60
DEL N1-N2	The computer removes lines N1 through N2 from the program in your workspace.	DEL 10-50
HELP	The computer types a list of keywords for which it can provide help.	HELP
HELP NAME	The computer types information about the use of the keyword in VAX-BASIC.	HELP PRINT

Example 2.1 *Using BASIC Commands*

The sample dialogue below shows how to use a variety of the commands above.

```
NEW CUBE                                    NEW: Clears the workspace for
Ready                                            a new program named CUBE.

10 PRINT "Volume ="; 4 * 4 * 4
20 END
RUN                                         RUN:  Executes the program

CUBE (The current date and time)    Header Line

Volume = 64
Ready
15 PRINT "Area ="; 6 * 4 * 4         Add a new line

LISTNH                                      LISTNH: Lists all lines of the
                                                    program, but no
                                                    header.

10 PRINT "Volume ="; 4 * 4 * 4
15 PRINT "Area ="; 6 * 4 * 4
20 END
Ready
SAVE CUBE                                   SAVE:  Saves the program CUBE
                                                   on the disk.

EXIT                                        EXIT:  Leave BASIC

$ BASIC                                     BASIC: Reenter BASIC
VAX BASIC Version xx.x
Ready
OLD CUBE                                    OLD:   Retrieves a copy of
                                                   your program CUBE
                                                   from the disk.
```

These commands can be used in any order and any number of times during a BASIC work session. Remember that the BASIC commands work only while you are in BASIC.

Program Names

Many commands are followed by a *program name*. Program names can contain up to 39 letters, digits (0-9), dollar signs ($), and underscores (_). You can use either upper-case or lowercase letters in program names; VAX-BASIC treats all letters as upper-case. Thus, some legal program names are:

```
SQUARE    Program2    10$    P_Q    3KINGS
THISISONEOFTHELONGESTNAMESICOULDTHINKOF
```

The following names are NOT legal program names:

```
THISISONEOFTHELONGESTPROGRAMNAMESICOULDTHINKOF (46 characters)
NAME% (% is not allowed in a program name)
```

Program names should be recognizable by you. Your program names should help identify old programs so you can find them to make changes or run them again.

To see a list of all the BASIC programs you have saved, use the DCL command DIR. This is a VAX command that can be used in BASIC or at the DCL level after leaving BASIC. If you use DIR in BASIC, you should precede it with a dollar sign ($).

```
Ready
$ DIR
CUBE.BAS          SQUARE.BAS          NONAME.BAS
```

Other DCL commands that might be useful are given in Appendix D.

More on Mistakes—The EDIT Command

When a program line you have typed is incorrect, there are several options for correcting it. We have already talked about the DELETE key, but this is useful only while you are still typing the line. If you don't notice the mistake until you are done typing the line, a simple option is to retype the line. For example, if you have typed

```
20 PRINK "Hello"
```

you can retype it as

```
20 PRINT "Hello"
```

and the latter line will replace the former. (It's a good idea to LIST to make sure.)

Retyping long lines can be a bother. The EDIT command allows you to replace *parts* of lines with the correction. To edit the incorrect line 20 above, type

```
EDIT 20 /K/T
```

The computer will then print the corrected line.
Note the form of EDIT:

```
EDIT (line no.) / (character(s) to be removed) /
                         (character(s) to be inserted)
```

The slash (/) has been used as a *delimiter* symbol, enclosing the part to be removed. If the characters to be removed include a slash, some other character must be used as a delimiter. Any other printing character can be used, as long as it is not one of the characters to be removed.

To delete part of a line, but not insert anything, press ⟨RET⟩ immediately after the second delimiter in the EDIT command. For example, if the offending line is

```
30 PRINTSKY "Area = "; 6 * 5
```

type:

```
EDIT 30 /SKY/<RET>
```

This tells BASIC to delete SKY but not insert anything.

The EDIT command removes only the *first* occurrence of the character(s) you specify. Suppose you misspell TOTAL in the line

```
45  PRINT "TOTAR IS"; 1 + 3 + 5 + 7
```

and try to edit this line by replacing an R by an L:

```
EDIT 45 /R/L
```

The computer will print:

```
45 PLINT "TOTAR IS"; 1 + 3 + 5 + 7
```

(The first R in line 45 has been changed to L.) The proper way to edit the original line is:

```
EDIT 45 /AR/AL/
```

Even though you want to replace only one character, an R, you must specify two (at least) characters to specify which R should be removed (the one after A).

You can also make the previous correction by telling the computer *which* R to replace. Do this by typing a number after the last delimiter (/), as in

```
EDIT 45 /R/L/2
```

The 2 tells the computer to change the *second* R to L.

Often you will not be aware of a mistake until you type RUN and the computer gives you an error message, such as:

```
Diagnostic on listing line 2, BASIC line 20

20 PLINT "HELLO"
.........1

%BASIC-E-FOUND,1:  Found string constant when expecting one of:
                        "("
                        ","
                        "="
                        ";"
                        "::"
```

The error message may include part of your line with a numeral 1 pointing to the first place where BASIC could not make sense of your line. Notice that the 1 does not always mark the actual error, which in this case is the L in PLINT.

Syntax errors are often misprints; some will be immediately obvious to you, some will not. Generally, the first thing to do after getting an error "at line 20" message is to LIST 20 and scan the line for the mistake. Then use EDIT to correct the mistake (or retype the line).

EXERCISES A

Write a single program for each of the following:

1. Calculate the sum and product of the numbers 2, 4, 6, 8.
2. The circumference of a circle is $2\pi r$, where r stands for the radius. Calculate the circumference with radius 5 feet. (VAX-BASIC has a built in value for π. Use the word PI in place of π.)
3. A hammer costs $6.50 plus 4% sales tax. What is the total cost?
4. The area of a right triangle is one-half the base times the height. Calculate the area of a right triangle with base 6 and height 5.

2.3 GETTING DATA INTO PROGRAMS

The previous programs required you to put the precise number(s) you wanted into PRINT statements. To allow for more flexibility, we want programs that can use various data without our making major changes to the program. We discuss here several ways to get data into programs.

The formula for the area of a rectangle is

$$AREA = BASE * HEIGHT$$

This formula is appropriate for any rectangle, whatever the BASE and HEIGHT may be. (They must not be negative numbers, of course.) Thus, if you know the formula, you will be able to find the area of any rectangle, once you know the base and height.

Look at the program CUBE again.

```
10 PRINT "The volume of a 4-foot cube is "; 4 * 4 * 4
15 PRINT "Surface area = "; 6 * 4 * 4
20 END
```

The program works only for cubes of side 4. However, there are simple formulas for
the volume and surface area of any cube: VOLUME = SIDE * SIDE * SIDE; and
AREA = 6 * SIDE * SIDE. We should be able to write a program using these formulas; to do so, we need the concept of a *variable* in a computer program.

Nearly all programs use variables. While a program is running, different values
may be stored in the same memory location at different times. This memory location is
referred to as a *variable location*. The value in the location is the *value of the variable*.
The name given the location is called the *variable name*.

Thus, a variable name in a program is actually a name for the *location* in which a
specific number is stored. Sometimes the variable name is called the *address* of the
number. If we want to use a variable called SIDE with a value of 4, it is handy to think
of a number 4 placed in a box labeled SIDE, as in the following figure.

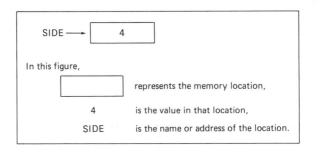

When we use the variable name SIDE in a program, the computer will use, in
place of SIDE, whatever number is in the box labeled SIDE. A great portion of learning how to program is learning how to get the right numbers into the right boxes.

The ASSIGNMENT Statement

To get the number 4 into a box labeled SIDE we use an *assignment statement:*

```
10 SIDE = 4
```

or

```
10 LET SIDE = 4
```

The keyword LET is optional in an assignment statement; we shall not use it.
If line 10 is the first statement in the program that uses the variable SIDE, then
the computer labels a certain storage location (our "box") as SIDE and stores the
number 4 in this location.

It is unfortunate that BASIC (like most other computer languages) uses the equals sign in an assignment statement. The statement

```
10 SIDE = 4
```

looks like a conclusion or solution in algebra. The statement should be read, "Put 4 in the location called SIDE." The computer must be able to calculate a number from whatever is on the right of "=", and it puts this number in a place labeled with whatever is on the left. The statements SIDE = 4 and 4 = SIDE would mean the same thing in algebra, but they do not mean the same thing in BASIC. The statement 4 = SIDE will result in an error message, because 4 is not a legal variable name. Only variable names can occur on the left side of the equals sign.

VAX-BASIC includes a multiple assignment statement. That is, several variables can be assigned the same value in one assignment statement. For example, the statement

```
10 SUM , TOTAL = 0
```

causes both variables, SUM and TOTAL, to have the value 0.

Similarly, if the variable START has already been assigned a value, several other variables can be given this same value by the statement

```
A , B , C , D = START
```

The only thing allowed before and after each comma is a single variable name. Any legal numerical *expression* can come after the equal sign. For now, think of a numerical expression as one or more numeric values (variables or constants), possibly combined with arithmetic operators. The following are examples of numerical expressions if X and SUM are numerical variables:

$$X \quad 2.5 \quad X + 2.5 \quad SUM * 10 - X + 16.5$$

Variable Names

As with program names, only certain strings of characters are legal variable names. A variable name must begin with a letter, but it can then contain an additional 30 characters, which may be letters, digits, periods, or underscores. Thus, the following are legal variable names:

P2   CIRCUMFERENCE   PAY_RATE   MR. JONES   P__.__

(Dollar signs also are legal inside variable names, but a dollar sign at the end of a variable name is a symbol for a special kind of variable, so we suggest that you do not use dollar signs until you learn about string variables.)

The following are NOT legal variable names:

MR JONES   (Space not allowed)

12P   (Letter must be first)

TOTAL__INCOME__FOR__THE__FOURTH__QUARTER   (Too long: 35 character

You can use lowercase as well as uppercase letters in variable names. VAX-BASIC considers RATE, Rate, and RaTe to be the same variable name. We will use only uppercase variable names in this text.

Some other special names, called *keywords* in BASIC, cannot be used as variable names. Keywords are words that have special meaning in BASIC, such as PRINT, LET, and END. There are many other keywords in VAX-BASIC. A complete list can be found in Appendix A.

Many of these keywords are words you would not think of using, but a few of them are likely candidates for variable names. PI, for example, is a keyword in VAX-BASIC. It stands for the constant 3.14159. . . . A simple abbreviation of the word "number" is NUM, but this is also a keyword in VAX-BASIC.

When you use a keyword for a variable name, VAX-BASIC gives an error message. For example, if one of your program lines is

```
20 NUM = 10
```

when you RUN the program, you will get an error message:

```
Diagnostic on listing line 2, BASIC line 20

        20 NUM = 10
.........1

%BASIC-E-FOUND 1: found keyword NUM when expecting a valid
                  statement

Ready
```

If you have a line:

```
25 END = 5
```

you will get the error message

```
Diagnostic on listing line 4, BASIC line 25

        25 END = 5

.........1
```

```
%BASIC-E-TEXFOLEND,1: text following end of program unit must be
on new BASIC line
```

Ready

The ....1 is VAX-BASIC's way of helping you pinpoint your error, but it is not always exceedingly helpful. The message also gives some hints. When you get a syntax error that is not immediately obvious to you, look in the keyword appendix to see if you have used a keyword for a variable name.

A word to the wise on variable names: Use names of *moderate* length that suggest what the variables are used for, such as SIDE, LENGTH, AREA, WEIGHT, INCOME, etc. A name of 31 characters is not practical. Conversely, names of one character will probably not convey much information to someone trying to understand the program.

More on Assignment

Often it is useful to put formulas in assignment statements. Consider the formula for weekly gross pay:

Weekly gross pay = (hours worked) times (hourly pay rate)

It would be reasonable to use the following variables:

GROSS for weekly gross pay;
HOURS for hours worked;
RATE for hourly pay rate.

The assignment statement to calculate GROSS is then

(line number) GROSS = HOURS * RATE

A simple program using this formula is then

```
10 HOURS = 37.5
20 RATE  = 6.50
30 GROSS = HOURS * RATE
40 PRINT "Gross = "; GROSS
50 END
```

This program works only for 37.5 hours and a pay rate of $6.50 per hour. However, if you want to use other figures, all you must do is change the assignment statements in lines 10 and 20.

Once again, be warned that line 30 *cannot* be written HOURS * RATE = GROSS, because HOURS * RATE is an expression, not a variable name, so it cannot occur on the left in an assignment statement.

The order of the lines in the program is important. Suppose our program were

```
10 HOURS = 37.5
20 RATE  = 6.50
30 PRINT "Gross = "; GROSS
40 GROSS = HOURS * RATE
50 END
```

When this program is RUN, the computer will type

```
GROSS =  0
```

This occurs because, at line 30, the variable GROSS has not been defined; it has not yet appeared on the left side of an assignment statement. It is conventional for BASIC to use a value of 0 for variables that have not been assigned a value. Line 30 tells the computer to type what is in the box labeled GROSS, and nothing has been put in that box yet.

The same sort of error occurs if the program is

```
10 HOURS = 37.5
20 GROSS = HOURS * RATE
30 RATE  = 6.50
40 PRINT "Gross = "; GROSS
50 END
```

The result of running this program will be

```
Gross =  0
```

because the computer will assume a value of 0 for RATE in line 20. (6.50 is not put into the RATE box until line 40.)

Often the computer will be able to run your program and give results, but the results are not what you want. It is important for you to be able to read your program from the computer's point of view to find out what happened. Anything in a program that causes incorrect results is called a bug and getting rid of these bugs is called debugging. A very common bug is the use of a variable on the right side of an assignment statement (or in a PRINT statement) before that variable has been assigned a value.

If you have ever been employed, you know that your gross pay is not what you receive; there are many deductions from gross pay before take-home pay (or net pay) is arrived at. Suppose the following deductions are made:

SOCIAL SECURITY	7.15% of Gross Pay
FEDERAL INCOME TAX	14.0% of Gross Pay
BLUE CROSS	$12.00 per week

A program to calculate these deductions and the net pay consists of several assignment and PRINT statements. Let us use the following variable names to represent the quantities to be calculated:

SOCSEC	for SOCIAL SECURITY
FIT	for FEDERAL INCOME TAX
BC	for BLUE CROSS
NET	for NET PAY

The following formulas are pertinent:

$$\text{SOCSEC} = .0715 * \text{GROSS}$$
$$\text{FIT} \quad = .14 * \text{GROSS}$$
$$\text{BC} \quad = 12$$
$$.\qquad.$$
$$.\qquad.$$
$$.\qquad.$$
$$\text{NET} \quad = \text{GROSS} - \text{SOCSEC} - \text{FIT} - \text{BC}$$

(Note that percents are changed to decimals by moving the decimal point 2 places to the left.)

The program to calculate and print a pay statement can then be written:

```
100 HOURS  = 37.5
110 RATE   = 6.5
120 GROSS  = HOURS * RATE
130 SOCSEC = .0715 * GROSS
140 FIT    = .14 * GROSS
150 BC     = 12
160 NET    = GROSS - SOCSEC - FIT - BC
170 PRINT "Gross pay", GROSS
180 PRINT "Social Security", SOCSEC
190 PRINT "Federal tax", FIT
200 PRINT "Blue Cross", BC
210 PRINT "Net pay", NET
220 END
```

Several points can be made concerning this program. First, notice that all the calculations were done first (lines 120-160), then all the PRINT statements (lines 170-210). This was not necessary, but it makes the program "cleaner," easier to read and understand. Second, the calculations for deductions (SOCSEC, FIT, and BC) could have been done in any order, since no one of them depends on any other. However, the calculations for SOCSEC and FIT must be made *after* the calculation of GROSS, because they do depend on the gross pay. NET must be calculated last because it depends on all the other variables.

Third, you should RUN this program to see that it does work. You should check the results with a calculator or paper and pencil. This may seem to be strange advice. Why use a computer if all results are to be checked by hand? In reality, if this program were to be used only one time, there would be no point in writing it; we would simply do the calculations by hand. The benefit of the program is that it can be used many times. For new values of hours and rate, just change lines 100 and 110. For checking purposes it is wise to put in values that make calculations easy, such as 40 hours and a rate of $10 per hour.

Finally, when you RUN this program, you will notice that not all of the numbers come out looking like dollars and cents. That is, not all of the numbers will have two digits after the decimal point. Nor will the computer print a $. We did not tell it to print one. We will deal with such problems later.

EXERCISES B

Write a program for each of the following:

1. Revise the pay statement program above to calculate a pay statement for a worker with 42 hours and a rate of $7.25 per hour. Run the program. Repeat with 30 hours and a rate of $5.30 per hour.

2. A Big Mac costs $1.29, french fries are $0.49, and drinks are $0.45. Write a program to calculate the total cost of 4 Big Macs, 3 orders of french fries, and 2 drinks. A 4% sales tax must be added to the total cost of the items to calculate the bill. Repeat this program for 2 Big Macs, 1 order of fries, and 2 drinks. The program should print out the number of each item, the total cost of the items, and the final bill.

2.4 OTHER WAYS TO GET DATA INTO PROGRAMS

Assignment statements are a legitimate way to get data into the computer, but changing data often requires searching through the program to find the assignment statements that need changing. Two better methods for getting data into programs involve three new BASIC keywords: INPUT and READ/DATA.

The INPUT Statement

The INPUT statement allows you to enter data while the program is running. Its simplest form is just the word INPUT followed by a variable name. The following trivial program illustrates its use.

```
10 INPUT N
20 PRINT "Your number was"; N
30 END
```

When this program runs, line 10 causes the computer to print a question mark (?) and wait for the user to type in a number (followed by RETURN). The number typed is assigned to the variable N (is placed in the box labeled N). Thus, if 12 is typed after the ?, the run (with your response underlined) looks like:

```
? 12
```

```
Your number was 12
```

Except for such trivial programs as the one above, it is bad form to write only INPUT N, because the person running the program might not know how to respond to the "?". The INPUT statement allows you to type literal text, giving some description of the expected data. For example, line 10 in the program above could be

```
10 INPUT "Please enter a number"; N
```

When the program runs, the computer will print

```
Please enter a number?
```

For an example involving a complete program, suppose you often buy several items of the same kind and want to calculate the total cost of a certain number of these items. (Ignore sales tax.) The variables in the program will be NUMBER for the number of items you wish, COST for the cost of one item, and TOTAL for the total cost. The program could be:

```
10 INPUT "How many items"; NUMBER
20 INPUT "Cost per item"; COST
30 TOTAL = NUMBER * COST
40 PRINT NUMBER; "Items at"; COST;
50 PRINT "yields a total cost of"; TOTAL
60 END
```

Assume you want 12 items at $6.25 each. When you type RUN, this is what should happen (your responses are underlined):

```
How many items ? 12 <RET>
Cost per item ? 6.25 <RET>
 12 items at 6.25 yields a total cost of 75
```

Notice that the INPUT statements in lines 10 and 20 have text in quotes immediately following the word INPUT but preceding the variable name. The text tells the user what kind of data the computer is "expecting." A question mark is not needed inside the quotes, because the INPUT statement automatically supplies one.

The semicolon (;) after the quoted text causes the question mark to be placed immediately after the last character inside the quotes. A comma could also be used. Then the question mark would be placed at the start of the next 14-column field.

Beginners are often confused about "who is asking what of whom" in an INPUT statement. This is probably because there are three "actors" involved: the programmer; the computer; and the user of the program. The student usually plays both the first and third parts, so with an INPUT statement you are, in effect, telling the computer to ask you a question. It often helps to imagine that the user of the program is someone other than yourself. Then you can translate the statement

```
INPUT "How many items"; NUMBER
```

as "Ask Susie Smith how many items she wants to buy and put whatever number she types into the box labeled NUMBER."

You might think line 40 is unnecessary, but it is a good idea to print out the data that you put into a program, so you can check that the computer is using the correct data. This practice is called "echo checking."

The INPUT statement also allows several numbers in response to a single question. Suppose you must calculate the mean of three numbers (add them up and divide by 3). A simple program that accomplishes this is:

```
10 INPUT "Enter three numbers"; A, B, C
20 PRINT "Your numbers are", A, B, C
30 PRINT "The mean of these numbers is "; (A + B + C) / 3
40 END
```

When this program is run, the computer will type

```
Enter three numbers?
```

and wait for you to enter three numbers, separated by commas, and RETURN. The first number is assigned to A, the second number to B, and the last to C. *Only* commas and spaces may be placed between the variable names (A, B, C) in the INPUT statement, and only commas and spaces may be placed between the numbers typed in response to INPUT.

VAX-BASIC is fairly tolerant of improper responses to INPUT statements. If you do not type in as many numbers as there are variables in the INPUT statement, the computer will type another question mark. Also, if you type too many numbers after the ?, the computer will ignore the extra numbers. For example,

```
10 INPUT A, B, C
20 PRINT A, B, C
30 END

RUNNH

? 3, 6, 8, 9
 3            6            8
```

Finally, if you notice a mistake before typing RETURN, the DELETE key can be used in the usual way.

EXERCISES C

Write programs that do the following:

1. Input the base and height of a rectangle. Calulate and print the area and perimeter of the rectangle.
2. Input five numbers and calculate their mean.
3. Input hours worked and hourly rate of pay and calculate: gross pay; federal tax (14% of gross); social security (7.15% of gross); and net pay (gross $-$ federal tax $-$ social security). Print out gross and net pay.
4. Input two positive numbers and find their harmonic mean. If the numbers are called x and y, their harmonic mean is

$$\frac{2}{1/x + 1/y}$$

   Use two statements to do the calculation. Calculate the denominator separately as DENOM, then divide 2 by DENOM.
5. Input four numbers. Print their sum and their product.
6. Ask for values for A, B, and C and solve the equation $Ax + B = C$. (Note that the value for A must not be zero.)

The READ and DATA Statements

When many numbers, say 20 or more, must be entered into a program, the INPUT statement is not the best way to enter them. With that many numbers, you are extremely likely to make a mistake. If you do not see the mistake until after you hit RETURN, your only recourse is to stop the program and start over.

The READ statement is similar to the INPUT statement in that the statement READ N causes the computer to look for a number to assign to the variable N, which is just what the statement INPUT N does. The difference is that, while INPUT causes the computer to wait for a number to be typed, the READ statement causes the computer to look for a number in a DATA statement inside the same program as the READ statement. A simple example:

```
10 READ X
20 PRINT "The number is "; X
30 PRINT "Its square is "; X * X
40 DATA 12
50 END

RUNNH

The number is  12
Its square is  144
```

When this program is run, line 10 causes the computer to look for the first number in a DATA statement, and assign this number to the variable X. The rest of the program prints the number and its square. Line 40 is actually ignored when line 30 has been executed. The DATA statement was already "used" by the READ statement in line 10.

After the RUN command, the computer first gathers all the numbers in DATA statements and places them in order in a list. When READ statements are encountered, the computer assigns the first number in the list to the first variable in a READ statement, the second number to the second variable, and so on. The DATA statement can appear anywhere in the program, even before the READ statement. We will usually put all DATA statements at the end of the program, so they do not distract a reader from the program flow.

As with INPUT, several variables can be assigned values with one READ statement. Variables in READ statements and numbers in DATA statements must be separated *only* by commas and spaces. There may be several READ statements and only one DATA statement (with several numbers), or conversely, there may be one READ statement with several DATA statements. There should be as many numbers in DATA statements as are required by the variable names in READ statements. If there are too few numbers, the computer will print an error message:

OUT OF DATA IN LINE xx

where xx is the number of the line with the READ statement for which the computer could not find a number.

Too *many* numbers in DATA statements will not cause an error message, but their presence means (probably) you have not properly thought out your program.

The following are three legitimate ways to assign values of 16.2 to the variable A, -3 to B, and 99 to C.

```
10 READ A, B, C        10 READ A, B         10 DATA 16.2, −3, 99
      .                       .                     .
      .                       .                     .
      .                       .                     .
80 DATA 16.2           40 READ C            50 READ A
90 DATA −3, 99         50 DATA 16.2                .
                       60 DATA −3.4                .
                       70 DATA 99.9         90 READ B, C
```

Suppose we have heights and weights of three people and want to calculate the mean height and mean weight. Assume heights are given in inches and weights in pounds. Let H1, H2, H3 represent the heights of the three people and let W1, W2, W3 represent their weights. The program could be:

```
10 PRINT "Program finds mean height and weight for 3 people"
20 READ H1, H2, H3
30 READ W1, W2, W3
40 PRINT "Mean height is"; (H1 + H2 + H3) / 3 ; "inches."
50 PRINT "Mean weight is"; (W1 + W2 + W3) / 3 ; "pounds."
60 DATA 64, 68, 72
70 DATA 118, 146, 185
80 END
```

```
RUNNH
```

```
Program finds mean height and weight for 3 people
Mean height is 68 inches
Mean weight is 149.667 pounds
```

After line 20 is executed, H1 will have the value 64, H2 the value 68, and H3 the value 72. After line 30 is executed, W1 will be 118, W2 will be 146, and W3 will be 185. There are many other ways to write the READ and DATA statements in this program. We have read all the heights first, then all the weights. If, instead, the data came to us as pairs, one height and weight for each person, the READ statements could be:

```
20 READ H1, W1
25 READ H2, W2
30 READ H3, W3
```

and the corresponding DATA statements could be

```
60 DATA 64, 118
65 DATA 68, 146
70 DATA 72, 185
```

We could even write one READ statement

```
READ H2, W1, W3, H3, H1, W2
```

and one DATA statement

```
DATA 68, 118, 185, 72, 64, 146
```

but this makes it difficult to see if the numbers are being assigned to the appropriate variables. This was only a small example. With many more numbers, is becomes quite important to set up the DATA statements so the data are easy to check.

Warning: Do not put a comma at the end of a DATA statement, because the computer will read a 0 after the comma. For example, if the READ and DATA statements in a program are

```
10 READ A, B, C
60 DATA 10, 20,
70 DATA 30
```

A will be 10 and B will be 20, but C will be 0. Similarly, if there is only one DATA line

```
60 DATA 10,,20, 30
```

A will be 10, B will be 0, and C will be 20. (The computer will read a 0 between the commas.) Along these same lines, write a number such as six thousand without a comma; write it as 6000.

EXERCISES D

Write programs for the following

1. Read 12 numbers. Find the sum of the first six numbers and the sum of the last six. Also find the quotient of the first sum divided by the second.
2. Redo Exercises C, substituting READ and DATA statements for the INPUT statements in those programs.
3. The sum of the fractions a/b and c/d is $(ad + bc)/bd$. Read the numerators and denominators of two fractions and print the sum as a fraction. [Do not divide to get a decimal; print the result as numerator, slash(/), denominator.]
4. A survey of three stores provided the following data on product costs.

Item	Store A	Store B	Store C
Eggs	.69	.79	.75
Milk	1.99	1.89	2.05
Bread	.39	.44	.40

Put store names and prices in data statements, and write a program that reads the data and writes the information as above. Include a fifth column labelled "AVERAGE PRICE," which gives the average price for the three stores. (Call the different egg prices EGGSA, EGGSB, EGGSC, and give similar names to the milk and bread prices.)
5. A company plans to paint the four sides of a rectangular building. One gallon of paint covers 450 square feet. Put the length, width, and height of a building in

data statements, and write a program to calculate the number of gallons of paint required to paint the building. (Assume the building has no windows, doors, or other gaps.)

Review Questions

1. Define the following terms:
   a. Algorithm.
   b. Delimiter.
   c. Syntax.
   d. Variable.
   e. Expression.

2. Mark the valid BASIC variables.

   a. 3X
   b. X
   c. SUM
   d. WEIGH1
   e. FIRST__Name

   f. MISS. SMITH
   g. GROSS PAY
   h. COLLEGETUITIONFOR1986.1987
   i. $PAY
   j. RATE

3. Which assignment statements are incorrect?
   a. 40.0 = HOURS
   b. GROSS__PAY = HOURS * RATE
   c. 3 * Y = 2
   d. C = A + B + C
   e. AREA = PIR2

4. a. Write an INPUT statement for each statement below.
   b. Write READ and DATA statements for each statement, using the data given.
   (1) Input three weights (45, 54, 63).
   (2) Input three numbers (1, 2, 3).
   (3) Input hours worked and pay rate (40, 3.65).
   (4) Input price of item and discount rate (45.72, .20).

5. Look at the following program that will print out the range of degrees in temperature for 5 days of the week. The raw data consists of the day of the week and the high and low temperatures for that day.

Day	DATA High	Low
MON	90	60
TUE	92	65
WED	88	58
THUR	86	60
FRI	86	62

PROGRAM

```
10 REM -- PRINT OUT THE WEEKDAYS AND THEIR TEMPERATURE RANGE
20 PRINT "TEMPERATURE RANGES"
30 PRINT
35 PRINT "DAY","RANGE"
40 PRINT
45 READ DAY$
50 READ HI,LO
55 RANGE = HI - LO
60 PRINT DAY$, RANGE
70 GO TO 40
```

Which DATA statements will give the correct output?

```
a. 100 DATA MON, TUE, WED, THUR, FRI
   110 DATA 90, 60
   120 DATA 92, 65
   130 DATA 88, 58
   140 DATA 86, 60
   150 DATA 86, 62
   160 END
b. 100 DATA MON, 90, 60
   110 DATA TUE, 92, 65
   120 DATA WED, 88, 58
   130 DATA THUR, 86, 60
   140 DATA FRI, 86, 62
   150 END
c. 100 DATA MON, 90, 60, TUE, 92, 65, WE, 88, 58
   110 DATA THUR, 86, 60, FRI, 86, 62
   120 END
d. 100 DATA MON, TUE, WED, THUR, FRI, 90, 60
   110 DATA 92, 65, 88, 58, 86, 60, 86, 62
   120 END
```

6. Match the BASIC commands with the results.

_ 1. LIST

_ 2. HELP

_ 3. OLD

_ 4. SAVE

_ 5. NEW

a. Places a copy of your program on the disk.

b. Erases your workspace for you to start a new program.

c. Computer copies your program from disk to workspace.

d. Information on BASIC keywords.

e. Types all the lines of the program at the terminal.

SUMMARY OF CHAPTER 2

CONCEPTS AND KEYWORDS INTRODUCED IN
THIS CHAPTER

Concepts	Related statements and keywords
1. Get data into programs	LET
	INPUT
	READ/DATA
2. Calculate and print numerical expressions	+, -, *, /
3. Use the BASIC commands	RUN
	LIST
	SAVE
	OLD
	NEW
	UNSAVE
	DELETE
	EDIT

3

Structure of a Program and Its Data

Chapters 1 and 2 explained the fundamental steps for writing BASIC programs. This chapter will examine problem analysis. Although small problems appear to need little analysis, it is best to go through the analysis phase before trying to write a program, because not all programs are five lines long. Many can become quite lengthy. Therefore, it is important to produce good programs that are easy to read, efficient, and correct. Each program module must be easy to follow and to maintain. This can best be achieved by using a standard program format and by using top-down structured program design.

3.1 A PROGRAM FORMAT

We will use the payroll program from Chapter 2 to provide a simple model for good program formatting. It begins with many comment lines that serve several purposes. First, they clearly state the name, date, and purpose of the program. Second, they describe any specific restrictions or qualifiers necessary to use the program. Third, all the variables and constants are listed and described.

Finally, the actual program appears with comments thorough enough for a reader to understand the program's logic without knowing BASIC. Within the program section, spacing should be used to set off specific sections. The rest of the program examples in this text are documented only with comments and spacing to set off the BASIC constructs. In this book the programs are not always completely documented, because they are usually quite short and are used exclusively for educational purposes.

Example 3.1 *Program Format*

```
100 !
    !================================================================
    !  TITLE          :PAYFORM
    !
    !  Author         :John Smith
    !  Written        :Jan. 26, 1980
    !  Modified       :June 12, 1982
    !  System         :VAX 11/780
    !  Purpose        :Print a pay form with constants
    !                     assigned to the variables
    !  Variables      :HOURS  - Hours worked per week, 37.5
    !                  :RATE   - Hourly pay rate, $6.50
    !                  :GROSS  - Gross pay, calculated as
    !                               Hourly rate * Hours worked
    !                  :SOCSEC - Social Security tax,
    !                               calculated as .0715 * GROSS
    !                  :FIT    - Federal income tax,
    !                               calculated as .14 * GROSS
    !                  :BC     - Blue Cross payment, $12.00
    !                  :NET    - Net pay, calculated as
    !                               GROSS - SOCSEC - FIT - BC
    !
    !================================================================
    ! Initialize variables.
110 HOURS = 37.5
120 RATE  = 6.5
130 BC    = 12
    !================================================================
    ! Compute values of other variables.
150 GROSS  = HOURS * RATE
160 SOCSEC = .0715 * GROSS
170 FIT    = .14 * GROSS
180 NET    = GROSS - SOCSEC - FIT - BC
190 !================================================================
200 ! Print out pay form.
210 PRINT "This program prints out a pay form."
220     PRINT "Gross pay      :"; GROSS      ! Gross pay
230     PRINT "Social security:"; SOCSEC
240     PRINT "Federal tax    :"; FIT
250     PRINT "Blue Cross     :"; BC
260     PRINT "Net pay        :"; NET        ! Final pay
300 END
```

As you can see, the payroll program is easy to follow and the comments are helpful. The rest of the programs in this book will conform to these same acceptable formatting conventions. However, to conserve space, we will usually write only one or two comment lines at the top of a program. Although BASIC does not require special program formats, the following standards will be followed for clarity in the book:

1. Programs of more than a few lines will be started at line 100 and will be increased by increments of 10.
2. Certain blocks of program statements will be constructed without line numbers, and margins will be used for clarity.
3. Letters will be uppercase in all program statements except for comments and quoted strings.

In addition, many simple forms of documentation are available for clarity. To *document* a program means to describe what is happening in the program. When you write a properly documented program, someone who knows very little about programming should be able to look at your program and know immediately what the goal of the program is and how the program is achieving that goal.

One of the simplest means of documenting is use of appropriate variable names. We have, for example, used the variable names GROSS, SOCSEC, FIT, HOURS, RATE, BC, and NET in the payroll program. (For illustrative purposes we sometimes use X, Y, Z or A, B, C for "any three numbers.") For several heights and weights we used H1, H2, H3 and W1, W2, W3; the name H2 should make you think of the height of the second person. Even when you do not want to write out a long variable name, use a letter or two that will remind you what the name stands for.

Not all documentation belongs in the program itself. It is a good idea to write out a description of the program; specify the goal of the program and the method used to achieve the goal. There are two major reasons for doing this. First, it will help you in writing the program by making clear what you are trying to do and how. Second, it will help users of your program understand how and when to use it. A further benefit is that you will be able to look at the program later and understand what you did.

There are two standard ways to document a program within the program itself: with PRINT statements and with comments.

The PRINT Statement

When printing results of a program, do not print a single number without explanation. Look at lines 130–180 of the payroll program as an example. Write PRINT statements that say something like:

```
The area is ...
The volume is ...
The mean is ...
Total cost ...
```

Use INPUT statements as PRINT statements (when INPUT is used). If you write

```
10 INPUT COST
```

all the computer will do is print a ? A better INPUT is

```
10 INPUT "What is the cost"; COST
```

or simply

```
10 INPUT "Cost"; COST
```

Finally , a PRINT statement can be used at the beginning of the program to tell the user what the program does. For example,

```
100 PRINT "Calculate the area and volume of a cube."
```

The REM Statement

The word REM stands for remark or reminder. When the first three characters in a line are the letters REM, the line is a *comment*. The computer ignores the line because REM indicates that the line is inserted only as a clarification for the programmer and/ or the user. The REM statement is referred to as a "non-executable" statement. The REM statement can be used much like an informational PRINT statement, but of course it will not cause anything to be printed when the program is run. For example:

```
100 REM This program calculates the mean of three numbers
```

or

```
100 REM-H1, H2, H3 are heights; W1, W2, W3 are weights.
```

or

```
100 REMARK: Problem 3 of the first assignment
```

For now, one or two REM statements at the beginning of the program will be all you need. Later, when your programs get longer and more complicated, you might want a dozen or more REMs.

The Exclamation Point

Comments can also be included at the end of regular statement lines. An exclamation point (!) in a line or at the beginning of a line signals the computer that the rest of the line is a comment and is to be ignored during the RUN. For example:

```
30 FEDTAX = 0.14 * GROSS        ! Calculate federal tax
```

or

```
10 INPUT "Radius"; RADIUS
20 CIRCUM = 2 * PI * RADIUS   ! VAX-BASIC has the value of pi in PI.
30 PRINT "Circumference ="; CIRCUM
40 END
```

The exclamation point is not a comment signal when it is included inside a quoted string, as in

```
PRINT "Hi! How are you?"
```

Also, the exclamation point cannot be used as a comment signal in a DATA statement.

3.2 TOP-DOWN DESIGN

A well formatted and documented program module is usually only one part of a much larger program. *Top-down structured programming* is a method that provides a procedure for designing programs. This organized form of program planning and design is also referred to as top-down design, top-down documentation, top-down implementation, and structured programming. Whatever it is called, it can be defined as the process of breaking a complex function into simpler hierarchical functions. Each level of the hierarchy refers to a complete task that is subordinate to the next level. The complete task is referred to as a *program module.*

In programming, a *module* is a self-contained unit that performs one specific task, which is usually part of a set of tasks required to accomplish a larger task. For example, a computer program might have a module for input, a module for processing information, and a module for printing output. A program that is divided into modules for analysis and implementation has a *modular design.*

A modular program lends itself to top-down design because, during the analysis of the problem, you start at the "top" with the most general module and then work "down" to the specific aspects of the program—as far down as a single line of code. The term *code* refers to the program statements in a program. Thus, *coding* means to write a program.

For example, suppose you are going to write a computer program to teach a

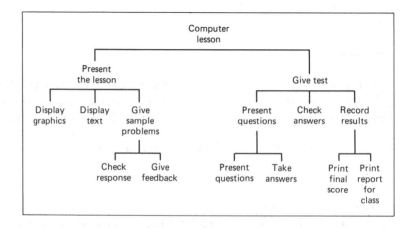

Figure 3.1   Hierarchical Design of Program Module

lesson on addition and to give a test after the lesson. The main module would activate a series of tasks. The first level of tasks could include presenting the lesson and giving the test. The next level of tasks would fall under either of the two previous levels. These could include presenting questions for the test or displaying graphics for the lesson. The hierarchical structure of the program module is shown in Figure 3.1.

Each block or module represents a section of code in a program. The individual modules can be broken down further with a flowchart. The flowchart describes each task by single actions. (If you have not already done some flowcharting, Appendix E explains the basics.) It is fairly easy to write a BASIC program from a flowchart, but if you did this for each task individually, the entire program would not work together to perform the main task. Therefore, with a structured progam the lower level tasks are activated from the main module. The program outline for the computer lesson would look like this:

Example 3.2 *Program Outline*

```
100 REM -- Main Module
    GOSUB 200          !Present the lesson
    GOSUB 300          !Give the test
    GO TO 999          !Go to the end of the program
200 REM -- Module to present lesson
    GOSUB 400          !Display graphics
    GOSUB 500          !Display text
    GOSUB 600          !Give a sample problem to try
    RETURN             !Return to main module to give test
300 REM -- Module to give test
    GOSUB 700          !Present question
    GOSUB 800          !Check answers
    GOSUB 900          !Record results
    RETURN
400 REM - Subroutine to display graphics
    REM - lines of code
    RETURN
500 REM - Subroutine to display text with graphics
    REM - lines of code
    RETURN
600 REM - Subroutine to give sample problems to try
    REM - lines of code
    GOSUB 950          !Check response
    GOSUB 960          !Give feedback
    RETURN
700 REM - Subroutine to present the questions
    REM - lines of code
    RETURN
800 REM - Subroutine to check the answers to the questions
    REM - lines of code
    RETURN
```

```
900 REM - Subroutine to record and report the results
    GOSUB 970          !Print final score
    GOSUB 980          !Print report for class
    RETURN
950 REM - Subroutine to check the response
    REM - lines of code
    RETURN
960 REM - Subroutine to give feedback on sample problems
    REM - lines of code
    RETURN
970 REM - Subroutine to print final score
    REM - lines of code
    RETURN
980 REM - Subroutine to print a class report
    REM - lines of code
    RETURN
999 END
```

The GOSUB statements send the program to the individual tasks. Each individual task is a separate program module, called a *subroutine*. The structure of the program is always controlled from the main module. After the execution of a subroutine a RE-TURN statement sends the computer back to the module calling the subroutine. Note that each subroutine can also have subroutines for the lower levels. The use of subroutines is explained in Chapters 6 and 7.

Structured program design is not difficult to implement. It is based on four main steps:

1. Analyzing the problem.
2. Writing the main module.
3. Writing the lower-level modules from the top down.
4. Testing and debugging.

Use these steps as you begin to implement the examples and exercises in this text. There are many books available that will provide you with more information on top-down design.

3.3 STRING VARIABLES AND CONSTANTS

All data used in a BASIC program have specific types. Numerical constants can contain digits, decimal points, plus and minus signs, and an exponentiation symbol E. String constants contain characters including letters, digits, blanks, commas, and special characters such as !, @, #, $, and so on. In this section we discuss string variables and constants. Numerical data will be covered in later sections.

To identify a string variable, use any legal variable name with a dollar sign ($) at the end: NAME$, ANSWER$, COLOR$, Z3$, and so on. The value of a string variable can be any string of characters (letters, numbers, spaces, @, #, $, etc.) up to

65,535 characters. In assignment statements, the values of string variables should be enclosed in quotes:

```
10 Z$ = "Hello"
```

This line causes the string of characters,

```
Hello
```

to be stored in a location labeled Z$.

A quoted string is called a *string constant*. "Hello" is a string constant in the same way 6.25 is a numerical constant. The characters can be upper- or lowercase letters, digits, or any printable character. If a later line in the program is

```
50 PRINT Z$
```

the computer will type

```
Hello
```

just as if line 50 had been

```
50 PRINT "Hello"
```

With INPUT statements, values of string variables may or may not be placed in quotes. The computer takes everything you type before a terminator such as ⟨RET⟩ as the value of the string variable. Consider the following program:

```
10 INPUT "What's your name"; NAME$
20 PRINT "Hello "; NAME$
30 END
```

Suppose your name is Ernestine Schwarzenegger. Then this is what should happen when the program is RUN:

```
What's your name? Ernestine Schwarzenegger <RET>
Hello Ernestine Schwarzenegger
```

You can have both numerical variables and string variables in the same INPUT statement. As before, variable names are separated by commas, and you should separate their values by commas too. A simple example program:

```
10 INPUT "Please give me your first name and age"; NAME$, AGE
20 PRINT "Hi there, "; NAME$
30 PRINT AGE; "is a nice age"
40 END
```

```
RUNNH
```

```
Please give me your first name and age? MARY, 18
Hi there, MARY
18 is a nice age
```

When the computer asks for your name and age, respond

```
MARY, 18 <RET>
```

The computer takes everything you type before the comma as the value of the variable
NAME$. Thus, the comma is also a terminator for string constants in INPUT.

When reading the value of a string variable from a DATA statement, the value
may or may not be enclosed in quotes. An example:

```
10 READ NAME$, HOURS, RATE
20 PRINT NAME$; " earned"; HOURS * RATE
30 DATA Mary Jones, 40, 6.50
40 END
```

When this program is RUN, the computer will respond

```
Mary Jones earned 270
```

Notice the space before earned inside the quotes (line 20). If this space were not
present, the computer would type

```
Mary Jonesearned 270
```

The computer does not leave a space before or after the values of string values, so if
you want a space between Jones and earned, you must put the space in. (See also the
previous program, where there is a space after 'there, '.) No space is needed after
earned because the next item to be printed is HOURS * RATE, which is a number.
VAX-BASIC automatically leaves a space before and after a printed number.

Warning: If your string contains a comma, then you must put quotes around the
string. Thus, to assign the value

```
Jones, Mary
```

to NAME$, you would respond "Jones, Mary" to an INPUT NAME$ or write DATA
"Jones, Mary" in conjunction with READ NAME$.

String manipulation will be discussed further in Chapter 10.

EXERCISES A

1. Write a program that asks for a first name and last name (two separate values) and types the full name with last name first and a comma between the names.
2. Joe Cool has four test grades in a course: 76, 84, 79, 91. Put Joe's name and his grades in a DATA statement. READ the DATA, calculate his average (mean) grade, and print the name and average grade.
3. At one point in the baseball season, Reggie Jackson had 135 hits in 380 times at bat, and Pete Rose had 142 hits in 425 times at bat. Calculate batting averages for these two players (batting average = hits/times at bat). Print out names and batting averages.
4. Write a program that asks whose birthday it is, and asks who is sending greetings. The program should then type a short birthday greeting to the first person from the second person.
5. Ask the names of the sender of a letter and the addressee. Print a business letter (a short one) in proper format.

3.4 REAL VARIABLES AND CONSTANTS

VAX-BASIC contains four main numerical data types: real, integer, packed decimal, and RFA (Record File Address). Each of these data types has certain characteristics that can help structure your programs more efficiently. This text uses primarily real numerical data (numbers with decimal points), but integers are discussed briefly later in this chapter. RFA and packed decimal are advanced topics, not covered in this text.

Real numbers are often called floating-point numbers and decimal numbers, among other things. For us, the main distinction between real numbers and integers is that a real number contains a decimal point, while an integer does not. For the computer, the distinction is important because integer and real values are stored differently. Integers are stored "in one piece" while real numbers are stored in two parts: one part for the digits of the number, and one part for the placing of the decimal point.

The situation is complicated by the fact that VAX-BASIC ordinarily considers a number such as 75 to be a real number and stores it as 75.0. Also, VAX-BASIC treats all the numerical variables we have mentioned as real variables. The real data type, usually written in uppercase as REAL, is BASIC's "default data type." That is, unless you take some positive step, BASIC assumes any variable you use is a REAL variable and any number you write is a real number. [One positive step to let BASIC know that you want a variable to be a string variable is to end the variable name with a dollar sign ($). There is a similar way to let BASIC know that a variable or a constant is an integer. This and another way to describe data types will be discussed later in this chapter.]

In the rest of this section any numbers or numerical variables we use will be real.

E-Notation

For very large, or very small, real values the computer switches from the standard decimal notation into an *exponential notation* or E-notation when printing numbers. Look at the following program.

```
10 REM -- Illustration of E-format
20 PRINT 33 * 30303
30 PRINT 2000 * 500
40 END
```

When this program is run, the computer will type

```
999999
.1E+07
```

The first number is printed in standard decimal notation, while the second is in E-notation. The $E+07$ means "multiply the preceding number by 10 to the 7th power" or "multiply the preceding number by 10 seven times." It is quite easy to multiply any number by 10; just move the decimal point one place to the right. Thus, $E+07$ can be interpreted as "move the decimal point seven places to the right." In other words

$$.1E+07 = 1,000,000 \text{ (one million)}$$

(If you have seen scientific notation, the E-notation is quite similar.)

This E-notation corresponds very closely to the way the computer stores real numbers. To store 1,000,000 (which we enter without commas as 1000000), the computer stores two items: the digit (1) and the exponent ($+7$). The notation also helps explain the term "floating-point number." We can write the number 12,345.6 in many ways, including:

$$12345.6E0 = 1234.56E+01 = 123.456E+02 = .123456E+05$$

In other words, the decimal point can "float" to any place inside the number.

As the example above indicates, VAX-BASIC causes the computer to switch into the E-notation at one million. More to the point, the switch occurs when more than six digits would have to be typed to express the number in standard notation.

For numbers typed in E-format, BASIC always begins the number with a decimal point, then a nonzero digit, up to five more digits, and the E with plus or minus a two-digit number. Notice that we said "up to five more digits"; BASIC will not type trailing zeros after a decimal point. If we try

```
PRINT 1111 * 2222
```

the computer will type

```
.246864E+07
```

The exact answer is 2468642, but BASIC will not type the seventh digit. If we did not know the exact answer, the best we could do would be to interpret .246864E+07 as 246860, with a little roundoff error.

A similar switch to E-format occurs when numbers get too small, which roughly means less than 0.1. The computer will not type the number 0.0002345 in standard notation. It will be typed instead .2345E−03. The negative sign after the E means divide by 10 to the third power, or "move the decimal point three places to the left."

Notice the word "roughly" in the first sentence of the last paragraph. If you type

```
PRINT 1 / 25
```

the computer responds with

```
.04
```

because 1/25 is exactly .04. However,

```
PRINT 1 / 24
```

will elicit

```
.434783E-02
```

which is .0434783 in standard notation. This latter number is bigger than .04, but it is only approximately equal to 1/24. In standard notation, VAX-BASIC does not like to type zeros immediately after a decimal point, but it will do so if it can perfectly represent the number with six or fewer digits.

EXERCISES B

1. a. Write the following numbers in VAX-BASIC E-format.

    (1) 875349123   (2) 0.000063425   (3) 1/5000000

   b. Write the following numbers in standard decimal notation.

    (1) .123456E+08   (2) .2E−06   (3) .3E+09

2. Write a program to find the number of seconds in a week and the number of seconds in a month of 30 days.

3. Write a program that types the following numbers and their reciprocals: 10, 11, 16, 18, 200, 5000, 250000.

4. How many digits will VAX-BASIC allow you to type in response to INPUT X? Write a "trivial" program that asks for INPUT, then PRINTs the number that was typed in at the ?. Experiment by putting in numbers of varying length.

5. The speed of light in a vacuum is 2.997925E+08 meters per second. What is this speed in miles per hour? (1 meter = 3.28084 feet.)

Arithmetic Operations

We have tried to keep arithmetic simple so far. Probably the only new symbol you have had to learn is the * for multiplication. We discuss here one further operation, exponentiation, and a little about more complicated expressions. We also introduce two simple functions often used in BASIC expressions.

Exponentiation is the operation of raising one number to a power. In algebra, a number to a power is usually written with the power as a superscript. That is, 10 to the fourth power is written as

$$10^4$$

which means "multiply 10 by itself 4 times," so

$$10^4 = 10 \times 10 \times 10 \times 10 = 10,000$$

Keyboards do not allow superscripts, so VAX-BASIC has a special notation to signify exponentiation. There are actually two notations. 10 to the fourth power can be written either as 10**4 or 10 ^ 4. (The symbol ^ is called a caret.) Some BASICs allow only the ^ notation.

When the power, or exponent, on a number is negative, we take the reciprocal of the given number, and raise it to the (positive) given power. That is, 10 to the −3 power is 1/10 to the third power, or 0.001.

Positive and negative numbers can be raised to any *integer* power, positive or negative. Zero cannot be raised to a negative power, since this would be tantamount to dividing by 0. Negative numbers cannot be given a noninteger exponent; (−4)**1.5 is not legal.

SQR Function

The 1/2 power is used often enough that there is a special function in BASIC to calculate it: the square root function denoted by SQR. (The square root and 1/2 power are actually calculated in different ways by VAX-BASIC, but that need not concern us.) This is the first function we discuss. There are many others in VAX-BASIC.

To get the nonnegative square root of a numerical expression, write SQR followed by the expression in parentheses; for example, SQR(4) or SQR(NUMBER) or SQR(A*B + C/2). The value of the expression must be a nonnegative number, otherwise an error will occur. SQR(*expression*) is not a statement by itself. It may occur on the right side of an assignment statement or in a PRINT statement, as in

```
30 Y = SQR(X)
```

or

```
50 PRINT "The square root is"; SQR(NUMBER)
```

The following program illustrates the SQR function and both exponentiation notations.

```
10 INPUT "Give me a nonnegative number"; NUMBER
20 PRINT "Number is"; NUMBER
30 PRINT "Square root is"; SQR(NUMBER)
40 PRINT "Fourth power is"; NUMBER**4
50 PRINT "Eighth power is"; NUMBER^8
60 END

RUNNH
```

```
Give me a nonnegative number ? 5 <RET>
Number is 5
Square root is 2.23607
Fourth power is 625
Eighth power is 390625
```

Notice that line 10 asks for a nonnegative number. If the number input is negative, line 30 will cause an error, because the computer is being told to take the square root of a negative number.

INT Function

Another function that we use often in BASIC expressions is *INT*. The INT function is invoked by its three letter name, followed by a numerical expression in parentheses, as in the following examples:

$$INT(6.3) \qquad INT(HOUR) \qquad INT(RATE * TIME / 60)$$

The expression in parentheses is called the *argument of the function*; it is what the function "operates on."

The value of INT(X) is the greatest integer which is less than or equal to X. For instance:

$$INT(6.7) = 6 \qquad INT(-3.2) = -4$$
$$INT(8) \ = 8 \qquad INT(-6) \ = -6$$
$$INT(5.1) = 5 \qquad INT(-2.9) = -3$$

Notice that, if the argument X is already an integer, then INT(X) has the same value as X. If X is not an integer, INT(X) is the first integer to the left of X on the usual number line.

$$-5 \quad -4 \quad -3 \quad -2 \quad -1 \quad 0 \quad 1 \quad 2 \quad 3 \quad 4 \quad 5$$

For positive arguments X, INT(X) can be thought of as "chopping off" the decimal part of X. This is not true for negative arguments, as can be seen from the example: INT(-3.2) = -4. [However, if you write -3.2 as $-4 + .8$, then INT($-4 + .8$) is -4, so the INT function still does "chop off" the *positive* decimal part of the number.]

The INT function has many uses, but two in particular will occur frequently in this book: rounding off and checking for exact divisibility.

You probably already know how to round positive numbers to integers in your head: 3.75 rounds to 4, 2.18 rounds to 2, and so on. If the decimal part of the number is more than .5, increase the integer part by 1; if the decimal part is less than .5, leave the integer part as it is. The troublesome case occurs when the decimal part is exactly .5. There are several possible options: round up, round down, or round to the even integer. We need a convention (an agreement) in this case, and we will agree to round up—or go to the right on the number line—when the decimal part of the argument is exactly .5.

Rounding to a whole number is easily accomplished by the statement

```
X = INT(X + .5)
```

That is, add .5 to the number to be rounded, then chop off the decimal part. To see that this statement does what it is intended to do, consider the following examples:

X	X + .5	INT(X + .5)
3.1	3.6	3
4.9	5.4	5
−2.6	−2.1	−3
−8.2	−7.7	−8

Often we want to round a number, not to an integer, but to a certain number of decimal places. Rounding to two decimal places occurs quite frequently when the numbers involved are intended to be dollars and cents. A generalization of this is given below, which rounds any X to two decimal places. An example value of 6.248 is used.

Operation	Result	Example
1. Move decimal two places to the right, or multiply by 10^2.	$X * 10^2$	624.8
2. Add .5 to result.	$X * 10^2 + .5$	625.3
3. Take INT of result.	$INT(X * 10^2 + .5)$	625
4. Move decimal two places to the left, or divide by 10^2.	$INT(X * 10^2 + .5) / 10^2$	6.25

Thus, to round X to two decimal places, use the statement

```
X = INT(X * 10^2 + .5) / 10^2
```

This method works for any number of decimal places. To round to N decimal places, just replace 10^2 with 10^N:

```
X = INT(X * 10^N + .5) / 10^N
```

Suppose a bank is to pay 9.75% interest on your balance of $268.34. A program is not really needed for this simple calculation, but let's write one to illustrate rounding.

```
10  INTEREST = 268.34 * .0975
20  REM -- Now round the interest to 2 places
30  INTEREST = INT(INTEREST * 100 + .5) / 100
40  PRINT "Interest ="; INTEREST
50  END

RUNNH
```

```
Interest = 26.16
```

(We have used the slightly simpler 100 in place of 102.) There is still a small problem in trying to print numbers that look like dollars and cents. VAX-BASIC does not type trailing zeros, so it will type a figure for $126.60 as 126.6. This problem will be dealt with later in Chapter 5.

Expressions

Expressions can become very complicated. Even when they are relatively short, it is not always clear how the computer will evaluate them. For example, what is the meaning of 8 / 4 / 2? If we first divide 8 by 4 to get 2, then divide this result by 2, the answer is 1. However, if we first divide 4 by 2 to get 2, then divide 8 by this result, the answer is 4. Mathematicians would simply say the expression 8 / 4 / 2 is ambiguous. If you type

```
PRINT 8 / 4 / 2
```

in VAX-BASIC, you will get the answer 1. It will benefit us to look a little closer at precisely how VAX-BASIC calculates expressions.

We have five operations and their symbols: add ($+$); subtract ($-$); multiply (*); divide (/); and exponentiate (** or ^). There is another operation, negation, that uses the same symbol ($-$) as subtraction. The expression -3 does not really mean subtract something, it means the negative of 3. When used this way, the minus sign is called a *unary* minus; it operates on one number. In contrast, the minus sign in $4 - 3$ does tell us to subtract 3 from 4.

When VAX-BASIC evaluates an expression that does not contain any parentheses, it sweeps across the expression from left to right several times, performing calculations in the following order:

Sweep Number	Operation
1	Exponentiation
2	Unary minus
3	Multiplication and division
4	Addition and subtraction

When two operations have the same priority, say two divisions, they are evaluated from left to right. This is why, according to BASIC, $8 / 4 / 2 = 1$. Similarly, $3 / 4 * 2$ is 1.5, because $*$ and $/$ have equal priority, and evaluation of equal priority operations is done from left to right (i.e., the division is done first in the expression $3 / 4 * 2$).

A very common mistake is writing $A / B * C$ when what is desired is $A / (B * C)$; that is, A divided by the product $B * C$. VAX-BASIC considers $A / B * C$ to be $(A / B) * C$. The surest way to get the desired result is to insert the parentheses, as in $A / (B * C)$. In VAX-BASIC, the same result can be obtained by writing $A / B / C$.

For a more complicated example, consider the expression:

$$-4**4 / 8 * 3 - 9 / 3 * 12 / 4$$

VAX-BASIC will perform the calculations in the order:

Sweep 1. The exponentiation (4**4) to obtain 256

Sweep 2. Unary minus to get -256: $-256 / 8 * 3 - 9 / 3 * 12 / 4$

Sweep 3.   a. Division by 8 to get -32: $-32 * 3 - 9 / 3 * 12 / 4$

        b. Multiplication by 3 to get -96 as the number
           before the second minus sign: $-96 - 9 / 3 * 12 / 4$

        c. Division of 9 by 3 to get 3: $-96 - 3 * 12 / 4$

        d. Multiplication by 12 to get 36: $-96 - 36 / 4$

        e. Division by 4 to get 9 as the number
           after the second minus sign: $-96 - 9$

Sweep 4. Subtraction of 9 from -96 to get -105 as -105
        the final result.

To make things clearer, it is wise to put some parts of expressions inside parentheses. The expression above should be clearer if it is written

$$- ((4**4) / 8) * 3 - (9 / 3) * (12 / 4)$$

Parenthesized expressions are evaluated first by VAX-BASIC, even before unary minus. When there are parentheses inside parentheses, the expression inside the innermost parentheses is performed first. In the example above, the innermost parentheses are those around 4**4.

When expressions become extremely long and complicated, it is often possible to simplify by breaking the expression into several parts. For instance, the statement

```
ANSWER = (4 * X * Y * Z - 3 / (X + Y + Z) +
         SQR(X**2 + Y**2)) / (3 / (X + Y + Z) * SQR(X**2 + Y**2))
```

might be more understandable when expressed as three statements:

```
A = 3 / (X + Y + Z)
B = SQR(X**2 + Y**2)
ANSWER = (4 * X * Y * Z - A + B) / (A * B)
```

EXERCISES C

1. Write a program that asks for a number and raises that number to the 2.5 power. What kind of numbers can be entered?

2. Write a program that asks for a number and raises it to the -4 power. What kind of numbers can be entered?

3. Write a program to calculate

$$\frac{3**4 - 4**3}{98/3 - 16/12} \quad \text{raised to the} \quad \frac{1/2 + 1/3}{1/2 - 1/3} \quad \text{power.}$$

4. If a and b are the lengths of the legs of a right triangle, the area of the triangle is $ab/2$ and the hypotenuse is the square root of $a^2 + b^2$. Write a program to calculate the area and hypotenuse of a right triangle, given the legs.

5. Write a program that asks the user for a number, asks to how many decimal places the user wants the number rounded, then prints the rounded value.

6. Write a program that rounds numbers to some number of places before the decimal point. Rounding to 1 place before the decimal means rounding to the 10's place, so 6928 would be rounded to 6930.

7. A taxi company charges $1.20 plus $.60 per mile or fraction of a mile. Write a program to calculate the fare for rides of given distances. Check the program with at least the distances 2.8, 9.1, and 6 miles. (You may assume miles are given to the nearest tenth.)

8. Write a program to find the solution(s) of a quadratic equation

$$ax^2 + bx + c = 0$$

Let $d = \sqrt{b^2 - 4ac}$. Generally, there are two solutions:

$$x_1 = \frac{-b - d}{2a} \quad \text{and} \quad x_2 = \frac{-b + d}{2a}$$

but these two solutions will be identical when $b^2 = 4ac$. Also, there will be no real solution if $b^2 - 4ac < 0$. Use the program for at least the following sets of values for A, B, and C:

A	B	C
2	−6	4
−1	2	−1
3	−2	4

You should get an error message for the third set of numbers. This simply means the equation has no solution. We will see how to deal with this problem more elegantly in Chapter 4.

9. A famous story concerns an ancient king who was so pleased with the game of chess that he offered the inventor of the game anything he desired, up to half his kingdom. The inventor, too smart for his own good, asked for "only a few grains of rice": one grain for the first square on the chess board; two grains for the

second; four grains for the third; eight grains for the fourth, etc., doubling the number of grains for each succeeding square. Write a program that types the number of grains required for the 64th square on the board. (The king obviously didn't have enough rice. He solved his problem by having the inventor put to death.)

10. If you invest a certain amount of money (call it PRINCIPAL) at an interest rate called RATE for N periods, at the end of that time you would have an amount of

$$PRINCIPAL * (1 + RATE)**N$$

This is the so-called compound interest formula. The RATE must be expressed as a decimal. That is, 8% would be .08. If one of your ancestors had invested $100 for you, at an annual rate of 6%, 180 years ago, how much money would you have today?

11. The distance between two points in the plane, (x, y) and (a, b) is the square root of

$$(x - a)^2 + (y - b)^2$$

Write a program to find the distance between (8, 1) and (5, -3) and the distance between (-9, 6) and (-4, -6).

12. Evaluate the polynomial $3x^4 + 5x^3 - 7x^2 + 12x - 9$ when $x = 5$.

13. If r is the radius of a circle, then the area of the circle is πr^2 and the circumference is $2\pi r$. Ask for the radius of a circle and print the values of the area and circumference.

14. Find the value of 10**50 divided by 2**60. The first number is too big for VAX-BASIC to store, so do some of the work by hand.

15. Find the value of 10**500 divided by 5**400. Do some of the work by hand.

3.5 INTEGERS

Integers are whole numbers, either positive, negative, or 0, without decimal points. Numbers in VAX-BASIC are either integers or real numbers.

Floating point numbers (decimal numbers) are stored in two parts: one part for the digits, and one part for the placing of the decimal point. Since integers have no decimal point, they are stored differently; all of the storage space is allocated to the digits. Because of the different ways integers and decimal numbers are stored, we need a way to distinguish between them. VAX-BASIC considers a number to be an integer if it is immediately followed by a percent sign (%). Thus, 8%, 6284%, and -12% are considered to be integers. Similarly, a percent sign at the end of a variable name signals that the variable holds integer values. Legal names for integer variables are GRADE%, N%, NUMBER.OF.WAYS%, or any legal variable name with % as the last character.

There are two major reasons for using integer variables in a program. First, the computer performs integer arithmetic faster than decimal-number arithmetic. In advanced work, when an operation is performed millions of times, it can be crucial to save a tiny fraction of a second for each operation. Second, integer arithmetic is exact, because there can be no roundoff error.

As far as you are concerned, integer addition, subtraction, and multiplication give results identical to results from decimal arithmetic with whole numbers. For example, the following two programs have identical output.

```
10 REM -- Integer variables        10 REM -- Decimal variables
20 A% = 12%                        20 A = 12
30 B% = 8%                         30 B = 8
40 PRINT "Sum"; A% + B%           40 PRINT "Sum"; A + B
50 PRINT "Difference"; A% - B%    50 PRINT "Difference"; A - B
60 PRINT "Product"; A% * B%       60 PRINT "Product"; A * B
70 END                            70 END
```

When either of these programs is run, the computer will print:

```
Sum 20
Difference 4
Product 96
```

Notice that the computer does not print % after integer values.

One difference in arithmetic for the two types of numbers is caused by the size restriction on the integers. If you type

```
PRINT 256000 * 256000
```

the computer will type .65536E+11, but if you type

```
PRINT 256000% * 256000%
```

the computer will respond with an error message, because 65536000000 is too large to be stored as an integer. The largest positive integer VAX-BASIC can store is 2,147,483,647 (a little over two billion), which is 1 less than 2 to the 31 power. This restriction should not cause you too much grief. Calculations resulting in numbers outside these numbers will result in errors: OVERFLOW if the number is too big, and UNDERFLOW if the number is too small.

The major difference in the two types of arithmetic lies in division. If you type PRINT 7% / 2%, the computer will print 3. That is, in integer division, the result is the number of times the divisor (2) is contained in the dividend (7). In third grade, you were taught something like "7 divided by 2 is 3 with remainder 1." The following program illustrates how you can get both the quotient and the remainder with integer division.

```
10 REM -- Integer division
20 INPUT "Give me two integers"; FIRST%, SECOND%
30 PRINT FIRST%; "is divided by "; SECOND%
40 PRINT "Quotient is "; FIRST% / SECOND%
50 PRINT "Remainder is "; FIRST% - SECOND% * (FIRST% / SECOND%)
60 END
```

When the program is run, suppose you enter the two numbers 93 and 8. (Do not put percent signs on the integers used as responses to INPUT.) Then the computer will type:

```
93 is divided by  8
Quotient is  11
Remainder is  5
```

The expression in line 50 probably seems strange. In algebra, the expression FIRST% − SECOND% * (FIRST% / SECOND%) would always be 0 because SECOND% * (FIRST% / SECOND%) would be FIRST%. However, follow the calculations the computer does when FIRST% is 93% and SECOND% is 8%. Then the expression becomes 93% − 8% * (93% / 8%). Now 8 goes into 93 eleven times, so 93% / 8% is 11%, and the expression becomes 93% − 8% * 11%, which is the same as 93% − 88%, or 5%.

Line 50 of the program also shows how we can check for exact divisibility of one integer by another. SECOND% exactly divides FIRST% if the remainder, FIRST% − SECOND% * (FIRST% / SECOND%), is 0.

We will not use integer arithmetic again in this book. (But later we will use some integer constants and variables when dealing with files.) Thus, when we say a certain value is an integer, we mean it is a whole number, and it will be stored as a floating point number.

EXERCISES D

1. Write a program that asks for a length in inches, then gives that length in feet and inches.
2. Without writing a program, determine the values of:
   a. (3% / 4%) * 6%
   b. (3% * 6%) / 4%
   c. 3% * (6% / 4%)

3.6 THE DECLARE STATEMENT

Up until now all the variable names used in the programs were automatically given the data type REAL unless they were followed by a dollar sign to indicate the STRING data type or a percent sign to indicate the INTEGER data type. The DECLARE statement can be used to explicitly assign a data type to a variable. The use of DECLARE statements at the beginning of a program makes the program clearer and more structured.

The DECLARE statement is nonexecutable and must precede any reference to the variables or constants. For clarity, we suggest using a separate declaration for each variable type, as follows:

```
100 DECLARE INTEGER I, J, K
110 DECLARE STRING ADDRESS, CITY, STATE
120 DECLARE REAL WEIGHT, HEIGHT
```

DECLARE statements can be used for *named constants*. All numbers and characters are constants. BASIC allows for both numeric and alphanumeric constants. Constants can be used in expressions in a program like variables if they are declared. If you are going to use the same constant several times in a program, it is wise to give the constant a name by declaring it as a named constant. Some examples of named constants in DECLARE statements are:

```
100 DECLARE REAL CONSTANT TAXRATE = .04
110 DECLARE INTEGER CONSTANT PERIOD = 52
```

An example of a program using a named constant TAXRATE is:

```
100 DECLARE REAL CONSTANT TAXRATE = .04
110 DECLARE REAL AMOUNT, COST
120 READ AMOUNT
130 COST = AMOUNT * TAXRATE
140 PRINT "The cost is "; COST
150 END
```

It is easy to decide when to declare a named constant by asking "Does the value of the quantity change during the execution of the program?"

DECLARE statements can also be used to allocate an exact amount of space in the memory of the computer. Integers can now be BYTE, WORD, or LONG length. This means that, in addition to one "box" or byte, you can allocate two bytes or four bytes. Floating point numbers can be SINGLE or DOUBLE. Some examples of DECLARE statements using these length qualifiers are:

```
100  DECLARE SINGLE SIDE, AREA
110  DECLARE DOUBLE VOLUME
120  DECLARE WORD NUMBER, TOTAL
130  DECLARE LONG SUM, QUOTIENT
```

The first two examples declare floating point variables, while the last two declare integer variables.

Declare statements can also be used for functions and arrays. This type of use is for an advanced discussion of BASIC. More information is available in the Digital VAX-BASIC documentation. Programs in this text will use DECLARE statements only when appropriate for the example and in lengthy problems. This convention is used since the programs are for teaching specific programming structures, not total progam format.

EXERCISES E

1. A common error when not using DECLARE statements is to confuse variables. What happens when you run the following program?

```
100 N% = 10%
110 PRINT N
120 END
```

2. Rewrite Example 3.1 using DECLARE statements. RUN the new program for several different constant values for HOURS and RATE. Why are HOURS and RATE considered constants in this program and not variables?

REVIEW QUESTIONS

1. List two ways to document a program.
2. Develop a top-down chart to keep track of the operations for a small business. These include INVENTORY, PAYROLL, ACCOUNTS RECEIVABLE, and ACCOUNTS PAYABLE.
3. What are the four main steps of program design?
4. Label string variables with an S, integer variables with an I, and real variables with an R.

   a. NAME$ f. SCHOOL
   b. X%   g. COLLEGE$
   c. XY   h. HOURS%
   d. WEIGHT   i. RATE
   e. HEIGHT%   j. FILE__NAME$

5. Evaluate the following BASIC expressions.

   a. 8 * 2 * 2 / 4
   b. (3 * 2)**2 + 6 − (4 / 2)
   c. 6**4 + 4 * 2 − 8
   d. 4 + (−8) * 6 + ((8 * 2) / 4 + 2)
   e. 6 + 2 − 7 * 8 + 6 / 3

6. Evaluate the following BASIC expressions for A = 2, B = 3 and C = 1.

   a. A / B + C * B
   b. C / A * B
   c. B**A + C
   d. A + B / C − A * C

SUMMARY OF CHAPTER 3

CONCEPTS AND KEYWORDS INTRODUCED
IN THIS CHAPTER

Concepts	Related Keywords and Symbols
1. Program format	REM ! (exclamation point) PRINT
2. Top-down design	
3. String variables and constants	$
4. Exponential notation	E
5. Functions	SQR INT
6. Integer variables and constants	%
7. Declare variables and constants	DECLARE

Program Control: Choice

4

The computer has followed a strict sequential order in executing all the programs we have written so far. It executes the lowest-numbered line first, then the next lowest-numbered line, continuing until it reaches the highest-numbered line (which should be the END statement) We can write much more powerful programs by using the capability of the computer to

1. Repeat a statement or group of statements many times (Loop)
   OR
2. Decide in one statement which of several statements to execute (Branch).

4.1 CHOICE

There are several types of choices. The simplest type is based on a single alternative. In programming we often ask whether the user wants instructions, or wants to play a game again. If the choice is "yes," then the instructions are printed out or the game is started again. Otherwise, no action is taken. As with all choice structures, a decision is made involving a comparison. This logic can be shown graphically as in Figure 4.1.

VAX-BASIC implements single-choice structures with IF . . . THEN statements.

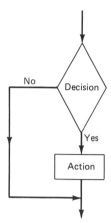

Figure 4.1 Single Action Choice

4.2 THE IF . . . THEN STATEMENTS

The Simple IF . . . THEN

The IF . . . THEN statement is one of the most powerful statements in BASIC. It allows you to write programs that can "make decisions." It is actually the programmer who makes the decisions, but the programs can take different actions, depending on which one of several conditions is true.

For a simple example, consider a program that asks for a number and prints the square of the number:

```
10 PRINT "Give me a number and I will give you its square."
20 INPUT "Number"; N
30 PRINT "Square ="; N*N
40 END

RUNNH

Give me a number and I will give you its square.
Number? 3
Square = 9
```

We will revise the program so that, after printing the square, it asks the user if she wishes to try another number:

```
10 PRINT "Give me a number and I will tell you its square."
20 INPUT "Number"; N
30 PRINT "Square ="; N*N
40 INPUT "Type YES to try again, NO to quit"; ANS$
50 IF ANS$ = "YES" THEN GO TO 20
60 END
```

```
RUNNH
```

```
Give me a number and I will tell you its square.
Number? 3
Square = 9
Type YES to try again, NO to quit?  YES
Number? 2.5
Square = 6.25
Type YES to try again, NO to quit?  NO
```

Notice the new lines 40 and 50. Line 40 asks the user to type YES to use the program again. Whatever string is typed will be assigned to the variable ANS$. In line 50, if ANS$ is "YES", the statement GO TO 20 directs the computer back to line 20 to ask for a number to be squared. If ANS$ is not "YES", line 50 directs the computer on to the next statement in the program, in this case the END statement.

The important point here is that, when the program is written, we do not know what is going to happen in line 50. Sometimes ANS$ will be "YES" and sometimes it will not. The user might want the square of one number or the square of many numbers. The program takes care of all possibilities. This has long been a standard use of the IF . . . THEN statement. In Chapter 6 we will see a better way to construct this kind of loop.

4.3 THE GO TO STATEMENT

In line 50 of the last program, the GO TO statement directs the flow of the program after the user chooses YES or NO. The GO TO statement can be used to repeat a section of a program or to skip over some lines of code. However, to write well structured programs, avoid overuse of GO TO. In the next two chapters we will illustrate several structures that will help you avoid GO TO.

When the GO TO statement is used by itself, it is called an *unconditional transfer*. Its form is simple: GO TO *xx,* where *xx* stands for a line number in the program. By itself, the GO TO statement is not particularly useful, but when combined with an IF . . . THEN statement a GO TO can be appropriately used.

The following example uses GO TO to repeat a section of a program. The program finds the squares of several numbers. We will print the numbers in one column with their squares in a second column.

Example 4.1 *A GO TO Loop*

```
10  PRINT "NUMBER", "SQUARE"
20  READ NUMBER
30  PRINT NUMBER, NUMBER ^ 2
40  GO TO 20
50  DATA 6.2, -3.4, 567, 86423, -0.054, 497, .023, 34.5
60  END
```

```
RUNNH
```

```
NUMBER          SQUARE
 6.2            38.44
-3.4            11.56
 567            321489
 86423          .746894E+10
-.054           .002916
 497            247009
 .023           .00529
 34.5           1190.25
%BAS-F-OUTOFDAT, Out of data
-BAS-I-FROLINMOD,   from line 20 in module NONAME
Ready
```

The loop in this program consists of lines 20 through 40. Notice that line 10 comes before the loop, so it will be executed only once. That is what we want; line 10 prints the headings for the columns. Lines 20 and 30 will be repeated many times; they are part of the loop that is created with the GO TO.

How many numbers and squares will be printed? However many there are in the DATA statement (8 in this case). The bad feature of this program is that it ends on an OUT OF DATA error, which is bad programming form, but it does point out another error message that you will probably see at least once or twice.

One last feature of this program should be pointed out. There are eight numbers in the DATA statement but only one variable name (NUMBER) in the READ statement. This is fine, because the READ statement will be repeated nine times, with the last repetition causing the error message. The first READ causes NUMBER to be 6.2; after 6.2 is dealt with, the second READ causes NUMBER to be -3.4. When -3.4 and its square are printed, the next READ causes NUMBER to be 567.

Thus a single variable name (or a single storage location) can have several different numbers assigned to it in a single program run. This feature makes possible more powerful programs. We could have found squares for hundreds of numbers simply by putting hundreds of numbers in DATA statements. But if each number had to have a different name, we would have to write each of these names in separate READ statements.

Sometimes it is necessary for programs to process large amounts of data. However, when testing a program you might want to stop a loop once you detect an error or find you are in an endless loop. You should suspect that the computer is in an endless loop when either it prints reams of unexpected results or you type RUN and nothing happens for a long time. The first thing to do is to stop the program from running. To do this, hold the CONTROL key down while striking the C key. The CONTROL key is usually on the lower left of the keyboard, near SHIFT. It might say CTRL. We usually indicate this action by CTRL-C. Remember, hold the CONTROL key down before hitting C. This will stop the program from running, and BASIC should respond with Ready. Then list the program and find out what made it loop. Often the culprit is a poorly placed GO TO statement.

4.4 IF RELATIONS

It should be obvious that a complete IF . . . THEN statement requires something after the word IF and something after THEN. After IF we need a relation which may or
may not be true. The possible relations and their symbols are:

Relation	Symbol
Equal	=
Less than	<
Greater than	>
Less than or equal	<=
Greater than or equal	>=
Not equal	<>

On either side of the relational symbol we need an expression, or a formula involving variables and/or constants. These expressions can be complicated, such as

$$(X + 16 * Y * Z) / (4 * X / 7 * X + 9 * Y / 5 * X)$$

or they can be as simple as a single variable X or a constant 2. The expressions can
involve strings as well as numbers.

VAX-BASIC allows almost any executable statement after THEN. In particular,
PRINT statements and assignment statements are often used:

```
50 IF GRADE >= 70 THEN PRINT "This is a passing grade"
```

or

```
80 IF LARGE > X THEN LARGE = X
```

A simple program involving the first statement is:

```
10 INPUT "Grade"; GRADE
20 IF GRADE >= 70 THEN PRINT "This is a passing grade"
30 IF GRADE < 70 THEN PRINT "This is a failing grade"
40 END

RUNNH

Grade?  10
This is a failing grade
Ready

RUNNH

Grade? 90
This is a passing grade
Ready
```

The intent of this program should be clear; tell whether a grade is passing (70 or above) or failing (below 70).

In many applications it is important to be able to tell the computer to decide which of two numbers is larger. A program to do this is as follows:

```
10 INPUT "Give me two different numbers"; A,B
20 LARGE = A
30 IF LARGE < B THEN LARGE = B
40 PRINT "The larger number is "; LARGE
50 END

RUNNH

Give me two different numbers? 3, 6
The larger number is  6
Ready
```

There are, of course, other ways to accomplish the same thing, but we shall be using logic similar to this later on. Line 20 may seem strange, but the logic behind it is this: Look at the number in A first; it must be the largest number so far because it is the only number we have looked at so far. Now compare this "largest number so far" to B. If it is less than B, then B is now the "largest number so far," so put the number in B into LARGE (LARGE = B). It is easy to extend this idea to handle three or four numbers:

```
10 INPUT "Give me three numbers"; A, B, C
20 LARGE = A
30 IF LARGE < B THEN LARGE = B
40 IF LARGE < C THEN LARGE = C
50 PRINT "The largest number is"; LARGE
60 END

RUNNH

Give me three numbers? 1, 2, 3
The largest number is 3
Ready
```

Another standard use of IF . . . THEN is to check INPUT. Sometimes only certain kinds of numbers can be used as data in a program; lengths and weights must not be negative; the day of the month must be between 1 and 31; the number of items bought must be an integer, and so on. The program to find the volume of a cube might begin:

```
10 INPUT "Give me the side of a cube"; SIDE
20 IF SIDE >= 0 THEN 50
30 PRINT "Side cannot be negative"
40 GO TO 10
50 (calculate and print volume)
   .
   .
   .
```

Line 20 checks to see that the value input for SIDE is greater than or equal to 0; if so, then the program goes to line 50 to do the desired calculations. [If not, the computer prints a warning (line 30) and returns to line 10 to ask for a value for SIDE again.] Notice also that line 20 has been shortened from "THEN GO TO 50" to "THEN 50".

The IF . . . THEN statement can also be used to "fix" our program to calculate squares for several numbers. We decide on a special number whose square we do not want and let that number serve as an *end-of-data flag* or *sentinel*. In this case, we know the square of 0 is 0, so 0 is a reasonable flag. The revised program follows.

Example 4.2 *End of Data Flag*

```
10 PRINT "NUMBER", "SQUARE"
20 READ NUMBER
25 IF NUMBER = 0 THEN 60
30 PRINT NUMBER, NUMBER^2
40 GO TO 20
50 DATA 6.2, -3.4, 567, 86423, -0.054, 497, .023, 34.5, 0
60 END

RUNNH

NUMBER          SQUARE
  6.2           38.44
 -3.4           11.56
  567           321489
  86423         .746894E+10
 -.054          .002916
  497           247009
  .023          .000529
  34.5          1190.25
Ready
```

This program is exactly the program used in the GO TO section, with two additions: the last number in the DATA statement is 0; and line 25 has been added. Line 25 says, "If the value of NUMBER is 0, go to the END statement." Again, the program is very general; put in as much DATA as you like, with 0 at the end. This device could as easily be used with INPUT instead of READ/DATA.

All the relations used for numerical variables can also be used for strings and string variables. The equals sign means what you think it means; the two strings have exactly the same characters in the same order. "ABC" is not the same as "ACB". One must be very careful about blanks. "MARY   " is not the same as "MARY" or " MARY". The difference is easy to see when you put quotes around the string but is nearly impossible to see when you type a string in response to INPUT on a screen.

When strings are composed entirely of capital letters, the less than sign (<) means "prior to, in alphabetical order." Thus the following relations are true:

"JOHN" < "MARY"

"HARRIET" < "HARRY"

"ABCD" > "ABC"

[The greater-than sign (>) means "after, in alphabetical order."]

Actually, a string can contain any character, not just capital letters, so we need an order of precedence for all characters. Such an order has already been established and is used by the VAX. It is called ASCII code. (ASCII stands for American Standard Code for Information Interchange.) You can find the entire code in Appendix B, but you do not need to know the entire code. For now, the following should suffice:

1. The uppercase letters are in alphabetical order.
2. The lowercase letters are in alphabetical order, and all the lowercase letters follow all the uppercase letters.
3. The digits, 0 through 9, are in standard numerical order and the digits are prior to all letters.
4. The blank, or space, comes before the digits and letters.

Thus, you can visualize the order of these characters as:

Blank or space

Digits: 0123456789

Uppercase letters: ABCDEFGHIJKLMNOPQRSTUVWXYZ

Lowercase letters: abcdefghijklmnopqrstuvwxyz

If you need to find where special symbols, such as ? and %, fit in, consult Appendix B.

Consider a program to find which of three strings is first in alphabetical order. (Assume the strings are composed entirely of capital letters.) This program is nearly identical to a program to find the smallest of three numbers. The only difference is the use of string variables instead of numerical variables.

```
10 INPUT "Give me three words separated by commas"; A$, B$, C$
20 FIRST$ = A$
30 IF FIRST$ > B$ THEN FIRST$ = B$
40 IF FIRST$ > C$ THEN FIRST$ = C$
50 PRINT FIRST$; " is first in alphabetical order"
60 END


RUNNH


Give me three words separated by commas? HORSE, BLUE, CAR
BLUE is first in alphabetical order
```

4.5 COUNTING WITH IF . . . THEN

The end-of-data flag is a handy device; it allows you to deal with several items of data without knowing in advance how many items there will be. When you do know, you can use the IF in a different way to control the program. Let's try the NUMBER-SQUARE program again, this time assuming in advance that there will be eight numbers to be squared. We introduce a new variable COUNTER that counts each number as it is read. (Do not use COUNT as a variable name; it is a keyword in VAX-BASIC.)

Example 4.3 *Counting with IF*

```
10 PRINT "NUMBER", "SQUARE"
20 COUNTER = 0
30 READ NUMBER
40 COUNTER = COUNTER + 1
50 PRINT NUMBER, NUMBER^2
60 IF COUNTER < 8 THEN 30
70 DATA 6.2, -3.4, 567, 86423, -0.054, 497, .023, 34.5
80 END

RUNNH

NUMBER          SQUARE
 6.2             38.44
-3.4             11.56
 567            321489
 86423          .746894E+10
-.054           .002916
 497            247009
 .023           .000529
 34.5           1190.25
```

Lines 20, 40, and 60 are the new lines, each one containing the variable COUNTER. Line 20 is called the initialization or initial statement. It starts COUNTER at the value 0 because, when line 20 is executed, no numbers have been counted yet. Line 20 is the "increment" line. The statement COUNTER = COUNTER + 1 would be nonsense in algebra, but this is BASIC programming, not algebra. The computer calculates a value for the expression on the right of the equals sign (adds 1 to COUNTER) and puts this value in the box on the left (COUNTER). The effect is simply to add 1 to the value of COUNTER.

Notice that the increment statement is placed immediately after the READ statement, so COUNTER increases by 1 each time a number is read. We could also say that COUNTER is counting the number of times line 30 is being executed. It is a good idea to put the increment statement immediately after (or before) whatever statement you want to count.

Line 60 is the check line. It checks the value of COUNTER by comparing it to the predetermined number 8. If fewer than 8 numbers haver been read, then the computer is directed back to line 30 to READ another number.

When you look at the program above, you should see a loop, lines 30 through 60. These lines will be repeated several times. The lines before the loop will be done only once. Some common mistakes involve putting lines that should be repeated outside a loop, and putting lines that should be executed once inside a loop.

You should follow the program above step by step for at least a few iterations until you see that it is working properly. One way to do this is to set up columns for all the variables in the program. Then read through the program, line by line, changing the values of the variables as the program directs. PRINT statements can be ignored or set off to the side; they will not change the values of variables.

In the program above, there are only two variables, COUNTER and NUMBER, so we begin with columns LINE, COUNTER, and NUMBER. When a line does not change the value of a variable, copy the last value of the variable.

Line	Counter	Number
20	0	
30	0	6.2
40	1	6.2
50	(Could be ignored; prints 6.2 and its square)	
60	(Back to 30, since COUNTER = 1, which is less than 8)	
30	1	−3.4
40	2	−3.4
60	2	−3.4
30	2	567
40	3	567

This should be enough to see that the program is working properly, at least at the beginning. Two or three iterations are generally enough to see if the loop is properly set up.

It is, however, important to consider what will happen when the loop should end. It is a very common mistake to have a loop repeat one too many or one too few times. From what we have already seen, it should be clear that, after lines 30 and 40 are executed the seventh time, COUNTER will be 7 and NUMBER will be .023. In line 50, COUNTER is 7, so the computer goes back to line 30 to READ the last number (34.5). Line 40 increases COUNTER to 8. Finally, in line 60, COUNTER is 8, so the relation COUNTER < 8 is false, and the computer will not go back to line 30, but drops down to the END statement. (Remember, DATA is not an executable statement.) Everything seems to be all right, but of course you will RUN the program and check the results.

We do not really need to know in advance how many repetitions of a certain process are desired. The program could ask for that information at the beginning. For instance,

```
10 INPUT "How many repetitions"; TOTAL
20 COUNTER= 0
30 (Any statement)
40 COUNTER = COUNTER + 1
50 (Any
.  desired
.  operations)
100 IF COUNTER < TOTAL THEN 30
.
.
```

Finally, we often want to count only some of the repetitions in a loop. Suppose we have a set of grades on a test and want the computer to count the number of passing grades. We will use COUNTER as before to count all the grades, and NRPASS (short for number passing) to count passing grades. Assume 70 or above is passing. We will write the program using INPUT, but READ/DATA could be used as well.

```
10 INPUT "How many grades"; TOTAL
20 COUNTER, NRPASS= 0
30 INPUT "Grade"; GRADE
40 COUNTER= COUNTER + 1
50 IF GRADE >= 70 THEN NRPASS = NRPASS + 1
60 IF COUNTER < TOTAL THEN 30
70 PRINT "The number of passing grades is"; NRPASS
80 END

RUNNH

How many grades? 4
Grade?  99
Grade?  63
Grade?  72
Grade?  96
The number of passing grades is 3
```

NRPASS is set to 0 in line 20 and is incremented in line 50 only in cases where the grade is at least 70. COUNTER controls the loop in lines 30 through 60 as before. Finally, the PRINT statement follows the loop.

In the preceding programs there was always one variable that did nothing but count how many times some operation was performed. Sometimes this counting variable, or loop counter, can be used to generate the desired data. Suppose we want a table of squares for the integers from 10 to 20. Instead of putting these numbers in a DATA statement or inputting them by hand, we can generate them as follows:

```
10 PRINT "NUMBER", "SQUARE"
20 NUMBER = 9
30 NUMBER = NUMBER + 1
40 PRINT NUMBER, NUMBER ^2
50 IF NUMBER < 20 THEN 30
60 END

RUNNH

NUMBER          SQUARE
  10             100
  11             121
  12             144
  13             169
  14             196
```

15	225
16	256
17	289
18	324
19	361
20	400

Similarly, let us write a program to find the sum of the integers from 1 to 100 inclusive. We use, as before, a counting variable called NUMBER, and a new variable called SUM to represent the sum of all the numbers.

```
10 SUM, NUMBER = 0
20 NUMBER = NUMBER + 1
30 SUM = SUM + NUMBER
40 IF NUMBER < 100 THEN 20
50 PRINT "The sum of the integers from 1 to 100 is"; SUM
60 END
```

```
RUNNH
```

```
The sum of the integers from 1 to 100 is 5050
```

Line 30 is the "new" line; each time a new value for NUMBER is generated, this line adds the value of NUMBER to the current value for SUM. That is, as the program progresses, SUM is the running total of all the NUMBERs generated so far. A variable used as SUM in line 30 is called an *accumulator*; it accumulates values of some other variables or expressions. A counting variable is just a special kind of accumulator; it accumulates 1's.

The factorial of a positive integer is the product of all the positive integers from 1 to that positive integer. That is,

$$3\text{-factorial is } 1 * 2 * 3 = 6$$
$$5\text{-factorial is } 1 * 2 * 3 * 4 * 5 = 120$$
$$8\text{-factorial is } 1 * 2 * 3 * 4 * 5 * 6 * 7 * 8 = 4320$$

The notation for a factorial of a number is that number followed by an exclamation point; 3-factorial is written as 3!. It should be easy to see that, if A is any integer bigger than 1, then $A! = A * (A-1)!$. For instance, $4! = 4 * 3!$ or $9! = 9 * 8!$. Thus we can "build" factorials by multiplying, in much the same manner as we built sums by adding. The following program calculates N! for any positive integer N that is INPUT.

```
10 NUMBER = 0
20 FACTORIAL = 1
30 INPUT "Positive integer"; N
40 NUMBER = NUMBER + 1
50 FACTORIAL = FACTORIAL * NUMBER
60 IF NUMBER < N THEN 40
70 PRINT N; "factorial is"; FACTORIAL
80 END
```

RUNNH

Positive integer? 5
5 factorial is 120

Notice particularly lines 20 and 50. Line 50 generates factorials for the numbers 1,
2, . . ., up to N. Line 20 assigns an initial value to FACTORIAL. Why is it 1, not 0?

EXERCISES A

Write one program for each of the following (use IF . . . THEN).

1. a. Read five numbers and print the largest. Follow the example in the book and
      do not use a counting variable.
   b. Read five numbers and print the largest. Use a counting variable to set up a
      loop.
2. Read three numbers and print them in increasing order.
3. Read five numbers. Print their sum, product, and mean. (Set up a loop.)
4. Read ten test scores. Print each failing score (below 70) and print the total number of failing scores.
5. Find the sum of the odd integers from 1 to 99, inclusive.
6. Print the table of factorials for the integers from 1 to 10. Print column headings.
7. Degrees Celsius is related to degrees Fahrenheit by the equation

$$C = (5 / 9) * (F - 32)$$

Read the Fahrenheit temperatures 32, 70, 100, −8, and 212 and convert them to
degrees Celsius. Use a loop. Print results in two columns, one for Celsius, one for
Fahrenheit.
8. Find the sum of all the integers between 100 and 300 that are divisible by 9. How
   many such numbers are there?
9. Find the sum of the squares of the first 50 integers:

$$1, 4, 9, 16, . . ., 2500$$

10. A checking account has a balance of $14.23 on October 1. The following trans-
    actions are made in October:

Oct. 3	$90.00 deposit
Oct. 7	$32.25 check
Oct. 12	$11.53 check
Oct. 20	$20.00 deposit
Oct. 27	$56.78 check

Use these numbers as data, with positive numbers indicating deposits, negative numbers representing checks. Use 0 as an end-of-data flag. Read the DATA and print the type of transaction and the balance after each transaction.

11. Input as many positive numbers as you wish, with a negative number as an end-of-data flag. Have the program count the number of positive numbers you entered, their sum, and their mean.

12. Find the smallest integer N for which

$$(1 / 2)**N < 0.001$$

Print both this integer and 1/2 to this power.

13. Certain factory workers are paid an hourly rate. If they work 40 hours or less per week, their gross pay is their hourly rate times hours worked. For each hour over 40, they receive 1.5 times their hourly rate. social security is deducted at 6.65% of gross, and federal and state taxes at 15% of gross (an oversimplification). For each of the following cases, print out a pay statement, including ID number, gross pay, social security, taxes, and net pay (gross pay minus deductions). Round to two decimal places.

Worker ID number	Hourly rate	Hours worked
35648	$4.25	36
63841	$6.12	44
75835	$5.60	40
82457	$4.90	40
90354	$5.20	48
98374	$5.55	37.5

14. Calculate the first 25 Fibonacci numbers: 1, 1, 2, 3, 5, 8, 13 , ... Each number is the sum of the two preceding numbers.

15. Read a list of 12 numbers from a data list. Print the position of the first number that is negative. For example, the list contains 4, 6, 8, 9, −9, 7, 8. The position of the first negative is 5.

4.6 EXTENDED IF . . . THEN

Logical Operators

VAX-BASIC allows the use of the logical operators AND, OR, NOT, and XOR in IF statements. Suppose, for instance, that a grade from 80 to 89 inclusive is to be called a B. If GRADE is the numeric value of the grade in a program, we might want to use a statement such as

```
IF GRADE >= 80 AND GRADE <= 89 THEN PRINT GRADE; "is a B."
```

The PRINT statement will be executed only if both relations, GRADE >= 80 and GRADE <= 89, are true. (Do not try to use IF 80 <= GRADE <= 89 . . .; it won't work.)

The OR operator is sometimes called the "weak OR" or "inclusive OR." The relation

$$X = 2 \text{ OR } Y = 3$$

is considered true if either $X = 2$ or $Y = 3$ or both. The XOR operator is called the "exclusive OR." The relation

$$X = 2 \text{ XOR } Y = 3$$

is true if exactly one of the statements, $X = 2$, $Y = 3$, is true. (It is not true if both $X = 2$ and $Y = 3$.)

The NOT operator negates whatever relation immediately follows it. In place of IF $X <> 2$ . . . we could write IF NOT $X = 2$ . . . . Compound expressions can also be negated by placing them in parentheses. The statement

```
IF NOT (X = 2 OR Y = 5) THEN 50
```

is equivalent to

```
IF X <> 2 AND Y <> 5 THEN 50
```

The following program segment checks to see whether a number is a possible grade before performing operations using the number. (Grades must be between 0 and 100.)

```
50 INPUT "Grade"; GRADE
60 IF NOT (GRADE < 0 OR GRADE > 100) THEN 90
70       PRINT "Not a possible grade"
80       GO TO 50
90 (Any operations)
```

An annulus or doughnut shape in the plane is defined by inequalities of the type

```
A < X^2 + Y^2 < B
```

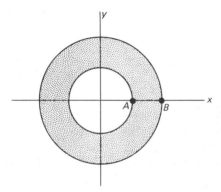

Figure 4.2   Diagram of an Annulus

where A and B are any two numbers such that A < B. A diagram of an annulus is shown in Figure 4.2. The following program determines whether a given point (X, Y) is in the annulus $2 < X^2 + Y^2 < 8$.

Example 4.4 *Determining Whether a Point Is in an Annulus*

```
10 INPUT "Give me the coordinates of a point"; X, Y
20 R = X^2 + Y^2
30 IF R > 2 AND R < 8 THEN PRINT "In annulus ";
40 IF R <= 2 OR R >= 8 THEN PRINT "Not in annulus ";
50 PRINT "X^2 + Y^2 between 2 and 8"
60 END


RUNNH


Give me the coordinates of a point? 1, 2
In annulus X^2 + Y^2 between 2 and 8
```

4.7 LOGICAL OPERATIONS

As with arithmetic operations, there is an order of precedence among logical relations. Also, there must be a hierarchy for the arithmetic operations, relations, and logical operations. The precedence in VAX-BASIC is:

> First, all arithmetic operations
>
> Second, all relations (less than, equals, etc.)
>
> Third, logical operations in the order:
>
> 1. NOT
> 2. AND
> 3. OR, XOR
> 4. IMP   (IMP and EQV are not
> 5. EQV   discussed in this text.)

Let A, B, C stand for relations. Then, according to the hierarchy for logical operations above, the expression

> A OR NOT B AND C

would be evaluated in the order:

> First, the NOT applied only to B;
> Second, the AND in "NOT B AND C";
> Third, the OR, applying to A and
> the result of "NOT B AND C".

The order of logical operations can be changed with the use of parentheses. Even if we do not want to change the order of evaluation of A OR NOT B AND C, the expression will be clearer if we insert parentheses to obtain

$$A \text{ OR (NOT B AND C)}$$

or even

$$A \text{ OR ((NOT B) AND C)}$$

Logical operators can also be used with strings. The following program types all names in DATA that begin with R. The numeral "6" is used as an end-of-data flag.

Example 4.5 *Logical Operations on Strings*

```
10 PRINT "Names beginning with R"
20 READ NAME$
30 IF NAME$ = "6" THEN 70
40    IF NAME$ >= "R" AND NAME$ < "S" THEN PRINT NAME$
50    GO TO 20
60 DATA "RALPH", "MARY", "RODNEY", "REBECCA", "SAM", "O'REILLY"
65 DATA "R2D2", "RHETT", "6"
70 END

RUNNH

Names beginning with R
RALPH
RODNEY
REBECCA
R2D2
RHETT
```

Notice particularly line 40. If the letter R were in a dictionary or telephone book, then it would be the first entry in the R category. We don't know what the last entry under R would be, but we do know that the first entry after all the R's is the letter S. Thus the IF in line 40 could be translated "if the name is at or after the first entry under R and before the first under S, then print the name."

It would be handy if VAX-BASIC also allowed an AND after a THEN. Often when a condition is true we would like to do more than one thing. Although AND cannot be used in this way, it is legitimate to type more than one statement on a line, separating statements by a backslash (\). The backslash can be read as the word "and". For example, checking a possible grade could be achieved in two lines:

```
50 INPUT "Grade"; GRADE
60 IF GRADE < 0 OR GRADE > 100 THEN PRINT "Bad value" \ GO TO 50
```

When the condition after IF is true, both the PRINT statement and the GO TO statement are performed. When the condition is false, the computer continues with the next line in the program and does not perform any of the statements after THEN. At the end of this chapter you will learn two structures more efficient than this one for dealing with multiple actions.

When the condition in the IF statement is long and the number of statements after THEN becomes large, it may be impossible to fit the entire statement on one line. VAX-BASIC allows an IF statement to be composed of several typed lines. We do this by pressing RETURN after THEN and continuing to type on the next line without starting with a new line number, as in the following example.

```
10 INPUT "Three numbers"; ABLE, BAKER, CHARLIE
20 IF ABLE < BAKER AND CHARLIE > ABLE * BAKER THEN <RET>
      PRINT "Example of continued IF statement"
30 END

RUNNH

Three numbers? 1, 2, 3
Example of continued IF statement
```

Line 20 of the program occupies two typed lines. The ⟨RET⟩ at the end of the first typed line and the omission of a line number on the next line tells the computer that the next typed line is still part of line 20. Also, notice that the blanks before the PRINT statement are legal and add to the clarity of the program format.

With two statements after THEN, place each statement on a separate line, as in

```
10 INPUT "Three numbers"; ABLE, BAKER, CHARLIE
20 IF ABLE < BAKER AND CHARLIE > ABLE * BAKER THEN <RET>
      PRINT "This is just an example of the use of" <RET>
      PRINT "two statements after THEN"
30 END
```

4.8 THE IF . . . THEN . . . ELSE STATEMENT

The IF . . . THEN structure can be extended to include two actions, one for the "yes" decision and one for the "no." This can be shown graphically with two action boxes, as in Figure 4.3.

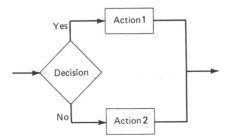

Figure 4.3   Two Action Choice

This decision block can be used for the comparison of two numbers or two strings.

User inputs two grades
If grade1 > grade2 then print grade1,
otherwise print grade2

Action 1 is to print grade1 while action 2 is to print grade2.

In VAX-BASIC the two-action choice structure is programmed with the IF . . . THEN . . . ELSE statement, exemplified by

```
50 IF A = B THEN 70 ELSE 90
```

or

```
80 IF GRADE < 70 THEN PRINT "Fail" ELSE PRINT "Pass"
```

When the condition after IF is true, the statement after THEN is executed. When the condition is false, the statement after ELSE is executed. The IF . . . THEN . . . ELSE structure chooses between two actions.

The IF . . . THEN . . . ELSE construction is not necessary in any sense. Anything that can be done with IF . . . THEN . . . ELSE could be done with IF . . . THEN and GO TO statements. However, the ELSE extension often makes the logic in a program clearer and more structured. Consider a program that asks for two numbers and tells which is larger. We could write the program in the following two ways (among others):

```
10 REM -- IF...THEN...ELSE
20 INPUT "Two different numbers"; A, B
30 PRINT "Larger number is ";
40 IF A > B THEN PRINT "first" ELSE PRINT "second"
50 END

RUNNH

Two different numbers? 3, 4
Larger number is second

10 REM -- IF...THEN with GO TO
20 INPUT "Two different numbers"; A,B
30 PRINT "Larger number is";
40 IF A > B THEN PRINT "first" \ GO TO 60
50 PRINT "second"
60 END

RUNNH

Two different numbers? 5, 4
Larger number is first
```

Both programs do the same thing, but the logic in the first program is a bit easier to see and is correctly structured.

Consider a program to read grades (again!). We will use a negative number as an end of data flag. The program is to print each grade along with PASS or FAIL and count the number NPASS of passing grades and the number NFAIL of failing grades.

Example 4.6 *Print and Count Passing and Failing Grades*

```
100 REM -- Print and count passing and failing grades
110 NPASS = 0
120 NFAIL = 0
130 READ GRADE
140 IF GRADE < 0 THEN 180
150 PRINT GRADE,     ! PASS or FAIL will be on same line as GRADE
160 IF GRADE < 70 THEN
        PRINT "Fail"
        NFAIL = NFAIL + 1
    ELSE
        PRINT "Pass"
        NPASS = NPASS + 1
170 GO TO 130
180 PRINT            ! Leaves a blank line before the next PRINT
190 PRINT NPASS;  "Passing grades"
200 PRINT NFAIL;  "Failing grades"
210 DATA 75, 92, 63, 54, 87, 79, 82, 73, 69, 69, 70, 100, 12, -1
220 END
```

The output of the program will be:

```
75          Pass
92          Pass
63          Fail
54          Fail
87          Pass
79          Pass
82          Pass
73          Pass
69          Fail
69          Fail
70          Pass
100         Pass
12          Fail

8 Passing grades
5 Failing grades
```

The main line in the program is line 160. When GRADE is below 70, this line causes the computer to print Fail and add 1 to NFAIL. When GRADE is not below 70, the statements after ELSE are executed: Pass is typed and 1 is added to NPASS.

Generally, an IF statement deals with two possibilities: the condition after IF is true or false. We can deal with several possibilities by using one or more IFs after ELSE. Suppose a grade of 95 or above is called an HONOR grade and Pass/Fail are as before. Then we could write

```
10 INPUT "Grade"; GRADE
20 IF GRADE >= 95 THEN PRINT "Honor"
   ELSE IF GRADE >= 70 THEN PRINT "Pass"
   ELSE PRINT "Fail"
30 END
```

After ELSE IF we are not required to have the condition GRADE < 95, because the computer gets to ELSE IF only when the condition GRADE >= 95 is false. Similarly, the computer gets to ELSE PRINT "FAIL" only when the two conditions GRADE >= 95 and GRADE >= 70 are both false.

Several of the programs we have already written can be cleaned up a little by using the ELSE in IF statements. The program dealing with points in an annulus could be written:

```
10 INPUT "Give me the coordinates of a point"; X, Y
20 R = X^2 + Y^2
30 IF R > 2 AND R < 8 THEN PRINT "In annulus";
                      ELSE PRINT "Not in annulus";
40 PRINT " 2 < X^2 + Y^2 < 8"
50 END
```

EXERCISES B

Write one program for each of the following (use IF . . . THEN . . . ELSE):

1. Input two numbers. Call the larger one LARGE and the smaller one SMALL. Print the quotient LARGE / SMALL unless SMALL = 0. If SMALL is 0, print a message: Can't divide by 0. (Have the program determine LARGE and SMALL.)

2. Input two positive integers, with the larger one first. Print a message and stop if the first is not larger. Call the larger number LARGE and the smaller number SMALL. Calculate LARGE! / SMALL! (! is factorial).

3. Read three names and type them in alphabetical order.

4. Students whose last names begin with A–M register at 9 A.M. Those with names beginning with N–Z register at 2 P.M. Ask a student her last name and tell her when to register.

5. Ask a student if she is enjoying programming. Print an appropriate response for the answers "YES", "NO", and any other answer.

6. Play a guessing game with the computer. You think of a number from 1 to 100

and have the computer "guess" the number. After the computer picks a number, it should ask if the number was high, low, or correct. If you respond that the number was high, the computer should pick a lower number. Have the computer continue picking numbers until it picks the correct number. When the computer prints its guess, you should respond with H, L, or C to indicate high, low, or correct, respectively. *Hint:* Begin with HIGH $=$ 100 and LOW $=$ 1. Let the computer's first GUESS $=$ 50. If that is too high, let HIGH $=$ GUESS and let the next "guess" be INT(GUESS + LOW)/2). A similar procedure is followed if GUESS is too low. This is a simple example of "binary searching"; the computer is searching for a number from 1 to 100 by cutting the range of the number in half with each guess.

7. A quadratic equation has the form Ax^2 + Bx + C = 0, with A not equal to 0. The discriminant D of the quadratic equation is

$$D = B^2 - 4 * A * C$$

The solution to the quadratic equation is often written as

$$X = (-B \pm SQR(D))/(2 * A)$$

There are actually three possibilities:

1. If D $\langle$ 0 there is no solution (in real numbers).
2. If D $=$ 0 there is one solution.
3. If D $\rangle$ 0 there are two solutions.

Write a program to solve a quadratic equation, given the coefficients A, B, and C. Test the program on (at least) the four cases:

A	B	C
2	12	18
3	-4	2
1	-7	12
0	1	2

8. Write a program that asks for the coordinates x, y of a point and tells whether the point is in one, both, or neither of the circles:

$$x^2 + y^2 = 16 \quad \text{and} \quad (x - 3)^2 + (y + 2)^2 = 25$$

[Consider "in" to mean either inside or on the boundary.] Test the program with the cases $(-3, 2)$, $(4, -1)$, $(2, -1)$, and $(-3, -2)$.

9. Letter grades are to be assigned to number grades as follows:

Range of numbers	Letter grade
90 or above	A
80 or above, but less than 90	B
70 or above, but less than 80	C
60 or above, but less than 70	D
below 60	F

Write a program to read several numerical grades. Print each grade along with the appropriate letter grade.

10. Write a program that asks for three different numbers and prints them in increasing order.

11. The three interior angles of a triangle sum to 180 degrees. Write a program that computes the third angle, given the other two in degrees. Also, tell whether the triangle is equilateral (all angles equal), isosceles (two of the three angles equal), or scalene (no two angles equal).

12. Write a program that asks the user to type in a grade-point average. Print out an appropriate message for the average. For example, with the range 3.5 to 4.0 you might print "GOOD WORK!"

4.9 BLOCK IF

Often IF . . . THEN . . . ELSE statements become quite complicated with many levels of choice. The *block IF* structure allows you to clarify your logic and create a structure for coding the decisions.

The general format of a block IF is:

```
Line #  IF condition THEN
             STATEMENT A

                  .
                  .
                  .

             STATEMENT B
        ELSE
             STATEMENT C

                  .
                  .
                  .

             STATEMENT D
        END IF
Line #  (rest of program)
```

Notice that a line number is needed only at the beginning of the IF block. From now on programs in this text will not use line numbers for statements inside a block IF structure.

An IF statement must be terminated, either by an END IF statement or by a line number. That is, even a single-alternative IF statement such as

```
IF X < Y THEN PRINT Y
```

requires a line number on the next line to terminate the IF. We will use END IF for all IF statements except single-alternative statements like this one.

The statements in a block IF can be any valid BASIC statements, even another

IF . . . THEN . . . ELSE sequence. An END IF can be used with an IF statement within a block IF.

Let's look at a salary example again, using the block IF structure.

```
100 READ N$, HR, RATE
110 IF HR > 40 THEN
        OVER = HR - 40
        OVERPAY = 1.5 * OVER * RATE
        SAL = 40 * RATE + OVERPAY
    ELSE
        SAL = HR * RATE
    END IF
120 PRINT N$, HR, RATE, SAL
130 DATA JONES, 35, 12.50
140 END
```

The following example is a complete program using the block IF structure. It calculates college tuition for in-state and out-of-state students.

Example 4.7 *College Tuition for In-State and Out-of-State Students*

```
100 REM -- Calculate in-state and out-of-state tuition
110 PRINT "   TUITION PROGRAM"
120 PRINT
130 PRINT "STUDENT", "TUITION"
140 READ NAME$, CREDITS, INOUT$
150 IF NAME$ = "EOD" THEN 230
160 !      Block IF Structure
170 IF INOUT$ = "IN" THEN
        IF CREDITS >= 10 THEN
            TUITION = 80 * CREDITS
        ELSE
            TUITION = 100 * CREDITS
        END IF
    ELSE
        IF CREDITS >= 10 THEN
            TUITION = 100 * CREDITS
        ELSE
            TUITION = 120 * CREDITS
        END IF
    END IF
180 PRINT NAME$, "$"; TUITION
190 GO TO 200
200 DATA Wilson, 8, IN, Tiffin, 17, IN
210 DATA Adams, 6, OUT, Davis, 16, OUT
220 DATA EOD, 0, X
230 END

RUNNH
```

TUITION PROGRAM

STUDENT	TUITION
Wilson	$ 800
Tiffin	$ 1360
Adams	$ 720
Davis	$ 1600

In this example the main block IF has two block IF statements inside, each with its own END IF statement. Only a single line number is used to start the block at line 170. The final END IF statement signals the end of the block IF structure. The GO TO in line 190 is used to repeat the code for determining tuition. In Chapters 5 and 6 you will learn additional ways to repeat code without a GO TO.

4.10 ON ... GO TO

We often use IF statements to control program flow, as with the statement:

```
IF X < 2 THEN 40 ELSE 80
```

This statement sends the computer to line 40 when the value of X is less than 2 and to line 80 when the value is 2 or more. This simple construction works well when there are just two alternatives, and it can be extended to handle several alternatives.

For example, suppose X can be only 1, 2, 3, or 4 and that each different value of X requires the computer to go to a different line. Then we could write:

```
IF X = 1 THEN 40
ELSE IF X = 2 THEN 80
ELSE IF X = 3 THEN 140
ELSE IF X = 4 THEN 160
END IF
```

A simpler way to achieve the same result is with an ON . . . GO TO statement:

```
ON X GO TO 40, 80, 140, 160
```

The general form of the ON . . . GO TO statement is:

```
ON <integer expression> GO TO Ln #, Ln #, ... OTHERWISE Ln #
```

When the value of the integer expression after ON is 1, control passes to the first line number after GO TO. When the value is 2, control passes to the second line number after GO TO, and so on. If the value is less than 1, BASIC gives an error message: ON statement out of range. If the value is greater than the number of line numbers after GO TO, control passes to the line number given after OTHERWISE.

Suppose you want your program to print different messages to freshmen, sophomores, juniors, and seniors. The program might be:

```
100 REM -- Illustrate ON...GO TO
110 PRINT "What is your class?"
120 PRINT "Please enter 1, 2, 3, or 4"
130 INPUT C
140 ON C GO TO 70, 90, 110, 130 OTHERWISE 120
150 PRINT "Freshmen are foolish"
160 GO TO 220
170 PRINT "Sophomores are silly"
180 GO TO 220
190 PRINT "Juniors are a joy"
200 GO TO 220
210 PRINT "Seniors are superb"
220 END

RUNNH

What is your class?
Please enter 1, 2, 3, or 4
? 5
Please enter 1, 2, 3, or 4
? 3
Juniors are a joy
```

Notice that the OTHERWISE 120 protects the program from ending on an error message if the user enters any integer but 1, 2, 3, or 4.

If the expression after ON is not an integer, VAX-BASIC will truncate the value to an integer. That is, ON C is equivalent to ON INT(C). A value of 1.99 would be truncated to 1, 3.7 to 3, and so on.

4.11 SELECT/CASE

The SELECT/CASE statement is one of the most versatile multiple decision structures. It can accommodate the benefits of ON . . . GO TO and eliminate the cumbersome block IF for multiple decisions. The structure of the SELECT/CASE statement is really just an expanded two action choice. Instead of two actions there are now multiple actions. This is shown graphically in Figure 4.4. The general format for the SELECT/CASE statement is:

```
Line #  SELECT <select expression>
            CASE <case value 1>
                Statements
            CASE <case value 2>
                Statements
            CASE <case value N>
                Statements
            CASE ELSE
                Statements
        END SELECT
```

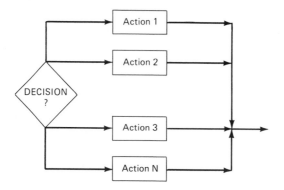

Figure 4.4   Multiple Action Choice

The keyword SELECT begins the block and the keyword END SELECT ends the block. Each CASE keyword establishes an alternative CASE. When the value after CASE matches the value of the SELECT expression, the block of code after that CASE will be executed. If the SELECT expression does not match any CASE, then the code after ELSE will be executed. If CASE ELSE is not included, the SELECT/CASE terminates and control passes to the statement after END SELECT.

Suppose you again want to print different messages to freshmen, sophomores, juniors, or seniors. The program rewritten with SELECT/CASE might be:

```
100 REM -- Illustrate SELECT/CASE
110 PRINT "What is your class?"
120 PRINT "Please enter 1, 2, 3, or 4"
130 INPUT C
140 SELECT C
        CASE 1
            PRINT "Freshmen are foolish"
        CASE 2
            PRINT "Sophomores are silly"
        CASE 3
            PRINT "Juniors are a joy"
        CASE 4
            PRINT "Seniors are superb"
        CASE ELSE
            GO TO 120
    END SELECT
160 END
```

You can also use a variety of CASE value ranges. For example you can stipulate a range with CASE 16 TO 24. You can also use relational operators, as in CASE < 15 for all values less than 15. CASE values that are not consecutive can also be listed separated with commas, as in CASE 3, 7 or CASE 7, 8, 11. The value following the CASE keyword can also be a string, as in CASE "SQUARE" or CASE "CLASS".

An equals sign is optional after CASE, as in CASE = 4. The value or values following CASE must match the data type of the SELECT expression. The following program uses SELECT with a string variable.

```
100 INPUT "Give me your last name"; NAME$
110 SELECT NAME$
          CASE "A" TO "LZZZZ"
               PRINT "Register at 9:00 AM"
          CASE "M" TO "ZZZZZ"
               PRINT "Register at 2:00 PM"
          CASE ELSE
               PRINT "Invalid name"
               GO TO 100
    END SELECT
120 END
```

There are many other opportunities where SELECT/CASE will make your programming task easier. The structure will help you to sort out multiple decisions. We will use the structure with a variety of examples throughout the rest of the book.

EXERCISES C

1. Write a program using IF blocks to compute employee bonuses. For each employee, read the employee name, weekly salary, number of years of service, and productivity rating (1 to 4). The bonus depends on the productivity rating of the employee and the number of years of service. Bonuses are determined as follows:

   If the productivity rating is a 3 or 4, the bonus is two weeks' salary. Otherwise the bonus is one week's salary.
   In addition, if an employee has 10 or more years of service, his bonus is increased by $200.
   If the employee has less than 2 years of service, his bonus is cut in half.
   No one is to receive a bonus less than $150.

2. Redo Exercise B9 in this chapter to obtain letter grades for numerical grades using an IF block.

3. Write a program using an IF block that computes discounts on sale items. The items are discounted based on the cost of the item.

Cost	Discount
1.00–99.99	5%
100.00–199.99	7%
200.00–299.99	9%
300.00 and above	10%

   Print out the original cost of the item, the amount of the discount, and the new cost after the discount.

4. Write a program using an IF block to classify boxes by weight. Use the following table:

Weight	Class
150–174	1
175–199	2
200–249	3
250 and above	4

Print an error message if the weight does not fall in one of these categories.

5. Write a program that asks the user which of four calculations she would like performed, then does that calculation. Use ON . . . GO TO and the following calculations.

1. Volume of a cube.   (User gives side)
2. Area of a circle.   (User gives radius)
3. Area of a triangle.   (User gives base and height)
4. Area of a trapezoid.   (User gives base and 2 heights)

6. Write a program to check that ON C GO TO is really ON INT(C) GO TO. Input decimal values (positive and negative) to branch to several alternatives.

7. Write a program using SELECT/CASE to compute the area of different shapes. Find the area of a square, rectangle, triangle, and circle.

8. Rewrite the employee bonus program in Exercise C1 above using SELECT/CASE.

9. Write a program to assign letter grades to numeric grades using SELECT/CASE. Also print out an appropriate message for each grade such as "Excellent" for an A.

10. Using the data given below, write a program to have the computer do the following:

(a) Calculate the cost of tuition, room, and board for students for a school in VA. Tuition is $80/credit for in-state students and $100/credit for out-of-state students, with a maximum tuition of $1500. Room and board is $2000 for Main Dormitory and $2500 for Randolph.

(b) Count the number of in-state and out-of-state students.

Name	State	Credits	Dorm
BEV STINSON	PA	14	RANDOLPH
LACY SMITHERS	CA	18	MAIN
ANN WATSON	VA	15	RANDLOPH
LISA SAUDERS	PA	15	MAIN
CATHY MATHEWS	VA	15	RANDOLPH
JESSICA HALL	VA	17	RANDOLPH

4.12 LINE NUMBERS REVISITED

As shown in this chapter, line numbers are not necessary for every line in a BASIC program. Even for programs written with line numbers, only the first statement in the program must have a line number. A program to calculate salary could be rewritten as follows:

```
100 PRINT ,,"SALARY PROGRAM"
    PRINT "NAME","HOURS","RATE","BLUE CROSS","SALARY"
    INPUT "Type in your name"; NAME$
    INPUT "Type in the hours worked"; HOURS
    INPUT "Type in the rate of pay"; RATE
    IF HOURS > 40
       THEN
          OVER = HOURS - 40
          SAL = 40 * RATE + OVER * RATE * 1.5
       ELSE
          SAL = HOURS * RATE
    END IF
    PRINT NAME$, HOURS, RATE, SAL
    END
```

We recommend against writing programs like this, unless you are using an editor to write and revise programs, because it is very awkward to use the EDIT command on a multistatement line. We assume from now on that you are writing programs with line numbers.

It is simpler to say which lines in a program *do* need line numbers. First, as we mentioned earlier, an IF statement that is not terminated with an END IF statement must be followed by a line with a line number.

Second, REM statements must be terminated by line numbers. If a REM statement is used to begin the preceding program, then two line numbers are needed. The program would start

```
100 REM -- Calculate salary
110 PRINT ,,"SALARY PROGRAM"
```

If the line number 110 were deleted, BASIC would consider the entire program to be a comment.

Third, a DATA statement should also be terminated by a line number on the following line.

Statement Labels

Statement labels may be used in place of, or in addition to, line numbers. Any legal variable name is also a legitimate statement label name. A *label* is a string that immediately precedes a statement. The statement can be on the same line as the label or on the following line. The label must be followed by a colon (:) to separate it from the following statement. For example, we could write

```
READLOOP:
    INPUT "Give me a number"; NUMBER
```

or

```
READLOOP: INPUT "Give me a number"; NUMBER
```

The colon after READLOOP is not part of the label name; it actually defines READ-LOOP as a statement label. However, when making reference to the label, the colon is not used, as in

```
GO TO READLOOP
```

Labels can be referenced anywhere line numbers could be referenced, with two exceptions:

a. In an IF . . . THEN or IF . . . THEN . . . ELSE statement, the keyword GO TO is required in order to reference a label. For example, in

```
IF ANSWER$ = "YES" THEN GO TO POSITIVE
```

the GO TO is required. With a line number one can write

```
IF ANSWER$ = "YES" THEN 20
```

b. The value of the ERL function (Error Line Function, described in Chapter 8) can be compared to a line number, but not to a label.

The following program illustrates the use of labels. The labels used are LOOP and FINISH. The program asks for names and ages and writes a message depending on the age.

```
100 PRINT "Give name and ages as requested."
    PRINT "Type STOP for name to end input"
    LOOP:
      INPUT "Name"; NAME$
      IF NAME$ = "STOP" THEN GO TO FINISH
200 INPUT "Age"; AGE
    SELECT AGE
        CASE 0 TO 20
           PRINT "You are young, "; NAME$
        CASE 21 to 40
           PRINT "Haven't hit middle age yet, "; NAME$
```

```
      CASE 41 TO 60
         PRINT "Enjoy yourself, "; NAME$
      CASE > 60
         PRINT "You are only as old as you feel, "; NAME$
   END SELECT
   GO TO LOOP
   FINISH:
      PRINT "Good bye"
   END
```

Notice that line 200 terminates the THEN statement in the preceding line. The END SELECT terminates the SELECT/CASE block.

Labels are useful for structuring the logic of a program. They allow for simpler program flow if used in programs without line numbers. In this text we will use only a few labels. We use line numbers mainly for easy reference to the lines when discussing programs but also for simplified editing with the EDIT command. We generally eliminate line numbers inside IF blocks, SELECT/CASE, and some other structures discussed in the next two chapters.

REVIEW QUESTIONS

1. Write an IF . . . THEN or IF . . . THEN . . . ELSE statement which will do the following.
   a. Print the value of variable Y if that value is greater than 10, otherwise print the value 2.
   b. Decrease CNT by 1 if the value of M is less than 100.
   c. Print "GOOD WORK" if the value of TEST is greater than 85, otherwise print "STUDY SOME MORE".
   d. Add 2 to SUM if A ⟩ B, subtract 2 from SUM if A ⟨ B, otherwise set SUM to 0.
   e. GO TO line 30 if X$ = "TRUE", otherwise set X$ to "FALSE".
2. Rewrite the following program using the block IF format.

```
10  READ A
20  IF A = 0 THEN 80
30  IF A > 0 THEN 60
40  PRINT " A is small"
50  GO TO 90
60  PRINT " A is large"
70  GO TO 90
80  PRINT " A is equal to 0"
90  END
```

3. The following program has several errors. Correct them all.

```
100  REM -- Program to compute wages for workers
110  READ N, HOURS, HOURLY_RATE
120  IF HOURS = -99 THEN GO TO 100
130  HOURS * HOURLY_RATE = WAGE
140  PRINT N, WAGE
150  GO TO 20
160  DATA ANNA HAVIALIND, 38, 10, BETSY REYNOLDS, 42, 12.5
170  DATA HENRY SIMMONS, 40, 8, LUCY ECKSTEIN, 40, 11
180  DATA STOP, -99
190  END
```

4. Mark the following relational expressions T or F for the following values: $X = 5$, $Y = 6$, $Z = 10$.

T	F	X < 6 AND Y < 6
T	F	X < 6 OR Y < 6
T	F	X = 5 OR Y = 7 OR Z > 34 / 56 + 2^5 - 978
T	F	X > 4 AND Y = 2^ -6 / 3 + 2.3 AND Z = 11
T	F	Y = 6 AND Z = 10

5. If the following statement is executed when the value of C is 3, what is the next line the computer will execute?

```
ON C GO TO 100, 150, 200, 250
```

SUMMARY OF CHAPTER 4

CONCEPTS AND STATEMENTS INTRODUCED IN THIS CHAPTER

Concept	Related statements
1. Single-action choice structure	IF . . . THEN
2. Two-action choice structure	IF . . . THEN . . . ELSE
3. Multiple-action choice structure	Block IF
	SELECT / CASE
4. Unconditional branch	GO TO
5. Control program flow	ON . . . GO TO
	IF
6. Labels	

5

Program Control: Repetition

In the last chapter we introduced the IF statements that allow us to control program flow based on certain sets of conditions being TRUE or FALSE. IF statements are very well suited to choosing one set of statements from several sets, but BASIC provides better methods for looping, or repetition of sets of statements. In this chapter we discuss the FOR and NEXT statements which provide for repetition of groups of statements.

5.1 REPETITION

We often write computer programs to repeat a tedious process numerous times. A structure that repeats a group of statements several times is called a *repetition structure* or a *loop*. This structure must have an action to repeat and a means of deciding when to stop repeating the action. In the last chapter we used IF statements to set up loops. Here we discuss the FOR/NEXT structure that sets up a loop to be performed a specified number of times. Figure 5.1 gives a graphic depiction of a FOR/NEXT loop.

At the beginning of the loop the repetition counter is set to a starting value. If the value is less than the final number of repetitions, the action is (or multiple actions are) performed. After the actions are completed, the loop counter is incremented and the loop repeated until the final value is reached. Then the loop is terminated and the program continues.

Two other forms of repetition will be discussed in Chapter 6.

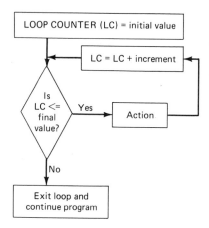

Figure 5.1   FOR/NEXT Structure

5.2 SIMPLE LOOPS

Strictly speaking, the FOR and NEXT statements are not necessary in BASIC; any program written with FOR and NEXT could also be written without them. However, they make many programs easier both to write and to read. An example:

```
10 FOR I = 1 TO 5
20     PRINT "Hello",
30 NEXT I
40 END
```

When this program is RUN, the computer will type

```
Hello        Hello        Hello        Hello        Hello
```

The FOR and NEXT statements in lines 10 and 30 cause line 20 to be repeated five times. We could accomplish the same thing with the following program using a counting variable and an IF statement:

```
10 I = 0
20 PRINT "Hello",
30 I = I + 1
40 IF I < 5 THEN 20
50 END
```

The FOR and NEXT statements should make it easier to see the loop(s) in a program. FOR begins the loop, NEXT ends the loop, and the statements in between (called the "body" of the loop) are the statements to be repeated. We indent the body of the loop as in line 20 in the first program above, because this will make the program easier to read.

The FOR statement has several parts. The word FOR, the equals sign, and the word TO must be present in every FOR statement. Between "FOR" and "=" there must be the name of a single numerical variable (I in the example above). After the equals sign and after "TO" there must be a numeric expression. Thus, we can write the form of the FOR statement as:

```
FOR <num. variable> = <num. expression> TO <num. expression>
```

The form of the NEXT statement is much simpler:

```
NEXT <numerical variable>
```

The only restriction on the NEXT statement is that the variable name in the NEXT statement must be the same as the variable name used in the corresponding FOR statement. This variable is called the *loop counter* or *loop control* variable.

In the program above the loop counter (I) had nothing to do with the statement in the body of the loop (Print "Hello",). This will often be the case, as in the program below.

Example 5.1 *A FOR Loop to Add 10 Numbers*

```
10 REM -- Find total of 10 numbers
20 TOTAL = 0
30 FOR K = 1 TO 10
       READ SCORE
       TOTAL = TOTAL + SCORE
40 NEXT K
50 PRINT "Total = "; TOTAL
60 DATA 35, 17, 48, 53, 67, 82, 35, 27, 91, 66
70 END

RUNNH

Total =   521
```

The loop counter K keeps track of how many times the body of the loop is done. Also, note that line numbers are not used for statements inside the FOR/NEXT block. This convention makes it easier to see the structure.

Often, however, the loop counter can be used to generate just the data you want to use. Loop counters are especially handy for setting up tables. Suppose you want a table of squares and square roots of the integers from 20 to 30. The following program types this table.

Example 5.2 *A Table of Squares and Square Roots*

```
10 REM -- Table of squares and square roots
20 PRINT "NUMBER", "SQUARE", "SQUARE ROOT"
30 FOR Z = 20 TO 30
       PRINT Z, Z*Z, SQR(Z)
40 NEXT Z
50 END
```

Z will have the value 20 when the PRINT statement in line 40 is first executed, then Z will become 21 and the PRINT statement will be executed again. Z will become 22, 23, and so on, until it reaches 30.

When there is only one statement in the body of the loop, VAX-BASIC permits a FOR statement to be "tacked on" to this statement with no NEXT required. The program above could be:

```
10 REM -- Table of squares and square roots
20 PRINT "NUMBER", "SQUARE", "SQUARE ROOT"
30 PRINT Z, Z*Z, SQR(Z) FOR Z = 20 TO 30
40 END

RUNNH
```

NUMBER	SQUARE	SQUARE ROOT
20	400	4.47214
21	441	4.58258
22	484	4.69042
23	529	4.79583
24	576	4.89898
25	625	5
26	676	5.09902
27	729	5.19615
28	784	5.2915
29	841	5.38516
30	900	5.47723

This device, called the *FOR modifier*, obviously can make programs shorter.

It is not necessary to know how many times a loop is to be performed before the program is written. As before, the program can ask for that information when it is running. For example:

Example 5.3 *Calculating a Mean*

```
10 PRINT "I will calculate a mean for you."
20 INPUT "How many numbers"; N
30 TOTAL = 0
40 FOR Q = 1 TO N
      INPUT "Number"; NUMBER
      TOTAL = TOTAL + NUMBER
50 NEXT Q
60 PRINT "The mean is"; TOTAL / N
70 END

RUNNH

I will calculate a mean for you.
How many numbers? 3
Number? 2
Number? 4
Number? 6
The mean is 4
```

STEP in FOR Statements

When we are using a variable only to count, it is natural to increment that variable by 1. It is often useful to be able to increment by some number other than 1, so BASIC allows a more general FOR statement in which we specify the value of the increment or step desired.

Suppose we want to add up the odd integers from 1 to 99. This can easily be done with a FOR loop using a *STEP clause,* as in the following program.

Example 5.4 *STEP in FOR Statements*

```
10 REM -- Sum of odd integers from 1 to 99
20 SUM = 0
30 SUM = SUM + NUMBER FOR NUMBER = 1 TO 99 STEP 2
40 PRINT "Sum ="; SUM
50 END

RUNNH

Sum = 2500
```

The new part of the FOR modifier in line 30 is "STEP 2". This clause tells the computer to increment by 2 instead of 1. Thus NUMBER will first be 1, then $1 + 2 = 3$, then $3 + 2 = 5$, and so on until NUMBER $= 99$.

Certain interest rates vary in steps of one-fourth of 1%. Suppose you want to know the simple interest on $1000 for one year for all possible interest rates between 12% and 14%, and suppose the interest rate can vary only in steps of 1/4%. The following program sets up such a table.

Example 5.5 *Interest Rates*

```
10 REM -- Interest on $1000, rates from 12% TO 14%, steps of 1/4%
20 PRINT "RATE IN %", "INTEREST IN DOLLARS"
30 PRINT RATE, 1000 * (RATE / 100) FOR RATE = 12 TO 14 STEP 1/4
40 END

RUNNH

RATE IN %     INTEREST IN DOLLARS
 12            120
 12.25         122.5
 12.5          125
 12.75         127.5
 13            130
 13.25         132.5
 13.5          135
 13.75         137.5
 14            140
```

(Notice we wrote RATE/100 in line 30 to change the rate from a percent to a decimal.) We could have written STEP 0.25 instead of STEP $1/4$ in line 30, but there is no harm in letting the computer do the calculation.

Because computer arithmetic can be inexact, some programmers recommend using only integer values after STEP. If you do use noninteger steps, it is wise to make the steps reciprocals of powers of 2: $1/2$, $1/4$, $1/8$, etc. The computer can calculate such steps exactly.

To see more precisely what the FOR and NEXT statements cause the computer to do, we will write a small program using FOR/NEXT and an equivalent program, with no FOR or NEXT, that executes as VAX-BASIC would execute the FOR/NEXT program. The program does nothing but type the values of the loop counter, but the point is to illustrate how FOR/NEXT controls the loop.

PROGRAM WITH FOR/NEXT   WITHOUT FOR/NEXT

```
15 FOR I = 1 TO 10 STEP 2     10 LIMIT = 10
       PRINT I                20 INCREMENT = 2
25 NEXT I                     30 I = 1
35 END                        40 IF I > LIMIT THEN 90
                              50     PRINT I
                              60 IF I + INCREMENT > LIMIT THEN 90
                              70 I = I + INCREMENT
                              80 GO TO 50
                              90 END
```

The first time the computer executes the FOR statement in line 15, VAX-BASIC does something equivalent to lines 10 through 40 in the second program:

```
10 The value 10 is assigned to a variable (LIMIT)
   so the computer can later check to see if the
   counter (I) is "over the limit."
20 The step size (INCREMENT) is assigned the value 2.
30 The counter (I) is set equal to the initial value (1).
40 The value of the counter (I) is compared to LIMIT.
   If it is greater than LIMIT, then the computer
   "jumps out of the loop" (goes to line 90).
```

The NEXT statement in line 35 of the first program is equivalent to lines 60, 70, and 80 of the second program:

```
60 Compare I + INCREMENT to LIMIT.  If I + INCREMENT is
   greater than LIMIT, the computer goes to the statement
   after NEXT (line 90).
70 Increment the value of the counter (I = I + INCREMENT).
80 GO TO 50.
```

What we have shown in the second program is not exactly what VAX-BASIC does. We have simplified a little. The point is that a loop requires initialization, incrementing, and checking, and it is important to notice that a check statement (line 40) comes before the body of the loop (line 50). Thus if you start a loop with

```
FOR I = 2 TO 1
```

the body of the loop will never be performed because the initial value 2 is over the limit 1. You are not likely to write FOR I = 2 TO 1 in a program, but you might write something like FOR I = INITIAL TO LIMIT and in some cases the value of INITIAL may be larger than the value of LIMIT.

Either program above just types the numbers 1, 3, 5, 7, 9 on five separate lines. You should notice that the number 10 (assigned to LIMIT in the second program) is *not* one of the values assigned to the counter I. Often it will be the last value that is assigned to the counter inside the loop, but it does not have to be.

Also, suppose we add to the first program the line

```
30 PRINT I
```

What number will be typed? To find out, look at line 50 in the second program when the value of I is 9. The number 9 is typed, then I + INCREMENT is compared to LIMIT in line 60. Since I + INCREMENT is 9 + 2 = 11 and LIMIT is 10, the computer leaves the loop with the value of I still 9. The general rule is: after a FOR/NEXT loop, the value of the loop counter is its last incremented value which is not beyond the limit of the loop.

Another warning: different versions of BASIC perform FOR/NEXT loops differently. When using a new version, you should find out what happens to the loop counter variable after the loop is performed and whether the loop counter is checked before the first iteration of the loop.

It is possible to have a loop counter begin with a large value and decrease to lower values by making the step size negative. For instance, you might want the higher numbers at the top of a table instead of at the bottom. To type the integers from 10 down to 1, you could write

```
10 FOR INTEG = 10 TO 1 STEP -1     ! INTEGER is a keyword
        PRINT INTEG
20 NEXT INTEG
30 END

RUNNH

10
9
8
7
6
5
4
3
2
1
```

With a negative step, the computer leaves the loop when the counter is *less than* or equal to the limit value. In the program above, the value of INTEG would be 1 after the entire loop is performed.

Finding the Smallest Number in a Set

Consider the problem of finding the smallest number in a list and its position in the list. We assume the list of numbers will be in a DATA statement, with a separate DATA statement giving the number of items in the list. We will need the following variables:

> NUMBER, representing the number of items in the list
> I, the loop counter
> SCORE, representing each number in the list
> SMALL, the smallest number in the list
> POSITION, the position of the smallest number in the list

As before, we have the computer look at the numbers one at a time, and at any given time, SMALL will be the smallest number the computer has seen so far. Similarly, POSITION will be the position of the smallest number so far.

Try to imagine being somewhere in the middle of the program as it is running. That is, several numbers have been looked at, but not all of them. SMALL and POSITION have some values (but we do not have to know what these values are). What needs to be done next? We must:

1. Look at the next number on the list.
2. Compare this number to SMALL.
   a. If this number is bigger than (or equal to) SMALL, we don't do anything with it but just go on to look at the next number in the list.
   b. If this number is smaller than SMALL, then it is the smallest number so far; its value must be assigned to SMALL and its position assigned to POSITION.

Now, how do we code what we have said? That is, how do we write VAX-BASIC statements that do what we have said in English? Point 1 is easy; to look at the next number, write READ SCORE. For point 2b, we can write

```
IF SCORE < SMALL THEN
   SMALL = SCORE
   POSITION = I
END IF
```

The point is that the loop counter I is the position of this SCORE, since I is just counting the number of scores read (so far). Of course, this SCORE might not be the smallest one in the list, but if a later SCORE turns out to be smaller, then SMALL and POSITION will be assigned new values.

What about point 2a? It says to go back and look at (READ) the next SCORE. Does that mean we need an ELSE clause or a GO TO directing the computer back to the READ statement? For both of these questions the answer is no. The NEXT statement will direct the computer back to the READ statement if the last SCORE has not yet been read, and it will send the computer to the statement after NEXT if this was the last SCORE. Thus the body of the loop has only a READ statement and an IF block:

```
READ SCORE
IF SCORE < SMALL THEN
    SMALL = SCORE
    POSITION = I
END IF
```

The rest of the program is easier, but there is still one sticky point. What should we use for an initial value for SMALL? If we don't specify anything, then we start with SMALL = 0, so if all the scores are positive, the final value of SMALL would be 0. (The condition after IF would never be true.) There are two reasonable ways to assign an initial value for SMALL. One is to choose a very large number—large enough so we can be practically certain that at least one of the scores will be smaller. We will begin with SMALL = 1E30, a rather large number. We have already agreed that NUMBER will be read from a DATA statement, so READ NUMBER will be on the first line. Finally, we put PRINT and DATA statements after the loop. The complete program follows.

Example 5.6 *Finding the Smallest Number in a Set*

```
100 REM -- Find the smallest number in a set of scores
110 POSITION = 1
120 READ NUMBER
130 SMALL = 1E30
140 FOR I = 1 TO NUMBER
        READ SCORE
        IF SCORE < SMALL THEN
            SMALL = SCORE
            POSITION = I
        END IF
150 NEXT I
160 PRINT "The smallest number is "; SMALL
170 PRINT "Its position is"; POSITION
180 DATA 6
190 DATA 38, -74, 502, 0, -86, 34
200 END
```

When this program is RUN, the output will be:

```
The smallest number is -86
Its position is 5
```

We said that there is another reasonable way to get an initial value for SMALL. Here it is: replace lines 120–140 above with

```
120 READ SMALL
130 FOR I = 2 TO NUMBER
```

In other words, read the first score in as SMALL. (The first number must be the small-est number so far.) Then, since the first score is dealt with outside the loop, begin the loop counter at 2 rather than 1. This method is better than the first method, which would not work if all the numbers were larger than 1E30.

You should see the program above as consisting of three parts: the loop itself (lines 140 to 150); and the parts before and after the loop. When you write programs involving one loop, you should think about one of these parts at a time. It is always a good idea to break a big problem down into several smaller parts. Very often it will be helpful to write the program "inside out." That is, concentrate on what goes inside the loop first, then consider what must come before the loop, and finally decide what comes after the loop. Of course, some programs will be so simple that you can just write them from beginning to end.

The RESTORE Statement

Consider the same problem as above, but suppose we also want to subtract the small-est number in the list from every number in the list. Since we already know how to find the smallest number, this is quite an easy problem. We just have to add a loop that subtracts SMALL from each number in the list. The problem arises from the fact that we must read all the numbers again, but one more READ statement will cause an out-of-data error. The solution to the problem is a new statement, RESTORE. This state-ment causes the next READ statement to begin with the first item in DATA. Then we simply read each number and subtract SMALL from it. Here is the program.

Example 5.7 *Reusing DATA with the RESTORE Statement*

```
100 REM -- Find the smallest number and subtract from each number
110 READ NUMBER
120 READ SMALL
130 FOR I = 2 TO NUMBER
        READ SCORE
        IF SCORE < SMALL THEN
            SMALL = SCORE
            POSITION = I
        END IF
140 NEXT I
150 PRINT "The smallest number is "; SMALL
160 PRINT "Its position is "; POSITION
170 RESTORE
180 READ NUMBER
190 PRINT
200 PRINT "Score - small equals"
```

```
210 FOR I = 1 TO NUMBER
          READ SCORE
          PRINT SCORE - SMALL
220 NEXT I
230 DATA 6
240 DATA 38, -74, 502, 0, -86, 34
250 END

RUNNH

The smallest number is -86
Its position is 5

Score - small equals
 124
 12
 588
 86
 0
 120
```

Notice that we simply inserted lines 170 to 220 in the previous program. You will often be able to use all or part of a program in this way to solve more complicated problems.

5.3 NESTED LOOPS

One loop can be placed inside another loop. In the program below, the Y loop is nested inside the X loop.

```
10 PRINT " X Y"
20 FOR X = 1 TO 2            ! X Loop starts
30      FOR Y = 1 TO 3       ! Y Loop starts
            PRINT X; Y
40      NEXT Y               ! Y Loop ends
50 NEXT X                    ! X Loop ends
60 END
```

Notice that FOR Y comes after FOR X, but NEXT Y comes before NEXT X. The entire Y loop must be inside the X loop, as shown by the indenting. When this program runs, the result is:

```
X  Y
1  1
1  2
1  3
2  1
2  2
2  3
```

First X is set to 1, then Y goes from 1 to 3. Then the Y loop is finished, so X goes to 2 and Y goes from 1 to 3 again. We say the inner loop variable changes faster than the outer loop variable. Here Y changes faster than X.

Suppose each of six students in a class has taken five tests, and we want to calculate the mean score for each student. We will put the students' names and scores in DATA statements. The variable STUDENT will control the outer loop, while TEST controls the inner loop. For each student we will calculate a TOTAL, so each student's mean will be TOTAL/5.

Example 5.8 *Calculating Means for Several Students*

```
100 REM -- Calculate mean score of 5 tests for 6 students
110 FOR STUDENT = 1 TO 6
        READ NAME$
        TOTAL = 0
        FOR TEST = 1 TO 5
            READ SCORE
            TOTAL = TOTAL + SCORE
        NEXT TEST
        PRINT "Average for "; NAME$; " is"; TOTAL/5
120 NEXT STUDENT
130 DATA "Mary Lee",     76, 85, 81, 73, 91
140 DATA "Larry Brown", 87, 93, 96, 89, 98
150 DATA "Conrad Crum", 47, 58, 69, 54, 71
160 DATA "Ruth Wright", 95, 93, 97, 91, 100
170 DATA "Joe Cool",     75, 78, 77, 76, 74
180 DATA "Jean Jones",  65, 87, 73, 92, 79
190 END

RUNNH

Average for Mary Lee is 81.2
Average for Larry Brown is 92.6
Average for Conrad Crum is 59.8
Average for Ruth Wright is 95.2
Average for Joe Cool is 76
Average for Jean Jones is 79.2
```

Notice that READ NAME$ and TOTAL = 0 are placed inside the STUDENT loop but before the TEST loop, because these statements must be performed once for each student. The same is true for the statement that prints results, except this statement obviously belongs *after* the TEST loop. We cannot print results for a student until after adding up the scores on the tests for that student.

Loops can be nested up to a maximum of 12 levels in VAX-BASIC. You will probably never need that many nested loops, but we will give a few examples using more than two loops.

Counting with Loops

How many ways can you buy a total of 3 gallons of milk if milk can be bought in quantities of 1 gallon, 1 quart, 1 pint, and 1 cup? (Remember the relationships: 2 cups = 1 pint; 2 pints = 1 quart; 4 quarts = 1 gallon.) You can, for example, buy 3 gallons, or 1 gallon and 8 quarts, or 4 quarts and 8 pints and 16 cups, among many other ways. You should at least start to do this problem by hand, to see what is involved. It is fairly easy to get the computer to count the ways for you. We will present first a rather simple-minded way to do the problem, then a refinement.

First, it should be clear that the number of gallons in one particular way can be 0, 1, 2, or 3. This suggests a loop FOR GALLON = 0 to 3, where GALLON represents the number of gallons. Similarly, the number of quarts can be any integer from 0 to 12, so we can use a loop FOR QUART = 0 TO 12. For pints and cups, we can use FOR PINT = 0 TO 24 and FOR CUP = 0 TO 48, respectively. Then inside the loops, we must check to see whether this particular combination of gallons, quarts, pints, and cups totals 3 gallons. If we express everything in terms of cups, then we need a total of 48 cups. Thus, inside the loops we put the statement

```
IF 16*GALLON + 4*QUART + 2*PINT + CUP = 48 THEN
   CNT = CNT + 1
END IF
```

Here is the entire program.

Example 5.9 *Counting with Loops; Simple-Minded Version*

```
100 REM -- Simple-minded version
110 REM -- Count number of ways to make 3 gallons
120 CNT = 0
130 FOR GALLON = 0 TO 3
140    FOR QUART = 0 TO 12
150       FOR PINT = 0 TO 24
160          FOR CUP = 0 TO 48
                 IF 16*GALLON + 4*QUART + 2*PINT + CUP = 48 THEN
                    CNT = CNT + 1
                 END IF
170          NEXT CUP
180       NEXT PINT
190    NEXT QUART
200 NEXT GALLON
210 PRINT "The number of ways to make 3 gallons is "; CNT
220 END
```

Most of the program lines are taken up with FOR and NEXT statements. There are four loops with the CUP-loop nested inside the other three loops. We have called the program simple-minded because we did not do much thinking before writing it. When the program runs, it will print:

```
The number of ways to make 3 gallons is 276
```

Now consider how many times the computer executed the body of the nested loops, the IF statement. The GALLON loop causes everything inside it to be done 4 times (GALLON = 0, 1, 2, 3). The QUART loop causes everything inside it to be done 13 times, the PINT loop 25 times, and the CUP loop 49 times. Thus the IF statement is executed $4 * 13 * 25 * 49 = 63,700$ times! Try running this program and see how long it takes before the result is printed. Let's look for a better way to do this problem.

As before, we start with the GALLON loop FOR GALLON = 0 TO 3. Assuming that some number of gallons has been chosen, how many quarts could there be? There could be as few as 0. At the upper end, 12 quarts equals 3 gallons, but for each gallon used, we must take 4 quarts away from the total of 12 quarts. That is, we can use a loop

```
FOR QUART = 0 TO 12 - 4*GALLON
```

When GALLON is 0, QUART goes from 0 to 12, and when GALLON is 1, QUART goes from 0 to $12 - 4 * 1 = 8$, and so on.

Now, having chosen some number of gallons and quarts, we must choose a number of pints. The smallest number for pints is 0 and the largest is 24, but for each gallon we must subtract 8 pints, and for each quart we must subtract 2 pints. Thus the PINT loop will begin with

```
FOR PINT = 0 TO 24 - 8*GALLON - 2*QUART
```

There are no more choices left. After choosing the number of gallons, quarts, and pints, there will always be only one possible number of cups. (For example, with 1 gallon, 3 quarts, and 2 pints, there would have to be 16 cups.) Since we are only counting the ways, not listing them, we do not even have to know how many cups there are. We just have to be sure that the gallons, quarts, and pints do not already add up to more than 3 gallons, and we have assured this by the subtractions in the FOR statements. So, although there seemed to be four variables originally, we need only three loops in the program.

What is in the body of the nested loops? Not much, just a counter. Here is the program.

Example 5.10 *Counting with Loops*

```
100 REM -- Count number of ways to make three gallons
110 CNT = 0
120 FOR GALLON = 0 TO 3
130     FOR QUART = 0 TO 12 - 4*GALLON
140         FOR PINT = 0 TO 24 - 8*GALLON - 2*QUART
                CNT = CNT + 1
150         NEXT PINT
160     NEXT QUART
170 NEXT GALLON
180 PRINT "The number of ways to make 3 gallons is"; CNT
190 END
```

The saving is considerable: no IF statement, one less loop, and the assignment statement (CNT = CNT + 1) is executed 276 times.

When this program runs, it should give the number of ways as 276. It is unlikely that you would want to see all 276 ways. However, with a video screen, you should include some PRINT statements in your program, and check some of the results to see that the program is running correctly. (Don't print all the ways on paper. Have mercy on the trees.) We would temporarily include the following lines in the program:

```
115 PRINT "GALLONS", "QUARTS", "PINT", "CUPS"
144                 CUP = 48 - 16*GALLON - 4*QUART - 2*PINT
146                 PRINT GALLON, QUART, PINT, CUP
```

When the revised program is RUN, some of the printed lines will be:

GALLONS	QUARTS	PINTS	CUPS
0	0	0	48
0	0	1	46
0	0	2	44
.	.	.	.
:	:	:	:
0	0	24	0
0	1	0	44
0	1	1	42
.	.	.	.
:	:	:	:
3	0	0	0

```
The number of ways to make 3 gallons is 276
```

Once you are satisfied that the program is running correctly, then take out the lines 115, 144, and 146.

Combinations

Another counting problem that can be done fairly easily using several loops is the problem of combinations. For instance, how many ways can five digits be chosen from the nine digits 1, 2, 3, 4, 5, 6, 7, 8, 9? We do not care about the order of the selected digits; that is, if we count 12368 as one possibility, then we do not want to count 23618 or 83126.

We will list all the combinations as well as count them, and when we list a single combination, we will put the numbers in increasing order. Let the variables A, B, C, D, E stand for the five selected digits. Then A can be any digit from 1 to 5. (If A were greater than 5, then there would not be room for four more digits, all greater than A.) B must be bigger than A, and the largest value for B is 6 (leaving room for 7, 8, and 9 after B).

Thus the B loop can begin with

```
FOR B = A + 1 TO 6
```

Similarly for C, D, and E:

```
FOR C = B + 1 TO 7
FOR D = C + 1 TO 8
FOR E = D + 1 TO 9
```

The program is, again, almost all loop statements.

Example 5.11 *Counting Combinations*

```
100 REM -- Count and list combinations of 9 digits, 5 at a time
110 TOTAL = 0
120 FOR A = 1 TO 5
130     FOR B = A + 1 TO 6
140         FOR C = B + 1 TO 7
150             FOR D = C + 1 TO 8
160                 FOR E = D + 1 TO 9
                        TOTAL = TOTAL + 1
                        PRINT A; B; C; D; E
170                 NEXT E
180             NEXT D
190         NEXT C
200     NEXT B
210 NEXT A
220 PRINT
230 PRINT "Number of combinations is"; TOTAL
240 END
```

The result of running this program is:

```
1  2  3  4  5
1  2  3  4  6
1  2  3  4  7
.  .  .  .  .
:  :  :  :  :
4  5  6  7  9
.  .  .  .  .
:  :  :  :  :
5  6  7  8  9
```

```
Number of combinations is 126
```

Again, do this problem on a video screen, not a hardcopy terminal. The results do not justify using so much paper. However, do include PRINT statements such as the one in the loop body as a way of checking the program, even if all you want is the total number of combinations, not a complete list of them.

EXERCISES A

1. Compute the value of $1 + 1/2 + 1/3 + 1/4 \ldots + 1/100$.

2. Read ten numbers and print the largest and smallest numbers.

3. Print the integers from 1 to 50 in 5 columns. Print headings on the columns: COLUMN 1, COLUMN 2, etc. Do this problem with (a) one loop, (b) two nested loops.

4. You put $10,000 in a money-market certificate. At the end of each year your account gains 16% interest, and then a check for $2000 is sent to you. Calculate the balance at the end of the year (after the check is sent to you) for ten years. (Round off.)

5. Calculate values of the function

$$y = 6x^4 - 4x^3 + 5x^2 - 7x + 2$$

for values of x between -2 and $+2$ in steps of $1/4$.

6. Write a program to compute the test averages and grades for students who have taken five tests each. Letter grades are to be assigned to the test averages using the rules in Exercise C9 in Chapter 4. Test the program on the following four students:

I. M. Grate	92, 89, 97, 87, 94
U. R. Nott	79, 81, 78, 83, 77
E. Z. Rider	86, 67, 74, 89, 85
M. I. Wright	45, 56, 38, 64, 61

7. (*Another payroll problem, with more complications*) Read an employee name, hours worked, hourly rate of pay, and Blue Cross status. Print a pay statement for the employee, giving name, gross pay, each deduction, and net pay. Round all results. The new rules are:

   a. An employee is paid twice his hourly rate for overtime (over 40 hours)
   b. Social Security is 7% of gross pay.
   c. An employee may have no Blue Cross, a single plan at $9.50 per week, or a family plan at $24.75 per week.
   d. State tax is 3% of gross pay.
   e. Projected yearly earnings (PYE) are used to calculate federal income tax. PYE = 52 * GROSS. The federal income tax withheld is:

       0% of gross if PYE is less than $6,000
       8% of gross if $6,000 <= PYE < $16,000
       16% of gross if $16,000 <= PYE < $24,000
       24% of gross if PYE >= $24,000

Test the program on the following employees.

Name	Hours	Hourly Rate	Blue Cross
R. G. JONES	40	1.25	NONE
H. A. SMYTH	42	8.50	SINGLE
R. U. BRITE	36.5	24.00	FAMILY
W. B. YEATS	43	5.95	FAMILY
E. E. CUMIN	30.5	12.45	SINGLE
B. B. CODIE	50.5	6.25	NONE

8. Calculate how many ways there are to make change for a dollar, using any combination of half-dollars, quarters, dimes, nickels, and pennies.

9. Find the number of ways to buy 100 fowl for $100 if ducks cost $2, hens cost $1, doves are 2 for $1, and sparrows are 10 for $1. (You cannot buy 50 cents' worth of sparrows or doves.)

10. Find four positive integers, x, y, z, and w, all less than 10, such that

$$x^3 + y^3 + z^3 = w^3$$

11. Write a table to show the compounded interest on $1000 for periods of time from one to five years and interest rates of 10, 12, 14, and 16 percent. Interest is to be compounded quarterly (4 times a year).

12. Write a program that simulates what a department-store cashier does to make change. Input an amount for a bill and the amount given by the customer. Print out the amount of change and the number of each coin and denomination of paper money that the customer receives in change. Let the customer give the cashier up to a $20 bill.

13. a. Count and print all the permutations of the digits 1, 2, 3. (A permutation is an ordered arrangement. Thus, 213 and 321 are two of the permutations.)
  b. Just count the permutations of the digits 1, 2, 3, 4, 5.

14. Redo Exercise 6 with three classes of students. Make the classes small, no more than 5 students. Get letter grades for each student as before. Also calculate the test average for each class and the test average for the three classes combined.

15. Write a program to find the area bounded by the x axis, the line $x = 2$, and the curve $y = SQR(x^4 + 3x^2)$. First, approximate this area with the sum of the areas of 8 rectangles. Then double the number of rectangles and approximate the desired area again. Keep doubling the number of rectangles and approximating until two successive approximations $A1$ and $A2$ are within $A1/1000$ of each other.

16. Read 10 scores and find the largest score. Then multiply this largest score by every one of the 10 scores.

5.4 PRINT FORMATS

Now that we can generate lots of output using a FOR/NEXT loop, it is appropriate to know how to format the output. Until now, the only spacing controls we have used in the PRINT command were the comma for wide spacing, the semicolon for single spaces, and blanks for formatting within quotes. In this section we discuss PRINT TAB and some variations of the PRINT USING statement.

The PRINT TAB Statement

The *TAB function* is used in a PRINT statement to produce precise spacing. The TAB moves the cursor or the printhead to a specified column. Its format is:

```
PRINT TAB <integer expression>
```

For example, the following program uses the TAB for spacing.

```
10 REM - TAB Statement
20 PRINT "012345678901234567890123456789012345678901234567890123456789"
30 PRINT "NAME"; TAB(10); "CLASS"; TAB(30); "GRADE"
40 END

RUNNH

012345678901234567890123456789012345678901234567890123456789
NAME      CLASS            GRADE
```

BASIC numbers the columns beginning with column 0, so TAB(10) actually moves the cursor or printhead to the eleventh column. Notice that the headings are spaced starting in column 0, column 10, and column 30.

Always follow the TAB with a semicolon to keep the cursor at the column given in the TAB. If a comma is used instead, then BASIC prints the item after the TAB at the beginning of the next print zone. Also, if a TAB statement moves the cursor to a position already passed, it has no effect. Notice that in the following program, NUMBER is placed immediately after SQUARE, since column 3 has already been passed.

```
10 REM -- TAB with no effect
20 PRINT "SQUARE"; TAB(3); "NUMBER"
30 END

RUNNH

SQUARENUMBER
```

Look at the two programs below to print the multiplication table for factors of 1 to 10. The first does not use TAB, so the columns do not line up correctly. The second uses TAB with a variable (4*J) argument which will move the cursor equally as J increases.

```
10 REM -- Program without TAB
20 FOR I = 1 TO 10
30     FOR J = 1 TO 10
           PRINT I * J;
       NEXT J
       PRINT
40 NEXT I
50 END
```

RUNNH

```
1  2  3  4   5   6   7   8   9  10
2  4  6  8  10  12  14  16  18  20
3  6  9 12  15  18  21  24  27  30
4  8 12 16  20  24  18  32  36  40
5 10 15 20  25  30  35  40  45  50
6 12 18 24  30  36  42  48  54  60
7 14 21 28  35  42  49  56  63  70
8 16 24 32  40  48  56  64  72  80
9 18 24 36  45  54  63  72  81  90
10 20 30 40  50  60  70  80  90 100
```

Example 5.12 *Printing Columns with TAB*

```
10 REM -- Program with TAB
20 FOR I = 1 TO 10
       FOR J = 1 TO 10
           PRINT TAB(4*J); I * J;
       NEXT J
       PRINT
30 NEXT I
40 END
```

RUNNH

```
1   2   3   4   5   6   7   8   9  10
2   4   6   8  10  12  14  16  18  20
3   6   9  12  15  18  21  24  27  30
4   8  12  16  20  24  28  32  36  40
5  10  15  20  25  30  35  40  45  50
6  12  18  24  30  36  42  48  54  60
7  14  21  28  35  42  49  56  63  70
8  16  24  32  40  48  56  64  72  80
9  18  27  36  45  54  63  72  81  90
10  20  30  40  50  60  70  80  90 100
```

PRINT USING with # and $

The PRINT USING statement gives the programmer more control over the appearance and location of data on a printed line. It provides a facility to create lists, tables, and forms. The general format is:

```
PRINT USING <string expression>, <Print list>
```

where the string expression is one of several format codes. The string expression can be followed by a semicolon as well as by the comma shown. This section will explain the pound sign (#) for reserving places for digits and the dollar sign ($). The other format codes are discussed in Chapter 10.

The *pound sign (#)* reserves places for each digit position. For example,

```
10 PRINT USING "#",1
20 PRINT USING "##", 12
30 PRINT USING "###", 123
40 PRINT USING "####",-123        ! Minus sign
50 END

RUNNH

1
12
123
-123
```

Notice that the pound signs are in quotes and that a pound sign must be included for the minus sign in line 40. If there are not enough digits to fill the field, then VAX-BASIC prints spaces before the first digit, as shown in the next series of PRINT USING statements.

```
10 PRINT USING "###", 1
20 PRINT USING "###", 10
30 PRINT USING "###", 100
40 END

RUNNH

  1
 10
100
```

However, if you include more digits than pound signs, the computer will print the entire number preceded by a percent sign (%) as a warning that the PRINT USING format was too small for the number.

```
10 PRINT USING "###", 12345
20 PRINT USING "###", 123
30 END

RUNNH

% 12345
123
```

The pound signs (#) can be combined with a decimal point. The placement of the decimal point tells the computer how many places on each side of the point are to be reserved.

If the number being printed has more digits in the decimal part, BASIC prints the number rounded to the number of decimal places reserved in the PRINT USING format. If the number has fewer decimal places than the number specified in the PRINT USING format, the number is filled with zeros. The PRINT USING statements below demonstrate these rules.

```
10 PRINT USING "##.###", 12.345      !all places used
20 PRINT USING "##.###", 12.34       !fill with zeros
30 PRINT USING "##.###", 12          !fill with zeros
40 PRINT USING "##.###", 12.3456     !rounding to three places
50 PRINT USING "##.##", 1.23         !spaces used to fill
60 PRINT USING "##.##", -1.23        !minus sign
70 PRINT USING "###.##", -1.23       !spaces and minus sign
80 END

RUNNH

12.345
12.340
12.000
12.346
 1.23
-1.23
 -1.23
```

The *dollar sign ($)* can also be included with the PRINT USING format. To print a number with a dollar sign before the first digit, start the PRINT USING field with two dollar signs. Since the dollar sign will precede the number, the minus sign will come at the end of the format and is referred to as a *trailing minus sign*. The following lines demonstrate these features of PRINT USING.

```
10 PRINT USING "$$##.##", 32.63      !extra space
20 PRINT USING "$$##.##", 325.75     !complete field filled
30 PRINT USING "$$##.##", 23256.81   !warning message
40 PRINT USING "$$##.##-", -325.75   !final minus sign
50 PRINT USING "$$##.##-", 325.75    !same as above, but plus
60 END

RUNNH

 $32.63
$325.75
% 23256.8
$325.75-
$325.75
```

Note that in line 10 the two dollar signs provide space for the dollar sign and one digit. Thus the first space is not filled, since there are only two digits (32) and the dollar sign, but four places have been reserved before the decimal point ($$##.) In line 50, the trailing minus sign causes a space to be printed after the last digit, since the number is positive.

The dollar sign is most useful in printing rounded money values. Compare the output of the following two programs to see the advantage of the PRINT USING. The only difference in the program is in line 40—one with and one without the PRINT USING. The PRINT USING statement is set up to print two formatted numbers with spaces between each format. This causes two columns to be printed. The program figures interest on $655.00 at 12.5% compounded semiannually for five years.

WITHOUT PRINT USING

```
10 P = 655
20 PRINT "YEAR", "INTEREST", "BALANCE"
30 FOR J = .5 TO 5 STEP .5
      I = P * .125 * .5
      P = P + I
      PRINT J, I, P
40 NEXT J
50 END
```

RUNNH

YEAR	INTEREST	BALANCE
.5	40.9375	695.938
1	43.4961	739.434
1.5	46.2146	785.648
2	49.103	834.751
2.5	52.172	886.923
3	55.4327	942.356
3.5	58.8972	1001.25
4	62.5783	1063.83
4.5	66.4895	1130.32
5	70.6451	1200.97

WITH PRINT USING

```
10 P = 655
20 PRINT "YEAR     INTEREST    BALANCE"
30 FOR J = .5 TO 5 STEP .5
      I = P * .125 * .5
      P = P + I
      PRINT USING "##.#     $$###.##     $$###.##", J, I, P
40 NEXT J
50 END
```

RUNNH

YEAR	INTEREST	BALANCE
0.5	$40.94	$695.94
1.0	$43.50	$739.43
1.5	$46.21	$785.65
2.0	$49.10	$834.75
2.5	$52.17	$886.92
3.0	$55.43	$924.36
3.5	$58.90	$1001.25
4.0	$62.58	$1063.83
4.5	$66.49	$1130.32
5.0	$70.65	$1200.97

EXERCISES B

1. Write a program to create a table of numbers from 1 to 10 with the square of each number, its square root, and its reciprocal. Use TAB to space the columns evenly.

2. Use the PRINT TAB function to prepare a formatted receipt.

3. Use the PRINT TAB function to space a line based on the values of the variables R and S. Let the first TAB be R, the second (S − R), and the third (S + R). Run the program for the values R = 3, S = 12, and T = 350. Print T, the value of T, and the value of T + 2 in the columns indicated by the three TAB functions.

4. Write a short program to determine the column specified by TAB(−3), TAB(−70), TAB(85), and TAB(200). Can you find the general rule for TAB arguments that are negative or larger than the number of columns set for your terminal?

5. Rewrite Exercise A4. Use PRINT USING for formatting the output.

6. Rewrite Exercise A7. Use PRINT USING for formatting the output.

5.5 DEBUGGING HINTS

We have been looking at the analysis and implementation phases of programming. Both these phases require you to run and test programs. The testing of a program usually means correcting errors or *debugging* the program. Here are some techniques you can use to help debug programs.

1. *Echo print all input data.* Echo printing lets you see if the values read in are what you thought they were. After the values are confirmed, the PRINT line can be deleted.

```
100 READ H1, W1, H2, W2,
110 PRINT "Values read are "; H1, W1, H2, W2
```

2. *Check data for incorrect values.* Checking provides a way for you to control data input. This means you can avoid dividing by zero or processing a negative number when only positive numbers are acceptable.

```
100 INPUT "Age", AGE
    IF AGE < 0 THEN
        PRINT "Age not correct"
        GO TO 100
    END IF
```

3. *Use parentheses.* Use parentheses to make your expressions clear and correct. Be careful that you write what you mean. For example, the following two arithmetic expressions are very similar but produce different results.

$$3 * (7 + 2) = 3 * 9 = 27$$
$$3 * 7 + 2 \quad = 21 + 2 = 23$$

4. *Check variables.* Check variables to make sure they match the data types. Don't assign a string value to a numeric variable.

5. *Use sample data.* Take sample data values and work them through your program by hand. This is called "playing computer." If the answer calculated by hand does not match the computer's answer, then recheck your math and your input data.

6. *Test the program.* Plan to test your program with appropriate test data. Test all sections of the code. Use data from all ranges (negative, positive, zero).

7. *Watch for infinite loops.* You probably have this problem when your program does not stop or if nothing seems to happen after you type RUN.

8. *PRINT statements.* Use PRINT statements to trace the flow of program execution. They can be placed at strategic points and deleted after the program runs correctly.

```
100 FOR X = 1 TO 20
110     PRINT "Loop pass"; X
120     SUM = SUM + X
130 NEXT X
```

Line 110 is used to see if the FOR/NEXT loop has been started and how many times it is repeated.

9. *Documentation.* Use documentation carefully and completely. As programs become more complicated, it is essential for you to use PRINT and REM statements for clarification. Identify the purpose and output for all major sections of code such as a FOR/NEXT loop.

These hints for debugging do work. Use them frequently and you will find that as your programs become more sophisticated you will not increase your debugging time.

REVIEW QUESTIONS

1. Which program segments have properly nested FOR/NEXT loops?

   a.
   ```
   FOR X = 1 TO 3
       FOR Y = 1 TO 5
           PRINT X*Y
       NEXT Y
   NEXT X
   ```

   b.
   ```
   FOR R = 1 TO 5
       FOR C = 1 TO 5
           PRINT R,C
       NEXT R
   NEXT C
   ```

   c.
   ```
   FOR X = 1 TO 5
       PRINT X
   NEXT X
   FOR I = 1 TO 3
       READ A
       PRINT A;
       FOR J = 1 TO 2
           READ B
           PRINT B;
       NEXT J
   NEXT I
   ```

   d.
   ```
   FOR A = S TO 1 STEP -1
       PRINT A;
       FOR B = 1 TO 5
           READ B
           PRINT A*B;
       NEXT A
   NEXT B
   ```

2. Using the following program, identify the parts of each loop in the program.

   ```
   10  READ X(J) FOR J = 1 TO 10
   20  FOR I = 9 TO 1   STEP -2
           PRINT X(I)
   30  NEXT I
   40  DATA 5, 3, 6, 4, 7
   50  END
   ```

	Loop 1	Loop 2
Counter variable		
Initial value for counter		
Increment amount		
End value for counter		
Section of code		

3. List three techniques for debugging a program. Give a program segment as an example of each.

4. How many times will the computer execute the body of the loops below? What will be printed in each case?

   a.
   ```
   FOR I = 2 TO 6   STEP 2
       PRINT I, I**2
   NEXT I
   ```

   b.
   ```
   FOR R = 1 TO 10
       FOR C = 1 TO 10
           PRINT R*C
       NEXT C
   NEXT R
   ```

c.   FOR J = 4 TO 1
          PRINT *, J
      NEXT J

d.   FOR X = 4 TO 0 STEP -.5
          PRINT "Your GPA is"; X
      NEXT X

5. Write a FOR/NEXT loop for each of the following conditions:
   a. Counter variable   J
      Initial value   1
      Increment amount   2
      End value for counter   7
      Loop body   PRINT J, J/2
   b. Counter variable   X
      Initial value   100
      Increment amount   -10
      End value for counter   1
      Loop body   PRINT X, Y*X

6. What will the following program print? What are the values for I and J after the loops have been executed?

```
FOR I = 1 TO 2
   FOR J = 1 TO 2
       PRINT I,J
   NEXT J
NEXT I
```

7. What output will the following programs produce with the PRINT USING statement?

a.   10 F$ = " ### ### ###"
      20 FOR I = 1 TO 5
      30   PRINT USING F$, I, I^2, I^3
      40 NEXT I
      50 END

b.   10 F$ = "   #.###"
      20 FOR I = 2 TO 6
      30   PRINT USING F$, 1/I
      40 NEXT I
      50 END

c.   10 READ ITEM, QUAN, COST
      20 V = QUAN*COST
      30 PRINT "ITEM   QUAN COS/ITEM   VALUE"
      40 PRINT
      50 F$ = "'######   #### $$#.## $$##.##"

```
60 PRINT USING F$, ITEM, QUAN, COST, V
70 DATA 321456, 56, 12.98
80 END
```

SUMMARY OF CHAPTER 5

CONCEPTS AND KEYWORDS INTRODUCED IN THIS CHAPTER

Concept	Related Statements and Keywords
1. The repetition structure	FOR/NEXT
	STEP
2. Repeated use of DATA	RESTORE
3. Format output	PRINT TAB
	PRINT USING (# and $)
4. Debugging programs	

More on Program Control

As programs become more complicated, it is necessary to consider more structured methods of designing and coding a problem. This chapter examines the WHILE and UNTIL structures and the use of subroutines for modular design.

Probably the most important principle of well-structured programs is that the computer should enter a structure at the top and leave it at the bottom. The computer should begin an IF block at the IF statement and end at END IF, and it should begin a FOR/NEXT loop at the FOR statement and exit at the NEXT statement. In particular, this means we should avoid the GO TO statement for branching. WHILE loops perform many functions that were accomplished with IF statements in Chapter 4, but the WHILE loops promote better program structure.

6.1 THE WHILE STRUCTURE

In the last chapter we examined the repetition structure with FOR/NEXT loops. The FOR/NEXT structure is easy to use and concise. However, sometimes the repetition of a set of actions is based upon certain conditions that can be checked with the WHILE and UNTIL structures, but not with a FOR/NEXT loop counter.

The WHILE statement tests the same kind of condition as the IF statement. A group of statements is executed as long as a certain condition is true. When the condition is no longer true, the repetition stops. The WHILE structure is shown graphically in Figure 6.1.

The WHILE structure begins by checking the condition. If it is true, then the actions are executed. After the actions have been executed, the program again checks the condition. If it is true, the actions are repeated. If the condition is no longer true,

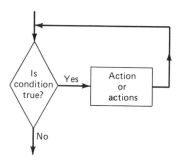

Figure 6.1   WHILE Structure

program control passes to the statements after the WHILE loop. It is important to remember that the condition is checked before *any* actions are executed.

Looping with WHILE

The concept of repetition is so important to programming that this section will look at some of the typical loops you will use in implementing your programs. The WHILE statement allows logical implementation of all types of loops.

The general format of the WHILE statement is

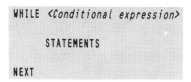

```
WHILE <Conditional expression>

     STATEMENTS

NEXT
```

The WHILE keyword marks the beginning of the loop. The loop is terminated with the NEXT statement. The conditional expression can be any legal BASIC relation. Within the WHILE/NEXT loop there can be a single statement or many statements.

Counting with WHILE

BASIC provides for a variety of ways to count. We have shown how to count with IF . . . THEN and FOR/NEXT loops. The following example program uses WHILE to count. A loop used for counting keeps track of how many times the loop is executed.

Example 6.1 *Counting with WHILE*

```
100 REM -- WHILE loop for counting
110 TOTAL = 0
120 READ NAME$
130 WHILE NAME$  <> "EOD"
140     TOTAL = TOTAL + 1
150     READ NAME$
160 NEXT
170 PRINT "The number of names read is"; TOTAL
180 DATA JANE, JACK, JOAN, JILL, EOD
200 END
```

Line 130 begins the loop with WHILE. The relational or logical expression is

```
NAME$ <> "EOD"
```

If this expression is true, BASIC executes the body of the loop (lines 140–150). If the expression is false, control passes to the statement after NEXT.

Notice that NEXT stands alone in line 160. A WHILE loop does not have a loop counter like FOR/NEXT, so there is not a variable after NEXT. The NEXT merely passes control back to the WHILE statement.

Since the WHILE condition is tested before the loop is executed, it is necessary to see that the condition to be tested is initialized before the WHILE loop begins. In the above program, line 120 reads a name before the WHILE statement. This READ statement is duplicated inside the loop. The initializing READ before WHILE is often called a *priming READ*.

Once the loop begins, the condition must be changed within the loop to insure that it will become false at some point. If not, you will have an infinite loop. Line 150 continues to read names until the EOD flag is read.

This WHILE loop, with an end-of-data flag EOD, is sometimes called a *sentinel-controlled loop*. This concept for stopping a loop was described in Example 4.2. It is a classic use of a WHILE loop.

A similar example sums a list of numbers. The following program sums a list of numbers and finds the mean, or average. The user enters as many numbers as desired, ending by entering the number zero.

Example 6.2 *Summing with WHILE*

```
100 REM -- WHILE loop to find the average of a list of numbers
110 PRINT "Please enter numbers, one at a time, ending with 0."
120 SUM, COUNTER = 0
130 INPUT "Number"; N
140 WHILE N <> 0
        SUM = SUM + N
        COUNTER = COUNTER + 1
        INPUT "Number"; N
150 NEXT
160 PRINT "The average of the list of numbers is"; SUM / COUNTER
170 END
```

Line 130 initializes the loop control variable N. Line 140 begins the WHILE loop by checking the condition

```
N <> 0
```

The control-variable value is changed by another INPUT statement within the body of the loop, just before the NEXT statement.

The COUNTER and SUM variables are initialized to 0. When the WHILE loop is completed, SUM will contain the sum of the values and COUNTER will contain the number of values.

It is not too difficult to decide when to use WHILE or FOR/NEXT. The following chart compares the two.

Action	WHILE	FOR/NEXT
Initialize loop counter	Initialized before loop	Initialized with FOR statement
Execute actions	Executed until condition is false	Executed for specified number of times
Update loop counter	Updated inside body of loop	Updated at NEXT statement
Final loop values	The first loop counter value that makes the WHILE condition false	The loop counter is equal to the final number of steps

The programs that follow compare the WHILE loop with a counter to the FOR/NEXT loop.

WHILE

```
100   X = 1
110   WHILE X < 5
         PRINT X;
         X = X + 1
120   NEXT
130   PRINT "Final X value is"; X
140   END
```

Initial loop-counter value 1
Test condition X < 5

Update loop counter

Final loop value is 5

```
RUNNH

1 2 3 4
Final X value is 5
```

FOR/NEXT

```
100   FOR X = 1 TO 5
         PRINT X;
120   NEXT X

130   PRINT "Final X value is"; X
140 END
```

Initial loop-counter value 1

Update loop counter and test if final step

```
RUNNH

1 2 3 4 5
Final X value is 5
```

The final value of X in both examples is 5. The WHILE loop repeated the loop body four times, but the FOR loop repeated five times.

Determining when to use a WHILE loop instead of a FOR/NEXT is usually a natural choice. If the loop involves only a single variable that increases or decreases by the same amount each iteration, the FOR/NEXT loop will be simpler. Use WHILE when the structure asks a question about a condition under which the loop should execute.

Loops without Counters

More natural uses of WHILE occur when there is not an obvious loop-counter variable, as in the following program.

Example 6.3 *Loops without Counters*

```
100 REM -- Use of WHILE without loop counter
110 X = 48
120 Y = 9
130 PRINT " X", " Y", "X - Y"
140 WHILE X > Y
        PRINT X, Y, X - Y
        X = 3 * X / 4
        Y = 4 * Y / 3
150 NEXT
160 PRINT "Final X is"; X
170 PRINT "Final Y is"; Y
180 END

RUNNH

X            Y            X - Y
48           9            39
36           12           24
27           16           11

Final X is 20.25
Final Y is 21.3333
Ready
```

Notice that there is no counter set in the program. X is decreasing and Y is increasing, but neither one changes by a fixed step size. A WHILE loop is thus more natural than a FOR/NEXT loop.

Notice, too, that the PRINT statements in lines 160 and 170 show us that the final X is less than the final Y, and the body of the loop is not executed when this condition is true (or when the condition X > Y is false).

Checking Input Data

A standard use of WHILE involves checking input data. For instance, suppose a program is to calculate the square root of an input value for a variable X. Then X must not be negative, or the program will crash attempting to calculate SQR(X). One way around this problem is a WHILE loop like the one in the following segment.

```
INPUT "Number"; X
WHILE X < 0
      PRINT "Number cannot be negative."
      INPUT "Number"; X
NEXT
PRINT "The square root is"; SQR(X)
```

If the number entered for the first INPUT statement is positive or zero, the WHILE loop will not be executed. If the number is negative, however, the WHILE loop *is* executed; the computer warns the user about negative input and asks for a new value for X. If the user is bullheaded and enters several negative numbers, the computer will remain in the loop until the user enters a nonnegative value. (Computers can be much more bullheaded than people.)

Nested WHILE Loops

As with FOR/NEXT, WHILE loops can be nested inside other WHILE loops or other structures such as IF blocks and FOR/NEXT loops. Look at the following program for calculating average grades. The outer WHILE loop reads names until the user enters "EOD", and the inner FOR/NEXT loop reads and sums the grades.

Example 6.4 *Calculating Grades; WHILE Loop with Nested FOR/NEXT Loop*

```
100 REM -- Calculate average grades for several students
110 READ NAMES
120 WHILE NAMES <> "EOD"
        PRINT NAMES
        SUM = 0
130     FOR TEST = 1 TO 5
            READ GRADE
            SUM = SUM + GRADE
140     NEXT TEST
        PRINT "Your average for five tests is"; SUM / 5
        READ NAMES
150 NEXT
160 DATA "Jane Smith", 98, 88, 78, 95, 85
170 DATA "Bob Taylor", 65, 73, 82, 78, 75
180 DATA "George Hines", 91, 93, 98, 89, 97
190 DATA "EOD"
200 END


RUNNH

Jane Smith
Your average for five tests is 88.8
Bob Taylor
Your average for five tests is 74.6
George Hines
Your average for five tests is 93.6
```

Here is a slightly more complicated version of the same idea. Suppose the program will use INPUT instead of READ. Grades should be between 0 and 100, so grade values can be checked with a WHILE loop of the form:

```
WHILE GRADE < 0 OR GRADE > 100
      PRINT "Grade must be between 0 and 100."
      INPUT "Please reenter grade"; GRADE
NEXT
```

Here is the complete program.

Example 6.5 *Calculating Grades; WHILE Loop with Nested FOR/NEXT Loop with Nested WHILE Loop*

```
100 REM -- Calculate average grades for several students
110 PRINT "This program will calculate average grades"
120 PRINT "on five tests for several students.  Enter"
130 PRINT "data as requested.  To stop, enter EOD for"
140 PRINT "the student name."
150 INPUT "Name"; NAME$
160 WHILE NAME$ <> "EOD"
      SUM = 0
      FOR TEST = 1 TO 5
          INPUT "Grade"; GRADE
          WHILE GRADE < 0 OR GRADE > 100
              PRINT "Grade must be between 0 and 100."
              INPUT "Please reenter grade"; GRADE
          NEXT
          SUM = SUM + GRADE
      NEXT TEST
      PRINT "Average for "; NAME$; " is"; SUM / 5
      INPUT "Name"; NAME$
170 NEXT
200 END
```

6.2 THE UNTIL STRUCTURE

The UNTIL structure is also used to create a loop or a repetition of code. UNTIL loops are similar to WHILE loops, but UNTIL loops are executed *until* a specified condition is true. The loop repeats as long as the condition is *not* true or as long as it is false. Once the condition becomes true, the loop is terminated. As with the WHILE loop, the condition is evaluated before the loop is begun and subsequently before each repetition. (See Figure 6.2.)

The UNTIL structure is not used very frequently in BASIC, because the WHILE is usually a more logical choice. The following are some examples to show the use of UNTIL.

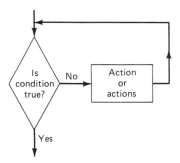

Figure 6.2   UNTIL Structure

UNTIL Loops

Consider the problem to find the smallest integer N for which 1 / 2**N is less than 0.001. The problem might be done with the following program.

Example 6.6 *UNTIL Loop*

```
10 REM -- Make 1 / 2**N < 0.001
20 N = 1
30 UNTIL 1 / 2**N < 0.001
40       N = N + 1
50 NEXT
60 PRINT "1/2 to the"; N; "power is"; 1 / 2**N
70 END

RUNNH

1/2 to the 10 power is .976563E-03
```

It seems natural to have the condition which determines when to stop in line 30, which sets up the loop. Line 30 could also have been

```
30 WHILE 1/2**N >= 0.001.
```

The two statements

```
UNTIL 1/2**N < 0.001
```

and

```
WHILE 1/2**N >= 0.001.
```

mean exactly the same thing.

The following two payroll programs also produce exactly the same results. The first one uses an UNTIL loop and the second a WHILE loop.

UNTIL

```
100 REM -- Using UNTIL
110 READ NAMES, HOURS, RATE
120 UNTIL NAMES = "DONE"
        WAGE = RATE * HOURS
        PRINT NAMES, HOURS, RATE, WAGE
        READ NAMES, HOURS, RATE
130 NEXT
140 DATA "Mr. Jones", 40, 12.3
150 DATA "Mrs. Ellis", 34, 10.0
160 DATA DONE, 0, 0
170 END
```

WHILE

```
100 REM -- Using WHILE
110 READ NAMES, HOURS, RATE
120 WHILE NAMES <> "DONE"
        WAGE = RATE * HOURS
        PRINT NAMES, HOURS, RATE, WAGE
        READ NAMES, HOURS, RATE
130 NEXT
140 DATA "Mr. Jones", 40, 12.3
150 DATA "Mrs. Ellis", 35, 10.0
160 DATA DONE, 0, 0
170 END
```

Run both these programs to convince yourself that they produce the same output.

Choosing between WHILE and UNTIL is a matter of personal preference. Use the one that seems more natural to you. Most of the examples in this text use WHILE, since that usually is more natural for us.

EXERCISES A

Use WHILE or UNTIL loops in the following problems.

1. Write a program to find the smallest integer N for which N-factorial is greater than 1000. Print both this integer and its factorial value.

2. Begin with X = 9. Then repeatedly let X = X + SQR(X) until X is larger than 100. Print the value of each X, the value of each X + SQR(X), and count the number of repetitions.

3. Write a program to compute the end-of-year interest on a savings account. Start the account with $10,000. Compute the interest at 10.5% annually. Print out the interest earned and the new balance in the account at the end of each year. The last balance printed should be the first balance over $20,000.

4. Write a program to read string values from DATA statements until a blank (" ") is read. Count how many words were read before the blank. Print each word read and the number of words read.

5. Write a program to read a list of numbers until a zero is read. Count the number of positive integers and the number of negative integers. Print the total number of integers read, the number greater than zero, and the number less than zero.

6. Write a program to compute the powers of 2 that are less than 5000. Print each number (X, say) and its power (2^X).

7. Write a program to calculate the product of the odd integers 1, 3, 5, and so on, until the first product is reached that is greater than 100,000. Print the highest integer in the product.

8. Redo Exercise A6 in Chapter 5 to find test averages and grades for students who have taken five tests.

9. Redo Exercise A7 in Chapter 5 (payroll problem).

6.3 STATEMENT MODIFIERS

Implied Loops

We have already discussed the FOR modifier, as in

```
PRINT X * X FOR X = 1 TO 10
```

WHILE and UNTIL can also be used as modifiers to create such loops. For example,

```
C = C + C UNTIL C > 10^3
```

will cause C to be summed with itself until its value is greater than 10^3. If the original C has a value greater than 10^3, then the statement will not be executed.

Another example, this time with WHILE:

```
X = (X + Y) / 2 WHILE (X - Y) > 0.1
```

If X is any number, then $(X + Y)/2$ is a number midway between X and Y. Thus each new X will be closer to Y until the first X is found such that $(X - Y) <= 0.1$.

Conditionally Executing Statements

The IF statement can also be used as a modifier, as in

```
PRINT X IF X <= 2
```

which is exactly equivalent to

```
IF X <= 2 THEN PRINT X
```

When IF is used as a modifier, it cannot be followed by THEN or ELSE, but the IF modifier can follow another IF . . . THEN or IF . . . THEN . . . ELSE. We can write, for example:

```
IF X < Y THEN PRINT NAME$ IF NAME$ < "Z"
```

or

```
IF C$ = "TRUE" THEN PRINT Y ELSE PRINT Z IF Z > Y
```

In each case, the IF modifier applies only to the clause immediately preceding it. That is, "IF Z > Y" refers only to PRINT Z; it has no impact on PRINT Y. PRINT Y will be executed if C$ is "TRUE", regardless of the truth value of Z > Y.

There is also an UNLESS modifier, which can be interpreted as IF NOT. That is, "UNLESS X = Z" means the same as "IF NOT X = Z" or "IF X < > Z". For example:

```
X = Y UNLESS X < Y
```

is equivalent to

```
X = Y IF X >= Y
```

Notice that a statement modified by an IF condition is executed when the condition is true, but a statement modified by an UNLESS condition is executed when the condition is false.

The IF and UNLESS modifiers can follow one another, as in:

```
PRINT NAME$ IF Z > X UNLESS NAME$ = "STOP"
```

VAX-BASIC evaluates the modifiers from right to left, so if the value of NAME$ is "STOP", then NAME$ will not be printed, regardless of the truth value of Z > X. Similarly, we can have:

```
X = X/2 UNLESS X > 1 IF N < 100
```

In order for X = X/2 to be executed, N < 100 must be true and X > 1 must be false.

FOR/NEXT Loops with Conditions

FOR/NEXT loops with WHILE and UNTIL conditions can also be used to control the execution of a multiple-action loop. An example of a FOR/WHILE loop is:

```
100 REM -- Using FOR-WHILE
110 FOR X = 0 WHILE NAMES <> ""
        INPUT "Type in a name or return to end"; NAMES
120 NEXT X
130 PRINT "The number of names read is"; X
140 END
```

```
RUNNH
```

```
Type in a name or return to end? Bob
Type in a name or return to end? Sue
Type in a name or return to end? Mary
Type in a name or return to end? Dick
Type in a name or return to end? <RET>
The number of names read is 4
```

The WHILE modifier in line 110 allows you to create a FOR loop without a set number of repetitions. The loop is terminated when the ⟨RET⟩ key is hit in response to INPUT. The ⟨RET⟩ assigns the null string ("") to NAME$.

The loop could have been written with UNTIL by changing line 110 to

```
110 FOR X = 0 UNTIL NAMES = ""
```

An example of a FOR-UNTIL loop is one for summing. The following program adds integers until the sum is greater than 5000.

```
100 REM -- Summing with FOR-UNTIL
110 FOR X = 0 UNTIL SUM > 5000
        SUM = SUM + X
120 NEXT X
130 PRINT "The sum is"; SUM
140 PRINT "The number of integers summed is"; X
```

FOR loops with WHILE or UNTIL modifiers are very rarely used. The WHILE or UNTIL structure can create the same logical block. In this text we will not use them except for these sample programs.

6.4 SUBROUTINES

GOSUB and RETURN

A *subroutine* is a part of a BASIC program that performs a specific task. The subroutines we discuss here are *internal* in the sense that the subroutine code occupies program lines. VAX-BASIC also contains *external* subroutines that are stored separately from the programs which use them.

Although a subroutine is part of a program, the subroutine code is placed in a separate section of the program and is executed only when the program *calls* the subroutine. After the computer executes the subroutine, it returns to the point in the program immediately after the statement that called the subroutine.

To call or use a subroutine beginning in, say, line 500 of a program, we use the statement GOSUB 500. This statement is very similar to the statement GO TO 500; the computer will go to line 500, but it will also remember the line number of the GOSUB statement so it can return to the statement following GOSUB after performing the task in the subroutine. Line 500 can contain any legal VAX-BASIC statement. We usually make this statement a comment indicating the start of the subroutine.

The end of a subroutine should always be a RETURN statement. This statement, too, is similar to a GO TO statement. It says, in effect, "GO TO the statement after the GOSUB statement that called this subroutine." The following program uses a subroutine to print two numbers in increasing order.

Example 6.7 *A Subroutine to Print Numbers in Increasing Order*

```
100 REM -- Subroutine prints two numbers in increasing order
110 INPUT "Two numbers"; X, Y
120 GOSUB 200
130 INPUT "Two numbers"; X, Y
140 GOSUB 200
150 GO TO 300
200 !  Begin subroutine
210     PRINT "Increasing order"
        IF X < Y THEN
            PRINT X, Y
        ELSE
            PRINT Y, X
        END IF
220 RETURN                  ! End of subroutine
300 END


RUNNH


Two numbers? 12, 3
Increasing order
 3               12
Two numbers? -12, 5
Increasing order
-12              5
```

For illustrative purposes, we used two GOSUB statements, in lines 120 and 140. Each one directs the computer to line 200 to begin the subroutine. In each case, the computer executes the lines of the subroutine until it comes to the RETURN statement. The first time the computer comes to RETURN, it returns to line 130, which is the statement following the GOSUB that called the subroutine. Then line 140 calls the subroutine again, so the computer executes the subroutine until RETURN is encountered. This time, the computer returns to line 150, the statement after the GOSUB that called the subroutine.

A word about the GO TO statement in line 150 is in order. If it were not present, then after the second execution of the subroutine, the computer would return to line 200, the line which would follow the second GOSUB. That is, the computer would begin executing the subroutine a third time. When the computer encountered RETURN for the third time, it would not know where to RETURN because it did not begin the subroutine by way of a GOSUB statement. This situation causes a *GOSUB-RETURN error,* analogous to having the computer encounter a NEXT statement without first encountering a FOR statement. Thus, we will always have a GO TO statement immediately preceding a subroutine (or the first of several subroutines), so the computer will not inadvertently begin executing the subroutine.

Suppose you have written a subroutine to calculate the values of the first five powers of a number X: X**1, X**2, X**3, X**4, and X**5. Further, suppose that your program must calculate these powers for variables with necessarily different names, say A, B, and C. This is not a major difficulty, since you can let X = A before calling the subroutine the first time, and similarly for B and C. The following program illustrates this idea.

Example 6.8 *A Subroutine to Print Five Powers of a Number*

```
100 REM -- First 5 powers of different variables; Subroutine
110 INPUT "Three numbers"; A, B, C
120 PRINT "Power"; I, FOR I = 1 TO 5
130 X = A
140 GOSUB 200
150 X = B
160 GOSUB 200
170 X = C
180 GOSUB 200
190 GOTO 300
200 REM -- Subroutine:  First 5 powers of X
210    PRINT
220    PRINT X**I, FOR I = 1 TO 5
230    PRINT
240 RETURN
300 END

RUNNH

Three numbers? 2, 3, 4
Power 1        Power 2        Power 3        Power 4        Power 5
2              4              8              16             32
3              9              27             81             243
4              16             64             256            1024
```

A complicated program will often look simpler if portions of the program are placed in subroutines. Consider the grade-calculating program of Example 6.5. That program began with four PRINT statements giving instructions to the user. With that many instructions or more, it is reasonable to put the instructions in a subroutine.

Recall that the main structure of that program was a WHILE loop within a FOR/NEXT loop within another WHILE loop. The structure should look cleaner if the interior loops are placed in subroutines. The following program illustrates these ideas.

Example 6.9 *Subroutine Version of Example 6.5*

```
100 REM -- Calculate average grades for several students
110 GOSUB 200              ! Give instructions
120 INPUT "Name"; NAME$
130 WHILE NAME$ <> "EOD"
        GOSUB 300          ! Read grades and calculate sum
        PRINT "Average for "; NAME$; " is"; SUM / 5
        INPUT "Name"; NAME$
140 NEXT
150 GO TO 400
200 !!!!!!!!!!!!!!!!!!!!!!!!!!!!!!!!!!!!!!!!!!!!!!!!!!!!!!!!!
210 !  Subroutine; Give instructions.
220 PRINT "This program will calculate average grades"
230 PRINT "on five tests for several students.  Enter"
240 PRINT "data as requested.  To stop, enter EOD for"
250 PRINT "the student name."
260 RETURN
300 !!!!!!!!!!!!!!!!!!!!!!!!!!!!!!!!!!!!!!!!!!!!!!!!!!!!!!!!!
310 !  Subroutine; Read grades and calculate sum.
320 SUM = 0
330 FOR TEST = 1 TO 5
        INPUT "Grade"; GRADE
        WHILE GRADE < 0 OR GRADE > 100
            PRINT "Grade must be between 0 and 100."
            INPUT "Please reenter grade"; GRADE
        NEXT
        SUM = SUM + GRADE
340 NEXT TEST
350 RETURN
400 END
```

The *main program* is everything in the program except the subroutines. Here the main program runs from line 100 through line 150. The structure of the main program should be clearer with the subroutines removed. Notice that each GOSUB contains a comment explaining what the target subroutine will do.

The ON . . . GOSUB Statement

The *ON . . . GOSUB statement* looks exactly like an ON . . . GO TO statement with GOSUB in place of GO TO. It chooses one particular subroutine from several, depending on the value of a variable. Here is a fairly trivial example that determines which subroutine to call for producing a bill.

Example 6.10 *Example of ON . . . GOSUB*

```
100 REM -- Example of ON ... GOSUB
110 REM -- Produce bill for late, no charge, current
120 INPUT "Type in 1, 2 or 3 for bill and 4 to end "; X
130 ON X GOSUB 200, 300, 400, 500
140 GOTO 500
200 !   Subroutine for late
    PRINT "Your payment is overdue."
210 RETURN
300 !    Subroutine for no charge
    PRINT "Your account shows no charge."
310 RETURN
400 !     Subroutine for current charges
    PRINT "Your bill shows current charges."
410 RETURN
500 END


RUNNH


Type in 1, 2 or 3 for bill and 4 to end ? 2
Your account shows no charge.
Type in 1, 2 or 3 for bill and 4 to end ? 4
```

Notice that additional information could be computed and printed once the subroutine is called. This program does not check for incorrect INPUT at line 120, but such checking can easily be added to the program. The use of ON . . . GOSUB allows for simplified program control with subroutines.

EXERCISES B

1. Write a program to read six names and ages. Print both the name and age if the age is less than 18. Print only the name if the age is above 40 and the name follows S in the alphabet. Print only the age if the age is more than 18 and the name comes before P in the alphabet.

2. Use the WHILE modifier to calculate the sum for numbers being INPUT until the given number is less than 8.

3. Write a program with a FOR-UNTIL loop that repeats until the loop counter is greater than the SQR(X).

4. Write a program to read a list of words. Print all words that come at or after R in the alphabet. Assume all words begin with an uppercase letter. Continue to read words until the word END is read. Use a loop modifier.

5. Write a program to find all the powers of 2 that are less than 5000. Use the WHILE modifier. Rewrite the program with the UNTIL modifier.

6. Write a program to read test scores until a negative test score is read. Find the mean of the scores. Use a FOR-WHILE loop.

7. Write a program that asks for names of three runners and their times in a race. The program should print the names in the proper order of finish. (Lowest time is first, of course.) Use a subroutine to order and print the names.

8. Redo Exercise A7 in Chapter 5 (the payroll problem) with subroutines to calculate gross pay, Blue Cross deduction, and federal income tax.

9. Write a program that uses three subroutines to draw a square, rectangle, or triangle with asterisks, as in

```
*********        *************         *
*********        *************        **
*********        *************        ***
*********        *************        ****
*********        *************        *****
```

Ask the user which figure to draw. Use ON . . . GOSUB.

REVIEW QUESTIONS

1. What is wrong with each of the following WHILE or UNTIL loops?

   a.   ```
         SUM = 0
         INPUT X
         WHILE X > 0
             SUM = SUM + X
             INPUT X
         NEXT X
         ```

   b.    ```
         UNTIL N = 0
             PRINT N
             READ N
         NEXT
         ```

   c.   ```
         X = 0
         WHILE X = 1 TO 3
             PRINT X
             X = X + 1
         NEXT
         ```

   d.    ```
         READ X
         WHILE X > 0
             PRINT X
         NEXT
         READ X
         ```

2. Study the following four programs that use subroutines. Answer the questions that follow based on the programs.

A.
```
100 FOR I = 1 TO 3
110     READ X, Y
120     GOSUB 300
130 NEXT I
140 GO TO 999
300 PRINT I; X + Y
310 RETURN
500 DATA 3, 5, 8
510 DATA 6, -2, 1
999 END
```

B.
```
110 A = 15
120 B = 20
130 IF A < B THEN 150
140 GOSUB 200
150 GOSUB 300
160 GO TO 999
200 PRINT A - B
210 RETURN
300 PRINT B - A
400 RETURN
999 END
```

C.
```
100 FOR I = 1 TO 4
110     GOSUB 200
120     PRINT 2
130 NEXT I
140 GO TO 999
200 LET S = 0
210 FOR J = 1 TO I
220     LET S = S + J
230 NEXT J
240 RETURN
999 END
```

D.
```
10   PRINT "Menu"
20   PRINT "1. Add"
30   PRINT "2. Subtract"
40   PRINT "3. End"
50   INPUT "Choice"; CH
60   ON CH GOSUB 100, 200, 300
70   GO TO 10
100 REM Add Subroutine
110 INPUT X, Y
120 SUM = X + Y
130 PRINT SUM
140 RETURN
200 REM Subtract Subroutine
210 INPUT X, Y
220 DIFF = X - Y
230 PRINT DIFF
240 RETURN
300 END
```

a. In program A, at which line will the subprogram begin execution?

b. After line 310 in program A, at which line will program execution resume?

c. How many subroutines are in program B?

d. In program C, how many loops are there?

e. How many subroutines are in program D?

f. To which line does the subroutine Add in lines 100–140 of program D return after the RETURN is executed?

g. Explain how the ON . . . GOSUB works in line 60 of program D. (Be sure to identify the variable.)

3. Using the two relations $X >= 12$ and NAME$ = "STOP", write a WHILE loop that will continue to execute for each condition below.

a. At least one relation is true.

b. Both relations are true.

c. Neither is true.

d. One is true and one is false.

4. Convert the following block IF program segment to a single ON . . . GOSUB statement.

```
IF X = 1 THEN
    GOSUB 100
ELSE IF X = 2 THEN
    GOSUB 200
ELSE IF X = 3 THEN
    GOSUB 300
ELSE
    GOSUB 400
END IF
```

5. Convert the WHILE loops into UNTIL loops.

a.
```
    COUNT = 0
    READ X
    WHILE X > 0
        PRINT X
        COUNT = COUNT + 1
        READ X
    NEXT
```

b.
```
    READ A, B
    WHILE A > 0 AND B > 0
        IF A > B THEN
            PRINT Z - B
        ELSE IF A < B THEN
            PRINT A + B
            READ A,B
        END IF
    NEXT
```

SUMMARY OF CHAPTER 6

CONCEPTS AND KEYWORDS INTRODUCED IN THIS CHAPTER

Concepts	Related keywords and statements
1. The WHILE and UNTIL loop structures	WHILE/NEXT UNTIL/NEXT
2. Counting with loops	
3. Statement modifiers for implied loops	FOR . . . WHILE FOR . . . UNTIL
4. Conditionally executing statements	UNLESS
5. Subroutines	GOSUB RETURN ON . . . GOSUB

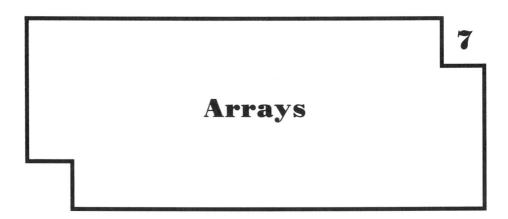

Arrays

7

We have often used a variable such as GRADE to represent many numbers in a program. Of course, at any given instant during execution, GRADE can contain only one number. However, we can input a value for GRADE, determine whether that value represents a passing or failing grade, then input a new value. The new value "forces out" the old one; the computer does not remember old values for GRADE once a new value has been assigned to GRADE. This approach uses only one storage space in the computer. It also permits efficiency in writing the program, since we do not have to use 50 different variables names to store 50 grades.

7.1 ONE-DIMENSIONAL ARRAYS

There are, however, applications in which it is more efficient or even necessary to have the computer store many different values of a variable at the same time. An earlier exercise asked you to calculate the first 25 Fibonacci numbers: 1, 1, 2, 3, 5, ... Each number in the sequence is the sum of the previous two numbers. Mathematically, we would represent the Fibonacci numbers by capital F's with subscripts:

$$F_1, F_2, \ldots , F_n$$

Keyboards do not allow us to type subscripts, but we can "subscript" by writing the subscript in parentheses following the variable name. Thus we can write F(1), F(2), F(N) for the first, second, and Nth Fibonacci numbers, respectively. Also, the "rule" becomes

$$F(N) = F(N-1) + F(N-2)$$

136

A variable used with subscripts in programming is an *array variable* or just an array. When the variable uses one subscript at a time, we call it a *one-dimensional array,* or a list. When you plan to use an array in a program, you should let the computer know by using a DIM (for dimension) statement at the beginning of the program. The DIM statement tells the computer to reserve storage for a subscripted variable and gives the largest subscript that may be used in the program. To reserve storage space for $F(1)$, $F(2)$, . . . , $F(25)$ we would use the statement

```
10 DIM F(25)
```

The computer will not regard DIM F(100) as an error if you calculate only the first 25 numbers; it allocates storage space for subscripts up to 100. You will simply have allocated much more storage than you plan to use. This is analogous to putting more numbers in DATA statements than you plan to READ; it wastes space.

The number in parentheses after DIM is called the size of the array. In most versions of BASIC, the size must be an integer constant, but VAX-BASIC also allows a numeric variable. With a constant, the DIM statement is called a *declarative DIM statement.* In most of our examples we will use declarative DIM statements, which must have a lower line number than any other reference to the array.

A program to calculate the first 25 Fibonacci numbers with subscripted variables is given below and is really quite simple.

Example 7.1 *Calculating Fibonacci Numbers with an Array*

```
10 REM -- First 25 Fibonacci numbers:  Subscripted variable F
20 DIM F(25)
30 F(1) = 1
40 F(2) = 1
50 FOR I = 3 TO 25
      F(I) = F(I-1) + F(I-2)
60 NEXT I
70 PRINT  F(I); FOR I = 1 TO 25
80 END

RUNNH

1  1  2  3  5  8  13  21  34  55  144  233  377  610  987  1597
2584  4181  6765  10946  17711  28657  46368  75025
```

Obviously, this program could be written without subscripted variables, but its logic is much simpler with them. Notice how the loop counter I automatically generates the subscripts.

The Executable DIM Statement

With the declarative DIM statement, the programmer must choose a number for the size of the array that is large enough for any conceivable application of the program. Programmers often choose sizes such as 100 or 500, hoping the user will not have a larger array. Users, on the other hand, often have very small arrays, so quite a lot of storage space is wasted. It is also possible that a user will have a larger array than the program specifies, in which case the program crashes.

The *executable DIM statement* contains a variable size. A typical application asks the user to specify the number of elements in the array, then dimensions the array to this number. The following program illustrates the point. It reads an array and prints it in reverse.

Example 7.2 *The Executable DIM Statement*

```
100 INPUT "How many elements"; TOTAL
110 DIM A(TOTAL)
120 INPUT "Element"; A(I) FOR I = 1 TO TOTAL
130 PRINT "The array in reverse is:"
140 PRINT A(I); FOR I = TOTAL TO 1 STEP -1
150 END
```

Subscript Bounds

Normally, array subscripts in BASIC begin with zero. You can set both lower and upper bounds on array subscripts by using the keyword TO in the DIM statement, as in

```
DIM A(5 TO 10)
```

which sets up an array with lowest subscript 5 and highest subscript 10. The array then contains six elements, A(5), A(6), . . . , A(10).

For example, at times we wish to deal with several recent years, and it would be handy to use subscripts corresponding to the years. We can deal with a company's earnings for the years 1984 through 1986 with an array EARNINGS dimensioned by

```
DIM EARNINGS(1984 TO 1987)
```

This idea is incorporated in the following program, which simply reads earnings for the four years and prints them.

Example 7.3 *Subscript Bounds in a DIM Statement*

```
100 REM -- Illustrate subscript bounds in DIM statement
110 DIM EARNINGS(1984 TO 1987)
120 PRINT " YEAR", "EARNINGS"
130 FOR YEAR = 1984 TO 1987
        READ EARNINGS(YEAR)
140 NEXT YEAR
150 FOR YEAR = 1984 TO 1987
        PRINT YEAR, EARNINGS(YEAR)
160 NEXT YEAR
170 CLOSE #1
180 DATA 18.5, 19.2, 20.1, 22.3
200 END
```

```
RUNNH
```

YEAR	EARNINGS
1984	18.5
1985	19.2
1986	20.1
1987	22.3

Searching an Array

String variables can be subscripted, too. Suppose we have a (very small) bank with six savings accounts. Each account has simply a name and a balance. We will put the names and balances in DATA statements and read them as subscripted variables NAME$ and BALANCE. We will write a program that allows a bank employee to enter a name, NEWNAME$, and find out the balance in the account with that name.

If the value of NEWNAME$ matches one of the NAME$ element values, we can find out which element with the following scheme:

```
INPUT "Whose account"; NEWNAME$
K = 1
WHILE NEWNAME$ <> NAME$(K)
    K = K + 1
NEXT
PRINT "Balance is"; BALANCE(K)
```

The WHILE loop increments the position counter K until NAME$(K) has the same value as NEWNAME$.

There is a problem, of course. What if the bank employee enters a name that does not match one of the NAME$ values? Then the WHILE loop will increment K to 7 and compare NEWNAME$ to NAME$(7), which does not exist. We need to exit from the loop if K becomes too large, so the WHILE statement should be:

```
WHILE NEWNAME$ <> NAME$(K) AND K < 6
```

[When K is 5, the computer should increment it to 6 and compare NEWNAME$ to NAME$(6), but when K is 6, the computer should exit the loop.]

The exit from the WHILE loop could be caused by one of two conditions: either NAME$(K) has the same value as NEWNAME$ or K has gone beyond the number of accounts. Thus, after the WHILE loop we place an IF block to determine which of these conditions was met:

```
IF NEWNAME$ = NAME$(K) THEN
    PRINT "Balance is"; BALANCE(K)
ELSE
    PRINT "Can't find an account by that name"
END IF
```

Here is the complete program.

Example 7.4 *Searching an Array of Bank Accounts*

```
100 REM -- Bank accounts
110 DIM NAME$(6), BALANCE(6)
120 FOR N = 1 TO 6
        READ NAME$(N), BALANCE(N)
130 NEXT N
140 ANSWER$ = "YES"
150 WHILE ANSWER$ = "YES"
160    INPUT "Whose account"; NEWNAME$
170    K = 1
       WHILE NEWNAME$ <> NAME$(K) AND K < 6
           K = K + 1
       NEXT
       IF NEWNAME$ = NAME$(K) THEN
           PRINT "Balance is"; BALANCE(K)
       ELSE
           PRINT "Can't find an account by that name"
       END IF
180    INPUT "Another name (YES or NO)"; ANSWER$
190 NEXT
200 DATA "Jones",   865.23, "Smith", 16.50
210 DATA "White", 1569.65, "Brown", 89.00
220 DATA "Black",   255.68, "Green", 8560.75
230 END


RUNNH

Whose account? Brown
Balance is 89
Another name? YES
Whose account? White
Balance is 1569.65
Another name? YES
Whose account? Allen
Can't find an account by that name
Another name? NO
```

This program might not seem very general, but it does give a general method for searching an array. Line 170 contains the entire search process. This particular program used precisely 6 accounts, but you can easily change that 6 to an N.

You do not have to use a DIM statement for subscripted variables if the largest subscript that will occur in the program is 10 or less. Only when you need large amounts of storage does the computer need to know ahead of time the amount of storage you need. However, we suggest that you DIM *all* subscripted variables as a reminder to yourself that certain variables *are* subscripted.

A DIM statement belongs at the beginning of a program; it is part of initialization or preparation. When you dimension a variable, say DIM GRADE(20), the computer sets aside storage for 21 variables, GRADE(0) to GRADE(20). In the two previous programs we ignored the 0 subscript, and you will often do this. It is more natural to begin counting with 1. Sometimes, however, the variable with 0 subscript has a natural use.

Suppose, for instance, that we have many numbers in DATA statements. We know that the numbers are either 0, 1, 2, or 3, and we want to count the number of occurrences of each of those digits. We *could* do something like the following:

```
100 REM -- Not the greatest way to count 0s, 1s, 2s, and 3s
110 N0, N1, N2, N3 = 0
120 FOR I = 1 TO 30
        READ X
        IF X = 0 THEN N0 = N0 + 1
        IF X = 1 THEN N1 = N1 + 1
        IF X = 2 THEN N2 = N2 + 1
        IF X = 3 THEN N3 = N3 + 1
130 NEXT I
140 PRINT "0 occurred "; N0; "times."
150 PRINT "1 occurred "; N1; "times."
160 PRINT "2 occurred "; N2; "times."
170 PRINT "3 occurred "; N3; "times."
180 DATA 3, 2, 3, 0, 3, 2, 1, 1, 2, 3
190 DATA 2, 3, 1, 2, 0, 2, 1, 2, 0, 2
200 DATA 1, 0, 2, 3, 2, 1, 2, 0, 2, 3
210 END
```

Notice line 120 and lines 140–170. In both cases something very similar is being repeated four times. When you see repetitions like this in a program, look for ways to avoid them. Loops and/or subscripted variables will often be the answer. In this case, instead of four separate variables N0, N1, N2, N3, it would be better to use one subscripted variable N with subscripts running from 0 to 3. The trick is: if X is a digit from 0 to 3, then N(X) counts the occurrences of X. Thus, instead of the four IF statements in line 120, we need only one statement: $N(X) = N(X) + 1$. The revised program follows.

Example 7.5 *An Array of Counters*

```
100 REM -- Counting number of digits 0, 1, 2, 3
110 DIM N(3)
120 N(I) = 0 FOR I = 0 TO 3
130 FOR I = 1 TO 30
        READ X
        N(X) = N(X) + 1
140 NEXT I
150 FOR I = 0 TO 3
        PRINT I; "occurred"; N(I); "times."
160 NEXT I
170 DATA 3, 2, 3, 0, 3, 2, 1, 1, 2, 3
180 DATA 2, 3, 1, 2, 0, 2, 1, 2, 0, 2
```

```
190 DATA 1, 0, 2, 3, 2, 1, 2, 0, 2, 3
200 END

RUNNH

0 occurred 5 times
1 occurred 6 times
2 occurred 12 times
3 occurred 7 times
```

We saved only 3 lines, but consider how many we would have saved if there had been 10 or 20 categories instead of 4.

Logic and Truth Tables

In logic, statements are often represented by letters—P, Q, R, etc.—and each statement may be true or false. If the truth values of P and Q are known, then the truth values of more complicated expressions, such as NOT(P OR NOT Q), can be determined. In this example, suppose P and Q are both True. Then P OR NOT Q is True because P is True, and a True statement OR any other statement is True. Thus NOT(P OR NOT Q) is False.

The logic of true/false relations can be turned into a rather simple arithmetic by letting the number 0 stand for "False" and the number 1 stand for "True." That is, in the computer we will assign 1 to P to indicate "the statement P is true" and 0 to P to indicate "the statement P is false." To get the appropriate number for P AND Q, simply multiply $P*Q$. This product will be 1 when, and only when, both P and Q have the value 1—that is, when the statements P and Q are both true.

To get NOT P, use $(1 - P)$. If $P = 1$, NOT P will be 0, and if $P = 0$, NOT P will be 1, as it should be. Finally, to get the appropriate number for P OR Q, take $P + Q - P*Q$. (Check to see that this works for all possible values of P and Q.)

In a program, we cannot use P OR Q as a variable name because it contains spaces, so we will use PORQ to represent P OR Q, PANDQ to represent P AND Q, and NOTP for NOT P.

To get "all possible" values for P, we will use a loop FOR P = 0 TO 1, and similarly for Q. We will use a subscripted variable TRUTH$ with just two values: TRUTH$(0) = "False" and TRUTH$(1) = "True". The program will print out a "truth table." That is, all possible values of True or False will be assigned to P and Q, then the appropriate value will be calculated for the statements P AND Q, P OR Q, and NOT P. The program follows.

Example 7.6 *Truth Tables*

```
100 REM -- Truth table for (P AND Q), (P OR Q), and (NOT P)
110 DIM TRUTH$(1)
120 TRUTH$(0) = "False"
130 TRUTH$(1) = "True"
140 PRINT "  P", "  Q", "P AND Q", "P OR Q", "NOT P"
150 PRINT
```

```
160 FOR P = 0 TO 1
        FOR Q = 0 TO 1
            PANDQ = P*Q
            PORQ = P + Q - P*Q
            NOTP = 1 - P
            PRINT TRUTH$(P), TRUTH$(Q), TRUTH$(PANDQ),
            PRINT TRUTH$(PORQ), TRUTH$(NOTP)
        NEXT Q
170 NEXT P
180 END
```

```
RUNNH
```

P	Q	P AND Q	P OR Q	NOT P
False	False	False	False	True
False	True	False	True	True
True	False	False	True	False
True	True	True	True	False

Here the use of a subscripted variable saved us from several IF statements, such as

```
IF PANDQ = 1 THEN PRINT "True", ELSE PRINT "False",
```

More complicated expressions involving P and Q could also be evaluated. For example, to evaluate NOT(P OR NOT Q), let NOTQ represent NOT Q, let PONQ repesent (P OR NOT Q), and let NPONQ represent the entire expression. Then we can evaluate the entire expression in three steps:

```
NOTQ = 1 - Q
PONQ = P + NOTQ - P*NOTQ
NPONQ = 1 - PONQ
```

Alternatively, we can evaluate the entire expression in one step:

```
NPONQ = 1 - (P + (1 - Q) - P*(1 - Q))
```

Sorting

A major application of subscripted variables occurs in sorting problems. A list of numbers or names is given, and the problem requires them to be put in increasing numerical order or alphabetical order. We will write a program to sort a list of numbers. Alphabetizing is almost an identical problem; the variable names just have to contain dollar signs. We will read ten values for a subscripted variable X and sort the values into increasing order. A program such as this should work for any number of values, but we leave this generalization as an exercise.

Almost any sorting scheme involves switching the values of two variables. Suppose X(I) and X(J) are two variables in a program and we want to switch their values;

the value for X(I) is to be assigned to X(J) and the value for X(J) is to be assigned to X(I). It is tempting to begin X(I) = X(J), but this will not work. After the statement X(I) = X(J) is executed, both variables have the value that was originally in X(J), and the value that was originally in X(I) has been lost.

The solution is to store the original value of X(I) in a temporary variable TEMP with the statement TEMP = X(I). Then put the value of X(J) into X(I) with the statement X(I) = X(J). Finally, assign the value in TEMP to X(J) with X(J) = TEMP. Thus switching the values of X(I) and X(J) involves three statements:

Code for Switch	Diagram of Switch
1. TEMP = X(I)	TEMP ←——1——→ X(I)
2. X(I) = X(J)	3 ↓ ╱ 2
3. X(J) = TEMP	X(J)

A rough outline of our method is as follows:

1. Find the smallest value in the variables X(1), X(2), . . . , X(10) and put this value in X(1). We will accomplish this by comparing each X(I) to X(1) and switching when we find a value smaller than the value in X(1). When this step is finished, we will not have to look at X(1) again.

2. Find the smallest value in X(2), X(3), . . . , X(10) and put this value in X(2). As before, do this by comparing X(3), X(4), etc. to X(2), and switch values when one of these variables has a value smaller than X(2).

3. Find the smallest value in X(3), X(4), . . . , X(10) and put this value in X(3). Use the same method as before.

4. Find the fourth smallest, fifth smallest, and so on. We stop here because we are repeating almost the same thing as in the previous steps.

Consider what step 2 tells us to do: compare X(2) with X(3), X(4), X(5), . . . , X(10) and switch values when one of these variables has a smaller value than X(2). This can easily be done with a loop counter J going from 3 to 10:

```
FOR J = 3 TO 10
    IF X(J) < X(2) THEN
        TEMP = X(J)
        X(J) = X(2)
        X(2) = TEMP
    END IF
NEXT J
```

Similarly, step 3 could be done with the same type J loop:

```
FOR J = 4 TO 10
    IF X(J) < X(3) THEN
        TEMP = X(J)
        X(J) = X(3)
        X(3) = TEMP
    END IF
NEXT J
```

You should by now be able to imagine a J loop for each step. There would actually be nine such loops, not ten, because, once the first nine numbers are in their proper order, the last number X(10) must be the largest number. Of course, we do not plan to write nine separate J loops. Look at the two loops and see what they have in common and how they differ. The FOR statements begin with FOR J = 3 and FOR J = 4, but otherwise they are the same. By the same token, the IF statements are identical except that, where one has three occurrences of X(2), the other has X(3). Now consider that we are finding a value for X(2) on the second step, a value for X(3) on the third step, and so on. Then it should seem reasonable to use a variable STP in place of the 2 and 3 in the IF statements above. Also, the 3 and 4 in the FOR statements can be replaced by STP + 1. (Don't use STEP as a variable name; it is a reserved keyword.) Now all the J loops can be written:

```
FOR J = STP + 1 TO 10
    IF X(J) < X(STP) THEN
        TEMP   = X(J)
        X(J)   = X(STP)
        X(STP) = TEMP
    END IF
NEXT J
```

We have already noted that we need to do nine steps, so we enclose the J-loops in a STP-loop FOR STP = 1 TO 9:

```
FOR STP = 1 TO 9
    FOR J = STP + 1 TO 10
        IF X(J) < X(STP) THEN
            TEMP   = X(J)
            X(J)   = X(STP)
            X(STP) = TEMP
        END IF
    NEXT J
NEXT STP
```

That is the heart of the program. We need to do some initial work: REM; DIM; READ the values of the array X. We also need to put in the data and print out the results. The program follows.

Example 7.7 *Sorting an Array*

```
10 REM -- Sort 10 numbers into ascending order
20 DIM X(10)
30 READ X(I) FOR I = 1 TO 10
40 FOR STP = 1 TO 9
      FOR J = STP + 1 TO 10
         IF X(J) < X(STP) THEN
            TEMP   = X(J)
            X(J)   = X(STP)
            X(STP) = TEMP
         END IF
      NEXT J
   NEXT STP
50 PRINT "The values in ascending order are:"
60 PRINT X(I); FOR I = 1 TO 10
70 DATA 34, -42, 49, 66, -52, -12, 68, 26, -6, 39
80 END

RUNNH

The values in ascending order are:
-52 -42 -12 -6  26  34  39  49  66  68
```

There are hundreds of different methods for sorting numbers. Some are minor modifications of this method, and some are very different. We do not claim that this method is the most efficient or the easiest; there are many ways that will sort faster. However, this method, a type of *selection sort,* is logically one of the simplest, and for 10 or 20 numbers you would not notice that this program runs slower than most of the very efficient methods.

EXERCISES A

1. Modify the sort program so that it will sort any number of values (up to 200 values). The program should read the number of values that are to be sorted. [Another change you might want to make is: Put the PRINT statement in line 50 before the nested loops, delete line 60, and put a statement PRINT X(STP); inside the STP-loop.]
2. Write a program to sort names into alphabetical order.
3. Write a program that sorts numbers into descending order.
4. The sort program works if there are duplicate values. (Try it.) Write a program that sorts numbers into increasing order and discards duplicate values. (If there are several identical values, only one of them should be printed.)
5. Write a program to type out a truth table for the statements NOT (P AND Q), P OR NOT (P OR Q)), and P AND NOT (P AND Q).

6. Write a program that asks you to enter digits (0, 1, 2, . . . , 9), stops when you enter a negative number, and counts the number of times each digit occurred.

7. Put four numbers in a list A and three numbers in a second list B. Calculate all possible products of a number from A times a number from B.

8. Calculate the median of a list of numerical values. When there is an odd number of values, the median is the middle value of the *ordered* values. When there is an even number of values, the median is the mean (or average) of the middle two values in the ordered list. [*Hint:* N is even if INT(N/2) = N/2.]

9. Read two lists, A and B, each of which is already in ascending order. Make and print a third list C which contains all the values in A and B arranged in ascending order. This is called *merging* the two lists A and B. Do not use a sort procedure. Keep three counters, say IA, IB, and IC, for the lists A, B, and C. Let C(1) be the smaller of A(1) and B(1). If B(1) was smaller than A(1), then increment IB, otherwise increment IA. Increment IC in either case.

10. a. Get the computer to play (but not very well) a game of Tic-Tac-Toe with you. Number the boxes from 1 to 9 as follows:

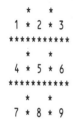

You go first. Let the computer's strategy be to choose the smallest number that has not already been taken. Have the computer print the board after every two moves, putting an X in for you, O for itself. Play the game several times. Be friendly—let the computer win at least once. (You don't have to program the computer to tell who won, but it should tell you if you pick a square that has already been taken.)

   b. Get the computer to keep track of wins or draws for the program in part a. This is much harder.

11. Set up bank accounts for five people by reading five names and five balances into two lists. Process several transactions; for each transaction, input a name and an amount to be withdrawn or deposited. After all transactions are completed, type out all the account names and new balances.

12. Read two lists of numbers, A and B, with the same number of values. Make all the A values positive, but let some of the B values be positive, some negative, and some zero. Find the smallest ratio A(I)/B(I) with a positive denominator. [In the ratio A(I)/B(I) the subscripts must be the same.]

13. Suppose you run a very small office supply store and have the following merchandise:

Merchandise	Quantity on hand	Price
Pen	3	$1.98
Pencil	8	$0.15
Eraser	6	$0.06
Notebook	5	$0.75
Ruler	7	$0.50

Set up your books by reading the information above into three lists. (Several arrays, related as these three are, are called *parallel arrays*.) Also, ask several customers what merchandise they want and how many. Give the total cost for the transaction, and update the inventory (subtract the number of items sold from quantity on hand). Take appropriate action if the customer asks for something you don't have. When all transactions are complete, print out the updated inventory.

14. Sort the inventory above into alphabetical order, keeping the appropriate quantity and price adjacent to the name of the merchandise.

7.2 ARRAY SUBROUTINES

Programs that deal with arrays can become long, so it is wise to use subroutines for parts of array programs. Many programs will have the structure of Figure 7.1.

We have read and printed several arrays without subroutines, but here we will write a subroutine for each part of the structure above, using a specific example.

Suppose we want a program to read names of salespeople and their weekly sales, then find and print the names and sales for the three highest sellers. We will first write a subroutine to find the three largest numbers in the sales array.

First, notice that our sorting algorithm (Example 7.7) can easily be modified to sort into descending order by reversing the inequality in the IF statement to read:

```
IF X(J) > X(STP) THEN   ! Change < to >
```

Second, we must keep the names adjacent to the sales figures whenever sales figures are switched. That is, if the sales data are in an array SALES and the names

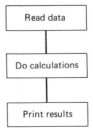

Figure 7.1   Program Structures

are in an array NAME$, then whenever we switch SALES(J) and SALES(STP), we must also switch NAME$(J) and NAME$(STP).

Finally, the sorting algorithm performs a complete sort, but it can easily be modified to find just the first three largest numbers, by performing just three steps, or by beginning

```
FOR STP = 1 to 3
```

Then our adapted sorting algorithm is as follows.

```
FOR STP = 1 TO 3
   FOR J = STP + 1 TO N
      IF SALES(J) > SALES(STP) THEN
         TEMP       = SALES(J)        ! Switch
         SALES(J)   = SALES(STP)      ! sales
         SALES(STP) = TEMP            ! values
                                      ! and
         TEMP$       = NAMES(J)       ! switch
         NAMES(J)    = NAMES(STP)     ! corresponding
         NAMES(STP) = TEMP$           ! names.
      END IF
   NEXT J
NEXT STP
```

This algorithm is the major part of the program, but of course the program must also dimension the arrays, read the input data, and print results. Reading the arrays is not difficult, but there are many ways to do it. We arbitrarily choose to have the names and sales in DATA statements, with

```
STOP, 0
```

as the end-of-data flag. Then the subroutine to read the data is as follows.

```
N = 1
READ NAMES(N), SALES(N)
WHILE NAMES(N) <> "STOP"
   N = N + 1
   READ NAMES(N), SALES(N)
NEXT
N = N - 1
```

N has counted the end-of-data flag, so it is decremented by 1 at the end of the loop.

Printing results is also rather simple. Here is the subroutine to do it.

```
PRINT
PRINT "The three people with highest sales are:"
PRINT
FOR I = 1 TO 3
    PRINT NAMES(I),
    PRINT USING "$$####.##", SALES(I)
NEXT I
```

Here are the subroutines in an entire program. Notice that the main program is almost entirely GOSUB statements.

Example 7.8 *Finding the Three Best Salespeople*

```
100 REM -- Find three top salespeople
110 DIM SALES(20), NAMES(20)
120 GOSUB 200      ! Input the array
130 GOSUB 300      ! Find three highest sales
140 GOSUB 400      ! Print results
150 GO TO 600
200 !!!!!!!!!!!!!!!!!!!!!!!!!!!!!!!!!!!!!!!!!!!!!!!!!!!!!!!!!!!!!!!
210 ! Subroutine; Read the array.
220 N = 1
230 READ NAMES(N), SALES(N)
240 WHILE NAMES(N) <> "STOP"
        N = N + 1
        READ NAMES(N), SALES(N)
    NEXT
250 N = N - 1
260 RETURN
300 !!!!!!!!!!!!!!!!!!!!!!!!!!!!!!!!!!!!!!!!!!!!!!!!!!!!!!!!!!!!!!!
310 ! Subroutine; Find three highest sales and the names
320 ! of the people who made these sales.
330    FOR STP = 1 TO 3
           FOR J = STP + 1 TO N
               IF SALES(J) > SALES(STP) THEN
                   TEMP      = SALES(J)       ! Switch
                   SALES(J)  = SALES(STP)     ! sales
                   SALES(STP) = TEMP          ! values
                                              ! and
                   TEMP$     = NAMES(J)       ! switch
                   NAMES(J)  = NAMES(STP)     ! corresponding
                   NAMES(STP) = TEMP$         ! names.
               END IF
           NEXT J
       NEXT STP
340 RETURN
400 !!!!!!!!!!!!!!!!!!!!!!!!!!!!!!!!!!!!!!!!!!!!!!!!!!!!!!!!!!!!!!!
410 ! Subroutine; Print results
```

```
420 PRINT
430 PRINT "The three people with highest sales are:"
440 PRINT
450 FOR I = 1 TO 3
        PRINT NAMES$(I),
        PRINT USING "$$####.##", SALES(I)
    NEXT I
460 RETURN
```

```
500 DATA  J. Rogers, 1235.41, R. Blackburn, 2426.21
510 DATA  M. Phillips, 2328.95, Z. Branovan, 1289.65
520 DATA  R. Reynolds, 1968.00, L. Martin, 3125.50
530 DATA  T. Cummings, 2479.12, D. Dork, 2762.53
540 DATA  C. Carlisle, 2685.90, STOP, 0
600 END
```

```
RUNNH

The three people with highest sales are:

L. Martin      $3125.50
D. Dork        $2762.53
C. Carlisle    $2685.90
```

The Shell Sort Subroutine

A sort subroutine is a fairly standard subroutine. Every programmer should have at least one sort subroutine available for use when needed. You could use the sort program given earlier as the basis for a sort subroutine. We give here another example of a sort subroutine, called *Shell* sort for its originator, Donald Shell. When there are a large number of items to be sorted, the Shell sort is quite a bit faster than our previous sort program.

      We do not give a lengthy explanation of the method, but there are a couple points to notice. First, instead of comparing adjacent numbers, such as A(I) and A(I + 1), this method compares numbers a certain gap apart: A(I) and A(I + GAP). The gap is denoted by the variable GAP in the subroutine, and GAP begins with value equal to half the number of items to be sorted. Then GAP is successively cut in half until it becomes 1, or less. Finally, a variable SORTFLAG is used: SORTFLAG begins with value 0 and is set to 1 when an exchange is made. When no exchange is made on one sweep across the numbers, then the GAP is cut in half.

```
300 ! Subroutine to sort list with Shell sort
310 GAP = N
320 WHILE GAP > 1
330     GAP = INT(GAP / 2)
340 ! Put numbers GAP positions apart in order.
        TOP = N - GAP
        SORTFLAG = 0
            WHILE SORTFLAG = 0
                SORTFLAG = 1
```

```
              FOR I = 1 TO TOP
                 NXT = I + GAP
                 IF A(I) > A(NXT) THEN
                    SORTFLAG = 0
                    TEMP    = A(I)
                    A(I)    = A(NXT)
                    A(NXT) = TEMP
                 END IF
              NEXT I
           NEXT
     NEXT
350 RETURN
```

Remember, this is only a subroutine and cannot run by itself. In particular, the main part of the program must dimension the list A and read in the values for A. However, the main benefit of writing this part of a program as a subroutine is that it is now quite general and can be used as a subroutine in any program that requires a list A of numbers to be sorted. This is, in fact, the main benefit of subroutines in general; they can be inserted into any program to solve part (sometimes all) of a complex problem. Thus, subroutines allow you to break a huge problem down into smaller parts, each of which can be solved with a particular subroutine.

Expressing Decimal Numbers in Binary Notation

When encountering a number such as 27, almost certainly you assume it is a base-10 number, whether or not you know what base 10 means; that is, you assume 27 means "two 10s plus seven 1s." Similarly, 475 means "four 10**2s plus seven 10s plus five 1s." To express a number in binary notation means to express it in powers of 2 rather than powers of 10 (or any other number).

The base 10 number 27 is equal to the following powers of 2:

$$16 + 8 + 2 + 1 \qquad \text{or} \qquad 2**4 + 2**3 + 2**1 + 2**0$$

To express this number in binary notation, simply write down a 1 for every power of 2 that is present and a 0 for powers of 2 that are missing, beginning with the highest power of 2 that is present. In the expression above, only the second power is missing from the powers from 0 to 4, so we would write 11011. That is,

$$27 \text{ (base 10)} = 11011 \text{ (base 2)}$$

As another example, the number 8 in base 10 is the same as 2**3, so the binary representation for that number begins with a 1 that is followed by three zeros, representing the fact that the second, first, and zero powers of 2 are "missing." So

$$8 \text{ (base 10)} = 1000 \text{ (base 2)}$$

It is not too difficult to write a program that converts a base-10 number into its representation as a binary or base-2 number. Simply find the largest power P of 2 in the number, and

1. Write a 1 in the P "place."

2. Start a subtotal equal to $2^\wedge P$.

Then check each smaller power I of 2 to see if it is present in the number. If the power of 2 is present,

1. Put a 1 in the I place for that power.

2. Add $2^\wedge I$ to the subtotal.

If the I power of 2 is missing, simply put a 0 in the I place.

    We illustrate this procedure for the decimal number 19. Let BINDIG(I) stand for the binary digit in place I, where I can be 0, 1, 2, . . . , up to the largest power of 2 contained in the number. Remember, the 0 place is on the right, and the highest power takes the leftmost place.

    The largest power of 2 in 19 is $16 = 2^\wedge 4$, so BINDIG(4) = 1, and we start the subtotal at 16. Now we check each power of 2 from the third power down to the zero power. For the third power, $2^\wedge 3 = 8$. But the subtotal is already 16, and $16 + 8 = 24$, which is greater than 19, so the third power of 2 is absent. Therefore we make BINDIG(3) = 0.

    The second power of 2 is also absent, because $16 + 2^\wedge 2 = 20$, which is greater than 19, so BINDIG(2) = 0.

    The first power is present because $16 + 2 = 18$, which is not greater than 19. Thus we set BINDIG(1) equal to 1 and add 2 to the subtotal, which now becomes 18.

    The zero power is present because $18 + 1 = 19$. Thus BINDIG(0) = 1. The binary representation of 19 is then 10011, the 0 and 1 digits stored in BINDIG(4), BINDIG(3), BINDIG(2), BINDIG(1), and BINDIG(0).

    There are many ways to find the largest power of 2 in a number. One of the simplest is to take successively higher powers of 2 until you reach the first power that is larger than the given number, then reduce that power by 1. Using the decimal number 19 as an example again, consider the powers of 2: 1, 2, 4, 8, 16, 32. Since 32, the fifth power of 2, is the first power larger than 19, we can begin with the fourth power of 2, or 16.

    Letting X represent the decimal number involved, we turn this algorithm into BASIC with the following code:

```
I = 1
WHILE 2^I <= X
    I = I + 1
NEXT
BIGPOWER = I - 1
```

    Here is the complete program. You will be asked to use part of it as a subroutine in the exercises.

Example 7.9 *Converting from Base 10 to Base 2*

```
300 REM -- Base 10 to base 2 conversion for positive integers
310 DIM BINDIG(20)
320 INPUT "Positive integer"; X
330 ! Find largest power of 2 contained in X
340 I = 1
350 WHILE 2^I <= X
        I = I + 1
360 NEXT
370 BIGPOWER = I - 1
380 ! Set this binary digit to 1 and start subtotal
390 BINDIG(BIGPOWER) = 1
400 SUBTOTAL = 2^BIGPOWER
410 ! Check each power from BIGPOWER - 1 down to 0
420 FOR I = BIGPOWER - 1 TO 0 STEP -1
        IF SUBTOTAL + 2^I > X THEN
            BINDIG(I) = 0
        ELSE
            BINDIG(I) = 1
            SUBTOTAL = SUBTOTAL + 2^I
        END IF
430 NEXT I
440 PRINT
450 PRINT BINDIG(I); FOR I = BIGPOWER TO 0 STEP -1
460 PRINT "is the binary representation for"; X
500 END
```

```
RUNNH

Positive integer? 4

1 0 0 is the binary representation for 4
```

VAX-BASIC allows arrays with more than one dimension. In fact, arrays can have up to 32 dimensions. We will discuss two-dimensional arrays in Chapter 13.

EXERCISES B

1. Write a program to use the Shell sort subroutine to sort a list of names into alphabetical order.

2. Rewrite the binary digit program of Example 7.9 without using an array.

3. Write a program that asks for two positive integers and gives the binary representations for these two integers and for their sum and their product. Use the program above as the basis for your subroutine. (A couple of lines should be deleted.)

4. Write a program that asks you for a list of numbers and prints them. The program should then ask you if there are any errors in the list. If there are errors, the program should ask you which elements are in error and give you a chance to correct the errors. The "error handler" should be in a subroutine.

5. Write a program to read two lists, A and B, that are already in increasing order. Put a subroutine in the program to merge the two lists into a list C in increasing order. Let C(1) be the smaller of A(1) and B(1), etc. Do not just put the two lists A and B together and sort.

6. Write a program that allows the user to play Tic-Tac-Toe with the computer. Use several subroutines to:

   a. Print the board.
   b. Check to see if either player has won.
   c. Get a move for the computer.

7. The median of a set of numbers is

   a. The middle number if there is an odd number of numbers in the set.
   b. The average of the middle two numbers if there is an even number of numbers in the set.

   Write a program to find the median of a set of numbers. Use a sort subroutine.

8. Write a subroutine to convert a positive integer into Roman numeral form. Then write a program that asks for two positive integers and writes Roman numeral forms for the two given numbers, their sum, and their product.

   a. Use *old Roman numeral* form, without subtraction. That is, 9 is VIIII and 95 is LXXXXV.
   b. Use *new Roman numeral* form, in which a single power of 10 (I, X, C) preceding a larger number denotes subtraction of that power. For instance, 9 is IX, 95 is XCV, and 1900 is MCM.

9. Write a program that asks the user which of three operations to perform on a list of numbers. Have the following subroutines perform the operations. The subroutines should be called with an ON . . . GOSUB statement:

   a. Order the list.
   b. Find average (mean) of the list.
   c. Find the median of the list.

REVIEW QUESTIONS

1. Write DIM statements for the following arrays.
   a. An array NAME$ with 100 names.
   b. An array of numbers from 1 to 10.
   c. An array with lowest subscript 100 and highest 999.
   d. An array X with a variable number of values referred to as QUANTITY.
   e. An array HEIGHT with 25 elements.

2. For the following array fill in the appropriate values.

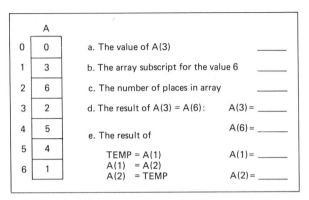

3. For X = True, Y = False and Z = True, what is the value of each of the logical expressions below?

a. NOT (X AND Y)

b. (X OR Y) OR (X OR Z)

c. (X OR Y) AND (Y OR Z)

d. NOT (X AND Y AND Z)

e. X OR Y OR Z

f. (X OR Y) AND (NOT Y)

4. What will array NUMBERS contain after the following code is executed?

```
DIM NUMBERS(5)
    FOR X = 1 TO 5
        NUMBERS(X) = X
    NEXT X
    FOR X = 1 TO 5
        FOR Y = 5 TO 1  STEP -1
            NUMBERS(X) = NUMBERS(Y)
        NEXT Y
    NEXT X
```

5. Write code to change the following array X so that every negative number in the array becomes −1, every positive number becomes 1, and every zero remains zero.

	X
1	0
2	−3
3	0
4	−6
5	7
6	8
7	−1
8	2
9	0
10	4

SUMMARY OF CHAPTER 7

The only keyword introduced in this chapter is DIM, which is used to specify the number of dimensions and the size of an array.

CONCEPTS INTRODUCED IN THIS CHAPTER

1. Defining (dimensioning) an array
2. Searching an array
3. Sorting an array
4. Manipulating an array
   a. Calculating array elements
   b. Using array elements as counters
   c. Using array elements for temporary storage

Terminal Format Files

Up to now, all data used by our programs were obtained through READ/DATA, assignment, or INPUT statements. These statements required that the data be part of the program or be typed on the terminal keyboard. However, many real applications require writing, reading, and updating large data sets. We can do these operations much more efficiently if the data sets are stored separately from the programs which use them. This separation is achieved with data files, which are stored by the computer in the same manner programs are stored.

Roughly, a *file* is simply a place to store information in a computer. The programs you write in BASIC become permanent files when you type SAVE. The computer then stores what you have written, using the name you have given. You can later call up the program by giving its name. The file name functions much like a variable name, giving the location in the computer where the file is stored.

We say an *array* is a *data structure* because it holds more than one value, and because it imposes some order on its values. A one-dimensional array has a linear, or sequential numerical order; element 2 follows element 1, element 67 follows element 66, and so on. The one-dimensional array is certainly an extremely important data structure.

A *data file,* or more simply a *file,* is an equally important data structure in programming. Just as an array allows us to refer to many related pieces of data with one name, a file allows us to store many related pieces of information in one place.

Probably the most important distinction between arrays and files is that files have an identity separate from the programs that use them. We sometimes say files are permanent while arrays are temporary. The values in an array are lost once the program defining the array has run. A file, on the other hand, remains in existence after any program that uses it has run.

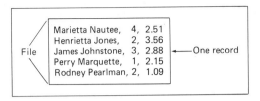

Figure 8.1   File Format

While the components of an array are its elements, the components of a file are called *records*. However, each array element stores just one value (number or string), but a record can hold several values. Also, while all elements of an array must have the same data type, the values in a record can have different types. Figure 8.1 depicts a file of five records in which each record holds a string, an integer, and a real number.

8.1 TERMINAL FORMAT FILES

To fully describe the file above, we must do more than just specify the records in it; we must tell how the file is organized. VAX-BASIC files can have five different organization types:

> TERMINAL FORMAT
> SEQUENTIAL
> INDEXED
> RELATIVE
> BLOCK I/O

We will discuss the first four types (treating relative files only briefly).

The simplest file in VAX-BASIC is a *terminal format file*, which looks just like lines typed at the terminal keyboard or printed on a terminal screen. Each line in a terminal format file is a record. VAX-BASIC programmers customarily refer to terminal format files and sequential files as two distinct types, but technically, a terminal format file is a special type of sequential file, a file in which one record follows another in sequence. Assuming the file above is a terminal format file, the sequence or order should be clear. The record with Marietta Nawtee is followed by the record with Henrietta Jones, and so on.

The word "sequential" has an even stronger implication here. If you want to read the record containing Perry Marquette, you must first read every record that comes before that one in the file. This "sequential access" is similar to the access you have to the selections on an audio cassette. If you want to hear the third song on a cassette, you must first pass over (play or fast-forward) the first two selections.

Similarly, if you want to create a file in which the third record contains James Johnstone, you must first put two other records in the file, then write the name James Johnstone in the third record. The position of a record in a sequential file is simply the order in which that record was placed in the file.

A terminal format file can be created either by running a VAX-BASIC program or by using an *editor*, a special program that helps users to create files. Some of the popular VAX editors are EDT, EVE, and LSE. If you know how to use one of these editors, or any other, you can create terminal format files with them. In this text we will discuss creating terminal format files only with BASIC programs.

The OPEN Statement

Before a program can do anything with a file, it must establish a connection between itself and the file. An *OPEN statement* connects a file to the program containing the OPEN statement. The simplest OPEN statement in VAX-BASIC is

```
OPEN "FILE.DAT" as #1
```

FILE.DAT is the name of the file to be opened, and #1 is the *channel number* or *logical unit number* of the file. The channel number establishes a connection between the program and the data file FILE.DAT. If a file named FILE.DAT already exists, this OPEN statement connects that file to the program. If such a file does not exist, the OPEN statement creates a file named FILE.DAT. Later in the program, you refer to the file by referring to the channel number. The channel number can be any integer from 1 through 99.

   You might want to think of the channel number as a physical line connecting the program to the file:

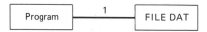

File names follow the same rules as BASIC program names. You have already seen the *extension* .BAS that BASIC appends to the name of your BASIC programs. An extension of three characters indicates the purpose of the file. Most VAX systems use certain default extensions, including .BAS for BASIC programs, .FOR for Fortran programs, and .PAS for Pascal programs. The extension .DAT is not one of the default extensions, but many programmers use .DAT for all data files.

   We will seldom use this simple form of the OPEN statement but will open files either "for input" or "for output." The words "input" and "output" refer to the program, which either takes data *in* from the file or puts data *out* to the file. To open a file for output, the OPEN statement takes the form

```
OPEN <filename> FOR OUTPUT AS #<channel number>
```

A specific example is

```
OPEN "SQUARE.DAT" FOR OUTPUT AS #1
```

This OPEN statement, with FOR OUTPUT, creates a data file SQUARE.DAT and prepares this empty file to receive output.

The PRINT # Statement

The PRINT # statement places data in an opened terminal format file. This statement has the form

```
PRINT #<channel number>, <data list>
```

For example, if N is a real variable in the program, we can write a record containing the values of N, its square, and its square root with the statement

```
PRINT #1, N, N*N, SQR(N)
```

The PRINT # USING Statement

The *PRINT # USING statement* acts exactly as the PRINT USING statement but writes to a terminal format file instead of a terminal screen. We could, for instance, write data to the file SQUARE.DAT with a statement of the form

```
PRINT #1 USING "### ###### ##.####", N, N*N, SQR(N)
```

The CLOSE Statement

The CLOSE statement breaks the connection between a program and a file. Its form is

```
CLOSE # <channel number>
```

An opened file should be closed when the program is finished with it.

Here is a small program that creates a file SQUARE.DAT and writes 20 records. Each record contains a number, its square, and its square root, with the numbers ranging from 1 to 20.

Example 8.1 *Creating a Terminal Format File*

```
100 REM -- Create a terminal format file containing a table of
110 REM -- squares and square roots for integers from 1 to 20.
120 OPEN "SQUARE.DAT" FOR OUTPUT AS #1
130 PRINT #1, "Number", "Square", "Square root"
140 FOR N = 1 TO 20
        PRINT #1, N, N*N, SQR(N)
    NEXT N
150 CLOSE #1
160 END
```

When this program is run, you will see only the familiar "Ready" to let you know that the run is complete. To see if the program has done its job, use the DCL TYPE command:

```
$ TYPE SQUARE.DAT
```

You should see the following:

```
Number          Square          Square root
1               1               1
2               4               1.41421
3               9               1.73205
4               16              2
5               25              2.23607
6               36              2.44949
7               49              2.64575
8               64              2.82843
9               81              3
10              100             3.16228
11              121             3.31662
12              144             3.4641
13              169             3.60555
14              196             3.74166
15              225             3.87298
16              256             4
17              289             4.12311
18              324             4.24264
19              361             4.3589
20              400             4.47214
```

The file looks exactly like the output that would be printed on your terminal screen if PRINT statements were used instead of PRINT # statements.

Reading a Terminal Format File

To read this file, a program should open the file *for input* with a statement such as

```
OPEN "SQUARE.DAT" FOR INPUT AS #2
```

The channel number could be any number from 1 to 99.
A record in a terminal format file is *read* with an *INPUT #* statement of the form

```
INPUT #<channel number>, <input list>
```

When the file is opened, VAX-BASIC sets up two record pointers, a *current record pointer* and a *next record pointer*. The current record pointer is initially undefined, and the next record pointer points to the first record in the file. Each INPUT # statement performs the following actions:

1. Reads the record pointed to by the next record pointer.
2. Sets the current record pointer to the record read.
3. Sets the next record pointer to the next record.

VAX-BASIC considers a record in a terminal format file to be a string of characters, so each record or line in the file SQUARE.DAT can be read with the INPUT # statement

```
INPUT #2, LINE$
```

Here is a short program which reads and prints the file SQUARE.DAT.

Example 8.2 *Reading a Terminal Format File*

```
100 REM -- Read and print SQUARE.DAT, containing a table of
110 REM -- squares and square roots for integers from 1 to 20.
120 OPEN "SQUARE.DAT" FOR INPUT AS #2
130 PRINT "Contents of file SQUARE.DAT:"
140 PRINT
150 FOR N = 1 TO 21
        INPUT #2, LINE$
        PRINT LINE$
     NEXT N
160 CLOSE #2
200 END
```

The LINPUT # Statement

The INPUT # statement with one string variable reads characters in a record until a data terminator is encountered. The end of a record in a file is a data terminator, just as the end of a line of DATA in a program. Closing quotes are terminators for string data, and commas are also data terminators for any kind of data, so if a record contains commas, the statement

```
INPUT #2, LINE$
```

will read only as far as the first unquoted comma.

For example, if a record has

"Murray Hill, NY", 12.35, 8.6

then the statement INPUT #2, LINE$ assigns to LINE$ the value

Murray Hill, NY

To overcome this difficulty, VAX-BASIC provides the LINPUT # statement, which reads an entire record into one string variable. The statement

```
LINPUT #2, LINE$
```

assigns to LINE$ precisely what is in the record, or

"Murray Hill, NY", 12.35, 8.6

Notice that all commas and quote marks are part of the value of LINE$.

We will not use the LINPUT # statement in the remainder of this text, but you should be aware of it if the need for it arises. (We will discuss the LINPUT statement, which reads string data from the terminal, in Chapter 10.)

Reading Several Values from One Record

While reading an entire line or record of data into one string variable is sometimes useful, this approach precludes using the separate numbers in the file. If we want to read the three numbers in one record into three numeric variables, the numbers must be separated by commas, just as they would be if the data were entered from a terminal with an INPUT statement.

Consider a data file in which each record is to contain a student name and three grades. When writing the data for one record, we must consider how the data will be read by a program that reads the file. For example, we can write a line of data as

```
Jane Austen, 86, 75, 92
```

just as we would write that same data in a DATA statement. We must supply the commas, which are necessary to separate data items.

Similarly, if we want the name written in the form

```
Austen, Jane
```

we must enclose the name in quotes, as in

```
"Austen, Jane"
```

to let the computer know that the comma is part of the name, not a data terminator. Thus our PRINT # statement might be

```
PRINT #2, '"'; NAME$; '",'; X; ","; Y; ","; Z
```

Suppose we want the name given in this latter form. The following program creates the specified data file.

Example 8.3 *Creating a Program-Readable Terminal Format File*

```
100 REM -- Create a terminal format file with each record
110 REM -- containing a student name and three grades.
120 REM -- Insert commas so a program can read the file.
130 OPEN "GRADE.DAT" FOR OUTPUT AS #2
140 PRINT "Enter student names and grades as requested."
150 PRINT "Enter name as last name, comma, first name,"
160 PRINT "and enclose the entire name in quotes, as in"
170 PRINT '"Carlisle, Pam"'
180 PRINT "To stop, enter ZZZZ in response to Name?"
190 INPUT "Name"; NAME$
200 WHILE NAME$ <> "ZZZZ"
```

```
      INPUT "Three grades"; X, Y, Z
      PRINT #2, '"'; NAME$; '"',; X; ","; Y; ","; Z
      INPUT "Name"; NAME$
   NEXT
210 CLOSE #2
300 END
```

After a sample run, you can use the DCL TYPE command to see the file. It might look like the following.

```
"Austen, Jane", 87 , 92 , 93
"Twist, Oliver", 68 , 73 , 71
"Flanders, Moll", 69 , 82 , 75
"Eyre, Jane", 84 , 89 , 82
"Chuzzlewitt, Martin", 62 , 47 , 70
```

Recall that VAX-BASIC prints numbers with a trailing space, and with a leading space if the number is positive.

To read a record from the file GRADE.DAT, the INPUT # statement could be

```
INPUT #3, NAME$, G1, G2, G3
```

where NAME$ could be any string variable name and G1, G2, and G3 could be any three real variable names.

Here is a program that reads the file GRADE.DAT and calculates the mean grade for each student.

Example 8.4 *Reading Several Values from a Record*

```
100 REM -- Read a terminal format file with each record
110 REM -- containing a student name and three grades.
120 REM -- Calculate mean grade for each student.
130 OPEN "GRADE.DAT" FOR INPUT AS FILE #3
140 FOR I = 1 TO 5
         INPUT #3, NAME$, G1, G2, G3
         MEAN = (G1 + G2 + G3) / 3
         PRINT NAME$; " has a mean grade of"; MEAN
      NEXT I
150 CLOSE #3
200 END
```

A sample run with the data file above would give:

```
Austen, Jane has a mean grade of 90.6667
Twist, Oliver has a mean grade of 70.6667
Flanders, Moll has a mean grade of 75.3333
Eyre, Jane has a mean grade of 85
Chuzzlewitt, Martin has a mean grade of 59.6667
```

Using an End-of-Data Record

The program above used a loop FOR I = 1 TO 5, because we knew the file contained exactly five records. Often a programmer does not know how many records a file will contain but wants to be able to read to the end of the file. An end-of-data record can be placed in the file to mark the end of the file.

The following program reads a name, hours worked, and hourly rate of pay for several employees and puts records into a file. The end-of-data record contains the word STOP and two zeros. Notice that the program asks for the name of the file, FILENAME$, then opens the file with OPEN FILENAME$ . . . .

Example 8.5 *Using an End-of-data Record*

```
100 REM -- Create a terminal format file containing names,
110 REM -- hours worked, and pay rates for several employees.
120 INPUT "Name of file to be created"; FILENAME$
130 OPEN FILENAME$ FOR OUTPUT AS FILE #3
140 PRINT "Enter names, hours, and rates as requested."
150 PRINT "Enter STOP for name to end input."
160 !    Get data and write records to the file.
170 INPUT "Name"; NAME$
180 WHILE NAME$ <> "STOP"
190    INPUT "Hours worked"; HOURS
200    INPUT "Hourly rate "; RATE
210    PRINT #3, NAME$; ","; HOURS; ","; RATE
220    INPUT "Name"; NAME$
230 NEXT
240 PRINT #3, "STOP"; ","; 0; ","; 0
250 CLOSE #3
300 END
```

With data for three people, the file might look like:

```
James Wilson, 40 , 6.5
Harold Harmon, 36 , 5.85
J. J. Johnson, 50 , 6.8
STOP, 0 , 0
```

The following program reads the file created in the previous program. We use a very simple calculation of gross pay as hours times rate, because the main point here is reading a file with an end-of-data record.

Example 8.6 *Reading a File with an End-of-Data Record*

```
100 REM -- Read a terminal format file containing names,
110 REM -- hours worked, and rates for several employees.
120 REM -- Calculate gross pay for each employee.
130 INPUT "Name of file with employee data"; FILENAME$
140 OPEN FILENAME$ FOR INPUT AS FILE #4
```

```
150 PRINT
160 PRINT "Name", "Hours", "Rate", "Gross Pay"
170 PRINT
180 !      Read records and calculate gross pay.
190 INPUT #4, NAME$, HOURS, RATE
200 WHILE NAME$ <> "STOP"
210    GROSS = HOURS * RATE
220    PRINT NAME$, HOURS, RATE, GROSS
230    INPUT #4, NAME$, HOURS, RATE
240 NEXT
250 CLOSE #4
300 END
```

The end-of-data record works well if the user of the data file is also its creator and plans ahead. Sometimes, however, you will have to read a large file created by someone else who has not put in an end-of-data record. The following program will read and print all the records in the file SQUARE.DAT but will end on an error.

Example 8.7 *Reading to the End of a File; Ending on an Error*

```
100 REM -- Read the terminal format file SQUARE.DAT created
110 REM -- earlier.  Assume that the number of records in the file
120 REM -- is unknown.  The program ends on an end-of-file error.
130 OPEN "SQUARE.DAT" FOR INPUT AS #2
140 PRINT "Contents of file SQUARE.DAT"
150    INPUT #2, X, Y, Z
160    PRINT X, Y, Z
170 GO TO 150
180 CLOSE #2
190 END
```

The error occurs after the program reads and prints the last record, because the GO TO in line 170 sends the computer back to line 150 to INPUT another record. Since no more records exist, the program ends on an end-of-file error, similar to an out-of-data error.

Error Handling

Ordinarily, BASIC takes care of runtime errors by terminating the run of the program and printing error messages. However, VAX-BASIC also provides a means by which the programmer can detect and deal with runtime errors.

The *ON ERROR GO TO statement* sends the computer to the *error handler,* a portion of the program that handles errors. This statement is placed before any other executable statement. The GO TO is followed by the line number where the error handler starts. An example is

```
100 ON ERROR GO TO 900
```

where the error handler begins at line 900.

VAX-BASIC contains a built-in function named *ERR*. This function takes an integer value corresponding to the most recent error encountered in a program. The value for the end-of-file error is 11. Since this is the only error we want to deal with, the error handler should begin with

```
IF ERR = 11% THEN
```

To "handle" this error requires us to do very little; we simply want the computer to continue at the CLOSE statement in line 180. We accomplish this with the statement

```
RESUME 180
```

This *RESUME statement* is similar to a GO TO statement and requires a line number after RESUME. It is used only in error handlers. Thus, the IF statement becomes

```
IF ERR = 11% THEN RESUME 180
```

The error handler requires one further addition. Program control passes to line 900 when any error occurs, not just the end-of-file error. If any other error occurs, we want VAX-BASIC to handle that error the way it normally does. We pass the error-handling responsibility back to VAX-BASIC with the statement

```
ON ERROR GO TO 0
```

Thus, the complete error handler is

```
IF ERR = 11% THEN RESUME 180 ELSE ON ERROR GO TO 0
```

The complete program now is as follows.

Example 8.8 *Reading to the End of a File*

```
100 REM -- Read a terminal format file to the end, using an error
110 REM -- handler to deal with the end-of-file error.
120 ON ERROR GO TO 900
130 OPEN "SQUARE.DAT" FOR INPUT AS #2
140 PRINT "Contents of file SQUARE.DAT"
150     INPUT #2, X, Y, Z
160     PRINT X, Y, Z
170 GO TO 150
180 CLOSE #2
190 GO TO 950
900 !!!!!!!!!!!!!!!!!!!!!!!!!!!!!!!!!!!!!!!!!!!!!!!!!!!!!!!!!!!!!!!!!!!!
910 !  Error handler to deal with end-of-file error; ERR number 11
920 !!!!!!!!!!!!!!!!!!!!!!!!!!!!!!!!!!!!!!!!!!!!!!!!!!!!!!!!!!!!!!!!!!!!
930 IF ERR = 11% THEN RESUME 180
                    ELSE ON ERROR GO TO 0
950 END
```

The code at line 930 will determine if the error was generated by the end-of-file error; if so, the program will close the file; otherwise, the error will be handled by the system because of ON ERROR GO TO 0. Notice the GO TO statement at line 190, which skips over the error handler to the END statement.

Searching a File

A standard file operation is finding a specific record in a file. Suppose, for example, that we have a simple payroll file in which each record contains a name, hours, and rate. We might want to find the record with a specific name.

For concreteness, let the variables in a record be NAME$, HOURS, and RATE, and let the name we want to find be SEARCHNAME$. Then it is a simple matter to find the appropriate record with a WHILE loop such as

```
WHILE NAME$ <> SEARCHNAME$
    INPUT #1, NAME$, HOURS, RATE
NEXT
```

We can then print the information from the appropriate record as soon as the computer exits from this WHILE loop, because the loop exit occurs when the values of NAME$ and SEARCHNAME$ match.

There is a problem with this approach. If the specified name is not in the file, the WHILE loop has no exit, so the program will crash on an end-of-file error. We take care of this problem with an error handler that informs the user that the file does not contain the given name. The complete program is as follows.

Example 8.9 *Searching a File for a Specific Record*

```
100 REM -- Search a terminal format file for a specific record.
110 ON ERROR GO TO 900
120 OPEN "PAYROLL.DAT" FOR INPUT AS FILE #1
130 PRINT "This program allows you to search the file"
140 PRINT "PAYROLL.DAT for a specific name."
150 PRINT
160 INPUT "Name"; SEARCHNAME$
170 PRINT
180 INPUT #1, NAME$, HOURS, RATE
190 WHILE NAME$ <> SEARCHNAME$
        INPUT #1, NAME$, HOURS, RATE
    NEXT
200 PRINT "Name", "Hours", "Rate"
210 PRINT NAME$, HOURS, RATE
900 !!!!!!!!!!!!!!!!!!!!!!!!!!!!!!!!!!!!!!!!!!!!!!!!!!!!!!!!!
910 !  Error handler; ERR number 11 is end-of-file.
    !!!!!!!!!!!!!!!!!!!!!!!!!!!!!!!!!!!!!!!!!!!!!!!!!!!!!!!!!
920 IF ERR = 11% THEN
        PRINT "That name is not in the file."
        RESUME 930
```

```
    ELSE ON ERROR GO TO 0
    END IF
930 CLOSE #1
950 END
```

Suppose the file PAYROLL.DAT is:

```
Jack Sprat, 42, 6.25
Mary Contrary, 38, 8.15
Jack Horner, 25, 3.35
Tom Piperson, 22, 4.80
Bo Peep, 60, 2.55
```

Then two runs of the program might go as follows:

```
RUNNH

This program allows you to search the file
PAYROLL.DAT for a specific name.

Name? Bo Peep

Name          Hours         Rate
Bo Peep         60          2.55

RUNNH

This program allows you to search the file
PAYROLL.DAT for a specific name.

Name? Willie Winkie

That name is not in the file.
```

The RESTORE # Statement

The RESTORE # statement sets the next record pointer to the beginning of the file so the next INPUT # statement reads the first record in the file. It works just like the RESTORE statement for data in DATA statements. The format is simple:

```
RESTORE #<channel number>
```

The previous program allows the user to search for just one record. We can use the RESTORE # statement to modify the program so the user can search for as many names as desired. The search procedure is enclosed in a loop beginning

```
WHILE SEARCH_NAMES <> "XXXX"
```

and the RESTORE # statement comes at the end of that loop.

Example 8.10 *Using RESTORE # on a Terminal Format File*

```
100 REM -- A terminal format file contains names, rates, and hours
110 REM -- worked for several employees.  Ask the user for a name
120 REM -- and print the record with that name, if it exists.
130 ON ERROR GO TO 900
140 OPEN "PAYROLL.DAT" FOR INPUT AS FILE #4
150 PRINT
160 PRINT "Whose record are you looking for?"
170 INPUT "Enter a name or XXXX to stop"; SEARCH_NAME$
180 PRINT
190 WHILE SEARCH_NAME$ <> "XXXX"
200 ! Read until record is found or until end of file.
210    INPUT #4, NAME$, HOURS, RATE
220    WHILE NAME$ <> SEARCH_NAME$
230       INPUT #4, NAME$, HOURS, RATE
240    NEXT
250    IF NAME$ = SEARCH_NAME$ THEN
          PRINT "Name", "Hours", "Rate"
          PRINT NAME$, HOURS, RATE
       END IF
260    PRINT
270    INPUT "Another name, or XXXX to stop"; SEARCH_NAME$
280    PRINT
290    RESTORE #4
300 NEXT
310 CLOSE #4
320 GO TO 999
900 !!!!!!!!!!!!!!!!!!!!!!!!!!!!!!!!!!!!!!!!!!!!!!!!!!!!!!!!!!!!!!!!!
910 !         Error handler; end-of-file ERR number is 11.
920 !!!!!!!!!!!!!!!!!!!!!!!!!!!!!!!!!!!!!!!!!!!!!!!!!!!!!!!!!!!!!!!!!
930 IF ERR = 11% THEN
       PRINT "Cannot find record with that name."
       RESUME 270
    ELSE ON ERROR GO TO 0
    END IF
999 END
```

The statement GO TO 999 in line 320 causes the computer to skip over the error handler to the END statement. If the computer were to execute the error handler, it would evaluate (ERR = 11%) as true if an end-of-file error had occurred during the program run. Then the computer would print the "Cannot find record" message and resume at line 270, putting the program into an infinite loop.

Therefore, place a GO TO statement before error handlers, just as you would before subroutines, so the computer does not "fall into" the error handler one extra time. This GO TO statement is not always necessary, as you can see by looking at Example 8.9, but sometimes it is crucial.

VAX-BASIC contains many more file operations, some of which will be discussed in Chapters 11 and 12.

More about Error Handling

It is a good idea to give error handlers the same beginning line numbers in all your programs. We generally use line 900 so we can start the program with ON ERROR GO TO 900. VAX-BASIC programmers who write very large programs often use line 19000.

By the same token, many programmers use the same line number on the END statement in every program they write. If you are quite sure all your line numbers will be three-digit numbers, then 999 is a reasonable number for the END statement. Then any GO TO statement that sends control to the END statement will be GO TO 999.

To use ON ERROR GO TO, you must know the error number corresponding to the error and take appropriate action. VAX-BASIC assigns each error an error number. These numbers and descriptions of each error are contained in the VAX-11 BASIC documentation. Some of the errors usually handled by the user are:

ERROR NUMBER	DESCRIPTION
11	End of file
161	Record too long
153	Record already exists
155	Record not found

We will deal with some of these errors later.

The ERL Function

At times the error number ERR does not give enough information to tell us where the error handler should send program control. A program could contain two sections of code that might cause an end-of-file error. The error handler should RESUME to one of two places, but we would not know which one. The built-in function *ERL* will tell us. ERL takes an integer value equal to the line number where the last runtime error occurred.

An error handler that uses ERL as well as ERR could be as follows:

```
IF ERR = 11% THEN
   IF ERL = 210% THEN
      RESUME 200
   ELSE IF ERL = 440% THEN
      RESUME 470
   END IF
ELSE
   ON ERROR GO TO 0
END IF
```

In almost every possible situation, the values of ERR and ERL together will pinpoint the error.

All the errors we deal with are concerned with files. There are many other errors, but most can be circumvented in different ways. For example, attempting to take the square root (SQRT) of a negative number is an error. However, you can easily circumvent this error with code such as the following.

```
WHILE X < 0
    PRINT "Value of X must not be negative".
    INPUT "New value for X"; X
NEXT
Y = SQRT(X)
```

The important thing is to be aware of possible errors like division by zero, and insert code to prevent them from "bombing" your program.

EXERCISES

In the exercises below, "file" means terminal format file. If you know how to create files with an editor, you can bypass part a of any problem, but we urge you to create a few files with BASIC programs.

1. a. Write a program that creates a file with the first record containing the header

    X   1/X   SQRT(X)   X-FACTORIAL

    and each succeeding record containing a real value, its reciprocal, its square root, and its factorial. Use X values from 10 to 20. Do not put commas between values, but line up entries in the table under the appropriate headings.

   b. Write a program that reads and prints the file above. You may assume that the file contains 11 records.

2. a. Write a program to create a file that contains the prime numbers in the range from 2 to 1,000, one prime number per record. Place an appropriate end-of-data record at the end of the file.

   b. Write a program that reads the file created in part a, and counts the number of prime numbers in the range from 2 to 1,000.

3. a. Write a program that creates an inventory file with the following records plus an appropriate end-of-data record. Place commas after each data item in records 3 through 9 so another program can read the separate values in each record.

	PART	PART	QUANTITY	REORDER	REORDER
Record 1:	PART	PART	QUANTITY	REORDER	REORDER
Record 2:	NUMBER	NAME	ON HAND	LEVEL	QUANTITY
Record 3:	1001	Frammis	142	125	144
Record 4:	1002	Gizmo	18	20	36
Record 5:	1003	Thingy	108	120	100
Record 6:	1004	Whatzis	62	84	50
Record 7:	1005	Gazoo	35	50	25
Record 8:	1006	Snew	64	50	36

b. Write a program that reads and prints the file created in part a, along with a column indicating whether the item should be reordered. (Reorder an item if the quantity on hand is below the reorder level.)

4. a. Write a program that creates a file with records containing three real numbers, separated by commas. Do not put in an end-of-data record.

b. Write a program that reads the file created in a, using an ON ERROR GO TO statement to detect the end of the file. For each record in the file, print the largest value in the record. Also print the largest and smallest of the values in the entire file.

5. a. Write a program to create a file with each record containing one real number. Do not put in an end-of-data record.

b. Write a program that reads the numbers in the file above into an array, using an ON ERROR GO TO statement to detect the end of the file. Sort the numbers and print the sorted array.

6. Write a program to read the file created in Exercise 3 and print all records with quantity on hand less than or equal to reorder level, then print all records with quantity on hand greater than reorder level. (Use the RESTORE # statement.)

REVIEW QUESTIONS

1. Which of the following are valid OPEN statements?
    a.   OPEN "FILE.DAT" FOR OUTPUT AS #1
    b.   OPEN ME AS #1
    c.   OPEN "CIRCLE.DAT" FOR INPUT AS #3
    d.   OPEN "NAME" AS #2
    e.   OPEN THE FILE "TODAY.DAT" FOR PRINTING AS #10

2. Write an OPEN statement for each of the following files.
    a. A file named SQUARE.DAT for output.
    b. A file named DATES.DAT for input and/or output.
    c. A file for input that contains charge account numbers.
    d. A file for output with names and addresses.

3. Write PRINT # statements to place data that will look like each sample below into an opened terminal format file.

    a.   X   X*2   X/2
         1   2   .50
         2   4   1
         3   6   1.5
         4   8   2
         5   10   2.5

    b.   "SMITH, JOHN"
         "JONES, DORIS"
         "DAYTON, BETH"
         "BROWN, MIKE"
         "THOMPSON, GREG"

c.   Grade 1   Grade 2   Grade 3

         98   100   99
         75   73   78
         86   53   85
         71   75   79
         75   85   92

4. Write an INPUT # statement to read each of the following terminal format files.

a.   Jack Smith, 39, 160
      Brian Jacobs, 36, 170
      Morris Garfinkle, 45, 150
      Larry Akman, 38, 180
      (These values are names, ages, and weights.)

b.   Height   Length   Area
         5   2   10
         3   20   60
         4   4   16
         7   5   35
         8   2   16

c.   Phone Number   Bill   Paid/Overdue
      774-2003   39.65   Paid
      563-2018   175.03   Overdue
      396-5411   25.67   Paid
      986-3321   102.75   Paid

5. Where will the program execution resume after entering the error handler with each of the given conditions?

```
IF ERR = 11 THEN
    IF ERL = 300 THEN
        RESUME 320
    ELSE IF ERL = 400 THEN
        RESUME 420
    END IF
ELSE
    ON ERROR GO TO 0
END IF
```

a. End of file and last INPUT # at line 300
b. End of file and last INPUT # at line 500
c. End of file and last INPUT # at line 400

SUMMARY OF CHAPTER 8

This chapter has introduced terminal format files, including the following concepts and VAX-BASIC statements:

Concepts	Related keywords
1. Creating a file	OPEN
	PRINT #
	PRINT # USING
	CLOSE
2. Reading a file	INPUT #
	LINPUT #
3. End-of-file error	ON ERROR GO TO
	RESUME
	ERR
	ERL
4. Rereading a file	RESTORE

Numeric Functions

We have already discussed two numeric library functions, SQR and INT. By *library* functions we mean functions that are part of VAX-BASIC or are *built into* VAX-BASIC. The random-number function RND will be discussed in Chapter 14. In this chapter we will define some numeric library functions and give program examples for most of them.

9.1 NUMERIC LIBRARY FUNCTIONS

Which functions will be most helpful to you? That depends on the type of problems you work. We recommend that you skim over this section, taking notice of what functions are available so you can find them if you need them later.

The ABS Function

The absolute-value function, ABS, gives the positive value of its argument. For instance, ABS(3.2) is 3.2, and ABS(−26.5) is 26.5. The definition of ABS is often given as:

```
ABS(X) =  X if X >= 0
ABS(X) = -X if X <  0
```

To take the absolute value of a number "by hand" is easy; just drop the minus sign if there is one.

When we want the distance between two numbers (the distance between two points on the number line), we usually want a positive value. Thus the distance between two numbers X and Y is usually given as ABS(X $-$ Y). It could as well be given as ABS(Y $-$ X). The distance between 1 and 6 is 5, which is the value of ABS(1 $-$ 6) and the value of ABS(6 $-$ 1). Also, in accounting it is useful to represent assets as positive numbers and liabilities as negative numbers. When a balance sheet is printed, however, negative numbers are not ordinarily used. The ABS function can be used to guarantee that all numbers printed are positive (or zero).

The ABS function enables us to give a complete solution to any quadratic equation

$$ax^2 + bx + c = 0$$

We often say that, if

$$b^2 - 4ac < 0$$

then the equation has no solutions. Actually, it has no *real* solutions, but it has *complex* solutions of the form RE $\pm$ IMi, where i is the square root of -1. RE is called the real part of the complex number and IM is the *imaginary part*.

If the coefficient values are stored in A, B, and C, then

```
RE = -B / (2*A)
```

and

```
IM = SQR(ABS(B^2 - 4*A*C) / (2*A)
```

Here is a program that solves quadratic equations.

Example 9.1 *Solving a Quadratic Equation*

```
100 PRINT "Enter coefficients a, b, c for a quadratic equation"
110 PRINT "  2"
120 INPUT "ax  + bx + c = 0   "; A, B, C
130 WHILE A = 0
        PRINT "First coefficient cannot be 0"
        INPUT "Enter new value for a"; A
140 NEXT
150 PRINT
160 D  = B^2 - 4*A*C
170 RE = -B / (2*A)
180 IM = SQR(ABS(D)) / (2*A)
190 IF D < 0 THEN
        PRINT "Two complex solutions"
        PRINT RE; "+"; IM; "i"
        PRINT RE; "-"; IM; "i"
    ELSE IF D = 0 THEN
        PRINT "One solution",   RE
    ELSE
        PRINT "Two real solutions"
        PRINT RE - IM
        PRINT RE + IM
```

```
   END IF
200 END
```

```
RUNNH
```

```
Enter coefficients a, b, c for a quadratic equation
ax² + bx + c = 0  ? 1, 1, 1
Two complex solutions
-.5 + .866025 i
-.5 - .866025 i
```

The MAX and MIN Functions

The MAX and MIN functions can take from two to eight arguments, with each argument being a numeric expression. MAX returns the value equal to the largest of its argument values, and MIN returns the smallest argument value. Some specific examples:

MAX(8, 3, 4, 5, 6)	is	8
MIN(8, 3, 4, 5, 6)	is	3
MAX(3 * 4, 64 / 4, 2 − 100)	is	16
MIN(3 * 4, 64 / 4, 2 − 100)	is	−98

Here is a short program illustrating the MAX and MIN functions.

Example 9.2 *The MAX and MIN Functions*

```
100 REM -- Calculate the largest and smallest of 4 numbers
110 PRINT "Enter 4 numbers, in any order."
120 PRINT "The largest and smallest will be calculated."
130 INPUT A, B, C, D
140 PRINT "The largest is "; MAX(A, B, C, D)
150 PRINT "The smallest is "; MIN(A, B, C, D)
160 END
```

The MOD Function

The MOD function takes two numeric arguments and returns the remainder when the first argument value is divided by the second argument value. The value returned takes the sign of the first argument. Thus:

MOD(8, 3)	is	2
MOD(−8, 3)	is	−2
MOD(14, 5)	is	4
MOD(14, −5)	is	4

The arguments of the MOD function do not have to be whole numbers. For instance, MOD(8.25, 2.5) is .75, because 2.5 goes into 8.25 three times, with remainder .75. Here is a simple program using the MOD function.

Example 9.3 *The MOD Function*

```
100 REM -- Find a remainder with the MOD function
110 INPUT "Enter two whole numbers"; A, B
120 PRINT "The remainder when "; A ; "is divided"
130 PRINT "by "; B ; "is "; MOD(A, B)
140 END
```

When this program is run, the result might be:

```
Enter two whole numbers? 123, 11
The remainder when  123 is divided
by  11 is  2
```

The SGN Function

The SGN function, like most VAX-BASIC functions, is used with an argument in parentheses: SGN(6.2); SGN(X); SGN(X**2 − Y**2). The value of the SGN function is

> +1   if the argument is positive
> −1   if the argument is negative
> 0   if the argument is 0

The SGN function is called the *signum* function (because "sign" would sound just like "sine"); it can be used to determine the sign of a numeric argument. The following program illustrates the use of the SGN function.

```
10 REM -- The SGN Function
20 READ X, Y, Z
30 DATA 4, -4, 8
40 PRINT "X + Y", "X - Y + Z", "X + 2 * Y"
50 PRINT X + Y, X - Y + Z, X + 2 * Y
60 PRINT "SGN(X + Y)", "SGN(X - Y + Z)", "SGN(X + 2 * Y)"
70 PRINT SGN(X + Y), SGN(X - Y + Z), SGN(X + 2 * Y)
80 END
```

```
RUNNH

X + Y           X - Y + Z          X + 2 * Y
0                 16                  -4
SGN(X + Y)      SGN(X - Y + Z)     SGN(X + 2 * Y)
0                  1                  -1
```

The FIX Function

The FIX function truncates (chops off the decimal part of) a number. It is identical to the INT function for positive or zero values of its argument. However, FIX(−9.53) is −9, while INT(−9.53) = −10. Like the other numeric functions, the argument for FIX can be any numeric expression, as in FIX(−12.79), FIX(A), or FIX(6*X − Y).

Trigonometric Functions

Three trigonometric functions are built into VAX-BASIC: SIN, COS, and TAN, which give the values of the sine, cosine, and tangent of their arguments. The arguments, usually considered to be angles, can be any numeric expressions, but VAX-BASIC assumes angles to be in radians. The following program reads several multiples of π and gives the sine, cosine, and tangent of the angles.

Example 9.4 *Trigonometric Functions: Radians*

```
10 REM -- SIN, COS, and TAN:  Angles read in radians
20 PRINT "RADIANS", "SINE", "COSINE", "TANGENT"
30 FOR I = 1 TO 7
        READ RANGLE
        RANGLE = PI * RANGLE
        PRINT RANGLE, SIN(RANGLE), COS(RANGLE), TAN(RANGLE)
40 NEXT I
50 DATA 0, 0.166667, 0.5, 0.333333, 0.75, 1.0, 1.33333
60 END

RUNNH
```

RADIANS	SINE	COSINE	TANGENT
0	0	1	0
.5236	.500001	.866025	.577352
1.5708	1	-.437114E-07	-.228773E+08
1.0472	.866025	.500001	1.73205
2.35619	.707107	-.707107	-1
3.14159	-.874228E-07	-1	.874228E-07
4.18878	-.86602	-.500009	1.73201

If you wish to state arguments for these functions in degrees, the arguments can be converted to radians. Since π radians equal 180 degrees, the conversion formula is:

$$\text{angle in radians} = (\pi/180) * (\text{angle in degrees})$$

However, you can cause VAX-BASIC to consider the arguments of the trigonometric functions as angles in degrees by using an *OPTION ANGLE* statement of the form

```
OPTION ANGLE = DEGREES
```

You may set angles to either DEGREES or RADIANS, but RADIANS is the default value, so the previous program did not require an OPTION ANGLES statement. The corresponding program to read angles in degrees would be:

Example 9.5 *Trigonometric Functions: Degrees*

```
10 REM -- SIN, COS, and TAN:  Angles read in degrees
20 OPTION ANGLE = DEGREES
30 PRINT "DEGREES", "SINE", "COSINE", "TANGENT"
```

```
40 FOR I = 1 TO 7
     READ DANGLE
     PRINT DANGLE, SIN(DANGLE), COS(DANGLE), TAN(DANGLE)
50 NEXT I
60 DATA 0, 30, 45, 60, 135, 180, 210
70 END

RUNNH
```

DEGREES	SINE	COSINE	TANGENT
0	0	1	0
30	.5	.866025	.57735
45	.707107	.707107	1
60	.866025	.5	1.73205
135	.707107	-.707107	-1
180	0	-1	0
210	-.5	-.866025	.57735

What do you suppose happens if you ask the computer to calculate the tangent of 90 degrees? Try it.

The ATN Function

The ATN function gives the arctangent of its argument; that is, it gives the angle whose tangent is the given argument. The value given by ATN is the principal value of the arctangent; it returns an angle in radians between $-\pi/2$ and $\pi/2$. Arguments can be in the range from $-1E38$ to $1E38$. For example:

Example 9.6 *The Arctangent Function ATN*

```
10 REM -- Arctangent
20 PRINT "Tangent", "Arctangent", "Arctangent"
30 PRINT "Value", "in Radians", "in Degrees"
40 FOR I = 1 TO 5
     READ X
     PRINT X, ATN(X), 180 * ATN(X) / PI
50 NEXT I
60 DATA 0, 1, -0.866, -8.92, 1000
70 END

RUNNH
```

Tangent Value	Arctangent in Radians	Arctangent in Degrees
0	0	0
1	.785398	45
-.866	-.71371	-40.8926
-8.92	-1.45915	-83.6034
1000	1.5698	89.9427

The statement OPTION ANGLE = DEGREES causes the ATN to return an Arctangent value in degrees. The following small program illustrates this point.

```
100 REM -- ATN Function
110 OPTION ANGLE = DEGREES
120 INPUT "Tangent value"; V
130 PRINT "The Arctangent of "; V ; "is "; ATN(V); "degrees."
140 END

RUNNH

Tangent value? -1
The Arctangent of -1 is -45 degrees.
```

Although the arcsine and arccosine are not part of the VAX-BASIC function library, you can calculate them if you know the sine or cosine of an angle. (There will, however, be an ambiguity in sign when the arccosine is calculated.) For example, the principal values for the arcsine function are the same as those for the arctangent; both range from $-\pi/2$ to $+\pi/2$ radians (or -180 to 180 degrees). Also, in this range, the cosine is always nonnegative. Thus, given the sine of an angle X, we can calculate the cosine by the formula

```
COS(X) = SQR(1 - SIN(X)**2)
```

Then the tangent of X is SIN(X)/COS(X) and the ATN function will give us the desired angle.

As an example, suppose the sine of an angle is .6 and we want to find the principal value of arcsine(.6). We first calculate

```
COS(X) = SQR(1 - .6**2) = .8
```

Then TAN(X) = .6/.8 = 0.75. Finally, ATN(.75) will give the desired angle. A simple program to do these calculations follows. Notice that we take care of the cases when the sine value is ± 1 first, because then the cosine value is zero and the tangent is infinite.

Example 9.7 *Calculating an Arcsine*

```
10 REM -- Calculating Arcsine using ATN function
20 OPTION ANGLE = DEGREES
30 INPUT "Sine value"; S
40 PRINT "Arcsine of your value is ";
50 IF S = 1 THEN
      PRINT 90;
   ELSE IF S = -1 THEN
      PRINT -90;
   ELSE
      C = SQR(1 - S^2)
      PRINT ATN(S/C);
```

```
   END IF
60 PRINT "degrees."
70 END

RUNNH

Sine value? 0
Arcsine of your value is  0 degrees.
```

The arccosine can be calculated in a similar way, but the cosine is positive in quadrants 1 and 4 and negative in the second and third quadrants, so the principal values of the arccosine are usually given in the range from 0 to π. This means that, when the cosine is negative, the ATN function applied to a negative value will give an angle in the fourth quadrant, when the angle should be in the second quadrant. It is a simple matter to get the angle in the proper quadrant by adding PI to it.

The following program is similar to the Arcsine program above. Notice that the Arcsine program calculated angles in degrees, while this program calculates angles in radians.

Example 9.8 *Calculating an Arccosine*

```
10 REM -- Calculating Arccosine with ATN
20 INPUT "Cosine value"; C
30 PRINT "The Arccosine of your value is ";
40 S = SQR(1 - C^2)
50 IF C = 0 THEN
      PRINT PI/2;
   ELSE IF C > 0 THEN
      PRINT ATN(S/C);
   ELSE
      PRINT ATN(S/C) + PI;
   END IF
70 PRINT "radians."
80 END

RUNNH

Cosine value? 1
The Arccosine of your value is  0

RUNNH

Cosine value? -1
The Arccosine of your value is  3.14159
```

The EXP Function

The small letter *e* is often used in mathematics to stand for a number approximately equal to 2.71828. The EXP function raises *e* to the power given by its argument; EXP(6) means "*e* raised to the 6th power." The argument can be any numerical expression in the range from −88 to +88. Arguments outside this range result in an error message (because e to the 89th power would be larger than 1E38).

There is no reserved keyword that gives the value for e as PI does for π. However, when the value of e is required in a problem, use EXP(1). Values of EXP(X) for several values of X are calculated by the following program.

Example 9.9 *Calculating Powers of* e

```
10 REM -- Powers of e
20 PRINT "Power", "EXP(Power)"
30 FOR I = 1 TO 5
       READ X
       PRINT X, EXP(X)
40 NEXT I
50 DATA 0, 1, -3, 4.6, 50
60 END


RUNNH


Power        EXP(Power)

0            1
1            2.71828
-3           .497871E-01
4.6          99.4843
50           .518471E+22
```

The LOG and LOG10 Functions

The LOG function is the inverse of the EXP function. That is, for a given argument X, LOG(X) is the power that would have to be placed on e to get the value X. Another way to put this is: EXP(LOG(X)) is X. The argument for the LOG function can be any numerical expression having a value between 1E-38 and 1E38. The powers of e are always positive, so LOG cannot have a negative or zero argument. In fact, the argument for LOG must not be closer to zero than 1E-38. The LOG function yields what are called the *natural* logarithms of numbers. Natural simply means that the base of the logarithms is e.

The LOG10 function gives logarithms to the base 10, or *common* logarithms. LOG10(X) is the power that would have to be placed on 10 to obtain the value X. Thus, for example, LOG10(100) is 2 because $100 = 10**2$, and LOG10(0.1) is −1 because $10**(−1) = 0.1$. As with the LOG function, arguments for the LOG10 function must be positive numbers between 1E-38 and 1E38.

Logarithms with any base satisfy the property

$$\log (A * B) = \log (A) + \log (B)$$

Also, for bases larger than 1, log (A) is less than A. These two facts enable us to calculate the logarithms of numbers larger than VAX-BASIC can store. For example, 80! is larger than 1E38 (about the largest number VAX-BASIC can store), but we can calculate the logarithm of 80! in the following way:

Example 9.10 *Calculating the Logarithm of a Large Number*

```
10 REM -- Calculation of LOG10(80!)
20 LOG80FAC = 0
30 FOR I = 1 TO 80
        LOG80FAC = LOG80FAC + LOG10(I)
40 NEXT I
50 PRINT "The log of 80! to the base 10 is"; LOG80FAC
60 END
```

```
RUNNH
```

```
The log of 80! to the base 10 is 118.855
```

We can also get BASIC to print values in E notation with exponents larger than 38. Suppose we are given the logarithm (base 10) of a large number; for concreteness, let the log be 67.3010. In theory, to find the value of the number X, we would write X = 10**67.3010. However, if we write this as a program line in VAX-BASIC, the computer will give us an error message, because 10**67.3010 is too large a number for VAX-BASIC.

We can overcome this difficulty by writing 10**67.3010 as (10**67)*10**0.3010). Now 10**67 is still too big for VAX-BASIC, but we know that it represents 10 to the 67th power or E67, so we can have VAX-BASIC print 10**67 or E67 without ever calculating it. So all we really need to do is have VAX-BASIC calculate 10**0.3010 and "tack on" the E67 or 10**67. The program to do this follows.

Example 9.11 *Calculating a Number too Large for VAX-BASIC*

```
10 REM -- "Calculate" 10**67.3010
20 PRINT "10**67.3010 = "; 10**0.3010; "E67"
30 END
```

```
RUNNH
```

```
10**67.3010 = 1.99986 E67
```

which is roughly the number 2 followed by 67 zeros.

The TIME Function

The TIME function in VAX-BASIC gives various times, depending on the argument supplied:

TIME(0)   gives the elapsed time since midnight in seconds. (But don't count on this being correct local time; some human being probably looked at a watch and supplied the computer with a starting time.)

TIME(1)   gives the current job's CPU time in tenths of a second. This is the amount of time the central processing unit (CPU) of the computer has spent on your behalf since you logged in.

TIME(2)   gives the elapsed time in minutes since you logged in.

If you want to know the amount of CPU time required by one of your programs, you can insert the statement PRINT TIME(1) at the beginning and end of the program. The difference between these two times in tenths of a second is the time spent on the program. You can use PRINT TIME(1) in the program as the first and second-last (just before END) lines.

The TIME function also accepts the arguments 3 and 4, but TIME(3) and TIME(4) are both 0. If you give any argument other than 0, 1, 2, 3, or 4 to TIME, VAX-BASIC will give an error message ("Not implemented", ERR = 250).

EXERCISES A

1. The distance between a point in the plane (u, v) and the line given by the equation $ax + by = c$ is the absolute value of

$$\frac{au + bv - c}{\text{SQR } (a^2 + b^2)}$$

Write a program to calculate the distance from a point to a line. Find at least the distances from (3, 4) to the line $4x - 3y = 5$, and from (−6, 8) to the line $3x + 7y = -4$.

2. If A and B are two numbers then the larger of them can be calculated by:

$$\text{LARGER} = \frac{(A + B + \text{ABS } (A - B))}{2}$$

Write a program that asks for two numbers and types the larger one.

3. Print a table for sine (x), cosine (x), and tangent (x) as x goes from 0 to 360 degrees in steps of 30 degrees. When cosine $(x) = 0$, the program should not try to calculate tangent (x), but should print Undefined.

4. Find the principal values of arccosine (.866) and arcsine (.9). Give answers in both degrees and radians.

5. A standard notation for triangles is to label the sides a, b, c and the angles A, B, C, where side a is opposite angle A, etc. The law of cosines states

$$c^2 = a^2 + b^2 - 2ab \cos (C)$$

with similar formulas for sides a and b. Write a program that accepts the values for sides a, b and the included angle C and gives the value for side c and angles A and B.

6. Write a program that accepts the three sides of a triangle and calculates the three angles. Use the law of cosines (given in the previous exercise).

7. Write a program that accepts a logarithm (base 10) and prints the antilogarithm. The program should be able to deal with logs larger than 38.

8. Find the values of 80! and 100! and print them in E-notation.

9. Write a program that asks for a number, then tells how many digits that number has before the decimal point. The program should work for both positive and negative numbers.

10. Write a program to print the value of EXP (100).

9.2 USER-DEFINED FUNCTIONS

Single-Line Function Definitions

You can create your own functions in VAX-BASIC programs by use of the DEF (for define) statement. The name of the defined function must begin with the letters FN and can contain up to 28 more letters, digits, underscores, or periods. For instance,

```
DEF FNPOLY(X) = X**2 + 3*X - 6
```

defines FNPOLY to be a function with one argument. The value of the function for that argument is: the argument squared, plus 3 times the argument, minus 6. The actual variable name used for the argument is immaterial; the argument is a dummy variable, or place-holder.

A very simple example:

```
10 DEF FNPOLY(ARGUMENT) = ARGUMENT**2 + 3*ARGUMENT - 6
20 PRINT "Value of the function at 6 is "; FNPOLY(6)
30 END

RUNNH

Value of the function at 6 is   48
```

In line 10 the computer is told how to calculate FNPOLY for any given number. This is the *function definition*. In line 20 the computer actually calculates the value for FNPOLY(6) by substituting 6 for ARGUMENT in the definition in line 10. This is called the *function invocation*. After line 10, which defines the meaning of FNPOLY, the function can be used as if it were one of the built-in VAX-BASIC functions. FNPOLY is, however, only defined in this program.

User-defined functions can have several (up to 255) arguments, such as

```
DEF FNAVG(A, B, C, D) = (A + B + C + D)/4
```

FNAVG has four arguments and gives their average or mean. A simple example of the use of this function is:

```
10 DEF FNAVG(A, B, C, D) = (A + B + C + D)/4
20 INPUT "Give me four numbers"; W, X, Y, Z
30 PRINT "Their mean is"; FNAVG(W, X, Y, Z)
40 END
```

```
RUNNH
```

```
Give me four numbers? 2, 9, 4, 8
Their mean is 5.75
```

Once again, the DEF statement in line 10 does not cause any calculation to be performed; it does not even cause the computer to look for values of the variables A, B, C, and D. These variable names are *local* to the DEF statement; you can use these names elsewhere in the program and the computer would not confuse them with the variable names in the DEF statement. (However, to avoid confusing yourself, use variable names in DEF that are not used elsewhere in the program.) For example, suppose we insert the following line in the program above:

```
35 PRINT A, B, C, D
```

When the revised program is run, the computer will type the average of the four numbers you put in, then it will type

```
0  0  0  0
```

because the variables A, B, C, D in line 35 were never given any values.

It is legitimate to use program variables in a DEF statement; just do not include such variables in the list of arguments for the function. For example,

```
10 DEF FNA(X) = X * MULTIPLIER
20 READ MULTIPLIER
30 FOR I = 1 TO 5
40     READ Z
50     PRINT FNA(Z),
60 NEXT I
70 DATA 12
80 DATA 6, 9, 2, 4.5, 8.25
90 END
```

```
RUNNH
```

```
72       108       24       54       99
```

The program would do exactly the same thing if lines 10 and 50 were changed to:

```
10 DEF FNA(X, Y) = X*Y
50     PRINT FNA(Z, MULTIPLIER),
```

The arguments in function *definitions* must be simple variable names, not array names or array element names. Constants such as 6 or PI, and expressions such as X*Y or X**3, also cannot appear as arguments in function definitions.

You can use VAX-BASIC's built-in functions in user-defined functions, such as

```
DEF FNROUND2(X) = INT(100*X + 0.5)/100
```

You can also use other user-defined functions, as in

```
DEF FNA(X) = X**3 - 64
DEF FNB(Z) = EXP(FNA(Z))
```

but you cannot use the function being defined, as in

```
DEF FNA(X) = EXP(FNA(X))   ! Illegal
```

It is not wise to define a function such as

```
DEF FNPROD(X, Y) = X*Y
```

because later in the program it will be easier to write FIRST*SECOND rather than having to write FNPROD(FIRST,SECOND) when you want to multiply two variables FIRST and SECOND. Also it will not generally be profitable to define a function if you use that function only once inside the program. If you have only one number to round, there is not much point in defining the function FNROUND2 above. However, it is definitely worthwhile to define FNROUND2 in the payroll problems where you should round GROSS, FEDTAX, SOCSEC, NET, etc.

The computer does not care where you put DEF statements in your program. It is going to deal with DEF statements before running your program in the usual sequence. (This is roughly the same way DATA statements are treated by the computer. DATA statements are "set aside" before the rest of the program is run.) However, for your benefit, you should put DEF statements at the beginning (or near it) of your programs. DEF statements are part of the initializing or preparatory stage, as are DIM statements.

Multiline Function Definitions

At times a single line is not long enough to define the function you need. VAX-BASIC allows function definitions to be spread out over several lines. A multiline function definition:

1. Begins with DEF FN*function-name(arguments)*.
2. Ends with the statement END DEF.
3. Has the function definition on one or more lines between DEF and END DEF.

(FNEND can be used in place of END DEF.)

   Here is a simple example that could have been a single-line function definition:

```
10 DEF FNQ(X, Y)
20     FNQ = X / Y
30 END DEF
40 PRINT FNQ(6, 3)
50 END
```

```
RUNNH
```

```
2
```

The program actually begins running in line 40, which directs the computer to the definition of the function FNQ. Notice that the function definition in line 20 has the function name FNQ with no arguments. A multiline function definition must contain a statement that assigns a value to the function name, and the function name in this statement appears without arguments. (If the function name is not assigned a value, then when the function is used in the program, it returns a value of 0.)
   Legitimate names for functions are the same in multiline definitions as in single-line definitions. The maximum number of arguments is also the same (255). There are, however, several distinctions to be made.
   A multiline function definition can contain loops and IF and GO TO statements. If a loop begins inside a multiline definition, it must also end inside that definition (after the DEF statement and before the END DEF statement). IFs and GO TOs which are inside the definition must not send the computer to a line outside the definition. Similarly, an IF or GO TO which is outside the definition must not transfer control to a line inside the definition. DATA statements inside the definition will be treated as if they were outside the definition. (The computer will take care of all DATA statements, in order, before dealing with DEF statements.)
   Suppose we want FNFACT(N) to be the value of N-factorial. Then we could write a program with a multiline definition as follows.

Example 9.12 *User-Defined Factorial Function*

```
10 REM -- Factorial using multiline function definition
20 DEF FNFACT(N)
       F = 1
       F = F * I FOR I = 1 TO N
       FNFACT = F
30 END DEF
40 REM -- Now start main program
50 INPUT "Give me a positive integer"; INGR
60 PRINT INGR; "factorial is"; FNFACT(INGR)
70 END
```

```
RUNNH
```

```
Give me a positive integer? 3
 3 factorial is 6
```

```
RUNNH
```

```
Give me a positive integer? 6
 6 factorial is 720
```

The main point of writing a function like this, which the program calls just once, is to make the main body of the code look simpler. In this example, the main body of the program starts at line 40.

The function is much more useful when the main body of the program invokes it several times. For example, suppose you must calculate an expression such as

```
(2 * A)! * B! * C! / (4*D)!
```

where A, B, C, D are some given positive integers. Then it would make sense to write the following program.

Example 9.13 *Several Invocations of a Factorial Function*

```
10 REM -- Calculation of expression with several factorials
20 DEF FNFACT(N)
       F = 1
       F = F*I FOR I = 1 TO N
       FNFACT = F
   END DEF
30 REM -- Read integers and print result
40 READ A, B, C, D
50 RESULT = FNFACT(2*A) * FNFACT(B) * FNFACT(C) / FNFACT(4*D)
60 PRINT "Result ="; RESULT
70 DATA 3, 5, 6, 3
80 END
```

```
RUNNH
```

```
Result = .12987
```

Notice that we used $F = F*I$ in the function definition, not FNFACT = FNFACT*I. As a general rule, do not use the function name on the right side of an assignment statement in the function definition. Values can be given *to* the function FNFACT, but it is not technically a variable.

Recursive Use of Multiline Functions

One of the major differences between multiline and single-line function definitions is that multiline functions are *recursive;* that is, they can call or use themselves.

A *recursive function definition* is one that defines terms of a function in terms of preceding terms. Earlier we defined the Nth Fibonacci number F(N) recursively as

$$F(N) = F(N - 1) + F(N - 2)$$

We also can define N-factorial, or FACTORIAL(N), recursively as

$$FACTORIAL(N) = N * FACTORIAL(N - 1)$$

In either case, we must specify some beginning terms nonrecursively. For the Fibonacci numbers, we specified that F(1) and F(2) should be 1. Similarly for the factorials, we specify that FACTORIAL(0) is 1. [We could also have started with FACTORIAL(1) as 1.]

The factorial function could be written recursively in the following way.

Example 9.14 *Recursive Factorial Function*

```
DEF FNFACT(N)
    IF N = 0 OR N = 1 THEN
        FNFACT = 1
    ELSE
        FNFACT = N * FNFACT(N-1)
    END IF
END DEF
```

The recursive function invocation is FNFACT(N − 1) in the statement

```
FNFACT = N * FNFACT(N-1)
```

where the function invokes itself with an argument (N − 1), one less than the original argument (N). This is a legitimate recursive use of FNFACT, because of the subscript N − 1.

Depending on the original value of N when the program first invokes the function, this function will call itself N − 1 times. If you try to calculate FNFACT(3), for example, the ELSE clause will try to calculate FNFACT as 3*FNFACT(2), causing the function to call itself with 2 in place of N. But the determination of FNFACT(2) involves the statement FNFACT = 2*FNFACT(1), so the function calls itself again to calculate FNFACT(1). Finally the function sets FNFACT(1) equal to 1. Then FNFACT(2) = 2*1 = 2, and FNFACT(3) = 3*2 = 6.

The computer must save the value of N each time the function calls itself. It does this by placing the N-values on a *stack*. The stack is a storage area, much like an array of N-values, with the first value at the bottom. We can picture this process as in Figure 9.1.

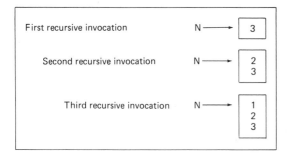

Figure 9.1 Growth of a Stack

From the figure, we can see that each new value on the stack pushes the preceding value(s) down. Therefore, such a stack is often called a *pushdown* stack.

A recursive function has two components. The obvious one is a part in which the function invokes itself. The other component must contain a stopping condition which causes the function to stop invoking itself. If this component were lacking, the function would fall into an *infinite recursive loop,* attempting to invoke itself over and over. In the example above, the stopping condition occurs when N is 0 or 1.

In our example, beginning with N = 3, the stopping condition occurs when N is 1. Then the IF condition (N = 0 OR N = 1) is true, so the computer executes the statement

```
FNFACT = 1
```

This is the first time FNFACT receives a value.

After setting FNFACT to 1, the computer removes the value 1 from the N stack and returns to the second function invocation. Now the value of N is 2 (the top value on the N stack), so the computer executes

```
FNFACT = N * FNFACT(N-1)
       = 2 * FNFACT(1)
       = 2 * 1
       = 2
```

Now the computer removes 2 from the N stack and returns to the first function invocation. The top (and only) value on the stack is 3, so N now takes the value 3. The computer executes

```
FNFACT = N * FNFACT(N-1)
           = 3 * FNFACT(2)
           = 3 * 2
           = 6
```

We illustrate this action by expanding Figure 9.1 to Figure 9.2.

Another example of a recursive function is one which computes the sum of integers from 1 to N. For example, if N is 5, the function would sum the integers from 1 to 5 for a total of 15. The program with this recursive function follows.

Example 9.15 *A Recursive Summing Function*

```
110 DEF FNSUM(N)
    IF N < 1 THEN
        FNSUM = 0
    ELSE
        FNSUM = FNSUM(N-1) + N
    END IF
120 END DEF
130 INPUT "What is the largest integer in the sum"; NUMB
140 PRINT "The sum is"; FNSUM(NUMB)
150 END
```

```
RUNNH
```

```
What is the largest integer in the sum? 20
The sum is 210
```

This function works very much like the factorial function, adding instead of multiply-ing numbers from 1 to N. The exit condition occurs when the function invokes itself with argument (N − 1) equal to zero.

Here is an example of a recursive string function which reverses the letters input by the user of the program. It also illustrates the EXIT DEF statement, which is equiv-alent to a GO TO statement that sends control to the line containing the END DEF statement.

```
DEF FNA$(CHAR$)
    INPUT "Character"; CHAR$
    IF CHAR$ = "." THEN EXIT DEF
    FNA$ = FNA$(CHAR$) + CHAR$
END DEF
```

The function FNA$ asks the user for a character. If the input character is any-thing but a period, the function recursively calls itself. The only purpose of this recur-sive call is to put the value CHAR$ on a stack. When the user enters a period, the stopping condition (CHAR$ = ".") is true, so the computer begins taking characters from the top of the stack and concatenating them with FNA$ according to the state-ment FNA$ = FNA$(CHAR$) + CHAR$.

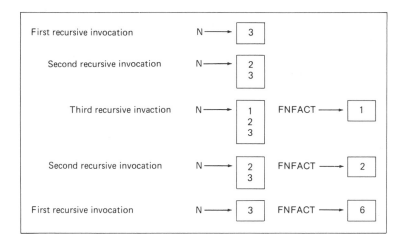

Figure 9.2   Growth and Decline of a Stack

Here is the function FNA$ in a complete program.

Example 9.16 *A Recursive Function to Reverse Characters*

```
100 REM -- Recursion
110 DEF FNA$(CHAR$)
120     INPUT "Character"; CHAR$
130     IF CHAR$ = "." THEN EXIT DEF
140     FNA$ = FNA$(CHAR$) + CHAR$
150 END DEF
160 PRINT "Input some characters, ending with a period."
170 REVERSE$ = FNA$("")
180 PRINT "Your characters in reverse order: "; REVERSE$
190 END


RUNNH
Input some characters, ending with a period.
Character? T
Character? O
Character? P
Character? .
Your characters in reverse order: POT
```

EXERCISES B

1. Redo the payroll problem (Exercise A7 in Chapter 5) to use a rounding function.
2. In each case below, write a program that defines and invokes (uses) the function described.
   a. FNMAX(X, Y) gives the larger of the two values of X and Y.
   b. FNDELTA(A, B) = A + B − 2*A*B.
   c. FNSINH(X) = (EXP(X) − EXP(−X))/2 (the hyperbolic sine of X).
   d. FNMEDIAN(A, B, C) gives the median or middle value of the numbers A, B, C when these numbers are in increasing or decreasing order.
   e. FNMOD(M, N) gives the remainder when the positive integer M is divided by the positive integer N.

REVIEW QUESTIONS

1. Write the output from the following program:

```
10  DEF FNAVG (A,B,C) = (A+B+C)/3
20  READ X,Y,Z
30  A = FNAVG (X,Y,Z)
40  PRINT A
50  DATA 3,7,5
60  END
```

2. Write a function definition for each function below.
   a. FNMIN(X, Y) gives the smaller of the values X and Y.
   b. FNDIV(X, Y) gives the integer part of the quotient of X divided by Y.
   c. FNPLACE(N, P) rounds a number N to the given number P of places.
   d. FNEXCH(N) gives the first three digits of a seven-digit phone number.

3. What are the following function values?
   a. ABS(−63.7)
   b. MAX(3,7,1,8)
   c. LOG(1)
   d. SQR(16)
   e. SGN(−6.2)
   f. FIX(−19.75)
   g. TIME(2)

4. True or False
   a. EXIT DEF is required in a single-line user-defined function.
   b. The DEF statement allows the user to create a function with any name.
   c. DEF SUM(A, B) = A + B is a valid function definition.
   d. A single-line user-defined function can be invoked only once in a program.
   e. A multiline function begins with DEF FN*name* and ends with END DEF.
   f. A recursive function is one which invokes itself.

SUMMARY OF CHAPTER 9

CONCEPTS AND KEYWORDS INTRODUCED IN THIS
CHAPTER

Concepts	Related statements and keywords
1. Numeric library functions	ABS
	MAX
	MIN
	MOD
	SGN
	FIX
	SIN
	COS
	TAN
	OPTION ANGLE
	ATN
	EXP
	LOG
	LOG10
	TIME
2. User-defined functions	DEF
	END DEF
	EXIT DEF
3. Recursive functions	

Strings and String Functions

We have already introduced string variables and discussed the meaning of the relations less than, equals, etc., when applied to strings. There are many more operations possible with strings. We shall deal with a few of these operations in this chapter.

10.1 MANIPULATING STRINGS

Concatenation

To *concatenate* two strings means to place the second string after the first. If the first string is "ABC" and the second string is "DEF", then the concatenation of the two produces the string "ABCDEF". The symbol for concatenation is the usual arithmetic plus sign (+). We can perform the concatenation above with the following program.

Example 10.1 *Concatenation*

```
100 REM -- Concatenation
110 A$ = "ABC"
120 B$ = "DEF"
130 C$ = A$ + B$
140 PRINT "The concatenation of "; A$; " and "; B$; " gives "; C$

RUN

The concatenation of ABC and DEF gives ABCDEF
```

198

All the string variables we have been dealing with have *dynamic* length; that is, the length of a string variable can change within a program. For example, we can use the statement A$ = "PAGO", which gives A$ a length of 4, and later in the program, the statement A$ = A$ + A$ will cause A$ to be the string "PAGOPAGO" which has a length of 8.

Notice that the plus sign is the only arithmetic operator which can be applied to strings. It does not make sense to multiply, divide, or subtract strings.

The LEN Function

The argument of the LEN function can be any string expression; the function returns an integer equal to the number of characters in the string expression. For example, if A$ = "HELLO", then LEN(A$) is 5. Use of the LEN function is illustrated in the following program:

Example 10.2 *The LEN Function*

```
100 REM -- LEN Function
110 PRINT "  STRING", "LENGTH OF"
120 PRINT "(WITHIN *S)", "STRING" \ PRINT
130 A$ = "Hello"
140 B$ = "Mary"
150 PRINT "*" + A$ + "*", LEN(A$)
160 PRINT "*" + B$ + "*", LEN(B$)
170 C$ = A$ + " " + B$
180 PRINT "*" + C$ + "*", LEN(C$)
190 END
```

```
RUN

    STRING      LENGTH OF
(WITHIN *S)     STRING

*Hello*          5
*Mary*           4
*Hello Mary*    10
```

The POS Function

The POS function gives the starting position of a substring inside a (usually larger) string. The POS function takes three arguments separated by commas: first, the string to be searched; second, the substring to be searched for; third, the position in the first string at which to begin searching.

For example, if A$ = "WHETHER 'TIS NOBLER" and B$ = "THE" then POS(A$, B$, 1) is 4 because the substring "THE" begins at the fourth character position in "WHETHER 'TIS NOBLER", when searching begins at the first position. The value of POS(A$, B$, 3) is also 4. Even though the search starts at position 3 of A$, the value of POS is calculated from the first position.

Notice that the first two arguments in POS must be string expressions. When the computer cannot find the specified substring inside the string, then POS takes a value of 0. Thus POS("ABC", "D", 1) will be 0. The value of POS("ABC", "A", 2) is also 0, because the "A" in the first string is in position 1, but the search starts at position 2.

The following program tells where the string "THE" first occcurs in an input string.

Example 10.3 *The POS Function*

```
100 REM -- Find THE with the POS function
110 INPUT "Give me a string (all caps)"; LINE$
120 P = POS(LINE$, "THE", 1)
130 IF P = 0 THEN PRINT "No THE ";
        ELSE PRINT "THE first occurs at position" ; P ;
140 PRINT "in your string."
150 END

RUNNH

Give me a string (all caps)? WE WERE THERE
THE first occurs at position 9 in your string.
```

You will not often want to search for a null string (""), but you should be aware that special rules apply when the second argument of POS is a null string. (Remember that BASIC assumes a string is null if you have not specifically given it a value.) The rules are:

CASE	VALUE OF POS(A$, "", START)
START > LEN(A$)	$1 + \text{LEN(A\$)}$
START $\leq$ 1	1
$1 < \text{START} < 1 + \text{LEN(A\$)}$	START
A$ = ""	1

The SEG$ Function

The SEG$ function gives a segment or substring of its string argument. SEG$ takes three arguments:

1. A string expression.
2. The starting position of the desired substring.
3. The ending position of that substring.

For example, SEG$("SWINGING", 2, 5) is "WING" because the characters in positions 2 through 5 in SWINGING are WING.

With SEG$, you can treat a string much like an array. The Nth character in the string A$ is SEG$(A$, N, N). The following program uses this idea to count the occurrences of E in an input string.

Example 10.4 *Counting Characters with SEG*

```
100 REM -- Counting Es with SEG$
110 INPUT "Give me a string (all caps)"; LINE$
120 TOTAL = 0
130 FOR N = 1 TO LEN(LINE$)
140    IF SEG$(LINE$, N, N) = "E" THEN TOTAL = TOTAL + 1
150 NEXT N
160 PRINT "Total number of Es is"; TOTAL
170 END

RUNNH

Give me a string? WHERE WERE WE THEN?
Total number of Es is 6
```

There are several extreme cases involving values of the integer arguments in the SEG$ function. They are dealt with as outlined below:

CASE	VALUE OF SEG$(A$, FIRST, LAST)
FIRST < 1	SEG$(A$, 1, LAST)
FIRST > LEN(A$)	"" (Null string)
LAST > LEN(A$)	SEG$(A$, FIRST, LEN(A$))

VAX-BASIC also has LEFT$ and RIGHT$ functions which behave like SEG$ but take only two arguments. LEFT$(A$, 4) gives the first four characters (or the four leftmost characters) in the string A$. It is equivalent to SEG$(A$, 1, 4). RIGHT$(A$, 5) gives the last five characters in A$ and is equivalent to SEG$(A$, LEN(A$) − 4, LEN(A$)). Use of these functions often yields simpler expressions than the SEG$ function.

The LINPUT and INPUT LINE Statements

Recall that in response to INPUT WORD$ you may use quotes or not, as you wish. When you use quotes, everything between the first and second set of quotes is taken as the value of WORD$. If you do not use quotes, everything you type up to the first comma (or ⟨RET⟩) is taken as the value of WORD$. You can get one type of quotation marks into the string by using the other kind as the delimiters of the string. That is, you can make the value of WORD$ equal to

```
SAY "HELLO"
```

by typing 'SAY "HELLO" '. The statements LINPUT and INPUT LINE allow you more freedom in putting both kinds of quotation marks as well as commas into the string.

Both LINPUT and INPUT LINE accept just one string variable value and store all characters you type, up to the line terminator ⟨RET⟩ in that variable. Thus, in response to these statements, do not use quotation marks of either kind unless you want quotation marks to be part of the string. The difference between LINPUT and INPUT LINE is that the line terminator ⟨RET⟩ is taken to be the last two characters in your string when INPUT LINE is used, while LINPUT does not include ⟨RET⟩ as part of the string.

As with INPUT, both LINPUT and INPUT LINE allow you to insert a prompt string before the string variable name, and a comma or semicolon after the prompt string has the same effect as a comma or semicolon in INPUT.

Here is a simple program showing the difference between INPUT and LINPUT or INPUT LINE.

```
10 INPUT A$
20 LINPUT B$
30 INPUT LINE C$
40 PRINT C$,
50 PRINT B$,
60 PRINT A$
70 END

RUNNH

? "HI"<RET>
? "HI"<RET>
? "HI"<RET>
"HI"
"HI"           HI
```

Notice that INPUT did not consider the quotes to be part of A$, but both LINPUT and INPUT LINE included the quotes. The difference between LINPUT and INPUT LINE can be seen in the placing of the words. After C$ was typed, the computer went to the next line before B$ was typed, because INPUT LINE caused C$ to have ⟨RET⟩ as its last characters. Notice that A$ was printed on the same line as B$ because LIN-PUT B$ does not include the ⟨RET⟩ as part of B$.

With the LEN function, we can see that the length of a string is longer when the string is input with INPUT LINE than when it is input with LINPUT. For example:

```
10 LINPUT "Word"; WORD$
20 PRINT "Length with LINPUT is"; LEN(WORD$)
30 INPUT LINE "Same word"; WORD$
40 PRINT "Length with INPUT LINE is"; LEN(WORD$)
50 END

RUNNH

Word? HELLO
Length with LINPUT is 5
Same word? HELLO
Length with INPUT LINE is 7
```

Notice that the ⟨RET⟩ is actually taken to be two characters, which represent a carriage return (CR) and a line feed (LF). We will generally use LINPUT in the remainder of the text, because normally we do not want those extra two characters CR and LF at the end of a string.

Simple Editing

Suppose you have made a typographical error in a string value and want to make a correction. The string functions we have been discussing will allow you to use the computer to help you make corrections.

Suppose, for definiteness, that the string variable you are dealing with is called LINE$. Further, suppose you want to remove from LINE$ the substring DELETE$ and put in its place the string ADD$. For concreteness, imagine that:

LINE$	is	"This is thare house"
DELETE$	is	"are"
ADD$	is	"eir"

We will call the corrected line NEWLINE$. Then the problem is to "calculate" NEWLINE$ from LINE$, DELETE$, and ADD$. Since, in this case, we know the values of all the variables, we can write:

NEWLINE$ = SEG$(LINE$, 1, 10) + ADD$ + SEG$(LINE$, 14, 19)

which means the same as

NEWLINE$ = "This is th" + "eir" + " house"

That is, we take NEWLINE$ to be an initial segment (from 1 to somewhere) of LINE$, plus the string to be inserted, plus the remainder of LINE$ (from somewhere to the end of LINE$). What we need to do, in general, is to express the integers 10 and 6 in terms of the variables LINES$, DELETE$, and ADD$.

Let P = POS(LINE$, DELETE$, 1). In our problem,

P = POS("This is thare house", "are", 1)

so P = 11. The first part of NEWLINE$ is to be the first part of LINE$, from position 1 to position 10. In general, we want the first part of LINE$ from position 1 to position $P - 1$, or

SEG$(LINE$, 1, $P - 1$)

Since we took out the string DELETE$ = "are", there are three positions "removed" from LINE$: positions P, $P + 1$, and $P + 2$. Thus the last segment of LINE$ begins at position $P + 3$, or P + LEN(DELETE$), and ends at position LEN(LINE$), so this segment can be expressed as

```
SEG$(LINE$, P + LEN(DELETE$), LEN(LINE$) )
```

This segment could also be expressed with the RIGHT$ function. (Try it.) Our general expression for NEWLINE$ now becomes

```
NEWLINE$ = SEG$(LINE$, 1, P - 1) + ADD$ +
           SEG$(LINE$, P + LEN(DELETE$), LEN(LINE$) )
```

This line is the heart of a program to correct a mistake. The complete program should now be easy to follow.

Example 10.5 *Simple Editing*

```
100 REM -- Correcting mistakes with string functions
110 LINPUT "Type a line"; LINE$
120 INPUT "Any mistakes (YES or NO)"; ANSWER$
130 IF ANSWER$ = "YES" THEN
        LINPUT "What needs to be deleted"; DELETE$
        P = POS(LINE$, DELETE$, 1)
        WHILE P = 0
           PRINT "Can't find error"
           LINPUT "What needs to be deleted"; DELETE$
           P = POS(LINE$, DELETE$, 1)
        NEXT
        LINPUT "What replaces it"; ADD$
        LDEL    = LEN(DELETE$)
        LLIN    = LEN(LINE$)
        FIRST$  = SEG$(LINE$, 1, P - 1)
        LAST$   = SEG$(LINE$, P + LDEL, LLIN)
        NEWLINE$ = FIRST$ + ADD$ + LAST$
        PRINT "The corrected line is:"
        PRINT
        PRINT NEWLINE$
     END IF
140 END


RUN

Type a line? He said, "Wear are we going?"
Any mistakes? YES
What needs to be deleted? era
Can't find the error
What needs to be deleted? ear
What replaces it? here
The corrected line is:
He said, "Where are we going?"
```

Notice that the program can correct only one mistake. In the exercises, you will be asked to modify the program so that it can correct several mistakes.

Also notice that you must fully specify the mistake. For example, suppose you run the program again and enter the line: Where ere we going? Then, in response to "What needs to be deleted?," you must not type simply an e, because this would cause the computer to replace the first e in Where. You can type " e" and answer the question "What replaces it?" with " a"; be sure to leave a space before the e and the a.

A more important question is: will the program work in all cases? In particular, what happens if the mistake is at the very beginning, or end, of the line? If the mistake is at the beginning, then the starting position of the error is 1, so the variable P in line 60 of the program will be 1. Then P—1 is 0, so the first part of NEWLINE$ is SEG$(LINE$, 1, 0), which is a null string according to the table above. Thus NEWLINE$ actually begins with ADD$, as it should. We leave it to you to verify that all is well if the error occurs at the end of the line. What is important is that extreme cases should be noticed, and programs should be checked to see that they behave properly with extreme cases.

EXERCISES A

1. Write a program to read an input string and print every other character (the second, fourth, and so on).

2. Write a program to read an input string and print the string in reverse.

3. Write a program to read an input line and change lowercase letters to uppercase. ASCII codes for lowercase letters run from 97 (a) to 122 (z), and for uppercase letters from 65 (A) to 90 (Z).

4. Modify the editing program in Example 10.5 to correct more than one occurrence of the same mistake. For instance, the phrase "THE STAY IN THE CAY WENT FAY.", should be corrected to read "THE STAR IN THE CAR WENT FAR."

5. Modify the editing program to make more than one correction in a string. After each correction, have the computer ask if more corrections are needed.

6. In a five-letter transposition cipher, each letter of the alphabet is simply replaced by the letter five places after it. For letters after Z, we simply begin the alphabet over at A. The following table illustrates this code.

Original letter: ABCDEFGHIJKLMNOPQRSTUVWXYZ
Replacement letter: FGHIJKLMNOPQRSTUVWXYZABCDE

Write a program to take a message, code it with a five-letter transposition key, and print out the coded message.

7. Write a program to decode a coded message using the table from the previous exercise.

8. Write a program to find two different strings in a paragraph and then switch the strings.

9. Write a program to count the number of occurrences of "ing" using POS. Each time an "ing" is found, start searching for the next occurrence one position to the right. Read several lines from a data file.

10. Write a program to find the number of occurrences of each vowel (a, e, i, o, u) in an input sentence. Make sure the program will work for any sentence.

Sample Run:

Input: `THE DOG JUMPED OVER THE FENCE.`

Output: `Vowel                Occurences`

```
A                 0
E                 6
I                 0
O                 2
U                 1
```

11. Product codes for a company have the following format:

$$\#\#\#-\#\#.\#\#-\#$$

The first number (###) is an inventory number.
The second number (##.##) is the price.
The third number (#) is the department number.

Write a program to print out a list of all inventory numbers and prices for the products in Department 2 using the data below. Do not print the "-" between the inventory number and the price.

> Data: 163-4.30-2
> 51-8.00-1
> 916-9.50-2
> 811-10.45-2
> 6813-5.33-1
> 333-.45-2

A sample line of output is:

`163      4.30`

10.2 STRING FUNCTIONS

VAX-BASIC includes many string functions in addition to those we have already discussed. Here are some of the more important ones.

The TRM$ Function

The *TRM$ function* takes one string argument and returns a string equal to that argument, except that trailing spaces and tabs are removed. For example, TRM$("Mary ") is "Mary". We will use this function on strings read from files in the next two chapters.

The EDIT$ Function

The *EDIT$ function* is a very powerful string editing function. EDIT$ takes two arguments, a string to be edited and an integer designating the type of editing to be done.

The editing functions corresponding to various integer values are given in the following table. The word "trim" means take off or delete.

Integer value	Editing function
1	Trim the parity bit (7) from each character.
2	Trim all spaces and tabs.
4	Trim all carriage returns, line feeds, form feeds, deletes, escapes, and nulls.
8	Trim all leading spaces and tabs.
16	Convert multiple spaces and tabs into a single space.
32	Convert lowercase letters to uppercase.
64	Convert square brackets to parentheses: [to (and] to).
128	Trim trailing spaces and tabs (same as TRM$).
256	Edit only characters not within quotation marks. If the string argument has only one quotation mark, edit only those characters preceding that quotation mark.

In addition, several editing functions can be combined by adding the integer values in the table above. EDIT$(A$, 288) combines the functions given for integer values 32 and 256 because 288 = 32 + 256. Also, the sum of 8 (trim leading blanks) and 128 (trim trailing blanks) is 136, so EDIT$(A$, 136) will trim both leading and trailing blanks from A$.

The following table gives examples of EDIT$(A$, I) for one string A$ and several values of I. The values of EDIT$(A$, I) are enclosed in asterisks, so you can see where leading and trailing spaces are removed.

```
Value
of A$      *  'Where     were      you, Charlie?', she asked.      *


    I      Value of EDIT$(A$, I)
```

I	Value of EDIT$(A$, I)
2	*'Wherewereyou,Charlie?',sheasked.*
8	*'Where were you, Charlie?', she asked. *
16	* 'Where were you, Charlie?', she asked. *
32	* 'WHERE WERE YOU, CHARLIE?', SHE ASKED. *
128	* 'Where were you, Charlie?', she asked.*
136	*'Where were you, Charlie?', she asked.*
256	* 'Where were you, Charlie?', she asked. *
288	* 'Where were you, Charlie?', SHE ASKED. *

The SPACE $ Function

The *SPACE $ function* takes an integer argument and returns a string containing that many blanks or spaces. That is, SPACE$(5) is "   ".

The STRING$ Function

The *STRING$ function* takes two integer arguments, N and A. STRING$(N, A) returns a string of N identical characters, with each character having the ASCII value A.

For example, STRING$(10, 66) is "BBBBBBBBBB", because 66 is the ASCII value for "B". You can use STRING$ even if you do not know the ASCII value for a character. For instance, to get a string of 40 dollar signs, use STRING$(40, ASCII("$")). (See the ASCII function below.)

The TIME$ Function

The *TIME$ function*, with argument 0, returns the current time as a string of the form "HH:MM XX", where HH stands for the hours, MM for the minutes, and XX for AM or PM. Thus, a specific value of TIME$(0) might be "12:42 PM". See the VAX-11 documentation for TIME$ arguments other than 0.

The DATE$ Function

The *DATE$ function*, with argument 0, returns the current date as a nine-character string of the form "DD-MMM-YY", where DD stands for the day, MMM for the month, and YY for the year.

Converting Data

BASIC has several built-in functions that convert string data to numeric data and vice versa. The basis for translating between numeric and string data is the ASCII code (see Appendix B), which assigns to each keyboard character an integer from 0 to 127. In particular, the ASCII code for a space is 32, and the ASCII codes for capital letters from A to Z are the numbers 65 to 90.

The *ASCII function* operates on string expressions and gives the ASCII value of the first character in the string. For example, the statement PRINT ASCII("HAROLD") in immediate mode causes the computer to type 72, which is the ASCII value for H. ASCII can be abbreviated to ASC.

The *CHR$ function* operates on an integer expression and returns the character which has this ASCII value. The argument of the CHR$ function will be reduced modulo 128. For example, both statements PRINT CHR$(65) and PRINT CHR$(193) will cause the computer to type the letter A. PRINT CHR$($-63$) will also cause A to be typed, since $-63 = 65 - 128$. CHR$ and ASCII are complementary functions in the sense that CHR$(ASCII("B")) is "B" and ASCII(CHR$(48) is 48.

A *numeric string* is a string whose characters are digits (0, 1, 2, . . . , 9), with possibly a leading plus or minus sign, a decimal point, and an exponent. Thus the following are numeric strings:

> "12345678987654321"
> "7.65743819654"
> "-3"
> "+999999999E-04"

The *VAL function* converts a numeric string to the corresponding real number. VAL("6.25") is the number 6.25. The *VAL% function* operates on integer numeric strings and returns the corresponding integer.

The *STR$ function* is the complementary function to VAL. STR$ takes a numeric argument and returns the corresponding string. For example, STR$(32) is "32" and STR$(1234567890) is ".123457E+10".

10.3 STRING ARITHMETIC FUNCTIONS

Sometimes we want to see numbers with more precision than VAX-BASIC types them. Several "string arithmetic" functions in VAX-BASIC allow you to treat strings of digits as numbers that can be added, subtracted, multiplied, and divided. The advantage is that the strings can be much longer than the number of digits (six) that VAX-BASIC normally prints. The disadvantage is that numeric string operations take much longer for the computer to execute than the usual arithmetic operations.

The SUM$ and DIF$ Functions

If A$ and B$ are two numeric strings, then SUM$(A$, B$) is a numeric string which represents the sum of the numbers in the numeric strings A$ and B$. Similarly, DIF$(A$, B$) is a numeric string representing the difference A$ "minus" B$. In either case, the strings A$ and B$ can contain up to 54 digits each plus optional signs and decimal point.

Here is a simple program illustrating SUM$ and DIF$.

Example 10.6 *The SUM$ and DIF$ Functions*

```
10 REM -- SUM$ AND DIF$
20 A$ = "12345678987654321"
30 B$ = "11111111111111111"
40 PRINT "Sum = "; SUM$(A$, B$)
50 PRINT "A$ - B$ = "; DIF$(A$, B$)
60 END

RUNNH

Sum = 23456790098765432
A$ - B$ = 1234567876543210
```

When A$ and B$ both represent whole numbers, then the precision of SUM$(A$, B$) and DIF$(A$, B$) is the precision of the larger whole number. If either A$ or B$ has a decimal point, then the precision of the sum and difference is determined in two parts:

a. The integer part takes the precision of the larger integer in A$ and B$.

b. The decimal part takes the precision of the more precise decimal part in A$ and B$.

In either case, padded zeros do not increase a number's precision. That is, 001 is less precise than 12, and 6.25 is more precise than 6.200. The statement

```
PRINT SUM$("987654321", "1.123456789")
```

will cause the computer to type 987654322.123456789.

EXERCISES B

1. Write a program that converts characters to ASCII code and vice versa. Ask whether the user wants to input an integer or a character, get the input, and perform the appropriate conversion.

2. Write a program that prints a short memo and includes the current date and time.

3. Write a program that asks for a number, reads the input into a string variable, converts that string to a number, and prints the number. Include an error handler to inform the user if the input string cannot be converted to a number. The ERR value for "Illegal number" is 52.

4. Write a program that determines whether an input string is a *palindrome*, a string that reads the same backward and forward. Some famous palindromes are:

   (a) ABLE WAS I ERE I SAW ELBA
   (b) A MAN, A PLAN, A CANAL: PANAMA
   (c) MADAM, I'M ADAM

   The palindrome in (a) does read exactly the same in either direction, including spaces, but (b) and (c) don't. Most palindromologists consider (b) and (c) to be palindromes because the *letters* read the same, ignoring spaces and punctuation marks.

   Read the input string with LINPUT, then delete all spaces and tabs and convert lowercase letters to uppercase with EDIT$. Finally, remove any characters which are not uppercase letters.

5. Write a program to count the number of words in several lines in a file. Add a single space at the end of the line, then use EDIT$ to trim leading spaces and convert all spaces and tabs to a single space. Consider each space to be the end of a word. Assume there are no hyphenated words.

6. Write a program to find the longest word in several lines in a file. As in the previous exercise, blanks can be used as word separators, but count only letters as parts of words, not periods, commas, quotes, and so on.

7. Write a program to compare SUM$(A$, B$) and DIF$(A$, B$) with A + B and A − B. Use 1234567 for A and A$, and 23.42567 for B and B$.

10.4 PRINTING STRINGS

The PRINT USING formats for strings allow centering, left and right justifying, specifying the number of characters, and printing extended fields.

Centering

Centering uses the character C. Just as pound signs reserve places for digits in numbers, each C reserves a place for a character. The sequence of C's is preceded by an apostrophe (') which also reserves a place for one character.

The center of the printed string falls at the center of the field of C's (counting the apostrophe). If the string cannot be exactly centered, BASIC prints the string one character off center to the left. The following small program illustrates centering.

Example 10.7 *Centering Strings with PRINT USING*

```
100 REM -- Illustrate centering with PRINT USING
110 A$ = "The Beginning"
120 Z$ = "The End"
130 PRINT USING "'CCCCCCCCCCCCCCCCCCCC"; A$  ! 20 C's
140 PRINT USING "'CCCCCCCCCCCCCCCCCCCC"; Z$  ! and '
150 END

RUNNH

    The Beginning
       The End
```

Both "The Beginning" and "The End" are centered in a field of 21 spaces, specified by the apostrophe and 20 C's.

Centering can help with form heading, as shown in the program below. Suppose we want items centered on a page or terminal screen with 80-character width. Then we need 79 C's to specify the PRINT USING format. Rather than type that many characters, we can use a variable CENTER$ with value

$$\text{""} + STRING\$(79, 67)$$

or an apostrophe followed by 79 C's. The following program illustrates this device.

Example 10.8 *Centering with a Variable PRINT USING Format*

```
10 A$ = "Term paper for Computer Science"
20 B$ = "Due March 31"
30 C$ = "By Jennifer Strauss"
40 CENTER$ = "'" + STRING$(79, 67)    ! ASCII("C") is 67
50 PRINT USING CENTER$; A$
60 PRINT USING CENTER$; B$
70 PRINT USING CENTER$; C$
80 END
```

```
RUNNH
```

```
                    Term paper for Computer Science
                           Due March 31
                         By Jennifer Strauss
```

As with numeric variables, PRINT USING with strings will "reuse" a format if there are more items in the print list than item specifications in the format. Thus, in place of lines 50–70 in the program above, we could write simply

```
50 PRINT USING CENTER$; A$, B$, C$
```

Left and right justification are implemented like centering, with L or R in place of C. Short fields are padded with spaces and larger fields (more characters than L's or R's) are truncated on the right to fit the field. Note the difference between the outputs of the left-justified PRINT USING in line 30 and the right-justified PRINT USING in line 60. Line 30 allows for six printed characters, while line 60 allows for five characters. Line 30 pads the names on the right, while line 60 pads on the left. (Compare ABE, JOHN, and WENDY in each case.)

Example 10.9 *Left and Right Justification with PRINT USING*

```
10 REM -- Left and Right Justification
20 PRINT "Output from left justify:"
30 PRINT USING "'LLLLL","ABE","JOHN","WENDY","DARRIN","HEATHER"
40 PRINT
50 PRINT "Output from right justify:"
60 PRINT USING "'RRRR","ABE","JOHN","WENDY","DARRIN","HEATHER"
70 END
```

```
RUNNH
```

```
Output from left justify:
ABE
JOHN
WENDY
DARRIN
HEATHE

Output from right justify:
   ABE
  JOHN
 WENDY
DARRIN
HEATHE
```

Combined PRINT USING Patterns

String and numeric PRINT USING formats can be combined to produce styled print-outs, as illustrated by the following program.

Example 10.10 *Combining String and Numeric Output*

```
100 REM -- PRINT USING with multiple forms
110 PRINT    "PRODUCT  STORE A  STORE B  STORE C  AVG PRICE"
120 STORE$ = "'LLLLLL  $$##.##  $$##.##  $$##.##    $$##.##"
130 FOR I = 1 TO 3
140     READ PRO$, P1, P2, P3
150     AVG_PRICE = (P1 + P2 + P3) / 3
160     PRINT USING STORE$; PRO$, P1, P2, P3, AVG_PRICE
170 NEXT I
180 DATA Eggs, .89, .83, .87, Milk, 1.99, 1.79, 1.85
190 DATA Hot dogs, 2.19, 1.89, 1.99
200 END
```

```
RUNNH
```

```
PRODUCT   STORE A  STORE B  STORE C  AVG PRICE
Eggs      $0.89    $0.83    $0.87      $0.86
Milk      $1.99    $1.79    $1.85      $1.88
Hot dogs  $2.19    $1.89    $1.99      $2.02
```

Notice how the quoted strings in lines 110 and 120 are lined up.

```
110 PRINT    "PRODUCT  STORE A  STORE B  STORE C  AVG PRICE"
120 STORE$ = "'LLLLLL  $$##.##  $$##.##  $$##.##    $$##.##"
```

This device makes it easy to see that the quantities printed under the format STORE$ will line up under the proper headers.

EXERCISES C

1. Write a program with PRINT USING to print out a paycheck and check stub. Be sure to include appropriate taxes and deductions on the stub of the check. (Refer to Exercise C1 of Chapter 2.)

2. Use the PRINT USING statement to create a business memo. Center the subject matter of the memo (i.e., Subject: _____) below the headings TO: and FROM:.

3. Use the PRINT USING statement to duplicate the financial statement below:

MARK COMPUTER(OTC)	19 1/8	EARNINGS PER SHARE	P/E MULTIPLE
Ind div.:	---	1986E: $1.30	1982E: 14.7X
Yield:	---	1985 : $0.70	1981 : 24.8
DJIA:	873.89	1984 : $0.24	1980 : ---

Quarterly earnings

Year	First	Second	Third	Fourth	Yearly
1982E	$0.256	$0.30	$0.367	$0.40	XXX.XX
1981	$0.148	$0.167	$0.215	$0.236	XXX.XX

(Note: Compute the yearly earnings, rounded to cents.)

4. Write a program to print the following data with PRINT USING statements. Have the data in a DATA statement and use variables in the PRINT USING lines. Round all dollar amounts to cents, left-justify the names and right-justify the status. Have each line appear with the headings and data as shown.

Name: TODD, JOHN   Account Number: 63875
                    Amount: $365.82   Status: Paid

Use at least the following data:

Smith, John	13654	$1335.32	Due
Jones, Betty	63581	$321.05 −	Overdue
Dickey, Jack	89765	$1987.367	Paid
Abbott, Mary	24689	$ 785.632	Due

5. Use PRINT USING to duplicate the title page from this book. Use the C format for centering.

6. Use the PRINT USING formats to generate a receipt for the store PEANUT BUTTER and BANANAS (center name and address) for the amount of $126.00 plus 4% tax. Include the date (Dec. 8, 1982) on the receipt and the descriptions and prices of each item as given:

1 skirt	$25.00
2 blouses	$12.50
	$17.50
1 jacket	$45.00
1 purse	$18.00
3 pair of socks	$ 8.00

The store's address is:

        123 Market Street
        Town, VA 01234

REVIEW QUESTIONS

1. What will be stored in X or X$ if AN$ = "ABCDEABC12345"?

```
a.    X$ = SEG$(AN$, 3, 6)
b.    X  = LEN(AN$)
c.    X  = POS(AN$, "2", 1)
d.    X  = POS(AN$, "C", 5)
e.    X$ = SEG$(AN$, 11, 11)
```

2. What is the output from the following program?

```
10   A$ = "MERRY "
20   B$ = "CHRISTMAS"
30   C$ = A$ + B$
40   PRINT C$
50   END
```

3. If X$ = "84" and Y = VAL(X$), what is stored in Y? Is Y a number or a character string?

4. Write a string function for each statement.

a. A function to extract the middle name from the string "SARA BETH JONES".

b. The total length of the strings "GOOD" and "BYE".

c. The position of the first hyphen in the social security number 283-50-8111.

d. The sum of the numeric values of strings "123" and "321".

5. What is the output from the following program?

```
10  INPUT "TYPE IN A STRING"; S$
20  L = LEN(S$)
30  FOR I = L TO 1  STEP -1
        PRINT SEG$(S$, I, I);
40  NEXT I
50  END
```

SUMMARY OF CHAPTER 10

CONCEPTS AND KEYWORDS INTRODUCED IN THIS CHAPTER

Concepts	Related keywords and symbols
1. Concatenate strings	+
2. Length of a string	LEN
3. Substrings	POS
	SEG$
4. Reading strings	LINPUT
	LINE INPUT
5. String editing functions	TRM$
	EDIT$
6. Display special strings	SPACE$
	STRING$
	TIME$
	DATE$
7. Convert from numeric to string data and vice versa	ASCII
	CHR$
	VAL and VAL%
	STR$
8. String arithmetic	SUM$
	DIF$
9. Printing strings	PRINT USING
	'C
	'L
	'R

11

Sequential Files

We said earlier that a terminal format file is a special kind of sequential file, one with *variable-length records*. That is, each record in a terminal format file contains a certain number of characters—a number that is called the *length* of the record—and different records can contain different numbers of characters. VAX-BASIC considers a record in a terminal format file to be a string of characters.

In this chapter we will discuss sequential files (and will say a little about relative files) in which each record contains the same type of information. We refer to these files as *mapped sequential files* but, as many writers do, will often call them simply sequential files. Since a terminal format file is a special kind of sequential file, many of the concepts discussed in this chapter apply to terminal format files.

11.1 MAPPED SEQUENTIAL FILES

In contrast to terminal format files, the records in a mapped sequential file must contain the same type of information *in the same order*. That is, if one record contains a character string followed by two numbers, then *every* record in the same file also contains a string *of the same length* followed by two numbers.

Suppose, for example, that you want to store information concerning five people. Then your data file will contain five records, one for each person. Suppose also that you want to store each person's name, height, and weight. Then each record will contain a string representing a name, a number representing height in inches, and a number representing weight in pounds. The separate parts of the record are called *fields*. That is, each record has a name field, a height field, and a weight field. The entire file might look like Figure 11.1.

```
                    FILE

Record 1    Mary Jones    62   110
Record 2    Ralph Brown   69   182
Recore 3    Bill Bailey   71   186
Record 4    Carry Nation  63   121
Record 5    Louis Leakey  70   164
```

Figure 11.1   File Format with Records

The records contain different information, but all records have the same type of information, in the same order. We say the records have the same *format*. When you use a mapped data file in a VAX-BASIC program, you must specify this format. That is, you must tell the computer what kind of information is stored in each record.

Describing a Record—The MAP Statement

The MAP statement in VAX-BASIC is used to allocate and describe the storage area for a data file. The descriptors used in the MAP statement describe the format of each record in a file.

A MAP statement for the file described above could be:

```
MAP (PHY) NAMES, HEIGHT, WEIGHT
```

The PHY in parentheses after MAP is the *name* of the MAP statement. There can be several MAP statements in one program, so a MAP name is used to distinguish one particular MAP statement from all others. The MAP name must be inside parentheses and must follow the conventions for variable names.

The statement

```
MAP (EMPLOY) EMP.NAMES, SOC_SEC_NO$, RATE, BLUECROSS%
```

defines a record with two strings, a real number, and an integer. The names of the variables should suggest what the strings and numbers represent: employee name; social security number, considered as a string; hourly rate of pay; and Blue Cross status. The variable names remind *you* what they stand for; the computer simply looks for two strings, a real number, and an integer.

MAP statements can contain any type of variable including subscripted variables. For example, the statement

```
MAP (SAMPLE) NAMES(3), D(4,4), X, Y$
```

defines a record format as:

    4 strings, NAME$(0) to NAME$(3)
    25 numbers, D(0,0) to D(4,4)
    1 number, X
    1 string, Y$

A MAP statement allocates storage for one record. This storage is called a *record buffer*. The storage space required for one string character is a *byte,* so a string of length *n* requires *n* bytes of storage. A numeric variable requires four bytes except in special circumstances. The statement

```
MAP (PHY) NAME$, HEIGHT, WEIGHT
```

above allocates space for a record buffer, as shown in Figure 11.2.

The variables named in a MAP statement are *buffer variables*. The buffer variables above are NAME$, HEIGHT, and WEIGHT. When NAME$, HEIGHT, and WEIGHT are given values in a program, the computer actually places these values in the record buffer. The program writes a record by copying the entire record buffer into a record in the file.

Generally, string variables in BASIC can hold strings of varying lengths; obviously, longer strings require more space for storage. String buffer variables, however, must have fixed lengths. If you do not explicitly specify the length of a string buffer variable, VAX-BASIC allocates space for 16 characters. Shorter strings are padded with blanks, and longer strings are truncated to 16 characters.

The amount of storage for string variables can be explicitly allocated in a MAP statement by appending an equals sign and a length to the variable name. Suppose we want to allocate 20 characters to the variable NAME$ and 11 characters to SOC.SEC.NO$. Then the appropriate MAP statement is:

```
MAP (EMPLOY) NAME$ = 20%, SOC.SEC.NO$ = 11%, RATE, BLUECROSS%
```

The percent signs are not strictly necessary but are recommended. Notice that the string variable names are followed by equals signs and the desired number of characters.

The OPEN Statement

The OPEN statement in VAX-BASIC can be used to create a file or to gain access to an existing file. The simplest form of the OPEN statement for sequential files is

```
OPEN <filename> AS FILE #<channel number>, MAP <MAP-name>
```

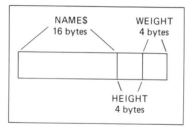

Figure 11.2 Map Format

The MAP clause in the OPEN statement signifies that the file will have mapped records and is not a terminal format file. For example, to OPEN a file for the MAP (EMPLOY) from the previous section, the statement would be

```
OPEN "EMP.DAT" AS FILE #1, MAP(EMPLOY)
```

The OPEN statement for mapped files *must* contain the word MAP followed by the appropriate MAP name.

The OPEN statement can contain an *organization clause,* such as

```
ORGANIZATION <organization type>
```

When it appears, the organization clause must be the first clause in the OPEN statement.

The file organization types we will discuss are SEQUENTIAL, RELATIVE, and INDEXED. The organization clause is not necessary for sequential files, because SEQUENTIAL is the default type—the type VAX-BASIC assigns if you do not specify a type. We will insert an organization clause in all OPEN statements for mapped files.

Record types, either FIXED-length or VARIABLE-length, can also be specified in the organization clause. VARIABLE is the default, so if you want fixed-length records, you must say so. Without going too deeply into the matter, let us say that fixed length records are easier for the computer to deal with, so we will use fixed length records. Our OPEN statement then becomes

```
OPEN "EMP.DAT" AS FILE #1,        &
ORGANIZATION SEQUENTIAL FIXED,    &
MAP(EMPLOY)
```

Notice that:

1. Clauses are separated by commas.
2. There is no comma between SEQUENTIAL and FIXED.
3. The ampersands (&) are necessary to signify continuation when the OPEN statement extends beyond one line.

11.2 CREATING A FILE

The PUT Statement

The *PUT statement* places data from a record buffer into a file. For a sequential file which has been opened on channel #1, the format of the PUT statement is simply

```
PUT #1
```

The first time PUT #1 is executed, the first record in the file is created. Each succeeding time PUT #1 is executed, the next successive record is created. The following program will OPEN a file and PUT in several records.

Example 11.1 *Creating a Sequential File*

```
100 MAP (NAMES) NAMES = 30%
110 OPEN "NAME.DAT" FOR OUTPUT AS FILE #1,    &
         ORGANIZATION SEQUENTIAL FIXED,       &
         MAP NAMES
120 PRINT "Enter a name or STOP when done."
130 INPUT "Name"; NAMES
140 WHILE NAMES <> "STOP"
        PUT #1
        INPUT "Name"; NAMES
150 NEXT
160 PUT #1
170 CLOSE #1
200 END


RUNNH


Enter a name or STOP when done.
Name? ROBERT E. LEE
Name? HANNIBAL HAMILCAR
Name? ULYSSES S. GRANT
Name? ALEXANDER THE GREAT
Name? STOP
```

When the program is RUN, you cannot tell what has happened. If everything has gone smoothly, a data file called NAME.DAT has been created. Notice that the word STOP has been put into the fifth record.

You can, however, look at this file at the VAX command level by using the TYPE command, $TYPE NAME.DAT. The file will be readable because the variable NAME$ is a string. If numeric variables were in the records, the characters displayed by the TYPE command would not be readable because of the format in which BASIC "puts" numbers (integer and floating point) in mapped sequential files.

Another example of a program that writes a file to disk is the one for the employee data described above.

Example 11.2 *Creating a Sequential Employee Data File*

```
100 MAP (EMPLOY) EMP.NAMES = 20%, SOC_SEC_NOS = 11%,   &
                 RATE, BLUECROSS%
110 OPEN "EMP.DAT" FOR OUTPUT AS FILE #1,   &
         ORGANIZATION SEQUENTIAL FIXED,     &
         MAP EMPLOY
120    INPUT "Employee list name"; EMP.NAMES
130    INPUT "Social Security number in form 111-22-3333"; SOC_SEC_NOS
140    INPUT "Rate"; RATE
```

```
150    INPUT "Blue Cross status: 1 for yes, 0 for no"; BLUE_CROSS%
160    PUT #1
170 INPUT "Are you done (YES or NO)"; ANS$
180 IF ANS$ = "NO" THEN 120
190 CLOSE #1
200 END

RUNNH

Employee name?  STEPHANIE SMITH
Social Security number, in form 111-22-3333? 241-21-4310
Rate? 3.35
Blue Cross status: 1 for yes, 0 for no? 1
Are you done (YES or NO)? YES
```

Notice in this program that after all the records have been put out to disk, the file is closed with the statement at line 190, CLOSE #1. VAX-BASIC will close open files when it encounters an END statement, but it is wise to put CLOSE statements in your program, because the program could terminate on an error without executing the END statement.

Finally, let's use a program to create an address file. Each address will consist of a name, a street address, a city and state, and a zip code.

The ACCESS APPEND Clause

The OPEN statement in the next program has a special feature, the ACCESS APPEND clause. If the file does not exist, this OPEN statement creates the file. For a file that already exists, this ACCESS clause sets the next record pointer to the end of the file, permitting you to add labels to the file each time you run the program.

Example 11.3 *Creating a Sequential Address File*

```
100 MAP (COLUMN) NAME$ = 30%, ADDRESS$ = 30%, CITY$ = 20%, &
            STATE$ = 2%, ZIP$ = 5%
110 OPEN "SLABELS.DAT;1" FOR OUTPUT AS FILE #1,    &
            ORGANIZATION SEQUENTIAL FIXED,         &
            ACCESS APPEND,                         &
            MAP COLUMN
120 PRINT "If you have made a mistake, type NO after 'OK?'"
130 PRINT "To stop, type STOP after Name?"
140 INPUT "Name"; NAME$
150 WHILE NAME$ <> "STOP"
        INPUT "Address"; ADDRESS$
        INPUT "City, State"; CITY$, STATE$
        INPUT "ZIP"; ZIP$
        INPUT "OK"; K$
```

```
      IF K$ = "NO" THEN
          PRINT "Reenter this label"
          INPUT "Name"; NAME$
          GO TO 160
      END IF
    PUT #1
    INPUT "Name"; NAME$
  NEXT
160 CLOSE #1
200 END
```

If you RUN this program, you will see the following at your terminal.

```
RUNNH

If you have made a mistake,type NO after 'OK?'
To stop, type STOP after Name?
Name? (you input) <RET>
Address? (you input) <RET>
City, State? (you input) <RET>
ZIP? (you input) <RET>
```

And then a repeat of Name?, Address?, City, State?, and ZIP?.

In the next section we consider how to read the files created by two of the examples in this section.

EXERCISES A

1. Write a program to put a list of novels out to a sequential file called NOVELS.DAT.

2. Write a program to create a file that contains an inventory. Each record should contain the inventory number, an item description, the price, the number on hand, and the number on order. Call the file INVENTORY.DAT.

3. Write a program to create a file of student records. Each record will contain the student's name, year, grade-point average, and major. Allow the file to be added to each time the program is run. Call the file STUDENTS.DAT.

11.3 READING A FILE

To read the file NAME.DAT created above, we begin with the same MAP and OPEN statements as in the program that created the file. There is some leeway, though. The MAP name, variable names, and channel numbers can be different. Also, the organization clause is not essential.

The GET Statement

The major difference, though, is that we want to *get* data from the file instead of putting data into the file. Thus we use a GET statement whose format is the same as the format of the PUT statement:

```
GET #<channel number>
```

The program to read the file and print its contents is as follows.

Example 11.4 *Reading a Sequential File*

```
100 MAP (GEN) GENERAL$ = 30%
110 OPEN "NAME.DAT" FOR INPUT AS FILE #2,   &
         ORGANIZATION SEQUENTIAL FIXED,     &
         MAP GEN
120 PRINT "CONTENTS OF FILE"
130 GET #2
140 WHILE GENERAL$ <> "STOP"
        PRINT GENERAL$
        GET #2
150 NEXT
160 CLOSE #2
200 END

RUNNH

CONTENTS OF FILE
ROBERT E. LEE
HANNIBAL HAMILCAR
ULYSSES S. GRANT
ALEXANDER THE GREAT
```

Notice how similar this program is to the program that created the file. The GET statement in line 140 is the major difference. Each time the computer executes GET #2, it places the contents of one record in the variable GENERAL$. The CLOSE #2 statement in line 160 is not strictly necessary, because the END statement automatically closes all open files, but it is good programming practice to close files when you are done with them. Programs can end on errors that leave files in an unreadable state.

Next we write a program that will read the file SLABELS.DAT and print each record as a label. We use an ON ERROR GO TO statement to handle the end-of-file error (ERR number 11). The program reads the records in a loop beginning WHILE 1%. VAX-BASIC considers any odd integer to be a true relation, so WHILE 1% sets up an infinite loop. The loop will not repeat indefinitely, because eventually the computer will read the last record in the file. The next GET #2 will cause an end-of-file error, which will be taken care of by the error handler.

Example 11.5 *Reading the Sequential Labels File*

```
100 ON ERROR GO TO 900
110 MAP (COLUMN) NAME$ = 30%, ADDRESS$ = 30%,    &
        CITY$ = 20%, STATE$ = 2%, ZIP$ = 5%
120 OPEN "SLABELS.DAT" FOR INPUT AS FILE #2,     &
        ORGANIZATION SEQUENTIAL FIXED,           &
        MAP COLUMN
130 C = 0
140 GET #2
150 WHILE 1%
        LET C = C + 1
        PRINT \ PRINT
        PRINT NAME$
        PRINT ADDRESS$
        PRINT TRM$(CITY$); ", "; STATE$; "  "; ZIP$
        GET #2
160 NEXT
900 !!!!!!!!!!!!!!!!!!!!!!!!!!!!!!!!!!!!!!!!!!!!!!!!!!!!!!!!!!
910 !       Error handler; End-of-file error is 11.
        !!!!!!!!!!!!!!!!!!!!!!!!!!!!!!!!!!!!!!!!!!!!!!!!!!!!!!!!!!
920 IF ERR = 11% THEN RESUME 930
                 ELSE ON ERROR GO TO 0
930 PRINT
940 PRINT "The number of labels printed is"; C
950 CLOSE #2
960 END
```

Notice that the program has a MAP statement identical to the MAP statement in the
program that created the file SLABELS.DAT. Also, the OPEN statement is identical
except that FOR INPUT replaces FOR OUTPUT. FOR INPUT is optional and tells
the computer that this file is being read *in*to the program.

    When this program runs, the labels will have the following format:

```
BOBBI SMITH
2114 LAKE ROAD
SALEM, VA  24153

TOM JONES
234 SALT STREET
JACKSON, MI  34567

The number of labels printed is  2
```

EXERCISES B

   1. Write a program to read the INVENTORY.DAT file (Exercise A2) and to print
      out the descriptions of all items that have fewer than ten on hand.

2. Write a program to read the file STUDENTS.DAT (Exercise A3) and to find separately the class grade-point averages for freshmen, sophomores, juniors, and seniors.

3. Write a program to read the file NOVELS.DAT (Exercise A1), alphabetize the novels, and put the names back out to a file NOVELSRT.DAT. Remember to OPEN two files and to use different channel numbers in the OPEN statements.

4. Write a program to find and delete a record from the file STUDENTS.DAT. It is not possible to delete records from the "middle" of a sequential file without creating a new file. Therefore open two files, STUDENTS.DAT and NEW-STUD.DAT. The program should ask for the student name to be dropped, then read the file STUDENTS.DAT and copy every record except the one to be deleted into NEWSTUD.DAT. Have the program notify the user if the given name is not found in STUDENTS.DAT.

11.4 MODIFYING A RECORD

The UPDATE Statement

In order to modify a RECORD, the clause ACCESS MODIFY must be added to the OPEN statement in the program which handles the modifications. The UPDATE statement

```
UPDATE # <channel number>
```

performs the actual record modification. UPDATE replaces the last record read with the contents of the record buffer.

Suppose you have a file of budget information by department. These data are constantly changing. The following program reads in each record and then updates the requested information for a specific record in a sequential file.

Example 11.6 *Updating Records in a Sequential File*

```
100 ON ERROR GO TO 900
110 MAP (LIBRAR) SPENT$ = 8%, ON_ORDER$ = 8%,        &
              TOT_BUDGET$ = 8%, DEPT$ = 20%
120 OPEN "DEPT.DAT" AS FILE #1,                       &
          ORGANIZATION SEQUENTIAL,                    &
          ACCESS MODIFY, MAP LIBRAR
130 PRINT "To stop execution of the program, type QUIT when"
140 PRINT "asked if you want to update information." \ PRINT
150 !              Get a record.
160 GET #1
170 WHILE ANS$ <> "Q"
180    PRINT "DEPARTMENT"; TAB(22); "SPENT TO DATE";    &
            TAB(38); "ON ORDER"; TAB(50); "BUDGET"
190    PRINT
```

```
200     PRINT DEPT$; TAB(25); SPENT$; TAB(39); ON_ORDER$; &
                    TAB(50); TOT_BUDGET$
210     PRINT
220 !                   Request update.
230     INPUT "Would you like to update this information"; ANS$
240 !                   Check response.
250     LET ANS$ = SEG$(ANS$, 1, 1)
260     WHILE ANS$ <> "Y" AND ANS$ <> "N" AND ANS$ <> "Q"
            PRINT "Please answer YES, NO or QUIT (Y, N OR Q)"
            INPUT "Update this information"; ANS$
        NEXT
270     WHILE ANS$ = "Y"
280        PRINT
290        PRINT "Please select the column you want to update"
300        PRINT
310        PRINT "         S  : AMOUNT SPENT"
320        PRINT "         O  : ON ORDER"
330        PRINT "         B  : BUDGET"
340        INPUT "Column"; X$
350        WHILE X$ <> "S" AND X$ <> "O" AND X$ <> "B"
               INPUT "Please answer S, O, or B"; X$
           NEXT
360        SELECT X$
             CASE "S"
                PRINT
                INPUT "Enter the amount spent"; NEW_SPENT$
                PRINT
                LET SPENT$ = SUM$ (NEW_SPENT$, SPENT$)
                PRINT
                PRINT "You have spent "; SPENT$; "to date"
                PRINT
             CASE "O"
                PRINT
                INPUT "Enter the amount on order"; NEW_ON_ORDER$
                LET ON_ORDER$ = SUM$ (NEW_ON_ORDER$, ON_ORDER$)
                PRINT
                PRINT "You have "; ON_ORDER$; "to date"
                PRINT
             CASE "B"
                PRINT
                INPUT "Enter the budget change"; NEW_BUDGET$
                LET TOT_BUDGET$ = SUM$ (NEW_BUDGET$, TOT_BUDGET$)
                PRINT
                PRINT "You have budgeted "; TOT_BUDGET$; "to date"
                PRINT
           END SELECT
              Check to see if updating is complete.
           PRINT
           INPUT "Would you like to update another column"; ANS$
           LET ANS$ = SEG$(ANS$, 1, 1)
```

```
         NEXT
         UPDATE #1
380      GET #1
390 NEXT
900 !!!!!!!!!!!!!!!!!!!!!!!!!!!!!!!!!!!!!!!!!!!!!!!!!!!!!!!!!!!!!!!!!!!!!!!!
910 !           Error handler; End-of-file is error number 11.
920 !!!!!!!!!!!!!!!!!!!!!!!!!!!!!!!!!!!!!!!!!!!!!!!!!!!!!!!!!!!!!!!!!!!!!!!!
930 IF ERR = 11% THEN
         RESUME 940
    ELSE
         ON ERROR GO TO 0
    END IF
940 PRINT "End of File.  Now closing."
950 CLOSE #1
960 END
```

An example of the possible output is:

```
To stop execution of the program, type QUIT when
asked if you want to update information.

    DEPARTMENT        SPENT TO DATE    ON ORDER       BUDGET

 COMPUTER SCIENCE     200.00           300.00         400.00

Would you like to update this information ? YES

Please select the column you want to update

  S:  AMOUNT SPENT
  O:  ON ORDER
  B:  BUDGET
Column? S

Enter the amount ? 12

You have spent 212    to date

Would you like to update another column ? YES

Please select the column you want to update

  S:  AMOUNT SPENT
  O:  ON ORDER
  B:  BUDGET
Column? O

Enter the amount on order ? 18

You have 318     to date
```

```
Would you like to update another column ? YES

Please select the column you want to update

   S:  AMOUNT SPENT
   O:  ON ORDER
   B:  BUDGET
Column? B

Enter the budget change ?  23

You have budgeted 423      to date

     DEPARTMENT              SPENT TO DATE  ON ORDER      BUDGET

     STATISTICS             500.00         700.00        800.00

Would you like to update another column ? QUIT
```

Although this is a lengthy program, it shows how to UPDATE items in a single record. Since this file has sequential organization, each record must be read in the order it was stored in the file DEPT.DAT. Therefore, the computer gets each record in order until it reaches the end of the file or until the user answers QUIT. Also, note that the program allows a change to each item in a record before the updated record is placed in the file with the UPDATE #1 statement.

The program is also useful for reviewing arithmetic string functions. The use of SUM$ was necessary, since the items in each record are stored as string variables according to the MAP. The use of string variables allows you to use the TYPE command at the VAX command level to review the file. If real or integer variables had been used, the file would not be in readable form at the command($) level. The use of the SEG$ function allows for easy response checking. Finally, in studying this program it is important to remember that this program is written to *update* an *already existing file*.

The FIND Statement

In a given situation you might know that the particular record you want is record number 30. With small sequential files, there is no harm in reading the 30th record with code such as

```
FOR I = 1 TO 30
    GET #1
NEXT I
```

However, with truly large files it can take a long time to read the 8500th record with

```
FOR I = 1 TO 8500
    GET #1
NEXT I
```

The FIND statement allows you to skip over records faster than a GET statement. Its form is

```
FIND #<channel number>
```

FIND moves the current and next record pointers as GET does, but it does not actually read the record (copy the record into the record buffer). Thus we can read the 8500th record much faster with code such as

```
FOR I = 1 TO 8500
   FIND #1
NEXT I
GET #1
```

Notice that one GET statement is required to copy the desired record into the record buffer.

Deleting Records

You cannot physically delete a record from the "middle" of a sequential file. Most programs that purportedly allow the user to delete single records from a sequential file use one of the following strategies.

1. Some special mark is placed in the record to signify that it is "deleted." For instance, if one of the fields in a record is NAME$, then NAME$ might be assigned the value "XXXXXXXXXXXXXXXXXXXX". Programs that read the file then ignore records with that value in the NAME$ field.
2. Two files are opened, the original (input) file and an output file. The program reads and prints each record from the input file and asks the user if the record should be deleted. If the user answers "NO", the record is copied into the output file, otherwise it is not.

The SCRATCH Statement

The SCRATCH statement allows the user to delete records *at the end* of a sequential file. Its form is

```
SCRATCH #<channel number>
```

SCRATCH deletes all records from the current record to the end of the file. There must *be* a current record or the SCRATCH command will cause an error. Recall that a current record is established by a successful GET or FIND; in particular, there is no current record immediately after an OPEN statement.

Before the SCRATCH statement can be used in a program, the OPEN statement must contain an *ACCESS SCRATCH* clause. The following segment shows how to delete all records, from the 30th record on, from a sequential file.

```
OPEN "XXXX.DAT" AS FILE #3,              &
    ORGANIZATION SEQUENTIAL FIXED,       &
    MAP PQRS, ACCESS SCRATCH
FOR I = 1 TO 30
    FIND #3          ! Or GET #3
NEXT I
SCRATCH #3
CLOSE #3
END
```

The SCRATCH statement does not change the physical size of the file. It causes the current record pointer to be undefined but leaves the next record pointer pointing to the location of the first deleted record, the 30th record in our example. If you PUT a new record immediately after the SCRATCH statement, that record occupies the same space as the old 30th record.

EXERCISES C

1. Write a program to create the file DEPT.DAT. Then update the file with the program in this section. Finally, change the update program to print out column totals for TOT_BUDGET$, SPENT, and ON_ORDER$.

2. Write a program to update the INVENTORY.DAT file previously created (Exercise A2). Allow the user to change the price and/or the number on order.

3. Write a program to update the STUDENTS.DAT file previously created (Exercise A3) to change the grade-point average and/or the major. In addition print out grade-point averages by year.

11.5 RELATIVE FILES

This section on relative files is quite short, because we believe that VAX-BASIC indexed files are much more important. However, some versions of BASIC include only sequential and relative files. If you are working with such a BASIC version, this section will introduce you to relative files.

The major distinction of a relative file is that each record has an associated positive integer called the *record number*. In working with relative files, you specify a record by its record number, as in

```
PUT #1, RECORD = 12%
```

which puts record number 12 into the file opened on channel 1. We also have

```
GET #2, RECORD = 5%
```

which reads record number 5 from the file on channel 2.

Records should be numbered consecutively from 1 to the largest record number, in order to conserve storage space. BASIC allows you to have, say, two records with numbers 1 and 1000. But then the file contains 998 empty records, thus wasting much storage space.

Creating a Relative File

Creating a relative file is simple. The OPEN statement will contain the clause OR-GANIZATION RELATIVE FIXED, and the PUT statement must contain a RE-CORD specifier giving the number of the record being placed in the file, as in

```
PUT #2, RECORD 6%
```

which puts record number 6 into the file opened on channel 2. We usually use a variable for the record number, as in

```
PUT #2, RECORD R%
```

where the integer variable R% holds the record number.

Here is a short program which creates a relative file. Each record contains a six-character string, a real number, and an integer.

Example 11.7 *Creating a Relative File*

```
100 REM -- Create a relative file
110 MAP (INVEN) CODE$ = 6%, COST, QUANTITY%
120 OPEN "INVENTORY.DAT" FOR OUTPUT AS FILE #2,    &
        ORGANIZATION RELATIVE FIXED,               &
        MAP INVEN
130 PRINT "Give record numbers when asked.  Use 0 to stop."
140 INPUT "Record number"; R%
150 WHILE R% <> 0%
    INPUT "Inventory code  "; CODE$
    INPUT "Cost of item    "; COST
    INPUT "Quantity on hand"; QUANTITY%
    PUT #2, RECORD R%
    INPUT "Record number (0 to stop)"; R%
    NEXT
160 CLOSE #2
200 END
```

Reading a Relative File

There are several ways to read a relative file. If you know the records in the file are numbered from 1 to some number N, you can read the entire file with a loop such as

```
FOR R% = 1% TO N%
    GET #1, RECORD R%
NEXT R%
```

The following program asks for a record number and prints just the record with that number. The ON ERROR statement is used to detect an unsuccessful GET. The ERR value 155 indicates a "Record-not-found" error, which can be caused by a GET statement with a RECORD number that does not match any record number in the file.

Example 11.8 *Reading a Relative File*

```
100 REM -- Read single records in a relative file
110 ON ERROR GO TO 900
120 MAP (INVEN) CODE$ = 6%, COST, QUANTITY%
130 OPEN "INVENTORY.DAT" FOR INPUT AS FILE #2,    &
        ORGANIZATION RELATIVE FIXED,              &
        MAP INVEN
140 INPUT "Which record do you want to see (0 to stop)"; R%
150 WHILE R% <> 0%
160    GET #2, RECORD R%
170    PRINT \ PRINT CODE$, COST, QUANTITY% \ PRINT
180    INPUT "Another record number or zero to end"; R%
190 NEXT
200 CLOSE #2
210 GO TO 999
900 !!!!!!!!!!!!!!!!!!!!!!!!!!!!!!!!!!!!!!!!!!!!!!!!!!!!!!!
910 !   Error handler; ERR = 155 is Record-not-Found.
920 !!!!!!!!!!!!!!!!!!!!!!!!!!!!!!!!!!!!!!!!!!!!!!!!!!!!!!!
930 IF ERR = 155% THEN
        PRINT "Record not found"
        RESUME 180
    ELSE ON ERROR GO TO 0
    END IF
940 !!!!!!!!!!!!!!!!!!!!!!!!!!!!!!!!!!!!!!!!!!!!!!!!!!!!!!!
999 END
```

The DELETE Statement

One major benefit of using relative files is the capability to delete a single record from the "middle" of a file, which is not possible with sequential files. This is often a necessary operation on a file in situations like the following: a student graduates or leaves school; a bank account is closed; or a store eliminates an item from its inventory.

The DELETE statement for relative files has a simple form:

```
DELETE <channel number>
```

For a file opened on channel number 2, we have

```
DELETE #2
```

The DELETE statement deletes the current record, the last record obtained by a (successful) GET or FIND statement. The following program illustrates its use.

Example 11.9 *Deleting Records from a Relative File*

```
100 REM - Demonstrate record delete in a relative file
110 ON ERROR GO TO 900
120 MAP (INVEN) CODE$ = 6%, COST, QUANTITY%
130 OPEN "INVENTORY.DAT" AS FILE #2,          &
        ORGANIZATION RELATIVE FIXED,          &
        MAP INVEN
140 INPUT "Which record do you want to delete"; R%
150 WHILE R% <> 0%
160 !        Locate record in file.
170    GET #2, RECORD R%
180 !        Delete that record from file.
190    DELETE #2
200    INPUT "Next record to delete or zero to end"; R%
210 NEXT
220 CLOSE #2
230 GO TO 999
900 !!!!!!!!!!!!!!!!!!!!!!!!!!!!!!!!!!!!!!!!!!!!!!!!!!!!!!!
910 !  Error handler; ERR = 155 is Record-not-Found.
920 !!!!!!!!!!!!!!!!!!!!!!!!!!!!!!!!!!!!!!!!!!!!!!!!!!!!!!!
930 IF ERR = 155% THEN
       PRINT "Record not found"
       RESUME 200
    ELSE ON ERROR GO TO 0
    END IF
940 !!!!!!!!!!!!!!!!!!!!!!!!!!!!!!!!!!!!!!!!!!!!!!!!!!!!!!!
999 END
```

This program will delete records by number until the user enters a zero to end the file operation. If a record number is not valid, the error handler will print a message and send the computer to line 200 to continue the program.

Assume the file INVENTORY.DAT has the following records:

Record 1	N3261	3.25	350
Record 2	A6178	7.39	200
Record 3	Z2211	1.72	809
Record 4	T224A	11.75	50

After running the above program and deleting Record 2, the file will contain only the following three records:

Record 1	N3261	3.25	350
Record 3	Z2211	1.72	809
Record 4	T224A	11.75	50

The file will, however, have a blank cell where Record 2 had previously been.

In addition, relative files can be changed, created, or read with the same procedures as sequential files. For example, a relative file can be updated without reading each record, as in the LIBRARY program.

Example 11.10 *Updating Records in a Relative File*

```
100 REM -- Update a relative file
110 ON ERROR GO TO 900
120 MAP (LIBRAR) SPENT$ = 8%, ON_ORDER$ = 8%,       &
                TOT_BUDGET$ = 8%, DEPT$ = 20%
130 OPEN "DEPT.DAT" FOR INPUT AS FILE #7,           &
         ORGANIZATION RELATIVE FIXED,               &
         MAP LIBRAR
140 INPUT "Which record to update (negative number to stop)"; R%
150 WHILE R% > 0
160     GET #7, RECORD R%
170     PRINT "Total budget for "; DEPT$ ; " is"; TOT_BUDGET$
180     INPUT "Revised budget is "; TOT_BUDGET$
190     UPDATE #7
200     INPUT "Next record (negative number to stop)"; R%
210 NEXT
220 CLOSE #7
230 GO TO 999
900 !!!!!!!!!!!!!!!!!!!!!!!!!!!!!!!!!!!!!!!!!!!!!!!!!!!!!!!!!!
910 !   Error handler; ERR = 155 is Record-not-Found.
920 !!!!!!!!!!!!!!!!!!!!!!!!!!!!!!!!!!!!!!!!!!!!!!!!!!!!!!!!!!
930 IF ERR = 155% THEN
        PRINT "Record not found"
        RESUME 200
    ELSE ON ERROR GO TO 0
    END IF
940 !!!!!!!!!!!!!!!!!!!!!!!!!!!!!!!!!!!!!!!!!!!!!!!!!!!!!!!!!!
999 END
```

This program updates the total budget item on the specified record. The program is stopped by entering a negative record number. To RUN the program, the *relative* file LIBRARY.DAT must already exist. That is, we cannot use this program to operate on the *sequential* file LIBRARY.DAT created earlier.

For this program to be useful, the user must know the record number for each department. This is the major shortcoming of relative files. VAX-BASIC programmers seldom use relative files now, preferring to use indexed files which allow users to ask for a record by specifying some of the information in that record.

EXERCISES D

1. Rewrite the Library Update Program to use a relative file with update by department code (i.e., record number).

2. Write a program to create a relative file to keep charge-account records. Include in each record the account number, the present amount charged and the charge limit. Have the program put out the records to a file BANK.DAT.

3. Write a program to read the file created in Exercise 2 by record number or record by record. Use error handlers to check for end-of-file and incorrect record number.

4. Write a program to add a record to the file BANK.DAT. Use an error handler to detect if the record being PUT into the file already exists (ERR = 153).

REVIEW QUESTIONS

1. Write a MAP statement for each set of data.
   a. Name, age, weight, height
   b. Grade1, grade2, grade3, GPA
   c. Name (20 characters)
      Phone number (13 characters)
      City (20 characters)
      State (2 characters)
      Zip (2 characters)
   d. Account #
      Charge
      Date due and date paid (Each seven characters)
      Status of account (CURRENT, DELINQUENT, or DORMANT)

2. If you want to change a record in a sequential file opened as file #1% and have had the user input new data into the variable to be changed, what statement writes the changes into the file on disk?
   a.   FIND #1%
   b.   GET #1%
   c   UPDATE #1%
   d.   MODIFY #1%
   e.   CHANGE #1%

3. The following program has numerous errors. Underline them and make appropriate changes. The program is to read and print all entries in a sequential file.
```
20    REM Program to read a sequential file of names
30    MAP (NAME) NAM% = 20$, AGE
40    OPEN "NAME.DAT" AS FILE #2%, MAP N
50    GET #1%
60    PRINT NAME$, AGE%
70    GO TO 50
19000 IF ERR = 12% AND ERL = 50 THEN
         GO TO 19100
      ELSE
         ON ERROR GO TO 0
      END IF
```

```
19100 PRINT "END OF FILE"
19200 CLOSE #6%
19300 END
```

4. Which of the following OPEN statements are valid?

    a.
```
OPEN "PHONE.DAT" FOR INPUT AS FILE #2, &
        ORGANIZATION SEQUENTIAL FIX,     &
        MAP NUMBERS
```
    b.
```
OPEN "NAMES.DAT" AS FILE #2, &
        MAP NAMES
```
    c.
```
OPEN MYFILE.DAT FOR OUTPUT/INPUT AS FILE #3, &
        MAP SONGS
```
    d.
```
OPEN "MUSIC.DAT" FOR INPUT AS FILE #1, &
        ORGANIZATION SEQUENTIAL FIXED    &
```

SUMMARY OF CHAPTER 11

CONCEPTS AND VAX-BASIC KEYWORDS INTRODUCED
IN THIS CHAPTER

Concept	Related statements and keywords
1. Define a record	MAP
2. Create a mapped sequential file	OPEN PUT ACCESS APPEND
3. Read a mapped sequential file	GET WHILE 1%
4. Update a record	ACCESS MODIFY UPDATE
5. Create a relative file	ORGANIZATION RELATIVE PUT #, RECORD R%
6. Read a relative file	GET #, RECORD R%
7. Delete a record in a relative file	DELETE

8. Handle errors:
    End of file
    Record already exists
    Record not found
	
	ERR = 11%
	ERR = 153%
	ERR = 155%

Indexed Files

The previous two chapters on files examined terminal format files, sequential files, and relative files. One of the most versatile files in VAX-BASIC is an indexed file. This chapter presents some longer programs to demonstrate the use of indexed files.

12.1 CREATING AND READING AN INDEXED FILE

If you are concerned with finding a record that contains specific values, indexed files are the easiest files to use. You can ask for a record by specifying the contents of a field of that record, called a *key field*. For example, if social security number is a key field, you can ask for the record containing social security number 123-44-5656. Or if name is a key field, you can request the record with name LESLIE HORNBY.

Indexed files have fixed-length records and use MAP statements identical to the ones we have already used for sequential and relative files. The OPEN statement for indexed files requires the clause ORGANIZATION INDEXED, to which we append the word FIXED, and a *key-field clause* of the form

```
PRIMARY KEY <key field>
```

Indexed files must have at least one key, known as the *primary key*. They can also have alternate keys, but for the moment we deal with just one key.

For example, suppose the MAP statement for an indexed file named PERSONNEL.DAT is

```
MAP (EMPLOY) NAME$ = 20%, SSN$ = 11%, RATE, BCSTAT$ = 6%
```

and SSN\$ is the desired key field. Then an appropriate OPEN statement is

```
OPEN "PERSONNEL.DAT" FOR OUTPUT AS FILE #1,      &
      ORGANIZATION INDEXED FIXED,                &
      MAP EMPLOY,                                &
      PRIMARY KEY SSN$
```

The primary key values must be unique (later we discuss the capability to allow duplicate key values). That is, if one record contains the social security number 123-45-6789, then no other record may contain that same value. NAME\$ could also be a primary key, but SSN\$ is better, because social security number is unique to each individual, while two people could have exactly the same name. Key fields can be either integer or string, but cannot be real, so RATE is not a possible key field.

An attempt to write a record with the same primary key value as an existing record will cause a fatal error, with ERR number 134. Therefore, we will include an error handler to take care of this possibility.

The PUT statement for indexed files is identical to that for a sequential file, simply PUT #1. Although this PUT statement seems to say nothing about the primary key field, records in the file are ordered by primary key value.

The following program illustrates these MAP, OPEN, and PUT statements in the creation of an indexed file. This program, like most of those in this chapter, will be relatively long, so we will make extensive use of subroutines.

Example 12.1 *Creating an Indexed File*

```
100 ! Create a personnel file, an indexed file with each record
110 ! containing an employee name, social security number, pay
120 ! rate, and Blue Cross status.  Social security number is
130 ! the primary key.
140 ON ERROR GO TO 900
150 !
160 GOSUB 300       ! MAP and OPEN statements
170 GOSUB 400       ! Print description of program
180 GOSUB 500       ! Read and write data
190 CLOSE #1
200 GO TO 999
300 !!!!!!!!!!!!!!!!!!!!!!!!!!!!!!!!!!!!!!!!!!!!!!!!!!!!!!!!!!!!!!!!!!!
310 !   Subroutine; Define records and open file.
    !!!!!!!!!!!!!!!!!!!!!!!!!!!!!!!!!!!!!!!!!!!!!!!!!!!!!!!!!!!!!!!!!!!
320 MAP (EMPLOY) NAME$ = 20%, SSN$ = 11, RATE, BCSTAT$ = 6
330 OPEN "PERSONNEL.DAT" FOR OUTPUT AS FILE #1,      &
            ORGANIZATION INDEXED FIXED,              &
            MAP EMPLOY,                              &
            PRIMARY KEY SSN$
340 RETURN
400 !!!!!!!!!!!!!!!!!!!!!!!!!!!!!!!!!!!!!!!!!!!!!!!!!!!!!!!!!!!!!!!!!!!
410 ! Subroutine; Print description of program.
    !!!!!!!!!!!!!!!!!!!!!!!!!!!!!!!!!!!!!!!!!!!!!!!!!!!!!!!!!!!!!!!!!!!
```

```
420 PRINT
    PRINT  "This program reads data and writes an indexed file"
    PRINT  "PERSONNEL.DAT.  Each record contains a name, social"
    PRINT  "security number, hourly rate of pay, and Blue Cross"
    PRINT  "status (FAMILY, SINGLE, or NONE).  Enter data as "
    PRINT  "requested.  To stop, enter STOP for name."
    PRINT
    RETURN
500 !!!!!!!!!!!!!!!!!!!!!!!!!!!!!!!!!!!!!!!!!!!!!!!!!!!!!!!!!!!!!!!!!!!
510 ! Subroutine; Read data and write to the personnel file.
    !!!!!!!!!!!!!!!!!!!!!!!!!!!!!!!!!!!!!!!!!!!!!!!!!!!!!!!!!!!!!!!!!!!
520 INPUT "Name"; NAME$
530 WHILE (NAME$ <> "STOP")
          INPUT "Social Security number "; SSN$
          INPUT "Hourly pay rate         "; RATE
          PRINT "Blue Cross status:"
          INPUT "FAMILY, SINGLE, or NONE"; BCSTAT$

          PUT #1

540       INPUT "Name"; NAME$
    NEXT
    RETURN
900 !!!!!!!!!!!!!!!!!!!!!!!!!!!!!!!!!!!!!!!!!!!!!!!!!!!!!!!!!!!!!!!!!!!
910 !   Error handler; Duplicate primary key has ERR number 134.
920 !!!!!!!!!!!!!!!!!!!!!!!!!!!!!!!!!!!!!!!!!!!!!!!!!!!!!!!!!!!!!!!!!!!
930 IF ERR = 134% THEN
        PRINT "An existing record has that social security number."
        PRINT "Please enter another record."
        RESUME 540
    ELSE
        ON ERROR GO TO 0
    END IF
    !!!!!!!!!!!!!!!!!!!!!!!!!!!!!!!!!!!!!!!!!!!!!!!!!!!!!!!!!!!!!!!!!!!
999 END
```

A program that reads an indexed file should have a MAP statement equivalent to the one in the program that created the file. "Equivalent" means the MAP variables should have the same types and lengths; the names could, of course, be different.

The OPEN statement, too, can be identical, except that FOR INPUT replaces FOR OUTPUT. It is not essential to specify the primary key in the OPEN statement, because the computer can determine the primary key when it opens the file.

The Keyed GET Statement

The major new statement required here is the *keyed GET* statement, which has the form

```
GET #<channel number>, KEY #<key number> <relation> <value>
```

The channel number is familiar, but several parts of this statement are new:

1. *Key number.* In VAX-BASIC the primary key number is 0, so we write KEY #0.
2. *Relation.* Possible relations and their meanings are:

Relation	Meaning
EQ	Equal
GT	Greater than
GE	Greater than or equal

"Equal" and "greater than" mean the same as = and > when applied to integer data, or to string data in which *value* is the same length as the key field. In our case we will ask for an exact match of a given social security number, so we will use EQ.
3. *Value.* This is the value we hope to find in the key field of a record. It is the social security number the user asks for, so we will call it ASKSSN$.

Finally, our GET statement will be

```
GET #2, KEY #0 EQ ASKSSN$
```

When the length of ASKSSN$ is less than the length of the key field SSN$, we say the GET statement is seeking a *generic match*. If, for instance, the user specifies a value for ASKSSN$ as "123-45", the GET statement above will read the first record whose key field begins with "123-45", if such a record exists. Thus, even if you do not remember an entire social security number, you might be able to retrieve the proper record if you can remember the first several digits.

If the length of ASKSSN$ is more than the length of the key field, an error occurs, with ERR value 145.

The following program reads the personnel file created above. The program asks the user for a social security number and prints the record with that number. If no such record exists, the program informs the user. Asking for a nonexistent record is a fatal error, so the program uses an error handler to determine if the specified record exists. The ERR value for a nonexistent record is 155.

Example 12.2 *Reading an Indexed File by Key Value*

```
100 ! Read a personnel file, an indexed file with each record
110 ! containing an employee name, social security number, pay
120 ! rate, and Blue Cross status.  Ask the user to specify a
130 ! social security number, and print the record with that number.
140 ! Social security number is the primary key.
150 !!!!!!!!!!!!!!!!!!!!!!!!!!!!!!!!!!!!!!!!!!!!!!!!!!!!!!!!!!!!!!!!!
160 ON ERROR GO TO 900
170 GOSUB 300    ! Define records and open file
180 GOSUB 400    ! print description of program
190 GOSUB 500    ! Main loop
200 CLOSE #2
```

```
210 GO TO 999
300 !!!!!!!!!!!!!!!!!!!!!!!!!!!!!!!!!!!!!!!!!!!!!!!!!!!!!!!!!!!!!!!!!!!
310 ! Subroutine; Define records and open the data file.
    !!!!!!!!!!!!!!!!!!!!!!!!!!!!!!!!!!!!!!!!!!!!!!!!!!!!!!!!!!!!!!!!!!!
320 MAP (EMPLOY) NAME$ = 20%, SSN$ = 11%, RATE, BCSTAT$ = 6%
330 OPEN "PERSONNEL.DAT" FOR INPUT AS FILE #2,      &
            ORGANIZATION INDEXED FIXED,             &
            MAP EMPLOY,                             &
            PRIMARY KEY SSN$
340 RETURN
400 !!!!!!!!!!!!!!!!!!!!!!!!!!!!!!!!!!!!!!!!!!!!!!!!!!!!!!!!!!!!!!!!!!!
410 ! Subroutine; Print description of program.
    !!!!!!!!!!!!!!!!!!!!!!!!!!!!!!!!!!!!!!!!!!!!!!!!!!!!!!!!!!!!!!!!!!!
420 PRINT
    PRINT "This program reads data from the indexed file"
    PRINT "PERSONNEL.DAT.  Each record contains a name, social"
    PRINT "security number, hourly rate of pay, and Blue Cross"
    PRINT "status.   Enter a social security number as requested."
    PRINT "To stop the program, enter STOP."
    PRINT
    RETURN
500 !!!!!!!!!!!!!!!!!!!!!!!!!!!!!!!!!!!!!!!!!!!!!!!!!!!!!!!!!!!!!!!!!!!
510 !          Main loop; continue until user enters STOP.
520 !!!!!!!!!!!!!!!!!!!!!!!!!!!!!!!!!!!!!!!!!!!!!!!!!!!!!!!!!!!!!!!!!!!
530 INPUT "Social security number (or STOP)"; ASKSSN$
540 PRINT
550 WHILE (ASKSSN$ <> "STOP")
            GET #2, KEY #0 EQ ASKSSN$
            PRINT  "Name:                "; NAME$
            PRINT  "Social security number: "; SSN$
            PRINT  "Hourly rate:         "; RATE
            PRINT  "Blue Cross status:   "; BCSTAT$
    !
560         INPUT "Social security number (or STOP)"; ASKSSN$
            PRINT
570 NEXT
    RETURN
900 !!!!!!!!!!!!!!!!!!!!!!!!!!!!!!!!!!!!!!!!!!!!!!!!!!!!!!!!!!!!!!!!!!!
910 !      Error handler; Check for nonexistent record.
920 !!!!!!!!!!!!!!!!!!!!!!!!!!!!!!!!!!!!!!!!!!!!!!!!!!!!!!!!!!!!!!!!!!!
930 IF ERR = 155 THEN
        PRINT "There is no record with that social security number."
        PRINT
        RESUME 560
    ELSE
      ON ERROR GO TO 0
    END IF
999 END
```

Updating an INDEXED File

We have already used an OPEN statement with an ACCESS MODIFY clause to allow sequential file updates. The same clause works for indexed files. The UPDATE statement is the same, too. In fact, the entire updating procedure is the same except for one change; in an indexed file, a key value cannot be changed (without a special provision, which we discuss later). Instead, the old record must be deleted, with the same DELETE statement we have already used, then an entirely new record placed in the file with a PUT statement.

The program is very similar to the last one, with an added subroutine to perform the updating. The main part of the subroutine is a SELECT statement:

```
PRINT "What needs to be changed?"
INPUT "Enter NAME, SSN, RATE or BC"; CHANGE$
SELECT CHANGE$
    CASE = "NAME"
        INPUT "New name"; NAME$
        UPDATE #2
    CASE = "SSN"
        INPUT "New social security number"; SSN$
        DELETE #2
        PUT #2
    CASE = "RATE"
        INPUT "New rate"; RATE
        UPDATE #2
    CASE = "BC"
        INPUT "Enter new Blue Cross status"; BCSTAT$
        UPDATE #2
    CASE ELSE
        PRINT "Could not understand your response."
        PRINT "No change has been made."
END SELECT
```

Here is the entire program.

Example 12.3 *Updating an Indexed File*

```
100 ! Read a personnel file, an indexed file with each record
        containing an employee name, social security number, pay
        rate, and Blue Cross status.  Ask the user to specify a
        social security number, and print the record with that number.
        Inform user if no record contains that social security number.
        Social security number is the primary key.

        Also give user the option to change any field in the record.
110 !!!!!!!!!!!!!!!!!!!!!!!!!!!!!!!!!!!!!!!!!!!!!!!!!!!!!!!!!!!!!!!!!!!!!!!!!
120 ON ERROR GO TO 900
130 GOSUB 300       ! Define records and open file.
140 GOSUB 400       ! Print description of program
```

```
150 GOSUB 500      ! Main loop
160 CLOSE #2
170 GO TO 999
300 !!!!!!!!!!!!!!!!!!!!!!!!!!!!!!!!!!!!!!!!!!!!!!!!!!!!!!!!!!!!!!!!!!!!!!!!
310 ! Subroutine; Define records and open the data file.
    !!!!!!!!!!!!!!!!!!!!!!!!!!!!!!!!!!!!!!!!!!!!!!!!!!!!!!!!!!!!!!!!!!!!!!!!
320 MAP (EMPLOY) NAME$ = 20%, SSN$ = 11%, RATE, BCSTAT$ = 6%
330 OPEN "PERSONNEL.DAT" AS FILE #2,          &
            ORGANIZATION INDEXED FIXED,       &
            MAP EMPLOY,                       &
            ACCESS MODIFY,                    &
            PRIMARY KEY SSN$
340 RETURN
400 !!!!!!!!!!!!!!!!!!!!!!!!!!!!!!!!!!!!!!!!!!!!!!!!!!!!!!!!!!!!!!!!!!!!!!!!
410 !                 Print description of program.
    !!!!!!!!!!!!!!!!!!!!!!!!!!!!!!!!!!!!!!!!!!!!!!!!!!!!!!!!!!!!!!!!!!!!!!!!
420 PRINT
    PRINT "This program reads data from the indexed file"
    PRINT "PERSONNEL.DAT, and allows you to modify records."
    PRINT "Each record contains a name, social security number,"
    PRINT "rate of pay, and Blue Cross status.  Enter a social"
    PRINT "security number as requested.  To stop, enter STOP."
    PRINT
430 RETURN
500 !!!!!!!!!!!!!!!!!!!!!!!!!!!!!!!!!!!!!!!!!!!!!!!!!!!!!!!!!!!!!!!!!!!!!!!!
510 ! Subroutine; Main loop - continue until user enters STOP.
    !!!!!!!!!!!!!!!!!!!!!!!!!!!!!!!!!!!!!!!!!!!!!!!!!!!!!!!!!!!!!!!!!!!!!!!!
520 INPUT "Social security number (or STOP)"; ASKSSN$
530 PRINT
540 WHILE (ASKSSN$ <> "STOP")
            GET #2, KEY #0 EQ ASKSSN$
            PRINT   "Name:                   "; NAME$
            PRINT   "Social security number: "; SSN$
            PRINT   "Hourly rate:            "; RATE
            PRINT   "Blue Cross status:      "; BCSTAT$

            PRINT
            INPUT "Do you want to modify this record"; ANS$
            PRINT
            A$ = SEG$(ANS$, 1, 1)
            IF A$ = "y" OR A$ = "Y" THEN GOSUB MODIFYRECORD
550         PRINT
            INPUT "Social security number (or STOP)"; ASKSSN$
            PRINT
560 NEXT
570 RETURN
600 !!!!!!!!!!!!!!!!!!!!!!!!!!!!!!!!!!!!!!!!!!!!!!!!!!!!!!!!!!!!!!!!!!!!!!!!
610 !       Subroutine to change any field of the record
    !!!!!!!!!!!!!!!!!!!!!!!!!!!!!!!!!!!!!!!!!!!!!!!!!!!!!!!!!!!!!!!!!!!!!!!!
```

```
620 MODIFYRECORD:
        PRINT "What needs to be changed?"
        INPUT "Enter NAME, SSN, RATE or BC"; CHANGE$
        SELECT CHANGE$
          CASE = "NAME"
              INPUT "New name"; NAME$
              UPDATE #2
          CASE = "SSN"
              INPUT "New social security number"; SSN$
              DELETE #2
              PUT #2
          CASE = "RATE"
              INPUT "New rate"; RATE
              UPDATE #2
          CASE = "BC"
              INPUT "Enter new Blue Cross status"; BCSTAT$
              UPDATE #2
          CASE ELSE
              PRINT "Could not understand your response."
              PRINT "No change has been made."
        END SELECT
630 RETURN
900 !!!!!!!!!!!!!!!!!!!!!!!!!!!!!!!!!!!!!!!!!!!!!!!!!!!!!!!!!!!!!!!!!!
910 !        Error handler; Check for nonexistent record.
920 !!!!!!!!!!!!!!!!!!!!!!!!!!!!!!!!!!!!!!!!!!!!!!!!!!!!!!!!!!!!!!!!!!
930 IF ERR = 155 THEN
        PRINT "No record contains that social security number."
        PRINT
        RESUME 550
     ELSE
        ON ERROR GO TO 0
     END IF
999 END
```

12.2 ALTERNATE KEYS

In addition to the primary key, alternate keys may be designated in an indexed file. Suppose, for example, we want to create a file in which each record contains a book title, the author's last name, the author's first name, and the year of publication of the book. The MAP statement could be

```
MAP (BOOKS) TITLE$ = 25%, AUTHORLAST$ = 20%,    &
      AUTHORFIRST$ = 10%, YEAR$ = 4%
```

Let the book title be the primary key, and let the author's last name and year of publication be two alternate keys. We specify an alternate key with an *alternate key clause* in the OPEN statement. This clause for AUTHORLAST$ would be

```
ALTERNATE KEY AUTHORLAST$
```

We have the power to allow duplicates and/or changes for key values. Since we might well have more than one book by the same author, and more than one book published in any given year, we should definitely allow duplicates for these two keys. The clause for AUTHORLAST$ is then

```
ALTERNATE KEY AUTHORLAST$  DUPLICATES
```

Notice that DUPLICATES is *not* preceded by a comma.

We could also allow changes to the alternate key field AUTHORLAST$ by adding the term CHANGES to the alternate key clause, as in

```
ALTERNATE KEY AUTHORLAST$  DUPLICATES CHANGES
```

This is more a matter of taste. Even if we do not allow changes to the alternate keys, we can still make changes later by deleting an old record and inserting a new one. We will not allow changes to our alternate keys in this program.

The complete OPEN statement then is

```
OPEN "BOOK.DAT" FOR OUTPUT AS FILE #1,            &
      ORGANIZATION INDEXED FIXED,                 &
      MAP BOOKS,                                  &
      PRIMARY KEY TITLE$,                         &
      ALTERNATE KEY AUTHORLAST$  DUPLICATES,      &
      ALTERNATE KEY YEAR$  DUPLICATES
```

The alternate key mentioned first, AUTHORLAST$, automatically becomes key number 1, or the first alternate key. YEAR$ is key number 2, or the second alternate key. Except for the OPEN statement, the program that creates the file does not mention either primary or alternate keys.

Here is the complete program.

Example 12.4 *Creating an Indexed File with Alternate Keys*

```
100 REM -- Create an indexed file with alternate keys.
            Primary key is title.  Alternate keys are
            author's last name and year of publication.
110 MAP (BOOKS) TITLE$ = 25%, AUTHORLAST$ = 20%,    &
              AUTHORFIRST$ = 10%, YEAR$ = 4%
120 OPEN "BOOK.DAT" FOR OUTPUT AS FILE #1,           &
          ORGANIZATION INDEXED FIXED,                &
          MAP BOOKS,                                 &
          PRIMARY KEY TITLE$,                        &
          ALTERNATE KEY AUTHORLAST$  DUPLICATES,     &
          ALTERNATE KEY YEAR$  DUPLICATES
130 PRINT "Enter data as requested.  Press return"
140 PRINT "for title to exit the program."
150 LINPUT "Title"; TITLE$
160 WHILE TITLE$ <> ""
        PRINT
        INPUT "Author's last name "; AUTHORLAST$
```

```
        PRINT
        INPUT "Author's first name"; AUTHORFIRST$
        PRINT
        INPUT "Year of publication"; YEAR$

        PUT #1
        PRINT
        LINPUT "Title"; TITLE$

    NEXT
170 CLOSE #1
200 END
```

We could now write a program to read the file BOOK.DAT using any of the three keys. To read the file according to the author's last name, simply use a GET statement of the form

```
GET #2, KEY #1 EQ ASKNAME$
```

where KEY 1 is the first alternate key, AUTHORLAST$, and ASKNAME$ is the name the user requested.

We will leave that program for the exercises and turn to another major feature of indexed files; it is almost a trivial matter to print the records of an indexed file sorted by any key.

An indexed file can also be read sequentially—that is, with a GET statement that does not contain a key clause. The following code will read the file BOOK.DAT from beginning to end.

```
GET #1
WHILE 1
    PRINT TITLE$; TRM$(AUTHORLAST$); ", ";
    PRINT AUTHORFIRST$; TAB(55); YEAR$
    GET #1
NEXT
```

The first GET reads the first record in the file according to the primary key, TITLE$. When the first GET statement in a program contains no key clause, VAX-BASIC assumes the user wants the record that has the first *primary* key value.

The second GET statement, inside the WHILE loop, uses the primary key because the previous GET used the primary key. For a GET after the first one in a program, VAX-BASIC uses the key used by the *previous* GET statement and gets the next record in order according to that key. Thus, this code will read and print the file in order by primary key and is the heart of the next program.

Example 12.5 *Reading an Entire Indexed File Sequentially*

```
100 REM -- Read an indexed file with alternate keys.
           Primary key is title.  Alternate keys are
           author's last name and year of publication.
```

```
110 ON ERROR GO TO 900
120 GOSUB 300       ! Define records and open file
130 GOSUB 400       ! Main loop
300 !!!!!!!!!!!!!!!!!!!!!!!!!!!!!!!!!!!!!!!!!!!!!!!!!!!!!!!!!!!!!
310 Subroutine; Define records and open file.
    !!!!!!!!!!!!!!!!!!!!!!!!!!!!!!!!!!!!!!!!!!!!!!!!!!!!!!!!!!!!!
320 MAP (BOOKS) TITLE$ = 25%, AUTHORLAST$ = 20%,      &
                AUTHORFIRST$ = 10%, YEAR$ = 4%
330 OPEN "BOOK.DAT" AS FILE #1,                       &
        ORGANIZATION INDEXED FIXED,                   &
        MAP BOOKS,                                    &
        PRIMARY KEY TITLE$,                           &
        ALTERNATE KEY AUTHORLAST$  DUPLICATES,        &
        ALTERNATE KEY YEAR$  DUPLICATES
340 RETURN
400 !!!!!!!!!!!!!!!!!!!!!!!!!!!!!!!!!!!!!!!!!!!!!!!!!!!!!!!!!!!!!
410 Subroutine; Read and print records.
    !!!!!!!!!!!!!!!!!!!!!!!!!!!!!!!!!!!!!!!!!!!!!!!!!!!!!!!!!!!!!
420 PRINT TAB(5); "Title"; TAB(25); "Author"; TAB(55); "Year"
430 PRINT STRING$(60%, 45%)
440 GET #1
450 WHILE 1%
        PRINT TITLE$; TRM$(AUTHORLAST$); ", ";
        PRINT AUTHORFIRST$; TAB(55); YEAR$
        GET #1
460 NEXT
470 RETURN
900 !!!!!!!!!!!!!!!!!!!!!!!!!!!!!!!!!!!!!!!!!!!!!!!!!!!!!!!!!!!!!
910 ! Error handler; ERR number 11 is end-of-file.
    !!!!!!!!!!!!!!!!!!!!!!!!!!!!!!!!!!!!!!!!!!!!!!!!!!!!!!!!!!!!!
920 IF ERR = 11% THEN RESUME 930 ELSE ON ERROR GO TO 0
930 CLOSE #1
999 END
```

The following output is typical of what the program might do. Notice that the records are ordered alphabetically by title.

```
    Title                Author                Year
------------------------------------------------------------
Absolom, Absolom        Faulkner, William       1964
Cannery Row             Steinbeck, John         1945
Death in the Afternoon  Hemingway, Ernest       1932
East of Eden            Steinbeck, John         1979
Farewell to Arms, A     Hemingway, Ernest       1929
For Whom the Bell Tolls  Hemingway, Ernest      1940
Great Gatsby, The       Fitzgerald, F. Scott    1925
Last Tycoon, The        Fitzgerald, F. Scott    1941
Of Mice and Men         Steinbeck, John         1937
Pearl, The              Steinbeck, John         1945
Sanctuary, The          Faulkner, William       1967
Tender Is the Night     Fitzgerald, F. Scott    1933
```

To get the file printed in order by author's last name, we would need to start with a GET statement containing a KEY #1 clause. In order to get the first record by author's last name, we can use the GET statement

```
GET #1, KEY #1 GE " "
```

because all last names will come after " " in ASCII order. When the GE relation appears in a GET statement, the computer reads the *first* record whose key value satisfies the relation. In this case, the computer starts with the first record whose AUTHORLAST$ value comes at or after " ". That should be the first record in alphabetical order by author's last name.

We can do the same for YEAR$. In our program, we will ask the user to choose:

1. Book title
2. Author's last name
3. Year of publication

Then we will use the following IF block to read the first record.

```
IF CHOICE% = 1% THEN
    GET #1
ELSE IF CHOICE% = 2% THEN
    GET #1, KEY #1 GE " "
ELSE IF CHOICE% = 3% THEN
    GET #1, KEY #2 GE " "
END IF
```

The rest of the records can then be read with a WHILE loop and error handler to handle the end of the file, as before.

Example 12.6 *Sequentially Reading an Indexed File with Alternate Keys*

```
100 REM -- Read an indexed file with alternate keys.
          Primary key is title.  Alternate keys are
          author's last name and year of publication.
110 ON ERROR GO TO 900
120 GOSUB 300          ! Define records and open file
130 GOSUB 400          ! Print instructions
140 GOSUB 500          ! Get key choice and print file
300 !!!!!!!!!!!!!!!!!!!!!!!!!!!!!!!!!!!!!!!!!!!!!!!!!!!!!!!!!!!!!!!!
310 ! Subroutine; Define records and open file.
    !!!!!!!!!!!!!!!!!!!!!!!!!!!!!!!!!!!!!!!!!!!!!!!!!!!!!!!!!!!!!!!!
320 MAP (BOOKS) TITLE$ = 25%, AUTHORLAST$ = 20%,     &
              AUTHORFIRST$ = 10%, YEAR$ = 4%
330 OPEN "BOOK.DAT" AS FILE #1,                      &
          ORGANIZATION INDEXED FIXED,                &
          MAP BOOKS,                                 &
          PRIMARY KEY TITLE$,                        &
          ALTERNATE KEY AUTHORLAST$  DUPLICATES,     &
          ALTERNATE KEY YEAR$  DUPLICATES
340 RETURN
```

```
400 !!!!!!!!!!!!!!!!!!!!!!!!!!!!!!!!!!!!!!!!!!!!!!!!!!!!!!!!!!!!!!!!!
410 ! Subroutine; Print instructions.
    !!!!!!!!!!!!!!!!!!!!!!!!!!!!!!!!!!!!!!!!!!!!!!!!!!!!!!!!!!!!!!!!!
420 PRINT "You may see the file BOOK.DAT ordered by"
    PRINT "1.  Book title"
    PRINT "2.  Author's last name"
    PRINT "3.  Year of publication"
    PRINT
430 RETURN
500 !!!!!!!!!!!!!!!!!!!!!!!!!!!!!!!!!!!!!!!!!!!!!!!!!!!!!!!!!!!!!!!!!
510 ! Subroutine; Get choice and print file on specified key.
    !!!!!!!!!!!!!!!!!!!!!!!!!!!!!!!!!!!!!!!!!!!!!!!!!!!!!!!!!!!!!!!!!
520 INPUT "Please choose 1, 2, or 3"; CHOICE%
    PRINT TAB(5); "Title"; TAB(25); "Author"; TAB(55); "Year"
    PRINT STRINGS$(60%, 45%)
530 IF CHOICE% = 1% THEN
        GET #1
    ELSE IF CHOICE% = 2% THEN
        GET #1, KEY #1 GE " "
    ELSE IF CHOICE% = 3% THEN
        GET #1, KEY #2 GE " "
    END IF
540 WHILE 1%
        PRINT TITLES$; TRM$(AUTHORLAST$); ", ";
        PRINT AUTHORFIRST$; TAB(55); YEAR$
        GET #1
550 NEXT
560 RETURN
900 !!!!!!!!!!!!!!!!!!!!!!!!!!!!!!!!!!!!!!!!!!!!!!!!!!!!!!!!!!!!!!!!!
910 ! Error handler; ERR number 11 is end-of-file.
    !!!!!!!!!!!!!!!!!!!!!!!!!!!!!!!!!!!!!!!!!!!!!!!!!!!!!!!!!!!!!!!!!
920 IF ERR = 11% THEN RESUME 930 ELSE ON ERROR GO TO 0
930 CLOSE #1
999 END
```

If the user chooses "1. Title," the output will be the same as that from the previous program. If the user chooses "2. Author's last name," the output will be:

```
        TITLE                AUTHOR                  YEAR
    --------------------------------------------------------
    Absolom, Absolom      Faulkner, William          1964
    Sanctuary, The        Faulkner, William          1967
    Tender Is the Night   Fitzgerald, F. Scott       1933
    Great Gatsby, The     Fitzgerald, F. Scott       1925
    Last Tycoon, The      Fitzgerald, F. Scott       1941
    For Whom the Bell Tolls  Hemingway, Ernest       1940
    Death in the Afternoon   Hemingway, Ernest       1932
    Farewell to Arms, A   Hemingway, Ernest          1929
    Cannery Row           Steinbeck, John            1945
    East of Eden          Steinbeck, John            1979
    Of Mice and Men       Steinbeck, John            1937
    Pearl, The            Steinbeck, John            1945
```

Records with the same author's last name are printed in the order they were placed in the file.

If the user chooses "3. Year," the output will be:

```
    TITLE                   AUTHOR                      YEAR
    ---------------------------------------------------------------
    Great Gatsby, The       Fitzgerald, F. Scott        1925
    Farewell to Arms, A     Hemingway, Ernest           1929
    Death in the Afternoon  Hemingway, Ernest           1932
    Tender Is the Night     Fitzgerald, F. Scott        1933
    Of Mice and Men         Steinbeck, John             1937
    For Whom the Bell Tolls Hemingway, Ernest           1940
    Last Tycoon, The        Fitzgerald, F. Scott        1941
    Cannery Row             Steinbeck, John             1945
    Pearl, The              Steinbeck, John             1945
    Absolom, Absolom        Faulkner, William           1964
    Sanctuary, The          Faulkner, William           1967
    East of Eden            Steinbeck, John             1979
```

(Those years, by the way, correspond to *some* edition of the book, not necessarily the first.)

Compound Key Fields

We generally think of a key field as being *one* of the fields specified in a MAP statement. Actually, a key field can be a combination of such fields. For example, if LASTNAME$ and FIRSTNAME$ are MAP variables, we can use one key field consisting of the LASTNAME$ field together with the FIRSTNAME$ field by placing in the OPEN statement the clause

```
PRIMARY KEY (LASTNAME$, FIRSTNAME$)
```

One reason for making such a compound key is that LASTNAME$ might have duplicate values in a data set, but LASTNAME$ and FIRSTNAME$ together have unique values.

The following program creates a compound key in an address file. Otherwise, there is nothing new in the program.

Example 12.7 *Creating a File with a Compound Key Field*

```
100 REM -- Create an indexed file with alternate keys.
            Primary key is (LASTNAME, FIRSTNAME).
            Alternate key is BIRTHDAY.
110 MAP (ENTRY) LASTNAME$ = 12%, FIRSTNAME$ = 10%,    &
                BIRTHDAY$ = 6%, ADDRESS$ = 20%,        &
                CITY$ = 15%, STATE$ = 2%, ZIP$ = 5%,   &
                AREACODE$ = 3%, PHONE$ = 8%
```

```
120 OPEN "ADDRESS.DAT" FOR OUTPUT AS FILE #1,              &
          ORGANIZATION INDEXED FIXED,                      &
          MAP ENTRY,                                       &
          PRIMARY KEY (LASTNAME$, FIRSTNAME$),             &
          ALTERNATE KEY BIRTHDAY$ DUPLICATES
130 PRINT "Enter data as requested.  Press return"
140 PRINT "for last name to exit the program."
150 INPUT "Last name"; LASTNAME$
160 WHILE LASTNAME$ <> ""
        PRINT
        INPUT "First name"; FIRSTNAME$
        PRINT
        INPUT "Birthday (as JAN 06, for example)"; BIRTHDAY$
        PRINT
        INPUT "Street address"; ADDRESS$
        PRINT
        INPUT "City"; CITY$
        PRINT
        INPUT "Two-letter state designation"; STATE$
        PRINT
        INPUT "Zip code"; ZIP$
        PRINT
        INPUT "Area code"; AREACODE$
        PRINT
        INPUT "Phone number"; PHONE$

        PUT #1
        PRINT
        INPUT "Last name"; LASTNAME$

    NEXT
170 CLOSE #1
200 END
```

Suppose we want to read the file ADDRESS.DAT near the beginning of a month and find the names of people with birthdays in that month. The idea is similar to reading an entire indexed file by an alternate key, but here we want to read just a portion of the file sequentially.

We will ask the user for the month, BIRTHMONTH$, then get the first record in that month with the keyed GET statement

```
GET #1, KEY #1 EQ BIRTHMONTH$
```

This keyed GET statement illustrates a difference between the relational operators $=$ and EQ. BIRTHMONTH$ will be three characters long (JAN, FEB, and so on), but the key field BIRTHDAY$ has six characters. The EQ requires a match on just the three characters in BIRTHMONTH$. This is a generic match that does not use all the characters in the key field.

We read the rest of the records with birthdays in that month with the sequential GET statements in the following code.

```
GET #1
WHILE SEG$(BIRTHDAY$, 1, 3) = BIRTHMONTH$
    GOSUB PRINT_ENTRY
    GET #1
NEXT
```

Here, however, we must compare SEG$(BIRTHDAY$, 1, 3) to BIRTHMONTH$, because BIRTHDAY$ and BIRTHMONTH$ are not equal under the = relation.

We will need an error handler to take care of two possible errors. The keyed GET statement might be attempting to find a nonexistent record (ERR number 155), and the sequential GET statements might be attempting to read past the end of the file (ERR number 11).

Here is the entire program.

Example 12.8 *Reading a Portion of an Indexed File*

```
100 REM -- Read an indexed file with an alternate key.
            Primary key is (LASTNAME, FIRSTNAME).
            Alternate key is BIRTHDAY.
110 ON ERROR GO TO 900
120 GOSUB 200          ! Define records and open file
130 GOSUB 300          ! Print instructions
140 GOSUB 400          ! Get month and print records
150 CLOSE #1
160 GO TO 999
200 !!!!!!!!!!!!!!!!!!!!!!!!!!!!!!!!!!!!!!!!!!!!!!!!!!!!!!!!!
210 ! Subroutine; Define records and open file.
    !!!!!!!!!!!!!!!!!!!!!!!!!!!!!!!!!!!!!!!!!!!!!!!!!!!!!!!!!
220 MAP (ENTRY) LASTNAME$ = 12%, FIRSTNAME$ = 10%,     &
               BIRTHDAY$ = 6%, ADDRESS$ = 20%,         &
               CITY$ = 15%, STATE$ = 2%, ZIP$ = 5%,    &
               AREACODE$ = 3%, PHONE$ = 8%
230 OPEN "ADDRESS.DAT" FOR INPUT AS FILE #1,           &
            ORGANIZATION INDEXED FIXED,                &
            MAP ENTRY,                                 &
            PRIMARY KEY (LASTNAME$, FIRSTNAME$),       &
            ALTERNATE KEY BIRTHDAY$  DUPLICATE
240 RETURN
300 !!!!!!!!!!!!!!!!!!!!!!!!!!!!!!!!!!!!!!!!!!!!!!!!!!!!!!!!!
310 ! Subroutine; Print instructions.
    !!!!!!!!!!!!!!!!!!!!!!!!!!!!!!!!!!!!!!!!!!!!!!!!!!!!!!!!!
320 PRINT "This program will read the file ADDRESS.DAT"
    PRINT "and print all entries with birthdays in a  "
    PRINT "given month.  Enter X to exit the program. "
    PRINT
330 RETURN
400 !!!!!!!!!!!!!!!!!!!!!!!!!!!!!!!!!!!!!!!!!!!!!!!!!!!!!!!!!
```

```
410 ! Subroutine; Get month and print records.
    !!!!!!!!!!!!!!!!!!!!!!!!!!!!!!!!!!!!!!!!!!!!!!!!!!!!!!!!!!!!!!!!!!
420 INPUT "Month of birthday (as JAN, FEB, etc.)"; BIRTHMONTH$
430 WHILE BIRTHMONTH$ <> "X"
        GET #1, KEY #1 EQ BIRTHMONTH$
        GOSUB PRINT_ENTRY

        GET #1
        WHILE SEG$(BIRTHDAY$, 1, 3) = BIRTHMONTH$
            GOSUB PRINT_ENTRY
            GET #1
        NEXT

440     PRINT
        INPUT "Month of birthday (or X to stop)"; BIRTHMONTH$
    NEXT
450 RETURN
500 !!!!!!!!!!!!!!!!!!!!!!!!!!!!!!!!!!!!!!!!!!!!!!!!!!!!!!!!!!!!!!!!!!!
510 !        Subroutine to print data from one record.
    !!!!!!!!!!!!!!!!!!!!!!!!!!!!!!!!!!!!!!!!!!!!!!!!!!!!!!!!!!!!!!!!!!!
520 PRINT_ENTRY:
        PRINT
        PRINT FIRSTNAME$; " "; LASTNAME$;
        PRINT TAB(35); "Birthday: "; BIRTHDAY$
        PRINT ADDRESS$
        PRINT TRM$(CITY$); ", "; STATE$
        PRINT ZIP$;
        PRINT TAB(35); "Phone: "; AREACODE$; "-"; PHONE$
        PRINT
        PRINT
530 RETURN
900 !!!!!!!!!!!!!!!!!!!!!!!!!!!!!!!!!!!!!!!!!!!!!!!!!!!!!!!!!!!!!!!!!!!
910 ! Error Handler; End-of-file (11), Record-not-found (155).
    !!!!!!!!!!!!!!!!!!!!!!!!!!!!!!!!!!!!!!!!!!!!!!!!!!!!!!!!!!!!!!!!!!!
920 IF ERR = 11% THEN
            RESUME 440
        ELSE IF ERR = 155% THEN
            PRINT
            PRINT "No one has a birthday in that month."
            RESUME 440
        ELSE ON ERROR GO TO 0
        END IF
999 END
```

The DELETE Statement

The DELETE statement for indexed files works like the DELETE statement applied to relative files, except that the storage space occupied by the deleted record is actually removed from the file. The record to be deleted must be the current record—the last record read by a successful GET statement.

The RESTORE Statement

VAX-BASIC keeps indexes for each key in an indexed file. Therefore, a RESTORE statement for an indexed file can restore the file on any one of the keys. If you do not specify a key, VAX-BASIC assumes you want the primary key. To restore the file on the primary key, use the statement

```
RESTORE #1, KEY #0
```

or just

```
RESTORE #1
```

To restore the file on an alternate key, you must specify the key number. For instance, to restore the file on the second alternate key, use the statement

```
RESTORE #1, KEY #2
```

Using DIR to Determine File Characteristics

If you create many files, there will come a time when you forget how a file was created and what characteristics it has. You can use the DIRECTORY command, abbreviated DIR, in DCL to find out some properties of the file. After the DCL dollar sign, type DIR/FULL and the name of the file. The command

```
$ DIR/FULL PERSONNEL.DAT
```

will produce something like

```
Directory FACULTY:[PUBLISHER.REVISION]

PERSONNEL.DAT;3          File ID:  (2735,9,0)
Size:           9/9      Owner:    [SWRK,PUBLISHER]
Created:  19-JUL-1986 12:20  Revised:  19-JUL-1986 12:21 (1)
Expires:  <None specified>  Backup:    <No backup done>
File organization:  Indexed, Prolog: 3, Using 1 key
File attributes:    Allocation: 9, Extend: 0, Maximum bucket size
                    2, Global buffer count: 0, No version limit
Record format:      Fixed length 41 byte records
Record attributes:  Carriage return carriage control
Journaling enabled: None
File protection:    System:RWED, Owner:RWED, Group:, World:
Access Cntrl List:  None
```

We will not discuss all the information here, just two lines that answer a couple of the more important questions you might have. The line beginning with "File organization" tells you that this is an indexed file with one key. The "Record format" line says the records have fixed length of 41 bytes.

EXERCISES

1. a. Write a program that creates an indexed file with one key. Each record should contain a student name and grade point average GPA (a real number between 0.00 and 4.00). Name is the primary key.
   b. Write a program to read the file created in part a. The user should give a name and the program should either print the record with that name or inform the user that no such record exists.
   c. Write a program to read sequentially the file created in part a. For each student, calculate a rating as follows:
      (1) If the GPA is 3.60 or above, the rating is "Highest honor".
      (2) If the GPA is 3.20 or above, but less than 3.60, the rating is "Honor".
      (3) If the GPA is below 2.00, the rating is "Ineligible to graduate".
   The program should print each student's name, GPA, and rating.

2. Write a program that opens the file BOOK.DAT, asks the user which key to use, then asks for the desired key value. If the specified record exists, the program should print its contents. If not, the program should inform the user. You may use the program in the text to create the file BOOK.DAT.

3. a. Write a program to create an indexed file with two keys. Each record contains a name and a social security number, with social security number the primary key and name the (first) alternate key.
   b. Write a program to read the file created in part a. The program should ask if the user wants to specify a name or social security number, ask the user to specify the record, and either print the appropriate record or tell the user that no such record exists.

4. Write a program that reads the file BOOK.DAT and asks the user for a record to delete. Have the program print the record, if it exists, and ask the user to verify that the record should be deleted. You may use the program of Example 12.4 to create the file.

5. Write a program that uses an indexed file such as ADDRESS.DAT and allows the user these options:
   a. Add a record.
   b. Print the entire file by primary key.
   c. Print just one record.
   d. Modify a record.
   e. Delete a record.
   Use subroutines for each option. Options c, d, and e require the user to specify a record (by primary key, say). Include an error handler to take care of cases where the record asked for does not exist.

6. Create a master payroll file, an indexed personnel file like PERSONNEL.DAT, created in Example 12.1, and insert at least 10 records. Also create a weekly payroll transaction file, a sequential file with each record containing a social security number and hours worked for one week.
   Write a program that reads both files and writes the weekly payroll report. Have the program read each record from the weekly payroll file, find the matching record in the master file, and calculate the payroll data for that employee.

The program should contain an error handler to deal with the end of the weekly file and the case in which a social security number in the weekly file cannot be found in the master file.

The report should resemble the following outline.

Employee Name	Gross Pay	Federal Tax	Social Security	State Tax	Blue Cross	Net Pay
Whitney Houston	358.25	64.49	25.61	14.33	13.50	240.32

Use the following rules to calculate deductions. A single Blue Cross plan costs $13.50 per week, and a family plan is 37.50 per week. Tax rates are given as a percent of gross pay. The social security tax rate is 7.15%, and the state and federal tax rates are given in the tables below.

Gross pay	Federal tax rate		Gross pay	State tax rate
Gross < 150	0%		Gross < 150	0%
150 < = Gross < 250	7%		150 < = Gross < 300	2%
250 < = Gross < 300	11%		300 < = Gross	4%
300 < = Gross < 350	15%			
350 < = Gross < 400	18%			
400 < = Gross < 450	21%			
450 < = Gross < 500	24%			
500 < = Gross	27%			

7. The Dillon County library keeps track of all books that have been signed out of the library on the computer. Each record in the file contains the following information:
   (1) Card catalogue identification number (this is different for every book in the library)
   (2) Title of the book
   (3) Name of person who signed the book out
   (4) Date the book is due back
   (5) Whether the book is fiction or nonfiction
   Write a program with each of the following subroutines:
   a. A subroutine which will allow the librarian to enter today's date in the form DDMMYR and have the computer print out a list of all overdue books. Each line should list the title of the book, the name of the person who signed it out, and the due date.
   b. A subroutine to allow the librarian to print out an alphabetical list of all persons who have taken out nonfiction books. Do not list a name more than once.
   c. A subroutine which prints each individual's name followed by all of the books that person has signed out and the numeric total for each individual as well as the cumulative total.

Trial data:

```
14451 COMPUTER FUN          BOMBECK,IRMA   122986 NON
2998  READERS GUIDE         HALEY,ANNABETH 010187 NON
3551  GUINNESS WORLD RECORDS HALEY,ANNABETH 010187 NON
1345A TRAINS                JONES,BILL     121186 FIC
2334B THE SANTE FE          JONES,BILL     121186 NON
1199J TIGER'S EYE           MARRIS,EVAN    121486 FIC
788GB THE CRADLE            MARRIS,EVAN    121786 FIC
3558  ENCYCLOPEDIA (A)      RALEIGH,BOB    112186 NON
9887  A STITCH IN TIME      ROSS,SUSAN     010287 FIC
3344  THE KING'S GENERAL    ROSS,SUSAN     010287 FIC
3546  FAST COOKING          SMITH,BONNIE   121586 NON
23331 DIETING WITHOUT PAIN  SMITH,BONNIE   121586 NON
2445  CHOCOLATE DELIGHTS    SMITH,BONNIE   121586 NON
4556  LOW-CAL CHEESECAKE    SMITH,BONNIE   121586 FIC
3343  COUNT YOUR CALORIES   SMITH,BONNIE   121586 NON
8876  LAZY DAYS             WALTERS,JANE   121586 FIC
2543  HORROR STORIES        WILTON,JANE    121186 FIC
32665 BIKING FOR FUN        WINSTON,AL     112286 NON
4454  GUINNESS BOOK OF RECORDS WINSTON,AL  112286 NON
```

REVIEW QUESTIONS

1. Write an OPEN statement for each of the indexed files described.

   a. An inventory file with the item number as the primary key and the name as an alternate key that allows duplicates. The MAP name is TOYS and the file is for OUTPUT.

   b. A grade file with student ID as the primary key and the MAP name GRADES. The file is to be modified.

   c. A software file with program name as the primary key, the computer model as the first alternate key, and the software publisher as the second alternate key. The MAP name is PROGRAMS.

   d. A song file with the record number as the primary key and the song name as the alternate key. The MAP name is MUSIC.

2. *True or False.* In an indexed file:

   _____   The primary key may be changed.
   _____   The primary key may be duplicated.
   _____   The alternate key may be changed.
   _____   The alternate key may be duplicated.

3. Match the file function with the appropriate statement.

   a. UPDATE   1. Places a record in the file
   b. GET   2. Changes a record in the file
   c. PUT   3. Retrieves a record from the file
   d. DELETE   4. Removes a record from the file
   e. RESTORE   5. Sets the file to the original primary key
                    or a specified key

4. Using the following OPEN and MAP statements, what will be the result of each of the given actions? Each case is an independent example.

```
MAP (TOYS) INVENO$, NAME$, DESCR$ = 30%,
    PRICE, ONHAND%, ONORDER%
OPEN "INVENTORY.DAT" AS FILE #2,   &
    ORGANIZATION INDEXED FIXED,   &
    MAP TOYS
    ACCESS MODIFY,
    PRIMARY KEY INVENO$,          &
    ALTERNATE KEY NAME$ DUPLICATES
```

a.
```
INPUT "Type in inventory number to search for", SEARCHNO
GET #2, KEY #0 EQ SEARCHNO
```

b.
```
INPUT "INVENO", INVENO$
INPUT "TOY NAME", NAME$
INPUT "Description of toy", DESCR$
INPUT "PRICE", PRICE
INPUT "ONHAND", ONHAND%
INPUT "ON ORDER", ON ORDER%
PUT #2
```

c.
```
GET #2
INPUT "NEW ORDER", ON ORDER%
UPDATE #2
```

d.
```
GET #2
INPUT "NEW INVENTORY NO", INVENO$
DELETE #2
PUT #2
```

SUMMARY OF CHAPTER 12

CONCEPTS AND VAX-BASIC KEYWORDS INTRODUCED IN THIS
CHAPTER

Concepts	Related statements and keywords
1. Indexed files	
2. Create an indexed file	ORGANIZATION INDEXED FIXED
	PRIMARY KEY clause
	DUPLICATES
	CHANGES
3. Read an indexed file	Keyed GET statement
4. Sequential read of an indexed file	Sequential GET statement
5. Update a record	ACCESS MODIFY
	UPDATE
6. Alternate keys	ALTERNATE KEY clause
7. Deleting a record	DELETE
8. Restoring an indexed file	Keyed RESTORE statement

Two-Dimensional Arrays

VAX-BASIC permits arrays with up to 255 dimensions, but the most widely used arrays certainly are one-dimensional, with two-dimensional arrays in second place. In this chapter we discuss two-dimensional arrays, or matrices, as they are often called.

13.1 MATRICES

Double Subscripted Arrays

Consider the following table, which gives numbers of shirts on hand arranged by size and pattern.

Size	Pattern		
	Stripe	Check	Solid
SMALL	22	12	18
MEDIUM	28	17	19
LARGE	24	14	20
XLARGE	12	10	13

The numbers are laid out in a rectangular pattern and thus form a *two-dimensional array* or *matrix*. Matrices can be represented in the computer by variables with two subscripts. For instance, suppose you want to find the number of medium size shirts on hand in solid colors. Medium size shirts are listed in row 2 , so you first look in row 2. Solid colors are in column 3, so you look for the number in row 2, column 3, and find 19. Any number in the table can be identified by specifying the row and column in which it occurs.

We can then represent the table above by a variable SHIRT with two subscripts. It is conventional to give the row subscript first, so SHIRT(2, 3) is 19. Similarly, SHIRT(4, 1) is the number in the SHIRT table in row 4, column 1, so SHIRT(4, 1) is 12. What about the value of SHIRT(1, 4)? This would be the number in row 1, column 4 of the table, but there is no column 4, so SHIRT(1, 4) does not exist. This SHIRT matrix above has 4 rows and 3 columns. It is called a *4-by-3* matrix.

As with lists, matrices should be dimensioned with a DIM statement near the beginning of the program. An appropriate DIM statement for the example above is DIM SHIRT(4, 3). This tells the computer to set aside storage space for a matrix variable SHIRT whose first subscript will not be larger than 4, and whose second subscript will not be larger than 3.

When you specify just the upper bound for a subscript, VAX-BASIC always starts with subscript 0, so the computer will set aside 20 storage spaces, for five rows numbered 0 to 4 and 4 columns numbered 0 to 3. Again, you do not have to use the 0 subscript if you don't want to. Just remember it is there. A DIM statement is not necessary if both subscripts have an upper limit of 10, but we recommend using a DIM statement whenever you use subscripted variables.

Subscript Bounds

As with singly subscripted arrays, VAX-BASIC allows you to set both lower and upper subscript bounds by using the keyword TO in the DIM statement. One or both of the subscripts can be given lower and upper bounds, as in the following DIM statement:

```
DIM EARNINGS(1984 TO 1987, 4)
```

This statement dimensions a two-dimensional array EARNINGS with first subscript ranging from 1984 through 1987 and second subscript ranging from 0 to 4. The array EARNINGS could represent a company's quarterly earnings for the years 1984 through 1987. For example, EARNINGS(1986, 3) could represent the company's earnings in the third quarter of 1986.

The following program illustrates a simple use of this EARNINGS matrix. The program simply reads the values for the array EARNINGS and prints a table of these values. The use of nested loops is characteristic of matrix programs. In this program, YEAR represents the first subscript on EARNINGS and QUARTER represents the second subscript. The main portion of the program is the YEAR loop with the QUARTER loop nested inside.

Example 13.1 *Reading and Writing a Matrix*

```
100 REM -- Illustrate array bounds and matrix input and output
110 DIM EARNINGS(1984 TO 1987, 4)
120 PRINT , "FIRST", "SECOND", "THIRD", "FOURTH"
130 PRINT " YEAR", "QUARTER", "QUARTER", "QUARTER", "QUARTER"
```

```
140 FOR YEAR = 1984 TO 1987
        PRINT YEAR,
        FOR QUARTER = 1 TO 4
            READ EARNINGS(YEAR, QUARTER)
            PRINT EARNINGS(YEAR, QUARTER),
        NEXT QUARTER
        PRINT
150 NEXT YEAR
160 DATA 18.5, 19.2, 20.1, 22.3
170 DATA 21.2, 22.1, 21.9, 23.7
180 DATA 22.8, 23.1, 22.8, 23.9
190 DATA 23.8, 24.2, 24.1, 24.6
200 END
```

```
RUNNH
```

YEAR	FIRST QUARTER	SECOND QUARTER	THIRD QUARTER	FOURTH QUARTER
1984	18.5	19.2	20.1	22.3
1985	21.2	22.1	21.9	23.7
1986	22.8	23.1	22.8	23.9
1987	23.8	24.2	24.1	24.6

Except for illustrating the use of doubly subscripted variables and bounds on subscripts, this program could (and should) have been written without any subscripted variables.

The MAT READ Statement

Let us write a program segment that does nothing but read the values from the table above into the variable SHIRT. One way to do this is as follows.

```
10 REM -- Read values into a 4-by-3 matrix
20 DIM SHIRT(4,3)
30 FOR ROW = 1 TO 4
        FOR COLUMN = 1 TO 3
            READ SHIRT(ROW, COLUMN)
        NEXT COLUMN
   NEXT ROW

    .
    .
    .
50 DATA 22, 12, 18
60 DATA 28, 17, 19
70 DATA 24, 14, 20
80 DATA 12, 10, 13
90 END
```

Notice that it requires the five statements in line 30 just to read in the values for a matrix. VAX-BASIC has a special statement that allows the entire matrix to be read in one step. Line 30 could be replaced by MAT READ SHIRT. This is a special form of the READ statement called the *MAT READ statement*. In the statement MAT READ SHIRT, we did not have to specify subscripts for SHIRT. The DIM statement in line 20 has told the computer the size of the matrix SHIRT already. Thus the line

```
30 MAT READ SHIRT
```

could replace line 30 above. (MAT statements can be used only if *all* array subscripts have lower bound zero.)

It is permissible to use subscripts in a MAT READ statement. This amounts to redimensioning the matrix variable. Suppose, for instance, that we no longer wish to stock shirts in the XLARGE size. We can ignore the last row of the matrix by writing

```
20 DIM SHIRT(4, 3)
30 MAT READ SHIRT(3, 3)
```

This MAT READ statement instructs the computer to read only the first 3 rows (and 3 columns) of the matrix SHIRT. The subscripts in the MAT READ statement "override" the subscripts in the DIM statement. Matrices can be made smaller in this way, but they must not be made larger. That is, subscripts in the MAT READ statement must not be larger than the corresponding subscripts in the DIM statement. Also, be aware that READ SHIRT(3, 3) would mean "read one data value and assign it to row 3, column 3 of SHIRT".

Although VAX-BASIC always sets aside storage space for a 0 row and 0 column, the MAT READ statement does not assign any values to the 0 row or 0 column.

Now that we know how to read values for a matrix, let us write a small program to do something with the values. Suppose we want to know how many shirts of each size are on hand, and we don't care about the patterns. To find the number of small shirts we need to sum the numbers in the appropriate row. We will want a loop FOR ROW = 1 TO 4. Inside this ROW loop, we want to sum the values in a particular row, the row numbered ROW. To add the numbers in this row, consider the following segment:

```
SUM = 0
FOR COLUMN = 1 TO 3
    SUM = SUM + SHIRT(ROW, COLUMN)
NEXT COLUMN
```

We have done exactly this sort of thing before with a statement like SUM = SUM + X. All we have done here is to change X to SHIRT(ROW, COLUMN). Here is the entire program.

Example 13.2 *Summing Rows of a Matrix*

```
100 REM -- Find total number of shirts of each size
110 REM -- Sizes are rows, colors are columns
120 DIM SHIRT(4, 3)
130 MAT READ SHIRT
140 PRINT "SMALL", "MEDIUM", "LARGE", "XLARGE"
150 FOR ROW = 1 TO 4
        SUM = 0
        FOR COLUMN = 1 TO 3
            SUM = SUM + SHIRT(ROW, COLUMN)
        NEXT COLUMN
        PRINT SUM,
    NEXT ROW
160 DATA 22, 12, 18
170 DATA 28, 17, 19
180 DATA 24, 14, 20
190 DATA 12, 10, 13
200 END
```

When the program is run, the result will be:

```
SMALL          MEDIUM         LARGE          XLARGE
 52             64             58             35
```

Notice the comma after PRINT SUM, which causes the four values of SUM to be typed on the same line in four separate print fields. Also, we set up the DATA statements to look like the matrix we are dealing with. This makes it easier to check the values in the DATA statements.

The MAT PRINT Statement

To print out the values of a matrix by methods we already know requires at least five statements:

```
REM -- Print matrix in one column
FOR ROW = 1 TO 4
    FOR COLUMN = 1 TO 3
        PRINT SHIRT(ROW, COLUMN)
    NEXT COLUMN
NEXT ROW
```

The same thing can be accomplished in VAX-BASIC by using the statement

```
MAT PRINT SHIRT
```

PRINT statements allow three kinds of punctuation: commas, semicolons, and no punctuation mark. The MAT PRINT statement allows the same kinds of punctuation with roughly the same effects. With no punctuation mark at the end of a MAT PRINT statement, each value will be printed on a separate line.

If we want a printed matrix to look like a matrix, then we need to use either a comma or semicolon. With the "old" method we would write

```
REM -- Print matrix in rows and columns
FOR ROW = 1 TO 4
    FOR COLUMN = 1 TO 3
        PRINT SHIRT(ROW, COLUMN),    ! Could also use ;
    NEXT COLUMN                      ! in place of,
    PRINT
NEXT ROW
```

Notice the comma at the end of the PRINT statement, which causes each succeeding value to be printed in the next print field of 14 columns. The blank PRINT after NEXT COLUMN causes each new ROW to be started on a new line. The single statement

```
MAT PRINT SHIRT,
```

accomplishes exactly the same thing; that is, it would type the matrix as:

```
22          12          18
28          17          19
24          14          20
12          10          13
```

For closer spacing, the statement

```
MAT PRINT SHIRT;
```

causes the matrix to appear as:

```
22  12  18
28  17  19
24  14  20
12  10  13
```

The comma results in good-looking matrices as long as there are not too many columns. On devices that allow 70 spaces for output, matrices with more than five columns will not look good because the sixth column will be printed below the first column.

The semicolon allows you to squeeze more columns into a line, but if the numbers vary greatly in size (some one-digit numbers and some in E-format), the columns will not line up very well. In our shirt example, all the values have two digits, so the semicolon lines the values up nicely. The comma and semicolon should serve well for most matrices you encounter. For special cases, see the discussion of PRINT TAB in Chapter 5.

The MAT INPUT Statement

Values for a matrix can be entered from the keyboard while a program is running. The statement that accomplishes this is the *MAT INPUT statement.* Suppose we want to input values for a 2-by-3 matrix (a matrix with 2 rows and 3 columns) and type out the matrix. We can write:

```
10 REM -- Input and print a 2 by 3 matrix
20 DIM A(2, 3)
30 PRINT "Give me six numbers";
40 MAT INPUT A
50 MAT PRINT A;
60 END
```

When this program is run, the computer will type

```
Give me six numbers?
```

and wait for you to type in numbers, separated by commas, and followed by ⟨RET⟩. If you type

```
1, 2, 3, 4, 5, 6 <RET>
```

after the ?, the computer will type´

```
1  2  3
4  5  6
```

If you type only four numbers in response to the ?, say

```
2, 4, 6, 8 <RET>
```

the computer will type

```
2  4  6
8  0  0
```

That is, the computer will fill up the matrix with zeros. If you type too many numbers in response to a MAT INPUT statement, the computer will ignore the excess numbers. For string-variable matrices, if you do not enter enough values to fill up the matrix, the computer will have null or empty strings ("") for the unspecified values.

When you must input more data than can be typed on one line, you can end a line with an ampersand (&) and continue typing data on the next line. Without the ampersand, the computer takes the ⟨RET⟩ to be the end of the input. For example:

```
10 DIM PLAYERS$(3, 3)
20 MAT INPUT PLAYERS$
30 MAT PRINT PLAYERS$,
40 END
```

Suppose that in response to the ? you type:

```
? Sampson, Jordan, Jabbar, Johnson, Bird&
? Thomas, Olajuwon
```

Then the computer will type

```
Sampson      Jordan       Jabbar
Johnson      Bird         Thomas
Olajuwon
```

Since we entered only seven names, the computer has two empty strings [PLAYER$(3, 2) and PLAYER$(3, 3)].

As with MAT READ, the MAT INPUT statement can dimension or redimension a matrix. The following are equivalent; any one of them will cause the computer to accept values for a 3-by-4 matrix.

| DIM A(3, 4) | DIM A(5, 5) | (No DIM statement) |
| MAT INPUT A | MAT INPUT A(3, 4) | MAT INPUT A(3, 4) |

If there is no DIM statement, then MAT INPUT A would cause the computer to put the input values into a 10-by-10 matrix.

Finding the Largest Number in Each Column of a Matrix

Consider the problem of finding the largest number in each column of the matrix. We have already written programs to find the largest number in a set of numbers, but the matrix notation and the fact that there are several largest numbers make this problem a little more complicated.

We will need variables to represent row and column numbers. We will use ROW and COL. We could decide now to use, say, four columns and six rows, but let's try to write a more general program and let NRCOL represent the number of columns and NRROW stand for the number of rows. For the entire matrix, use A.

For the largest numbers we have a choice. We could use one variable, LARGE, to represent all the largest numbers (one at a time), or we can use a subscripted variable LARGE so all the largest values can be stored at the same time. We will choose the latter course, not because it is necessary here, but because this program is likely to be part of a larger program in which it would be necessary to know all the largest numbers in the columns.

It should be clear that we need a loop

```
FOR COL = 1 TO NRCOL
```

and that the calculation of the largest number in each column will take place inside this loop. We will begin writing the part of the program inside the COL loop. For whatever value COL has, the largest number in the column will be designated LARGE(COL), and we begin by letting LARGE(COL) have the value of the first number in the column. That is,

```
LARGE(COL) = A(1, COL)
```

because A(1,COL) is the first element in the column numbered COL. We then compare the values in the remaining rows to LARGE(COL), so we have:

```
LARGE(COL) = A(1, COL)
FOR ROW = 2 TO NRROW
    IF A(ROW, COL) > LARGE(COL) THEN
        LARGE(COL) = A(ROW, COL)
    END IF
NEXT ROW
PRINT "Largest number in column"; COL; "is"; LARGE(COL)
```

We finish the program by putting the COL loop around the segment above and getting values into the matrix A. We will read NRROW, NRCOL, and the matrix. The full program follows.

Example 13.3 *Finding the Largest Number in Each Column of a Matrix*

```
100 REM -- Find largest in each column of a matrix
110 READ NRROW, NRCOL
120 DIM A(NRROW, NRCOL), LARGE(NRCOL)
130 MAT READ A
140 FOR COL = 1 TO NRCOL
        LARGE(COL) = A(1, COL)
        FOR ROW = 2 TO NRROW
            IF A(ROW, COL) > LARGE(COL) THEN
                LARGE(COL) = A(ROW, COL)
            END IF
        NEXT ROW
        PRINT "Largest number in column"; COL; "is"; LARGE(COL)
    NEXT COL
150 DATA 3, 6
160 DATA 23, 42, 56, 53, 49, -6
170 DATA 42, 37, 21, -25, 44, -56
180 DATA 38, 64, 21, -89, -92, 42
190 END

RUNNH

Largest number in column 1 is 42
Largest number in column 2 is 64
Largest number in column 3 is 56
Largest number in column 4 is 53
Largest number in column 5 is 49
Largest number in column 6 is 42
```

Notice the executable DIM statement in line 120.

13.2 MATRIX CALCULATIONS

This section can be skipped by those not familiar with matrix calculations.

Many operations that are used for numbers can also be used with matrices: addition, subtraction, and multiplication, for instance. However, in order to add or multiply two matrices A and B, there are restrictions on the sizes of A and B.

In order for the sum $A + B$ to be defined, A and B must have exactly the same size or dimension. Then the sum of A and B is a matrix C of the same size with

$$C(I, J) = A(I, J) + B(I, J)$$

That is, the element of C in a particular position is the sum of the elements of A and B in that same position.

Subtraction of matrices is defined in the same way, with a minus sign instead of a plus sign. If matrices A and B have been assigned values in a program, then the sum C can be calculated in VAX-BASIC with the single statement

```
MAT C = A + B
```

Similarly, the difference $A - B$ can be calculated and stored in a matrix D with the statement

```
MAT D = A - B
```

Remember that all the matrices should have been dimensioned exactly the same way.

There are, of course, some default rules. If A and B were dimensioned 2 by 3, and D were not dimensioned, then

```
MAT D = A - B
```

implicitly dimensions D to be 2 by 3. Also, A and B can be redimensioned in the MAT statment. For example:

```
DIM A(5, 5), B(3, 4)
.
.
MAT D = A(3, 4) + B
```

In the MAT statement, the first 3 rows and 4 columns of the matrix A are added to the matrix B, which was dimensioned 3 by 4. As before, redimensioning cannot increase the size of a matrix, and by default, the largest subscripts are 10 for matrices not specifically dimensioned.

Matrices A and B can be multiplied in the order $A * B$ if the number of columns in A is the same as the number of rows in B. That is, if A is a 3-by-5 matrix, then B must be 5 by something. When A is M by N and B is N by P, the product $A * B$ is an M-by-P matrix. If A is 3 by 5 and B is 5 by 4, then $A * B$ is 3 by 4.

The element of $A * B$ in the I row and J column is

$$A(I, 1) * B(1, J) + A(I, 2) * B(2, J) + \ldots + A(I, N) * B(N, J)$$

where N is the common number of columns in A and rows in B. To calculate a product matrix without a MAT statement would require triple-nested loops in BASIC, but in VAX-BASIC the product can be calculated and stored in a matrix P with a single statement:

```
MAT P = A * B
```

When we speak of the size of a matrix, we are ignoring the 0 row and 0 column. When MAT statements are used to add, subtract, and multiply matrices, VAX-BASIC does not use either the 0 rows or 0 columns of the matrices.

The following program illustrates matrix addition, subtraction, and multiplication.

Example 13.4 *Matrix Addition, Subtraction, and Multiplication*

```
100 REM -- Addition, subtraction, and multiplication of matrices
110 DIM A(3, 4), B(3, 4), C(4, 3), D(3, 4), E(4, 4), F(3, 3)
120 MAT READ A, B, C
130 !   Calculate sum A + B
    MAT D = A + B
    PRINT
    PRINT "Sum A + B"
    PRINT
    MAT PRINT D;
140 !   Difference A - B
    MAT D = A - B
    PRINT
    PRINT "Difference A - B"
    PRINT
    MAT PRINT D;
150 !   Product B*C
    MAT F = B * C
    PRINT
    PRINT "Product B*C"
    PRINT
    MAT PRINT F;
190 !   Product C*A
    MAT E = C * A
    PRINT
    PRINT "Product C*A"
    PRINT
    MAT PRINT E;
200 !   Matrix A
210 DATA  3, -4, -6,  8
220 DATA -5,  3,  8, -2
230 DATA  7, -1,  6,  3
240 !   Matrix B
```

```
250 DATA 6, 8,  3,  1
260 DATA 7, 3,  5, -3
270 DATA 5, 3, -8,  4
280 !   Matrix C
290 DATA  5, 8, -4
300 DATA -6, 3,  1
310 DATA  3, 2,  5
320 DATA -3, 1,  2
400 END


RUNNH


Sum A + B

 9  4 -3  9
 2  6  13 -5
12  2 -2  7

Difference A - B

-3 -12 -9  7
-12  0  3  1
 2 -4  14 -1

Product B*C

-12  79  1
 41  72 -6
-29  37 -49

Product C*A

-53  8  10  12
-26  32  66 -51
 34 -11  28  35
  0  13  38 -20
```

Special Matrices

VAX-BASIC has several MAT statements that allow matrices to be initialized with certain special values. A *zero matrix* is a special matrix containing all zeros. To set a matrix *C* equal to a zero matrix, use the statement

```
MAT C = ZER
```

C should already have been mentioned in a DIM statement. If it was not, VAX-BASIC assumes a 10-by-10 matrix of zeros is wanted. *C* can also be dimensioned or redimensioned by putting subscripts on ZER as in

```
MAT C = ZER(3, 5)
```

Similarly,

```
MAT C = CON
```

places a 1 in every row and column of *C* (except the 0 row and 0 column). Also,

```
MAT D$ = NUL$
```

places null strings in each row and column of a string-variable matrix D$.

An *identity matrix* is a square matrix (number of rows equals number of columns) with a zero in every position except for the diagonal elements, each of which has a 1. To set a matrix *Q* equal to an identity matrix, use the statement

```
MAT Q = IDN
```

if *Q* has been dimensioned, or a statement such as

```
MAT Q = IDN(4, 4)
```

to dimension or redimension *Q* when creating the identity matrix.

Example 13.5 *A Zero Matrix, an Identity Matrix, and a Matrix of Ones*

```
10 INPUT "How many rows and columns for a zero matrix"; M, N
20 MAT A = ZER(M, N)
   PRINT
   MAT PRINT A;
   PRINT
30 INPUT "How many rows and columns for a matrix of ones"; R, C
40 MAT B = CON(R, C)
   PRINT
   MAT PRINT B;
   PRINT
50 INPUT "How many rows for an identity matrix"; R
60 MAT C = IDN(R, R)
   PRINT
   MAT PRINT C;
   PRINT
70 END


RUNNH

How many rows and columns for a 0 matrix?  2, 2

 0   0
 0   0
```

How many rows and columns for a matrix of ones? `3, 4`

```
1   1   1   1
1   1   1   1
1   1   1   1
```

How many rows for an identity matrix? `4`

```
1   0   0   0
0   1   0   0
0   0   1   0
0   0   0   1
```

The *transpose* of an M by N matrix A is an N by M matrix whose rows are the columns of A. To transpose a matrix A means to obtain its transpose. We can get the matrix D to be the transpose of A with the statement

`MAT D = TRN(A)`

The *inverse* of a matrix B is a matrix C such that $B * C$ and $C * B$ are identity matrices. Only square matrices can have inverses (but not all square matrices). To get the inverse C of matrix B the appropriate statement is

`MAT C = INV(B)`

Then C is a square matrix with the same size as B.

To multiply a matrix by a constant means to multiply every element in the matrix by that constant—an operation called *scalar multiplication*. To multiply every element in a matrix A by 6, use the statement

`MAT D = (6)*A`

(The constant multiplier must be placed in parentheses.)

Example 13.6 *Transpose, Inverse, and Scalar Multiples*

```
10 PRINT "Enter 8 numbers for a 4 by 2 matrix"
20 MAT INPUT A(4, 2)
   MAT B = TRN(A)
   PRINT "The transpose of your matrix is"
   PRINT
   MAT PRINT B;
30 PRINT "Give me 4 numbers for a 2 by 2 matrix"
   MAT INPUT C(2, 2)
   PRINT
40 IF C(1, 1)*C(2, 2) = C(1, 2)*C(2, 1) THEN
      PRINT "Sorry, I can't invert that"
      GOTO 30
```

```
      END IF
      MAT D = INV(C)
      PRINT "The inverse of your matrix is"
      MAT PRINT D;
50 PRINT
      PRINT "The result of multiplying your matrix by 6 is"
      MAT E = (6)*C
      MAT PRINT E;
60 END
```

RUNNH

Give me 8 numbers for a 4 by 2 matrix
? 4, 7, 9, -8, 5, -2, 7, -4

The transpose of your matrix is
 4   9   5   7
 7 -8 -2 -4

Give me 4 numbers for a 2 by 2 matrix
? 4, 4, 4, 4

Sorry, I can't invert that

Give me 4 numbers for a 2 by 2 matrix
? 2, 3, 1, 2

The inverse of your matrix is

 2 -3
-1   2

The result of multiplying your matrix by 6 is

24 30
36 42

The IF statement in line 40 may look strange, but we said that not all square matrices had inverses, so this line is just protecting us from trying to invert a matrix that does not have an inverse. If you know about determinants, you will realize that the IF statement is checking to see if the determinant of the matrix is 0, in which case the matrix does not have an inverse.

There is one more function which is often useful in dealing with matrices. Associated with every square matrix is a number called the *determinant* of the matrix. We will not go into the details of how the determinant of a matrix is calculated. VAX-BASIC calculates the determinant of each matrix inverted and stores the value of the determinant in a variable called DET. (Thus, DET is a keyword in VAX-BASIC, and cannot be used as a variable name.) You can find the determinant of a square matrix *A* with an inverse by the following device:

```
MAT C = INV(A)
DETER = DET
PRINT "The determinant of A is"; DETER
```

Unfortunately, when DET is 0, the matrix *A* has no inverse, so if the determinant of *A* is 0, the statement MAT C = INV(A) will cause an error message to be printed and the program will stop without printing the value of DET. The ERR number for attempting to invert a noninvertible matrix is 56, so you can use an error handler and set DETER to 0 when the matrix cannot be inverted.

The MAT functions fall roughly into three categories, listed below.

Operations on two matrices	Initializing one matrix	Operations on one matrix
MAT C = A + B	MAT A = ZER	MAT B = TRN(A)
MAT D = A - B	MAT B = IDN	MAT C = INV(A)
MAT P = A * B	MAT C = CON	MAT B = (12)*A
	MAT D$ = NUL$	

Simultaneous Equations

A set of equations such as

$$2x + 3y - 4z = 9$$
$$5x - 2y - 3z = 8$$
$$x + 4y - 4z = 8$$

is called a system of *simultaneous linear equations.* A solution for such a system is a set of values for *x, y,* and *z* such that this one set of values simultaneously satisfies the three equations. In matrix notation, this set of equations can be represented by

```
A * X = B
```

where *A* is the 3-by-3 matrix of coefficients, *X* is the 3 by 1 matrix (or vector) of unknowns, and *B* is the 3 by 1 vector of constants on the right side of the equations. That is, we have:

Matrix A			Vector X	Vector B
2	3	-4	x	9
5	-2	-3	y	8
1	4	-4	z	8

The system has a unique solution when the matrix *A* has an inverse. Call the inverse of *A* the matrix *C.* Then the solution of the system is given by

```
X = C * B
```

Here is a program to find the solution of this system.

Example 13.7 *Solving a Simultaneous System of Equations*

```
10 REM -- Solution of simultaneous system (3 by 3)
20 DIM A(3, 3),B(3, 1),X(3, 1),C(3, 3)
30 MAT READ A, B
40 MAT C = INV(A)
50 MAT X = C * B
60 PRINT "The solution is "
   PRINT " X= "; X(1, 1)
   PRINT " Y= "; X(2, 1)
   PRINT " Z= "; X(3, 1)
70 DATA 2,  3, -4
   DATA 5, -2, -3
   DATA 1,  4, -4
   DATA 9,  8,  8
80 END

RUNNH

The solution is
 X = 4
 Y = 3
 Z = 2
```

You should check to see that these values do satisfy all three of the equations. Also, remember that this method works only when the coefficient matrix is square and has an inverse. The requirement that *A* be square simply means that there must be as many equations as there are unknowns. The requirement that *A* have an inverse is more complicated. The computer will let you know when *A* does not have an inverse by giving an error message when it tries to calculate INV(A) in line 40.

EXERCISES

For each problem, write a single program.

1. In the shirt example, calculate and print the total number of shirts of each pattern.

2. READ the size of a matrix and the values in the matrix. Find the largest number in the matrix.

3. INPUT a 4-by-4 matrix and print the sum of each row, the sum of each column, and the sum of the diagonal elements. (A diagonal element is an element with equal subscripts.)

4. In the shirt example, suppose small shirts cost $10, medium shirts cost $10.50, large shirts cost $11.00, and extra large shirts cost $11.50. Find the total value of the shirts on hand. Some appropriate matrix multiplication will make the calculations fairly short.

5. A magic square is an *N*-by-*N* matrix with elements 1, 2, 3, . . . , $N * N$, arranged in such a way that every row, every column, and both diagonals add up to the same total. Input the digits from 1 to 9 in some order into a 3-by-3 matrix. Print the square and tell whether it is a magic square.

6. Revise the Tic-Tac-Toe problem (Exercise A10 in Chapter 7) to use a 3-by-3 matrix for the board. Does this make keeping track of wins or draws easier or harder?

7. Read a 3 by 4 matrix. Find the product of this matrix times CON(4, 1) and the product of CON(1, 3) times this matrix. Say in words what happens when a matrix is multiplied on the right or the left by a CON vector.

8. Find the determinants of a 2 by 2 and a 3 by 3 matrix.

9. Solve the system of equations:

$$\begin{aligned} 3x + 4y + 5z - 2w &= -21 \\ 2x - 3y - 2z + 2w &= 21 \\ x + 5y + 3z &= -12 \\ 3y + 4z + 6w &= 9 \end{aligned}$$

10. In a matrix game, a matrix is written down, player *R* chooses a row, player *C* chooses a column, and the players simultaneously announce their choices. Then player *R* pays player *C* the amount in dollars found in the chosen row and column. Thus, if the matrix is

$$\begin{array}{rrrr} 2 & -3 & 4 & -3 \\ 5 & -2 & -4 & 1 \\ -4 & 3 & -1 & 2 \end{array}$$

and player *R* chooses row 1 and player *C* chooses column 3, then player *R* pays player *C* $4, the amount in row 1, column 3. When there is a negative amount in the position indicated by the choice of a row and a column, then player *R* receives this (positive) amount from player *C*. A conservative strategy for player *R* is to look at the largest number in each row, then choose the row which has the smallest of these largest numbers. Write a program that finds the largest number in each row, then finds the smallest of these numbers, and tells which row holds this smallest number.

11. Seven students in a class each took 5 tests. Read in a 7 by 5 matrix corresponding to the scores on the tests. Calculate the mean grade for each student and the mean grade for each test. Also, for each test score, calculate how far above or below the mean for the test that score is. Display these last results as a matrix.

12. Answers on a questionnaire are often cross-tabulated. That is, a matrix display is given showing the number of people who responded with each possible pair of answers to questions 1 and 2. For example, suppose question 1 is, "Are you male or female?" The obvious possible answers are "male" or "female." Suppose question 2 is, "Are you in favor of ERA?", with possible answers "yes," "no," and "don't know." Then the results of asking 50 people these questions might result in the following cross-tabulation:

	Question 2		
	Yes	No	Don't Know
Question 1 Male	11	9	2
Question 1 Female	18	6	4

Make up two hypothetical questions (or use these two) and answers given by 30 people. Print a cross-tabulation of the results. You might code answers as strings or numbers (e.g. 1 for yes, 2 for no, 3 for don't know). Which seems better?

REVIEW QUESTIONS

1. What will be the output from each of the following programs?

    a.
    ```
        DIM DRESS(4, 4)
    20  MAT READ DRESS
    30  PRINT "6", "8", "10", "12"
    40  MAT PRINT DRESS;
    50  DATA 30, 16, 25, 8
    60  DATA 12, 30, 15, 25
    70  DATA 16, 25, 20, 25
    80  DATA 20, 18, 11, 19
    90  END
    ```

    b.
    ```
    10  DIM A(4, 2)
    20  MAT READ A
    30  MAT PRINT A;
    40  PRINT MAXIM = MAX(A(1,1), A(1,2), A(1,3), A(1,4))
    50  PRINT MINIM = MIN(A(2,1), A(2,2), A(2,3), A(2,4))
    60  DATA  5, -2,  8, -9
    70  DATA -5,  7, -8  10
    80  END
    ```

    c.
    ```
    10  DIM A(3, 2), B(3, 2), C(3, 2)
    20  MAT READ A, B
    30  MAT C = A + B
    40  MAT PRINT A
    50  DATA 2, 1, 3, 4, 5, 6
    60  DATA 6, 5, 4, 3, 1, 2
    70  END
    ```

2. What is the size of each array below?

	Number of Rows	Number of Columns	Total Number of Elements
a. DIM A(14, 7 TO 10)	_____	_____	_____
b. DIM PHONE$(100, 4)	_____	_____	_____
c. DIM XYZ(−3 TO 2, 3)	_____	_____	_____
d. DIM R$(3 TO 5, 6 TO 9)	_____	_____	_____

3. *True or False.*

a. To set a matrix equal to the zero matrix use the statement MAT C = LEN.

b. The first value in the DIM statement is the number of columns and the second is the number of rows.

c. MAT READ A(2, 3) is equivalent to

```
FOR R = 1 TO 2
    FOR C = 1 TO 3
        READ A(R,C)
    NEXT C
NEXT R
```

d. To multiply two matrices (*A* and *B*), the number of columns in *A* must be the same as the number of rows in *B*.

4. The following program segment has a major flaw. Correct it and explain why it was incorrect.

```
210  REM -- Print the sum for each row
220  S = 0
230  FOR R = 1 TO 5
240      FOR C = 1 TO 5
250          S = S + A(R,C)
260      NEXT C
270      PRINT S
280  NEXT R
```

SUMMARY OF CHAPTER 13

CONCEPTS AND KEYWORDS INTRODUCED IN THIS CHAPTER

Concepts	Related statements and keywords
1. Matrix or two-dimensional array	
2. Reading matrices	MAT INPUT
	MAT READ
3. Printing matrices	MAT PRINT
4. Matrix calculations	MAT statements with +, −, and *
5. Initializing special matrices	ZER
	CON
	IDN
	NUL$
6. Obtain matrices related to a given matrix	INV
	TRN
7. Determinant of a matrix	DET

Random Numbers, Simulation, and Games

We discuss here the VAX-BASIC *RND function* and some of its applications to simulation and games. Generating a random number with RND is quite simple, but simulating real events with random numbers can become very involved.

14.1 THE RND FUNCTION

RND is one of the few VAX-BASIC functions that does *not* take an argument. The function can be used on the right hand side of an assignment statement, such as X = RND, or Y = 1 + INT(10*RND). It can be used in PRINT statements, such as PRINT 6*RND, or IF statements such as IF RND < .5 THEN PRINT "YES" ELSE PRINT "NO". When used, RND has an "unpredictable" value between 0 and .999999, inclusive. For simplicity we shall often say that RND takes a value from 0 to 1, but you should remember that it never gets quite as large as 1. Also, we shall call the numbers we get from RND "random" numbers, although "pseudorandom" would be more truthful.

To generate ten random numbers from 0 to 1 is as simple as:

```
10 PRINT RND, FOR I = 1 TO 10
20 END
```

On our VAX system, when this program is run, the result is:

.76308	.179978	.902878	.88984	.387011
.475943	.882193	.18578	.6388	.269213

You might get different results, but try running the program twice. You will get the same ten numbers the second time. (This is enough to prove that the numbers are not truly random.) To get different results each time a program is used, we need the statement RANDOMIZE or RANDOM near the top of the program:

```
10 RANDOMIZE
20 PRINT RND, FOR I = 1 TO 10
30 END
```

Now if this program is run several times, several different sets of numbers will be typed. The RANDOMIZE statement, in effect, tells the computer to pick a random starting number each time the program is run.

Programs containing RND do indeed seem to behave randomly, or unpredictably. The following program will respond pleasantly some of the time.

```
10 RANDOMIZE
20 INPUT "What's your name"; NAME$
30 IF RND < .7 THEN PRINT NAME$; " is a nice name."
              ELSE PRINT "I don't like the name "; NAME$
40 END
```

Try it several times. Roughly 70% of the time, RND should be less than .7, because 70% of the numbers from 0 to 1 are less than .7. The RND function generates numbers *uniformly*. That is, every possible number has roughly the same chance of occurring.

Random numbers between 0 and 1 are handy for dealing with probabilities, because probabilities are also numbers between 0 and 1. However, often we want random numbers in some range other than 0 to 1. To generate random numbers from 0 to 20, use 20*RND. (But remember that 20*RND will never be quite as large as 20, because RND can't be as large as 1.) If you want random (decimal) numbers between 0 and any number Z, use $Z*$RND. The most general rule is:

To get random decimal numbers from A to B, where A is less than B, use $(B - A)*$RND $+ A$.

The following program lets the user choose the limits A and B, then generates 15 random numbers from A to B and calculates their mean.

Example 14.1 *Generating Random Numbers: User Supplies Limits*

```
100 PRINT "I will give you 15 random numbers"
110 PRINT "between any limits you choose."
120 INPUT "Limits"; A, B
130 SUM = 0
140 FOR I = 1 TO 15
        Y = (B - A)*RND + A
        PRINT Y,
        SUM = SUM + Y
    NEXT I
```

```
150 PRINT \ PRINT
160 PRINT "The mean of the 15 numbers is"; SUM/15
170 END
```

```
RUNNH
```

```
I will give you 15 random numbers
between any limits you choose
Limits? 1, 2
   1.76308       1.17998        1.90288        1.88984        1.38701
   1.47594       1.88219        1.18578        1.6388         1.26921
   1.24668       1.13617        1.18302        1.78449        1.71652
```

```
The mean of the 15 numbers is 1.50944
```

If you want to use this program many times, insert a RANDOMIZE statement.

When someone says "Pick a number from 1 to 10," we generally assume the person means "Pick an *integer* from 1 to 10, inclusive." On many occasions we will want random integers in some range. To get random integers from 0 to 10, we would have to use INT(11 * RND). Notice that we multiply by 11, not 10, because 10 * RND will never be as large as 10. A simple way to remember this is to notice that there are 11 integers from 0 to 10. Generally, to get random integers from 0 to an integer N, use

```
INT( (N + 1) * RND )
```

Since we usually start counting with the number 1, we will often want to choose random integers from 1 to some number. To pick an integer from 1 to 10, first choose an integer from 0 to 9, then add 1. That is, we can get a random integer from 1 to 10 by using INT(10 * RND) + 1. (Ah, now we're back to multiplying by 10.) More generally, to get a random integer from 1 to N, use

```
INT(N * RND) + 1
```

Most generally (probably more generally than you wanted), to get a random integer from A to B inclusive, use

```
INT(B - A + 1) * RND) + A
```

(If A and B are integers, with A less than B, there are $B - A + 1$ integers from A to B inclusive.)

As a simple example, we will have the computer pick a random integer from 1 to 3 and ask you to guess the number.

Example 14.2 *A Guessing Game*

```
10 RANDOMIZE
20 Y = INT(3 * RND) + 1
30 PRINT "I am thinking of a number from 1 to 3."
```

```
40 INPUT "Guess what it is"; GUESS
50 IF GUESS = Y THEN
      PRINT "Great! You're psychic."
   ELSE
      PRINT "Sorry, the number was"; Y
   END IF
60 END
```

Run the program several times, at least until you get it to tell you both that you were right and that you were wrong.

There are times when we will want to choose several items from a list. One way to do this would be to number the items 1, 2, 3, etc., then put slips of paper with these same numbers on them in a hat, and have a blindfolded person draw numbers from the hat. (Remember the draft lottery?) This all sounds rather complicated. It is much easier to get the computer to "draw the numbers out of a hat." Incidentally, from now on, when we say something like "random number from 1 to 100," we shall mean *integer*. (If we want decimal numbers, we will specifically say so.)

A program that does nothing but pick ten random numbers from 1 to 100 is quite simple. Here it is.

```
10 REM -- Pick ten random numbers from 1 to 100
20 RANDOMIZE
30 PRINT INT(100 * RND) + 1; FOR I = 1 TO 10
40 END
```

```
RUNNH
```

```
 40  94  21  20  35  29  56  36  35  82
```

Often, this step of choosing random numbers is just a part of a larger program, and we need to save all the selected numbers. This can easily be done with subscripted variables. Just replace line 30 with

```
N(I) = INT(100 * RND) + 1 FOR I = 1 TO 10
```

and put in a DIM statement.

There is a possibility that two or more of the random numbers generated by the program above will be equal. Sometimes we don't care if there are "repeats," but sometimes we do. Suppose we pick ten people out of a group of 100. Obviously, we want ten *different* people. How can we guarantee that we get ten different numbers? In the example above, choosing ten people out of 100, we could simply run the program above. If it gives ten different numbers, fine. If not, run it again, and again if necessary, until it *does* give ten different numbers. We can't guarantee how many runs you would have to make, but almost certainly two or three would suffice.

This is not a very elegant way around the problem, though. Besides, what if we want to pick 99 out of 100? We might have to run the program several million times before we got 99 different numbers. So, of course, we will look for a better way. In fact, we will look for two better ways.

When we are looking for different random numbers, we often say we are "sampling without replacement." To use the analogy of the slips of paper in a hat, once a slip has been taken out of the hat, it cannot be selected again. This means that no number selected can match a number previously selected. And, of course, this gives us an idea for writing a program to accomplish the same thing.

Suppose the numbers we are selecting are in the range from 1 to some large number, and that we want relatively few of these numbers selected. To be concrete, suppose we want 50 numbers from 1 to 10,000, and we want the 50 numbers to be different. Then, each time we select a number, we will compare it to all the previously chosen numbers. If it matches a previously chosen number, then we discard it and choose a new number.

We said "compare it to all the previously chosen numbers." That implies we have saved all previously chosen numbers (by subscripting). So let's let an array R represent the 50 numbers to be selected. Obviously, we want a loop FOR I = 1 TO 50, and inside the loop we must select a number, different from all previous numbers, for R(I). To select a number in the range 1 to 10,000, we use the statement

```
X = INT(10000*RND) + 1
```

but before we assign this number X to R(I), we first check to see that it does not equal any of the previous numbers. The previous numbers are those elements of R with subscripts less than I, so to get subscripts for the previous numbers, we use a loop FOR J = 1 TO I − 1. The body of the I-loop is then:

```
140 X = INT(10000*RND) + 1
150 FOR J = 1 TO I - 1
160     IF X = R(J) THEN 140
170 NEXT J
180 R(I) = X
```

In line 160, if X is the same as any previously chosen number R(J), the computer goes back to line 140 to get a new "candidate" for R(I). The J loop goes until its normal completion only if X did not match any of the R(J) values, in which case line 180 assigns the number X to R(I). The entire program follows.

Example 14.3 *Drawing Random Numbers without Replacement*

```
100 REM -- Choose 50 different numbers from 1 to 10,000.
110 DIM R(50)
120 RANDOMIZE
130 FOR I = 1 TO 50
140     X = INT(10000 * RND) + 1
150     FOR J = 1 TO I - 1
160         IF X = R(J) THEN 140
170     NEXT J
180     R(I) = X
190 NEXT I
```

```
200 PRINT TAB(7 * (I - 1)); R(I); FOR I = 1 TO 50
210 END
```

```
RUNNH
```

```
2583  1823  4821  9277  7944  7521  2905  5295  3504  7478
4804  2353  8444  1990  3738  9220  1162  3707  8200  5782
8192  4391  7904  3947  725   8688  6627  1435  9219  1014
1187  8288  4036  9157  3254  3458  7609  5676  8221  6294
1081  5697  2864  5293  5897  7203  985   3953  8324  7404
```

Several points should be made concerning this program. First, it is not very general. In the exercises, you will be asked to make it more general by using variables instead of 50 and 10,000. Second, it is a pain to look through even 50 numbers to make certain that there are no duplicates. This pain can be alleviated by sorting the numbers, which you are also asked to do in the exercises.

Finally, notice line 150 FOR J = 1 TO I − 1. Does it bother you? It should at least make you ask, "What happens when I is 1?" Then line 150 is really saying FOR J = 1 TO 0. If you recall our discussion on FOR loops, you remember that the J loop is not executed in this case. That is, the first X will be assigned to R(1) without any checking in line 160. Fine. That's exactly what we want.

The program above works well when we take a relatively small fraction of the numbers in a given range. Suppose that we want to pick 500 numbers out of the numbers 1 to 500. (Why would we want to do this, you ask? We might be trying to put 500 people in a random order, or we might be trying to give 500 prizes to 500 people, and the prizes are worth different amounts, so we use the computer to assign prizes to people to avoid charges of personal prejudice.) If you use a modified form of the program above to select 500 numbers out of 500 numbers, the computer is going to be "spinning its wheels" for a long time trying to find the last few numbers. So when we are taking most of the numbers in a given range, a different approach is called for.

Consider the analogy of pieces of paper in a hat. When we take a piece of paper, we physically remove it from the hat so that it cannot be drawn again. Can we incorporate this idea in a program?

Suppose, for instance, we want to choose 95 numbers in the range from 1 to 100. We begin by "putting 100 numbers on pieces of paper." That is, we set up a subscripted variable with the values from 1 to 100. This is easily accomplished by a statement like

```
RANGE(I) = I FOR I = 1 TO 100
```

This makes RANGE(1) = 1, RANGE(2) = 2, . . . , RANGE(100) = 100. In other words, we start out with the numbers in order.

Now to choose the 95 numbers we use the following procedure:

1. Choose a number from 1 to 100 and put this number in the first position. That is, if the selected number is R, switch RANGE(R) and RANGE(1).

2. Choose a number R from 2 to 100 and switch RANGE(R) and RANGE(2).

3. Choose a number R from 3 to 100 and switch RANGE(R) and RANGE(3).

.

.

.

95. Choose a number R from 95 to 100 and switch RANGE(R) and RANGE(95).

At each step, all the numbers chosen on previous steps are removed from consideration. At step 95, for example, only six numbers remain to be chosen: RANGE(95), RANGE(96), . . . , RANGE(100).

The procedure outlined above requires a loop FOR STP = 1 TO 95. Inside the loop we must choose a random number from STP to 100. This can be done with

```
R = INT( (100 - STP + 1) * RND) + STP
```

Finally, we interchange RANGE(R) with RANGE(STP). The program follows.

Example 14.4 *Choosing "Most" of the Numbers in a Range*

```
100 RANDOMIZE
110 REM -- Select 95 numbers from 1 to 100
120 DIM RANGE(100)
130 RANGE(I) = I FOR I = 1 TO 100
140 FOR STP = 1 TO 95
150     R = INT( (100 - STP + 1)*RND) + STP
160     T = RANGE(R)
170     RANGE(R) = RANGE(STP)
180     RANGE(STP) = T
190 NEXT STP
200 PRINT "The 95 numbers are"
210 PRINT TAB(5 * (I - 1)); RANGE(I); FOR I = 1 TO 95
220 END


RUNNH

The 95 numbers are
 77  19  91  90  42  51  89  25  67  34  33  24  29  82  76  39
 68  50  96  54  27  36  8   93  63  56  100 35  43  40  86  37
 70  26  60  87  88  99  16  44  28  20  72  62  3   71  15  4
 64  98  95  94  18  11  49  74  58  41  59  84  81  12  30  80
 17  47  48  2   38  53  48  85  6   83  22  52  9   5   79  55
 32  61  1   69  57  92  75  7   21  66  13  23  65  14  10
```

Once again, the program is not general, and the numbers are not sorted. Those improvements are left as exercises.

There is a major distinction between this program and the previous one. In this program we subscripted the entire range of numbers from which we are selecting numbers. In the previous program we subscripted only the chosen numbers. If the range of the numbers is more than your computer can hold, then you have no choice but to use the first program. This is not much of a drawback; if you are selecting numbers from 1 to 1 million, you are not likely to choose a large fraction of those numbers.

When we are selecting *all* the numbers in a range, we are in effect randomly ordering the numbers in that range. This idea is useful in shuffling cards and, generally, in choosing random permutations of numbers. Notice that shuffling is the inverse of sorting; we begin with the numbers in order and proceed to mix them up.

EXERCISES A

1. Modify one of the random-number programs in this section so the random numbers generated are printed in increasing order.

2. Modify one of the random-number programs in this section so the computer will ask the user how many numbers are to be generated and the range of the numbers.

3. Generate 1000 random digits (0, 1, 2, . . . , 9) and count the number of times each digit appears.

4. Generate 50 different random integers from 1 to 100 and print them in increasing order. Use the following method:
   a. Begin with a subscripted variable with subscripts from 1 to 100.
   b. Generate a random number from 1 to 100. Call this number R.
   c. Check position R of the subscripted variable.
      (1) If position R has not already been chosen, put the number 1 in position R.
      (2) If position R has been chosen (it will have the value 1), then repeat step b.
   d. Repeat b and c 50 times.
   e. Print the positions that contain the value 1.

   Notice that this method avoids the problem of sorting the numbers after they are generated; the position numbers *are* in order.

5. Have the computer select a random number from 1 to 100 and ask the user to guess what the number is. The computer should then tell the user whether her guess was too high, too low, or just right. The user should be told to keep guessing until she gets the right number. The computer should keep track of how many guesses the user required to get the number.

14.2 SIMULATION AND GAMES

With the RND function the computer can be made to simulate or imitate many different processes that have random aspects. These processes can be as simple as tossing a coin or as complicated as dealing a bridge hand from a deck of cards. They can be as frivolous as rolling dice, or as serious as simulating the spread of a contagious disease or simulating the flight of a space ship. (NASA *does* simulate space flights many times on a computer before actual flights are made.)

A major goal in all simulations is realism. Something random must happen in a realistic way. We do not want coins to come up heads nearly every time, and we would not want a bowler to get a strike every time. To "make a coin come up heads" half the time, we would use a statement like

```
IF RND < .5 THEN PRINT "Heads" ELSE PRINT "Tails"
```

We would not use .9 in place of .5. In many problems the random numbers to use will be obvious, while in other problems there will be a wide range of choices that lead to "good" simulations.

A die, of course, is one-half of a pair of dice. When a die is tossed, it can "come up" 1, 2, 3, 4, 5, or 6. The six possibilities are equally likely, so each number from 1 to 6 should come up about one-sixth of the time. Let us use DIE to stand for the number that comes up. We could use logic like IF RND $<$ 1/6 THEN DIE $=$ 1, etc., but then we need 5 IF's to determine the value of DIE. It is simpler to generate a random number from 1 to 6 and let DIE be this number:

```
DIE = INT(6*RND) + 1
```

Then DIE should get each value from 1 to 6 roughly one-sixth of the time. Once we know how to "toss a die" on the computer, it is a simpler matter to toss it hundreds of times using a FOR statement. The program below simulates tossing a die 600 times and counts how many times each possible number came up. TOTAL(I) counts the total number of times I came up, where I can be any number from 1 to 6.

Example 14.5 *Tossing a Die*

```
100 RANDOMIZE
110 REM -- Toss a die 600 times and give frequencies
120 DIM TOTAL(6)
130 TOTAL(I) = 0 FOR I = 1 TO 6
140 FOR I = 1 TO 600
        DIE = INT(6*RND) + 1
        TOTAL (DIE) = TOTAL(DIE) + 1
150 NEXT I
160 PRINT "NUMBER", "FREQUENCY"
170 PRINT "------", "---------"
180 PRINT I, TOTAL(I) FOR I = 1 TO 6
190 END

RUNNH
```

NUMBER	FREQUENCY
1	95
2	107
3	92
4	95
5	99
6	112

Notice that the numbers do not come up with exactly the same frequency. We should be surprised if they did. But we do expect that each number will come up roughly one-sixth of the time.

Bowling

Bowling is a much more complicated example than die-throwing. Part of the complexity comes from the method of scoring, but generating good random numbers is also more complicated in bowling. For now we will ignore scoring and concentrate on getting the random numbers.

We use the ten-pin version of bowling. If all ten pins are knocked down with one ball, the bowler gets a strike. If fewer than ten pins fall on the first ball, the bowler is given a second ball. If the second ball knocks down all pins not knocked down by the first ball, the bowler gets a spare. The problem is to generate random numbers from 0 to 10 as possible numbers of pins knocked down by the first ball, and random numbers from 0 to the number of pins remaining to represent pins knocked down by the second ball.

Generating *some* random numbers to satisfy the requirements of the previous paragraph is not difficult. To get a random number from 0 to 10 for the first ball, use $R = INT(11 * RND)$. Then for the second ball (if necessary), there are $10 - R$ pins remaining, so generate a number from 0 to $10 - R$ by

```
S = INT( (10 - R + 1)*RND)
```

or

```
S = INT((11 - R) * RND)
```

In a full game of bowling, the bowler gets ten chances to throw at all ten pins. Each chance involves two throws unless the first throw is a strike, in which case the second throw is not necessary. The two attempts (sometimes one) constitute a "frame." Thus a full game of bowling involves ten frames. A program to give the results of each frame for ten frames is as follows.

Example 14.6 *Bowling*

```
100 REM -- Bowling: Results of ten frames
110 REM -- Poor bowler (or poor programmer)
120 RANDOMIZE
```

```
130 FOR FRAME = 1 TO 10
140     PRINT "Frame"; FRAME;
150     R = INT(11 * RND)        ! First ball
160     IF R = 10 THEN
            PRINT " Strike"
        ELSE
            S = INT((11 - R) * RND)        ! Second ball
            IF R + S = 10 THEN
                PRINT " Spare"
            ELSE PRINT R + S; "Pins"
            END IF
        END IF
170 NEXT FRAME
180 END

RUNNH

Frame 1   8 Pins
Frame 2   Spare
Frame 3   7 Pins
Frame 4   9 Pins
Frame 5   8 Pins
Frame 6   3 Pins
Frame 7   9 Pins
Frame 8   8 Pins
Frame 9   Strike
Frame 10  7 Pins
```

You should run the program several times. If you have ever bowled, the results should not appear too realistic. (If you have bowled only once in your life, maybe the program does appear realistic to you.) In any case, you should notice that there are very few strikes and not many spares either. The problem is that, on the first ball, every possibility from 0 to 10 is equally likely to occur, and on the second ball, every possibility from 0 to 10 − R is equally likely to occur. Someone who bowls as little as three or four times a year would do better than this. How can we change the probabilities to simulate a better bowler?

Let us try to simulate a very good bowler, someone who gets strikes or spares nearly all the time. First we deal with the problem of the first ball in a frame. Instead of generating random numbers from 0 to 10, we will get numbers from 1 to 100, thus giving us quite a bit of freedom in varying probabilities. For example, if we think this bowler should get a strike 48% of the time, we can let the numbers from 53 to 100 represent a strike (or ten pins on the first ball). Let us assume that 48% is reasonable. What about the other possibilities? When a very good bowler does not get a strike, he or she usually gets 7, 8, or 9 pins. We can get a probability of .14 for 9 pins by letting the numbers from 39 to 52 (14 numbers) represent the probability of getting 9 pins. We can continue in this way, asssuming "reasonable" probablities for each possible score. We will use the following table to determine what number of pins is knocked down on the first ball.

Number of pins on first ball	Range of numbers from 1 to 100	Theoretical probability
10	53–100	.48
9	39–52	.14
8	27–38	.12
7	18–26	.09
6	12–17	.06
5	7–11	.05
4	6	.01
3	4–5	.02
2	3	.01
1	2	.01
0	1	.01

Now, anyone can argue with the assignments. The important thing here is the method. First estimate the probability of a result, then choose that fraction of 100 numbers to represent the result. We chose 1 number (from 100 numbers) to represent 0 pins, because we are assuming that a very good bowler will get 0 pins .01 of the time. We chose 12 numbers to represent 8 pins because we assume the bowler gets 8 pins 12% of the time. If this problem meant a great deal to us, we would record scores for thousands of frames played by very good bowlers and see how often they got each possible score.

To store these numbers in the computer, we will use a subscripted variable PINS. PINS(1) will be 0, PINS(2) will be 1, etc., and PINS(53) through PINS(100) will all be 10. When a random number, say X, is chosen in the range from 1 to 100, then we will say that the number of pins knocked down is PINS(X). Since all values for X from 53 to 100 have PINS(X) = 10, then the bowler should get a strike 48% of the time.

To use this table in the bowling program, we change the program as follows:

Example 14.7 *Generating Nonuniform Random Numbers from a Table*

```
100 RANDOMIZE
110 REM -- Bowling: Results of ten frames
120 REM -- Set up table for probabilities of various
130 REM -- numbers of pins on the first ball
140 DIM PINS(100)
150 PINS(1) = 0 \ PINS(2) = 1 \ PINS(3) = 2
160 PINS(4), PINS(5) = 3
170 PINS(6) = 4
180 PINS(I) = 5 FOR I = 7 TO 11
190 PINS(I) = 6 FOR I = 12 TO 17
200 PINS(I) = 7 FOR I = 18 TO 26
210 PINS(I) = 8 FOR I = 27 TO 38
220 PINS(I) = 9 FOR I = 39 TO 52
230 PINS(I) = 10 FOR I = 53 TO 100
240 REM -- Now bowl the ten frames
250 FOR FRAME = 1 TO 10
260    PRINT "Frame"; FRAME;
270    X = INT(100 * RND) + 1
```

```
280     R = PINS(X)              ! New method for first ball
        IF R = 10 THEN
            PRINT " Strike"
        ELSE
            S = INT((11 - R) * RND)
            IF R + S = 10 THEN
                PRINT " Spare"
            ELSE PRINT R + S; "Pins"
            END IF
        END IF
290 NEXT FRAME
300 END


RUNNH


Frame 1 Strike
Frame 2 Strike
Frame 3 9 Pins
Frame 4 Strike
Frame 5 Strike
Frame 6 9 Pins
Frame 7 Strike
Frame 8 7 Pins
Frame 9 Strike
Frame 10 Strike
```

Most of the change in the program is due to lines 140–230, which store the values in the array PINS. The other change is in lines 270 and 280, where we first generate a random number X from 1 to 100, then let the number of pins R be the number in PINS(X). There should now be strikes nearly half the time. We have not, however, changed the method of getting random numbers of pins for the second ball, so there are still not enough spares.

Generating Nonuniform Random Numbers with a Function

The problem is: when 3 pins are left standing by the first ball, the method we are using for the second ball makes the possibilities 0, 1, 2, 3 equally likely on the second ball. We would like to increase the probability of 3 and decrease the probability of 0 pins. Let's consider a problem that does just the opposite. That is, let us try to give 0 a high probability and 3 a low probability.

Remember that RND gives values less than 1, and if a number less than 1 is squared, the result is smaller that the original number. That is, if $0 < Y < 1$, then $Y**2 < Y$. Then if we write

```
S = INT(4 * RND**2)
```

we will still get random numbers S from 0 to 3, but 0 will occur more than one-fourth of the time and 3 will occur less than one-fourth of the time. We can make S equal to 0

even more frequently by taking a power higher than 2. For example, we might take
S = INT(4 * RND**6). This "power method" makes the random numbers RND**6
pile up near 0. To get the numbers to pile up at the high end of the range, just subtract
the RND**6 from 1. That is, use

```
S = INT(4 * (1 - RND**6))
```

Of course, in the bowling program, we want a number from 0 to 10 − R, so we will use
the statement

```
S = INT((11 - R) * (1 - RND**6))
```

Try the bowling program with this statement for the number of pins on the second
ball. You should get more spares. Also, try some powers other than 6.

Even with these changes to the bowling program, you should not consider the
matter closed. In simulations, there is almost always room for improvement, and
much tinkering with probabilities is often necessary before everyone agrees that the
simulation is truly realistic.

Card Games; Shuffling a Deck of Cards

Many programmers enjoy simulating card games on the computer, and many card
games can be simulated. The computer can be made to play blackjack or poker with
an opponent, or the computer can play solitaire or bid a bridge hand, either alone or
with a partner. The starting point for any of these exercises is setting up a shuffled
deck of cards in the computer. The computer does not know anything about cards; it
deals with numbers. We, the programmers, are the ones who must make cards out of
numbers. One way to do this will be discussed here.

When you open a new pack of playing cards, the cards are in order. Reading
from the bottom of the deck, one usually finds the ace of clubs, 2 of clubs, etc., up to
the king of clubs, then the diamonds, beginning with the ace, then the hearts, and
finally the spades. We can number the cards from 1 to 52, so that 1 represents the ace
of clubs, 13 the king of clubs, 27 the ace of hearts, etc. Each card has a suit and a
denomination. Our problem is to find the particular suit and particular denomination
corresponding to any number from 1 to 52.

First let us concentrate on the suit. We can store the four suits in a subscripted
variable SUIT$. Explicitly, we want

$$\begin{aligned}
\text{SUIT\$}(0) &= \text{``clubs''} \\
\text{SUIT\$}(1) &= \text{``diamonds''} \\
\text{SUIT\$}(2) &= \text{``hearts''} \\
\text{SUIT\$}(3) &= \text{``spades''}
\end{aligned}$$

To find the suit corresponding to a certain number, we need roughly to divide the
number by 13 and take the integer part of the quotient. For example, 38 divided by 13
gives 2, so the suit for card 38 is suit number 2 or hearts. Similarly, 7 divided by 13
gives 0, so the card numbered 7 belongs in the 0 suit, clubs. This device fails for cards

numbered 13, 26, 39, and 52. We know, for example, that 26 should be the king of diamonds (suit 1), but 26 divided by 13 gives 2, so the rule we are using would put card 26 in the heart suit (suit 2). We can fix up the rule by first subtracting 1 from the card number, then dividing by 13. If we let SUIT stand for the number of the suit and CARD stand for the number of the card, then the rule is:

```
SUIT = INT( (CARD - 1)/ 13 )
```

This rule can be checked by writing a simple program and finding the suit corresponding to several numbers in the range from 1 to 52, as in the following program.

Example 14.8 *Card Games; Finding Suits for Various Numbers*

```
100 REM -- Find suit corresponding to various numbers
110 DIM SUITS$(3)
120 READ SUITS$(I) FOR I = 0 TO 3
130 ANS$ = "YES"
140 WHILE ANS$ = "YES"
150     INPUT "Number from 1 to 52"; CARD
160     SUIT = INT( (CARD - 1)/13 )
170     PRINT "The suit for"; CARD; "is "; SUITS$(SUIT)
180     INPUT "Try again (YES or NO)"; ANS$
190 NEXT
200 DATA clubs, diamonds, hearts, spades
210 END

RUNNH

Number from 1 to 52? 27
The suit for 27 is Hearts
Try again (YES or NO)? YES
Number from 1 to 52? 26
The suit for 26 is Diamonds
Try again (YES or NO)? NO
```

Next we must find the denomination corresponding to a card number. We will store the denominations in a subscripted variable DEN$ with DEN$(1) = "ace", DEN$(2) = "two", DEN$(3) = "three", . . . , DEN$(13) = "king". How do we find the denomination for a number such as 38? Numbers 1 to 13 stand for clubs, 14 to 26 are diamonds, and 27 to 39 are hearts, so card 38 is a heart. Which heart is it? We know that the number of the last diamond is 26, so card 38 is the 12th heart (12 = 38 − 26), and the 12th denomination is queen. Thus, 38 stands for the queen of hearts. In general, let DEN stand for the denomination number, and let CARD and SUIT be as before. Then

```
DEN = CARD - 13 * SUIT
```

We can now revise the suit program to print out both the suit and denomination of a card represented by a number from 1 to 52.

Example 14.9 *Card Games; Finding Suit and Denomination*

```
100 REM -- Print card suit and denomination
110 DIM SUIT$(3), DEN$(13)
120 READ SUIT$(I) FOR I = 0 TO 3
130 READ DEN$(I) FOR I = 1 TO 13
140 ANS$ = "YES"
150 WHILE ANS$ = "YES"
        INPUT "Number from 1 to 52"; CARD
        SUIT = INT( (CARD - 1)/13 )
        DEN = CARD - 13 * SUIT
        PRINT CARD; "is the "; DEN$(DEN); " of "; SUIT$(SUIT)
        INPUT "Try again (YES or NO)"; ANS$
    NEXT
160 DATA clubs, diamonds, hearts, spades
170 DATA ace, two, three, four, five, six, seven
180 DATA eight, nine, ten, jack, queen, king
190 END

RUNNH

Number from 1 to 52? 23
23 is the ten of diamonds
Try again (YES or NO)? YES
Number from 1 to 52? 44
44 is the five of spades
Try again (YES or NO)? NO
```

So far, we have done nothing random. We have simply been concerned with representing cards by numbers. The random part comes in when we try to shuffle the deck. Shuffling, like sorting, requires that the computer know all the numbers at one time, so we will subscript the variable CARD and begin with the cards in order. That is, we begin with

```
CARD(I) = I FOR I = 1 TO 52
```

and then shuffle the subscripted variable CARD. We have already seen how to get numbers from 1 to any number in random order, so let's write the program to shuffle and print a deck of cards.

Example 14.10 *Card Games; Shuffling a Deck of Cards*

```
100 REM -- Shuffle and print a deck of cards.
110 RANDOMIZE
120 DIM CARD(52), SUIT$(3), DEN$(13)
130 !         Read suits and denominations.
140 READ SUIT$(I) FOR I = 0 TO 3
150 READ DEN$(I) FOR I = 1 TO 13
160 !         Begin with deck "in order".
170 CARD(I) = I FOR I = 1 TO 52
```

```
180 !        Shuffle the deck
190 FOR I = 1 TO 52
200   R = INT(52 * RND) + 1  ! Get random card.
210   TEMP    = CARD(R)      ! Switch the random
220   CARD(R) = CARD(I)      !   card with
230   CARD(I) = TEMP         ! card numbered I.
240 NEXT I
250 !        Print the shuffled deck.
260 FOR I = 1 TO 52
270   SUIT = INT( (CARD(I) - 1)/13 )
280   DEN = CARD(I) - 13 * SUIT
290   PRINT  DEN$(DEN ); " of "; SUIT$(SUIT)
300 NEXT I
310 DATA Clubs, Diamonds, Hearts, Spades
320 DATA Ace, Two, Three, Four, Five, Six, Seven
330 DATA Eight, Nine, Ten, Jack, Queen, King
340 END


RUNNH


King of Hearts
Three of Diamonds
Four of Spades
Six of Clubs
   etc.
```

This program is just the beginning of any program to do something with a deck of cards. A couple of suggestions are in order. First, leave out the RANDOMIZE statement until you are sure the program is running properly. This will help you to see if the program is doing as it should. Second, leave in the PRINT loop (lines 260–300) for the same reason. If your program has the computer deal two hands, one to you and one to itself, you will then know what is in the computer's hand (and you will know if the computer dealt you the proper cards).

EXERCISES B

1. Modify the bowling program so the computer keeps score. A strike is scored as 10 points *plus* the number of pins knocked down by the next two balls. A spare is scored as 10 points plus the number of pins knocked down on the next ball. When the bowler gets a strike or spare in the tenth frame, he or she must roll two more balls or one more ball to get a final score.

2. Simulate tossing a pair of dice and print the total showing on the two dice. Repeat this 1000 times and count how many times each possible total comes up.

3. The game of craps is played by tossing a pair of dice. If the total on the dice for the first toss is:
   a. 7 or 11, the player is an immediate winner;
   b. 2, 3, or 12, the player is an immediate loser;

c. any total *not* given in a or b, then this total is called the player's POINT, and
play continues until the player tosses
   (1) this same point, in which case he wins;
        or
   (2) a total of 7, in which case he loses.
Write a program to simulate a game of craps.

4. Simulate one game of a tennis match. Let the server have probability of .55 of
winning each point. If you are not familiar with tennis scoring, use the following
rule: To win the game, a player must have 4 or more points *and* must be ahead of
her opponent by *at least* two points.

5. To get some idea of the probability of a tennis player's winning a game when we
know the probability of her winning a point, we can run the previous program
many times and count the fraction of games she wins. Write a program that
"runs" the previous program 1000 times and gives the fraction of times that the
server won the game.

6. Write a program to play some card game (or part of a game) with the computer.
It helps to play a game you know quite well; even then, programming a computer
to play cards is not easy. It is probably best to avoid games that require cards to
be removed from, and added to, hands. Some possibilities are:
   a. Get the computer to deal itself one bridge hand and make a reasonable bid.
   b. Have the computer deal two hands, one to you and one to itself, and play
      blackjack (twenty-one).
   c. Have the computer deal a five-card hand for poker and evaluate the hand (tell
      whether the hand contains a pair, a straight, a flush, etc.). If that's not too
      hard for you, get the computer to play draw poker with you.

7. First, simulate one play of a football game. Draw up a table, giving "all" the
possible things that can happen: gains of a certain number of yards; losses; fum-
bles; intercepted passes; etc. Then put "reasonable" probabilities on each of
these occurrences. When this program is running to your satisfaction, try several
plays until the team with the ball either makes a first down or has to give up the
football.

REVIEW QUESTIONS

1. Write BASIC statements to print the following:
   a. A nonnegative random number (not necessarily an integer) less than 4.
   b. A random number less than 3 but not less than −5.
   c. A random integer between 6 and 12, inclusive.
   d. A random number from the set [1, 3, 5, 7, 9].

2. What will be the output from each of the following programs? Just describe the
output in words, as for example: "Five random integers from 6 to 10 inclusive
will be printed on one line."
   a.   FOR I = 1 TO 5
            PRINT RND
          NEXT I

b.   FOR I = 1 TO 5
           PRINT 10*RND,
       NEXT I
c.   FOR I = 1 TO 5
           PRINT 10*RND + 20;
       NEXT I
d.   FOR I = 1 TO 5
           PRINT INT(10*RND + 100)
       NEXT I

3. Given that the RND function produces a "random number" X such that $0 \le X < 1$, what would be the range of Y if Y were assigned a value with the following statement?

Y = 5*RND - 2

SUMMARY OF CHAPTER 14

CONCEPTS AND KEYWORD INTRODUCED IN THIS CHAPTER

Concepts	Related keyword
1. Generate random numbers in a given range	RND
2. Generate random numbers with no duplicates	
3. Use random numbers to simulate real situations	
4. Use random numbers to play games	

Appendix A

Reserved Words in VAX-BASIC

Reserved words have special meanings in VAX-BASIC and cannot be used as names of variables, programs, functions, or subroutines.

RESERVED KEYWORD LIST

%ABORT	ACCESS	BINARY	CLOSE
%CDD	ACCESS%	BIT	CLUSTERSIZE
%CROSS	ACTIVATE	BLOCK	COLOR
%ELSE	ACTIVE	BLOCKSIZE	COM
%END	ALIGNED	BS	COMMON
%FROM	ALLOW	BUCKETSIZE	COMP%
%IDENT	ALTERNATE	BUFFER	CON
%IF	AND	BUFSIZE	CONNECT
%INCLUDE	ANGLE	BY	CONSTANT
%LET	ANY	BYTE	CONTIGUOUS
%LIBRARY	APPEND	CALL	CONTINUE
%LIST	AREA	CASE	COS
%NOCROSS	AS	CAUSE	COT
%NOLIST	ASC	CCPOS	COUNT
%PAGE	ASCII	CHAIN	CR
%PRINT	ASK	CHANGE	CTRLC
%SBTTL	AT	CHANGES	CVT$$
%THEN	ATN	CHECKING	CVT$%
%TITLE	ATN2	CHOICE	CVT$F
%VARIANT	BACK	CHR$	CVT%$
ABORT	BASE	CLEAR	CVTF$
ABS	BASIC	CLIP	DAT
ABS%	BEL	CLK$	DAT$

DATA	FNAME$	JUSTIFY	NOPAGE
DATE$	FNEND	KEY	NOREWIND
DEACTIVATE	FNEXIT	KILL	NOSPAN
DECIMAL	FONT	LBOUND	NOT
DECLARE	FOR	LEFT	NUL$
DEF	FORMAT$	LEFT$	NUM
DEFAULTNAME	FORTRAN	LEN	NUM$
DEL	FREE	LET	NUM1$
DELETE	FROM	LF	NUM2
DESC	FSP$	LINE	NX
DET	FSS$	LINES	NXEQ
DEVICE	FUNCTION	LINO	OF
DIF$	FUNCTIONEND	LINPUT	ON
DIM	FUNCTIONEXIT	LIST	ONECHR
DIMENSION	GE	LOC	ONERROR
DOUBLE	GET	LOCKED	OPEN
DOUBLEBUF	GETRFA	LOG	OPTION
DRAW	GFLOAT	LOG10	OPTIONAL
DUPLICATES	GO	LONG	OR
DYNAMIC	GOBACK	LSA	ORGANIZATION
ECHO	GOSUB	LSET	OTHERWISE
EDIT$	GOTO	MAG	OUTPUT
ELSE	GROUP	MAGTAPE	OVERFLOW
END	GT	MAP	PAGE
EQ	HANDLE	MAR	PATH
EQV	HANDLER	MAR%	PEEK
ERL	HEIGHT	MARGIN	PI
ERN$	HFLOAT	MAT	PICTURE
ERR	HT	MAX	PLACE$
ERROR	IDN	METAFILE	PLOT
ERT$	IF	MID	POINT
ESC	IFEND	MID$	POINTS
EXIT	IFMORE	MIN	POS
EXP	IMAGE	MIX	POS%
EXPAND	IMP	MOD	PPS%
EXPLICIT	IN	MOD%	PRIMARY
EXTEND	INACTIVE	MODE	PRINT
EXTENDSIZE	INDEX	MODIFY	PROD$
EXTERNAL	INDEXED	MOVE	PROGRAM
FF	INFORMATIONAL	MULTIPOINT	PROMPT
FIELD	INITIAL	NAME	PUT
FILE	INKEY$	NEXT	QUO$
FILESIZE	INPUT	NO	RAD$
FILL	INSTR	NOCHANGES	RANDOM
FILL$	INT	NODATA	RANDOMIZE
FILL%	INTEGER	NODUPLICATES	RANGE
FIND	INV	NOECHO	RCTRLC
FIX	INVALID	NOEXTEND	RCTRLO
FIXED	ITERATE	NOMARGIN	READ
FLUSH	JSB	NONE	REAL

RECORD	SEVERE	SUBROUTINE	UPDATE
RECORDSIZE	SGN	SUM$	USAGE$
RECORDTYPE	SHEAR	SWAP%	USEROPEN
RECOUNT	SHIFT	SYS	USING
REF	SI	TAB	USR$
REGARDLESS	SIN	TAN	VAL
RELATIVE	SINGLE	TEMPORARY	VAL%
REM	SIZE	TERMINAL	VALUE
REMAP	SLEEP	TEXT	VARIABLE
RESET	SO	THEN	VARIANT
RESTORE	SP	TIM	VFC
RESUME	SPACE	TIME	VIEWPOINT
RETRY	SPACE$	TIME$	VIRTUAL
RETURN	SPAN	TO	VPS%
RFA	SPEC%	TRAN	VT
RIGHT	SQR	TRANSFORM	WAIT
RIGHT$	SQRT	TRANSFORMATION	WARNING
RMSSTATUS	STATUS	TRM$	WHEN
RND	STEP	TRN	WHILE
ROTATE	STOP	TYP	WINDOW
ROUNDING	STR$	TYPE	WINDOWSIZE
RSET	STREAM	TYPE$	WITH
SCALE	STRING	UBOUND	WORD
SCRATCH	STRING$	UNALIGNED	WRITE
SEG$	STYLE	UNDEFINED	XLATE
SELECT	SUB	UNIT	XLATE$
SEQUENTIAL	SUBEND	UNLESS	XOR
SET	SUBEXIT	UNLOCK	ZER
SETUP	SUBSCRIPT	UNTIL	

Appendix B

ASCII Codes and Character Representation

Decimal code	Character	Decimal code	Character	Decimal code	Character	Decimal code	Character
0	NUL	32	SP	64	@	96	'
1	SOH	33	!	65	A	97	a
2	STX	34	"	66	B	98	b
3	ETX	35	#	67	C	99	c
4	EOT	36	$	68	D	100	d
5	ENQ	37	%	69	E	101	e
6	ACK	38	&	70	F	102	f
7	BEL	39	'	71	G	103	g
8	BS	40	(	72	H	104	h
9	HT	41	)	73	I	105	i
10	LF	42	*	74	J	106	j
11	VT	43	+	75	K	107	k
12	FF	44	,	76	L	108	l
13	CR	45	-	77	M	109	m
14	SO	46	.	78	N	110	n
15	SI	47	/	79	O	111	o
16	DLE	48	0	80	P	112	p
17	DC1	49	1	81	Q	113	q
18	DC2	50	2	82	R	114	r
19	DC3	51	3	83	S	115	s
20	DC4	52	4	84	T	116	t
21	NAK	53	5	85	U	117	u
22	SYN	54	6	86	V	118	v
23	ETB	55	7	87	W	119	w
24	CAN	56	8	88	X	120	x
25	EM	57	9	89	Y	121	y
26	SUB	58	:	90	Z	122	z
27	ESC	59	;	91	[	123	{
28	FS	60	<	92	\	124	|
29	GS	61	=	93	]	125	}
30	RS	62	>	94	^	126	~
31	US	63	?	95	_	127	DEL

Appendix C

VAX-BASIC Functions

C.1 BASIC FUNCTIONS

The following functions are in the text in the order they appear.

Chapter 3	SQR, INT
Chapter 5	TAB
Chapter 8	ERR, ERL
Chapter 9	ABS, MAX, MIN, MOD, SGN, FIX, SIN, COS TAN, ATN, EXP, LOG, LOG10, TIME
Chapter 10	LEN, POS, SEG$, LEFT$, RIGHT$, TRM$, EDIT$ SPACES$, STRING$, TIME$, DATE$, ASCII, CHR$ VAL, VAL%, STR$, SUM$, DIF$
Chapter 13	ZER, CON, NUL$, IDN, TRN, INV, DET
Chapter 14	RND

C.2 ADDITIONAL BASIC FUNCTIONS

The following are some additional functions supported by VAX-BASIC. For futher information on these and other functions check the Digital VAX-11 BASIC Documentation.

CCPOS	Returns the current character or cursor position on a specified channel.
COMP%	Compares two numeric functions.

303

CTRLC	Enables CTRL/C trapping.
ECHO	Enables echoing on a specified channel (see also NOECHO).
ERN$	Returns the name of the program unit (main program, subprogram, or DEF) containing the error.
ERT$	Returns the text of an error specified by an error number as input.
FORMAT$	Converts a numeric value to a string.
LOC	Returns a longword integer specifying the virtual address of a variable or symbol.
MAR	Returns the margin width of a specified channel.
MID$	Extracts a substring from a string by specifying the string's starting position and length.
NOECHO	Disables echoing on a specified channel.
NUM	Returns the row number of the last data element transferred into an array by a MAT I/O statement.
NUM2	Returns the column number of the last data element transferred into an array by MAT I/O statement.
NUM$	Evaluates a numeric expression and returns a string of characters formatted as the PRINT statement would format it.
NUM1$	Translates a number into a string of numeric characters.
PLACE$	Changes the precision of a numeric string; returns a numeric string, truncated or rounded to a specified value.
PROD$	Returns a numeric string that is the product of two numeric strings.
QUO$	Returns a numeric string that is the quotient of two numeric strings.
RCTRLC	Disables CTRL/C trapping.
RECOUNT	Contains the number of characters (bytes) read after each input operation.
STATUS	Accesses the status word containing characteristics of the last opened file.
SWAP%	Transposes an integer's two low-order bytes.
XLATE	Translates one string to another by referencing a table provided by the user.

BASIC does not operate independent of the rest of the computer system. Often it is necessary to move from within BASIC to the VMS system level, or DCL level. (DCL stands for Digital Command Language.) At this level, DCL prompts for input with the dollar sign ($). You can enter many commands that simplify your work with BASIC programs and help you to interact with the computer.

D.1 COMPILING AND EXECUTING A BASIC PROGRAM

Once a program has been created, debugged, tested, and saved by the programmer, it may be advisable to compile and link the program so that it can be RUN from the Digital Command Level. This increases the speed of the program execution and utilizes the VAX computer system most efficiently.

For example, assume the program given here has been saved in your acount in a directory with the BASIC SAVE command.

```
10 REM -- Sort 10 numbers into ascending order
20 DIM X(10)
30 READ X(I) FOR I = 1 TO 10
40 FOR STP = 1 TO 9
        FOR J = (STP + 1) TO 10
            IF X(J) < X(STP) THEN
                TEMP    = X(J)
                X(J)    = X(STP)
                X(STP) = TEMP
            END IF
```

```
     NEXT J
50 NEXT STP
60 PRINT "The values in ascending order are:"
70 PRINT X(I); FOR I = 1 TO 10
80 DATA 34, -42, 49, 66, -52, -12, 68, 26, -6, 39
90 END

RUNNH

The values in ascending order are:
-52  -42  -12  -6  26  34  39  49  66  68

SAVE  SORT
 Ready
 EXIT
$
```

The following sequences of commands will compile, link and execute the program SORT.

```
$ BASIC  SORT
$ LINK  SORT
$ RUN  SORT
```

These three commands will generate two new files in your directory and execute the program. The $ BASIC command creates a SORT.OBJ file which is a linkable object module produced from SORT.BAS (the highest version number). The $ LINK command creates an executable image file SORT.EXE from the SORT.OBJ file. The $ RUN command causes the SORT.EXE program to be executed. In addition to this simple procedure there are additional qualifiers that can be used with the BASIC, LINK, and RUN commands. The following is a list of some BASIC DCL command qualifiers:

QUALIFIER	USE
CHECK	Check for overflow
CROSS	Create a cross-reference listing
DEBUG	Enable VAX Debugger
DOUBLE	64 bits of precision for floating point data
LINES	Report line number of incorrect statements
LIST	Create a source listing
MACHINE	Include object codes in listing
OBJECT	Produce object file
WORD	16-bit integer (LONG is DEFAULT)

For example, the following command

```
$ BASIC / LIST = SORT.LIS / DOUBLE
```

creates a SORT.LIS listing and an object file SORT.OBJ with double-precision floating-point data.

Once in BASIC, an object module can also be created with the COMPILE command

```
$ BASIC
 VAX-11 BASIC
 Ready
 OLD SORT
 Ready
 COMPILE
 Ready
 EXIT
$
```

All the BASIC qualifiers can be used with the COMPILE Command.

The LINK command has its own set of qualifiers. The following is a list of some of the available options:

QUALIFIERS	USE
EXECUTE	Produce an executable image
MAP	Generate a MAP file
BRIEF	Generate a small MAP file
FULL	Generate a large MAP file
CROSS-REFERENCE	Produce a cross-reference
DEBUG	Include VAX Debugger

All the commands are further explained in the VAX-11 Linker, Debugger, and RUN Documentation.

D.2 OTHER USEFUL DCL COMMANDS

There are many other useful DCL commands. The following are just some of the very basic ones. You will probably need to use these at some time or other.

$ TYPE SORT.BAS

The BASIC program SORT will be listed on the screen.

$ PRINT SORT.BAS

The BASIC program SORT will be sent to the line printer. No text will appear on the screen, only a message that tells you your file will be printed. The message is usually

```
JOB SORT (queue LPA0, entry 110) started on SYS$PRINT
```

Other qualifiers can be used with the PRINT command to specify type of paper and number of copies.

```
$ PRINT/COPIES=2 SORT.BAS
$ PRINT/FORMS=0 SORT.BAS
```

$ DELETE

The DELETE command deletes specific files. When you use the command, you need to give the file name, file type, and *version number*.

```
$ DELETE SORT.BAS;7
```

Where SORT is the file name; .BAS is the file type; and ;7 is the version number.

$ DIR

The DIR command displays the full name of each of your files.

$ HELP

The HELP command will explain various topics about the VAX, the VMS operating system, and DCL. To invoke HELP, just type HELP at the dollar sign. This will print out the HELP topics. To get information about a specific topic, type

```
$ HELP DELETE
$ HELP TYPE
```

When you are finished reading the information on the screen, press ⟨RET⟩ until the $ appears.

$ RENAME

The RENAME command gives a file a new name. The format is

```
$ RENAME <old name> <new name>
```

as in

```
$ RENAME SORT.BAS LIST.BAS
```

$ COPY

The COPY command makes copies of a file. Sometimes this is necessary if you want to use part of an old program but still want the original after the changes are made. The form of the command is

```
$ COPY SORT.BAS NEWSORT.BAS
```

After using COPY you will have the original SORT.BAS file and the new file
NEWSORT.BAS in your directory.

D.3 USING THE EDITOR FROM WITHIN BASIC

Once you know the EDT editor, you can access the editor from within BASIC. The
following sequence shows the procedure for getting in and out of the editor.

```
$ BASIC

VAX BASIC V2.4

Ready

OLD SORT

Ready

LIST

(Program will be listed)

Ready

EDIT

1  10 REM -- Sort 10 numbers into ascending order

*C
```

The program appears on the screen. Now you can make any necessary changes. When
you are done, EXIT the editor and type SAVE. Then SAVE records the changes. Now
if you LIST the program, the changes will be there.

Appendix E

Flowcharting

Flowcharting is a simple but powerful tool for analyzing and representing the logical flow of a program. You should develop one before you write the computer program. You use the flowchart to break down a program module for coding. The flowchart and the process of developing it also give you a tool for debugging your program and graphically representing your program.

A flowchart consists of a pattern of symbols used to depict the logic of your program. There are many standard symbols, but the major ones are:

Symbol	What the Symbol Indicates	Statements
(rounded shape)	The start or end of a program	STOP, END
(rectangle)	A process or action	LET
(parallelogram)	Input or Output	INPUT, READ/DATA GET, PUT
(diamond)	A decision	IF. . .THEN. . .ELSE ON. . .GO TO SELECT/CASE BLOCK IF
(arrow)	The sequence of the program; the logical flow	

A simple flowchart for adding three numbers would be drawn as follows:

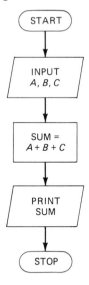

Here is an example of a flowchart with a decision. The problem is to find the sum of integers from 1 to 100.

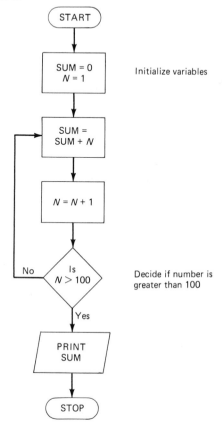

Flowcharts are not difficult to design, and they are useful both to you and to the program's user. When designing a flowchart, start with the general format and then add the details. Make sure the notation is useful to you and simplifies complicated process blocks. Make notes for clarification to the right of the flowchart.

Finally, here is a complete flowchart and program to read three numbers and determine whether or not they are in order. An output of "Yes" means they are in either increasing or decreasing order. An output of "No" indicates no order. The program is simple to state but difficult to flowchart. However, it is an excellent example for examining the logic of multiple decisions. Be sure you can follow the logic of the flowchart and the program. Try the BASIC program to make sure it works!

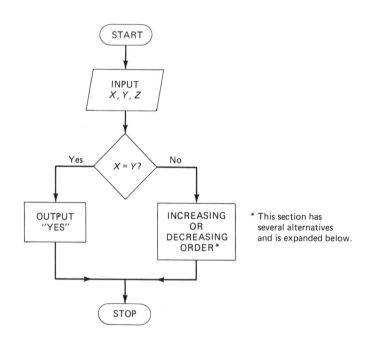

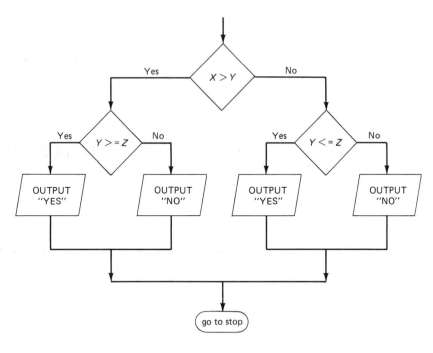

```
100   REM--Determine if 3 numbers are in order
110   INPUT "Type in 3 numbers"; X, Y, Z
120   IF X = Y AND Y = Z THEN
          PRINT "IN ORDER"
      ELSE
          IF X >= Y THEN
             IF Y >= Z THEN
                 PRINT "IN ORDER"
             ELSE
                 PRINT "NO ORDER"
             END IF                          (The lines show
          ELSE                                  the IF blocks.)
             IF Y <= Z THEN
                 PRINT "IN ORDER"
             ELSE
                 PRINT "NO ORDER"
             END IF
          END IF
      END IF
130   END
```

Obviously in one text you cannot learn every BASIC statement or command. Now that you understand the fundamentals of BASIC programming and some advanced concepts, it will not be difficult to learn other VAX-BASIC statements and features. A few of these are described below.

F.1 ITERATE AND EXIT

The ITERATE and EXIT statements give more explicit control of loop execution. ITERATE can be used only within a labeled FOR/NEXT, WHILE, or UNTIL loop. We will discuss EXIT only in conjunction with these loops, but it can also be used to exit from IF blocks, subprograms, function definitions, and SELECT blocks.

EXIT (*label*) is used to exit from a loop; it transfers control to the first statement following the NEXT statement that ends the labeled loop. The following loop will be exited if a value of 0 is read.

```
CHECK:
  FOR I = 1 TO 10
     READ Y
     EXIT CHECK IF Y = 0
     PRINT Y
  NEXT I
PRINT "Out of loop"
```

The EXIT CHECK statement sends the computer to PRINT "Out of loop", which is the first statement following NEXT I. FNEXIT is a similar statement for exiting from user-defined functions.

314

ITERATE can be used with or without a following label. The ITERATE statement is equivalent to a GO TO statement that sends the computer to the first NEXT statement after ITERATE. The following program takes the square root of all non-negative numbers in a DATA statement. A value of 0 is used as an end-of-data flag.

```
10  X = 1
    ROOT:
      WHILE X <> 0
        READ X
        ITERATE IF X < 0
        PRINT "The square root of"; X; " is"; SQR(X)
      NEXT
    DATA 17.4, -3.92, -4.26, 8.15, 92.7, -3.4, 64.7, 0
20  END
```

F.2 RECORD

The RECORD statement lets you name and define data structures in a BASIC program. You can use the RECORD name anywhere a BASIC data-type keyword is valid. The format is

```
RECORD rec-name
        rec-component
END RECORD [rec-name]
```

An example of the use of a record could be a club membership roster. Each member would have a record in the file. The following program shows how to define a RECORD and to access the information.

```
100 DECLARE MEMBER DUES_REC
110 RECORD MEMBER
      GROUP MEM_NAME
          STRING FIRST = 15
          STRING MIDDLE = 1
          STRING LAST = 14
      END GROUP MEM_NAME
      GROUP ADDRESS
          STRING STREET = 15
          STRING CITY = 10
          STRING STATE = 2
          STRING ZIP = 5
      END GROUP ADDRESS
120 END RECORD
130 INPUT "Type in your first name"; DUES_REC::MEM_NAME::FIRST
140 INPUT "Type in your middle initial"; DUES_REC::MEM_NAME::MIDDLE
150 INPUT "Type in your last name"; DUES_REC::MEM_NAME::LAST
160 PRINT "Thank you MR. "; DUES_REC::MEM_NAME::LAST
170 PRINT "Now please enter your address"
```

```
180 INPUT "Street"; DUES_REC::ADDRESS::STREET
190 INPUT "City"; DUES_REC::ADDRESS::CITY
200 INPUT "State"; DUES_REC::ADDRESS::STATE
210 INPUT "Zip"; DUES_REC::ADDRESS::ZIP
220 PRINT DUES_REC::ADDRESS::STREET
230 PRINT DUES_REC::ADDRESS::CITY; ", "; DUES_REC::ADDRESS::STATE; " ";
240 PRINT DUES_REC::ADDRESS::ZIP
250 INPUT "Is this your correct address (yes or no)"; ANS$
260 IF ANS$ = "NO" THEN GO TO 180 ELSE GO TO 270
270 END
```

The statements between RECORD and END RECORD are called a *RECORD block*.
You can access any part of the record by specifying the item you want. For example

```
DUES_REC::NAME::LAST
```

would access the last name of the club member.

F.3 OTHER PRINT USING FORMATS

PRINT USING provides special characters for printing numbers with *commas* and
numbers with *asterisks* to fill blank spaces. Some examples of this option are given
below.

```
10 PRINT "Several lines will be printed from line 20 using asterisks"
20 PRINT USING "**###"; 3, 45,678,98765,123456
30 PRINT "New formats with commas and dollar signs"
40 PRINT USING "##,###"; 1
50 PRINT USING "####,#.##", 12345
60 PRINT USING "#####,###.##", 1234567.83   !ROUNDS, 6 DIGITS
70 PRINT USING "##,###", 123
80 PRINT USING "$$#,##.##", 1234.56
90 END

RUNNH

Several lines will be printed from line 20 using asterisks
****3
***45
**678
98765
% 123456
New formats with commas and dollar signs
    1
12,345.00
1,234,570.00
   123
$1,234.56
```

Notice that in line 20 several numbers are listed, and they are all printed with asterisk format on separate lines. The last figure (1234.56) is too long, so the warning % appears. Lines 40–80 show the varied effects of the comma. Notice the comma can be placed anywhere to the left of the decimal point and one character (i.e , #.), then the comma is printed after every three digits. In line 70 there are only three digits to the left of the decimal, so the comma is suppressed and the line is space filled. Line 80 combines dollar signs with commas.

Also it is important to notice that in line 60, the number is rounded to six digits (1,234,570.00). To produce all digits (1234567.83) you need to COMPILE and LINK the program with /DOUBLE. This procedure is described in Appendix D). In general, PRINT USING in the interactive mode will print *only* six digits.

Finally, numbers can be printed with the *E* (*exponential*) format by placing four carets (^^^^) at the end of the PRINT USING field. The carets reserve space for the capital letter E, a plus or minus sign, and a two-digit exponent. The following line demonstrates several different numbers printed in E-format.

```
10 PRINT USING "###.##^^^^"; &
2,34,456,5678,87656,.35,.678,.0098,.00003

RUNNH

200.00E-02
340.00E-01
456.00E+00
567.80E+01
876.56E+02
350.00E-03
678.00E-03
980.00E-05
300.00E-07
```

New Data Types

VAX-BASIC supports 8-, 16-, and 32-bit integers within the language along with single and double floating-point numbers. The accompanying table gives the attributes of each type.

Type	Size	Maximum precision (decimal digits)	Internal size (bytes)
Integers			
BYTE	−128 to 127	3	1
WORD	32768 to 32767	5	2
LONG	−2147483648 to 214748367	10	4
Reals			
SINGLE	$.29*10^{-38}$ to $1.7*10^{38}$	6	4
DOUBLE	$.28*10^{-38}$ to $1.7*10^{38}$	16	8
GFLOAT	$.56*10^{-308}$ to $.9*10^{308}$	15	8
HFLOAT	$.84*10^{-4932}$ to $.59*10^{4932}$	33	16
String	0 to 65536		

These data types can be assigned to variables with the DECLARE statement.

F.4 THE OPTION STATEMENT

The OPTION statement is used to set a specific data type or subtype for a variable in a program. This feature is usually used when numeric accuracy is important; when six digits is not enough space. The statement is only one line in the program, and it must come before any BASIC statements other than remarks. For example, the following statement would specify that all computations be done with double-precision real numbers:

```
100 OPTION SIZE = REAL DOUBLE
```

The OPTION statement can be used with any data type.

F.5 USING ESCAPE SEQUENCES

Sometimes it is nice to be able to control the terminal screen as well as the print formats. This is done with special escape sequences that the computer sends to the terminal. The following strings, called *escape sequences,* will perform the indicated functions:

ESC + "[2J"	Erase the screen
ESC + "[K"	Erase the rest of the line
ESC + "[7m"	Turn on the reverse video
ESC + "[0m"	Turn off the reverse video

To use one of these escape sequences, PRINT the string. You can also assign the string to a variable and PRINT that variable, as in

```
ERASE$ = ESC + "[2J"
PRINT ERASE$
```

This sequence clears the terminal screen and positions the cursor at the upper left corner.

Answers to Even-Numbered Exercises

CHAPTER 1

Exercises A

2. a. PRINT "A", "B", "C", "D", "E"
   b. PRINT "A"; "B"; "C"; "D"; "E"
   c. PRINT "ABCDE"

CHAPTER 2

Exercises A

2. 100 PRINT "Circumference is "; 2 * PI * 5
   110 END

4. 100 PRINT "Area ="; 6 * 5/2
   110 END

Exercises B

2. 100 BIGM = 1.29
   110 FFR = .49
   120 DRINK = .45
   130 !
   140 NBIGM = 4
   150 NFFR = 3

```
160 NDRINK = 2
170 !
180 PRINT NBIGM; "Big Macs cost "; NBIGM * BIGM
190 PRINT NFFR; "French fries cost "; NFFR * FFR
200 PRINT NDRINK; "Drinks cost "; NDRINK * DRINK
210 PRINT "Total cost is "; NBIGM * BIGM + NFFR * FFR + NDRINK * DRINK
220 END
```

For the second part of the problem, put new data in lines 140–160.

Exercises C

2.
```
100 INPUT "Give me five numbers"; A, B, C, D, E
110 PRINT "Their mean is"; (A + B + C + D + E) / 5
120 END
```

4.
```
100 INPUT "Give me two positive numbers "; X, Y
110 PRINT "Harmonic mean is "; 2 / (1 / X + 1 / Y)
120 END
```

6.
```
100 PRINT "Give me 3 values for A, B, C. The first must not be 0."
110 INPUT "I will solve the equation AX + B = C"; A, B, C
120 PRINT "Solution for the equation is "; (C - B) / A
130 END
```

Exercises D

2. For example, for Exercise C1:

```
100 REM --  Area and perimeter of a rectangle
110 READ BASE, HEIGHT
120 PRINT "Area = "; BASE * HEIGHT
130 !
140 PRINT "Perimeter = "; 2 * (BASE + HEIGHT)
150 DATA 6,5
160 END
```

4.
```
100 PRINT "THIS PROGRAM PRINTS A TABLE OF PRICES OF ITEMS AT 3 STORES"
110 PRINT
120 PRINT
130 PRINT "ITEM","FOOD LION","KROGER","WINN DIXIE","AVERAGE"
140 PRINT
150 FOR X=1 TO 3
160    !I$=ITEM NAME, P1=PRICE @ FOOD LION, P2=KROGER, P3=WINN DIXIE
170 READ I$, P1, P2, P3
180    !A=AVERAGE
190    LET A=(P1+P2+P3)/3
200    !A1 IS AVERAGE ROUNDED OFF
210    LET A1=INT (A*100+.5)/100
220    PRINT I$, P1, P2, P3, A1
230 NEXT X
240 DATA EGGS, .69, .79, .75
```

```
250 DATA MILK, 1.99, 1.89, 2.05
260 DATA BREAD, .35, .40, .36
270 END
```

CHAPTER 3

Exercises A

2.
```
100 REM --  Mean of 4 grades
110 READ NAME$, G1, G2, G3, G4
120 PRINT NAME$ ; " has an average grade of "; (G1 + G2 + G3 + G4) / 4
130 DATA JOE COOL, 76, 84, 79, 91
140 END
```

4.
```
100 REM --  Birthday greeting
110 INPUT "Whose birthday is it"; NAME$
120 INPUT "Who is sending greetings"; SENDER$
130 !
140 PRINT "Happy birthday to you,"
150 PRINT "Happy birthday to you,"
160 PRINT "Happy birthday, dear "; NAME$ ; ","
170 PRINT "Happy birthday to you."
180 PRINT
190 PRINT "        Love from "; SENDER$
200 END
```

Exercises B

2.
```
100 REM --  Seconds in a week and month
110 SECPERDAY = 60 * 60 * 24
120 SECPERWEEK = 7 * SECPERDAY
130 SECPERMO = 30 * SECPERDAY
140 !
150 PRINT SECPERWEEK; "Seconds in a week"
160 PRINT SECPERMO; "Seconds in a 30-day month"
170 END
```

4.
```
100 INPUT "TYPE IN A NUMBER"; N
110 PRINT N
120 ! THIS PROGRAM IS CHECKING FOR NUMBER OF DIGITS
130 !      THAT VAX WILL PRINT IN AN INTEGER VALUE
140 END
```

Exercises C

2.
```
100 INPUT "Non-0 number"; N
110 PRINT N ; "to the -4 power is" ; N^-4
120 END
```

4.
```
100 REM --  Area and hypotenuse of a right triangle
110 INPUT "Legs of a right triangle"; A, B
120 !
130 AREA = A * B / 2
140 HYPOT = SQR(A^2 + B^2)
150 !
160 PRINT "Area ="; AREA
170 PRINT "Hypotenuse ="; HYPOT
180 END
```

6.
```
100 INPUT "Give me a big number"; B
110 PRINT "I will now round your number before the decimal point."
120 !
130 INPUT "How many places before the decimal point"; P
140 PRINT B ; "rounded is "; INT( B/10^P + .5) * 10^P
150 END
```

8.
```
100 REM --  Quadratic equation
110 INPUT "3 coefficients for quadratic equation"; A, B, C
120 !
130 D = SQR(B^2 - 4 * A * C)
140 X1 = (-B + D) / (2 * A)
150 X2 = (-B - D) / (2 * A)
160 !
170 PRINT "Solutions are "; X1, X2
180 END
```

10.
```
100 REM --  Compound interest
110 READ PRINCIPAL, RATE, PERIODS
120 !
130 BALANCE = PRINCIPAL * (1 + RATE)^PERIODS
140 !
150 PRINT "Balance is"; BALANCE
160 DATA 100, .06, 180
170 END
```

12.
```
100 PRINT "I will evaluate the polynomial 3X^4 + 5X^3 - 7X^2 + 12X - 9"
110 INPUT "What is the value of X"; X
120 PRINT "The polynomial value is "; 3*X^4 + 5*X^3 - 7*X^2 + 12*X - 9
130 END
```

14.
```
100 REM --  Value of 10 ** 50 / 2 ** 60
110 REM --  10 ** 50 causes overflow, so use 5 ** 50 / 2 ** 10
120 !
130 PRINT "10 ** 50 / 2 ** 60 ="; 5 ** 50 / 2 ** 10
140 END
```

Exercises D

2. a. 0   b. 4   c. 3

Exercises E

```
2. 100 !
       !=================================================================
       ! TITLE           :PAYFORM
       !
       ! Author          :John Smith
       ! Written         :Jan. 26, 1980
       ! Modified        :June 12, 1982
       ! System          :VAX 11/780
       ! Purpose         :Print a pay form with constants
       !                        assigned to the variables
       ! Variables       :HOURS  - Hours worked per week, 37.5
       !                 :RATE   - Hourly pay rate, $6.50
       !                 :GROSS  - Gross pay, calculated as
       !                            Hourly rate * Hours worked
       !                 :SOCSEC - Social security tax,
       !                            calculated as .0665 * GROSS
       !                 :FIT    - Federal income tax,
       !                            calculated as .14 * GROSS
       !                 :BC     - Blue Cross payment, $12.00
       !                 :NET    - Net pay, calculated as
       !                            GROSS - SOCSEC - FIT - BC
       !
       ! Subroutines called  :None
       !
       !=================================================================
       ! Initialize variables.
       !
   110 DECLARE REAL HOURS, RATE, BC, FIT, NET, GROSS, SOCSEC
   120 HOURS = 37.5
   130 RATE  = 6.5
   140 BC    = 12
   150 !=================================================================
       ! Compute values of other variables.
   160 GROSS  = HOURS * RATE
   170 SOCSEC = .0665 * GROSS
   180 FIT    = .14 * GROSS
   190 NET    = GROSS - SOCSEC - FIT - BC
   200 !=================================================================
   210 ! Print out pay form.
   220 PRINT "This program prints out a pay form."
   230     PRINT "Gross pay       :"; GROSS       ! Gross pay
   240     PRINT "Social security:"; SOCSEC
   250     PRINT "Federal tax    :"; FIT
   260     PRINT "Blue Cross     :"; BC
   270     PRINT "Net pay        :"; NET          ! Final pay
   280 END
```

CHAPTER 4

Exercises A

2.
```
100 REM --  Put 3 numbers in increasing order
110 READ A, B, C
120 !
130 IF A < B THEN 180
140      T = A
150      A = B
160      B = T
170 !
180 IF B < C THEN 230
190      T = B
200      B = C
210      C = T
220 !
230 PRINT "The numbers, in order, are "; A, B, C
240 DATA 37, -42, 0
250 END
```

4.
```
100 REM --  Print and count failing scores
110 CNT = 0
120 NFAIL = 0
130 READ SCORE
140 CNT = CNT + 1
150 !
160 IF SCORE >= 70 THEN 200
170 PRINT SCORE
180 NFAIL = NFAIL + 1
190 !
200 IF CNT < 10 THEN 130
210 PRINT "There were"; NFAIL ; "failing scores."
220 !
230 DATA 79, 68, 85, 91, 52, 73, 88, 95, 58, 76
240 END
```

6.
```
100 REM --  Factorials from 1 to 10
110 PRINT "INTEGER", "FACTORIAL"
120 !
130 FACT = 1
140 I = 0
150 I = I + 1
160 FACT = FACT * I
170 !
180 PRINT I, FACT
190 !
200 IF I < 10 THEN 150
210 END
```

8.
```
100 REM --  Sum and count numbers divisible by 9 between 100 and 300
110 SUM,CNT = 0
120 I = 99
130 I = I + 9
140 CNT = CNT + 1
150 SUM = SUM + I
160 !
170 IF I + 9 < 300 THEN 130
180 PRINT "Sum ="; SUM
190 PRINT CNT ; "numbers between 100 and 300 are divisible by 9."
200 END
```

10.
```
100 REM --  Checking account
110 PRINT "Date", "Transaction", "Amount", "Balance"
120 !
130 READ BALANCE
140 READ DTE$, TRANS
150 !
160 IF TRANS = 0 THEN 290
170 PRINT DTE$,
180 !
190 IF TRANS < 0 THEN PRINT "Check",
200 IF TRANS > 0 THEN PRINT "Deposit",
210 !
220 PRINT ABS(TRANS),
230 BALANCE = BALANCE + TRANS
240 PRINT BALANCE
250 GO TO 140
260 !
270 DATA 14.23, OCT. 3, 90.00, OCT. 7, -32.25
280 DATA OCT. 12, -11.53, OCT. 20, 20.00, OCT. 27, -56.78, X, 0
290 END
```

12.
```
100 REM --  Find smallest N for which (1/2) ** N < 0.001
110 N = 1
120 N = N + 1
130 !
140 IF (1/2) ** N >= 0.001 THEN 120
150 PRINT "(1/2) ** "; N ; "=" ; (1/2) ** N
160 END
```

14.
```
100 REM --  First 25 Fibonacci numbers
110 PRINT "The following numbers are the first 25 Fibonacci numbers."
120 !
130 A = 0
140 B = 1
150 PRINT B;
160 CNT = 1
165 FOR CNT = 1 TO 24 STEP 3
170    C = A + B
180    PRINT C;
190    A = B + C
```

```
200    PRINT A;
210    B = A + C
220    PRINT B;
240 NEXT CNT
260 END
```

Exercises B

2.
```
100 REM --  Calculate LARGE! / SMALL!
110 INPUT "Give me two integers with the larger one first"; LARGE, SMALL
120 !
130 IF LARGE <= SMALL THEN PRINT "Try again" \ GO TO 110
140 REM --  Instead of calculating factorials, do some mental arithmetic.
150 LS = 1
160 M = SMALL + 1
170 LS = LS * M
180 M = M + 1
190 !
200 IF M <= LARGE THEN 170
210 PRINT "Large!/Small! ="; LS
220 END
```

4.
```
100 INPUT "Give me your last name and I'll tell you when to register"; N$
110 !
120 PRINT "You register at ";
130 IF N$ < "N" THEN PRINT "9 am." ELSE PRINT "2 pm."
140 END
```

6.
```
100 REM --  Guess a number -- binary search strategy
110 PRINT "You think of a number between 1 and 100 and I'll try to"
120 PRINT "guess it. After my guess, you tell me if I'm too high,"
130 INPUT "too low or correct by typing H, L, or C. Got a number"; ANS$
140 !
150 HIGH = 100
160 LOW = 1
170 GUESS = 50
180 PRINT GUESS;
190 !
200 INPUT Z$
210 IF Z$ = "H" THEN HIGH = GUESS
    ELSE IF Z$ = "L" THEN LOW = GUESS
    ELSE IF Z$ = "C" THEN 240
    ELSE PRINT "PLEASE TYPE H, L, OR C."
220 GUESS = INT( (HIGH + LOW)/2 )
230 GO TO 180
240 END
```

8.
```
100 PRINT "I am looking for points in the circles X^2 + Y^2 = 16 and"
110 PRINT "(X - 3)^2 + (Y + 2)^2 = 25."
120 !
130 INPUT "Coordinates of a point (X,Y)"; X, Y
140 IF X^2 + Y^2 <= 16 THEN FIRST$ = "" ELSE FIRST$ = "not "
```

```
150 IF (X-3)^2 + (Y+2)^2 <= 25 THEN SECOND$ = "" ELSE SECOND$ = "not "
160 !
170 PRINT "The point is " ; FIRST$ ; "in the first circle and"
180 PRINT "is "; SECOND$ ; "in the second circle."
190 END
```

10.
```
100 REM --  Print 3 numbers in increasing order
110 INPUT "3 different numbers"; A, B, C
120 !
130 PRINT "The numbers in increasing order:";
140 IF A < B AND B < C THEN PRINT A, B, C
150 IF A < C AND C < B THEN PRINT A, C, B
160 IF B < A AND A < C THEN PRINT B, A, C
170 IF B < C AND C < A THEN PRINT B, C, A
180 IF C < A AND A < B THEN PRINT C, A, B
190 IF C < B AND B < A THEN PRINT C, B, A
200 END
```

12.
```
100 !PROGRAM TO PRINT APPROPRIATE MESSAGE FOR AN INPUT GPA
110 PRINT "TYPE -999 TO END PROGRAM "
120 INPUT "WHAT IS YOUR GPA";GPA
130 SELECT GPA
140   CASE -999
150     GOTO 450
160   CASE < 0
170     PRINT "DON'T TRY TO TRICK ME--TYPE IN A GPA BETWEEN 0 AND 4.0"
180   CASE 0 TO 1.5
190     PRINT "DO YOU EXPECT TO GRADUATE?????"
200     PRINT "BETTER START WORKING SINCE YOU'RE PAYING $10,000 TO BE HERE!!"
210   CASE 1.5 TO 2.0
220     PRINT "HA!  I CAN TELL YOU'VE BEEN WORKING REALLY HARD (HA! HA! HA!)"
230     PRINT "COME ON! GET WITH THE PROGRAM!!!!"
240   CASE 2.0 TO 2.5
250     PRINT "GEE, I CAN TELL WHO THE LIFE OF THE PARTY IS!"
260     PRINT "BETTER HAVE SOME PRIVATE PARTIES WITH THE BOOKS!!"
270   CASE 2.5 TO 2.999
280     PRINT "NOW JUST GIVE IT A LITTLE BIT OF EFFORT "
290     PRINT "AND YOU'LL BE AMAZED AT WHAT CAN HAPPEN"
300   CASE 3.0 TO 3.399
310     PRINT "PRETTY IMPRESSIVE, BUT--YOU'VE STILL GOT"
320     PRINT (3.4-GPA);"TO GO BEFORE THE DEAN IS IMPRESSED"
330   CASE 3.4 TO 3.999
340     PRINT "WOW! DEAN'S LIST--I'M REALLY IMPRESSED"
350     PRINT "JUST HOPE HARVARD LAW IS, TOO!!"
360   CASE 4.0
370     PRINT "TOO GOOD--YOU'RE MAKING THE REST OF US LOOK BAD"
380     PRINT "TAKE A DAY OFF AND GIVE US A BREAK, WILL YA?!"
390   CASE >4.0
400     PRINT "TRYING TO FOOL ME AGAIN, HUH?  WELL IT DIDN'T WORK!"
410     PRINT "GET A REAL GPA!"
420 END SELECT
```

```
430 PRINT
440 GOTO 120
450 END
```

Exercises C

2.
```
100 REM --  Assign letter grades to number grades
110 READ GRADE
120 !
130 IF GRADE > 0 THEN PRINT GRADE,      ! Negative is end-of-data flag
140 IF GRADE >= 90 THEN
        PRINT "A"
     ELSE IF GRADE >= 80 THEN
        PRINT "B"
     ELSE IF GRADE >= 70 THEN
        PRINT "C"
     ELSE IF GRADE >= 60 THEN
        PRINT "D"
     ELSE IF GRADE > 0 THEN
        PRINT "F"
     ELSE 180
150 GO TO 110
160 !
170 DATA 78, 89, 90, 95, 85, 76, 67, 14, 59, 60, 79, 70, -1
180 END
```

4.
```
100 REM --  Program to classify boxes by weight
110 CNT = 0
120 PRINT "Box #", "Weight", "Class"
130 PRINT
140 READ WEIGHT
150 CNT = CNT + 1
160 IF WEIGHT >= 150 AND WEIGHT <= 174 THEN
        CLASS = 1
     ELSE IF WEIGHT >= 175 AND WEIGHT <= 199 THEN
        CLASS = 2
     ELSE IF WEIGHT >= 200 AND WEIGHT <= 249 THEN
        CLASS = 3
     ELSE IF WEIGHT >= 250 THEN
        CLASS = 4
     ELSE
        CLASS = 0
     END IF
170 IF CLASS <> 0 THEN
        PRINT CNT, WEIGHT, CLASS
     ELSE
        PRINT "Error - box #"; CNT; "doesn't fit any category"
     END IF
180 PRINT
190 IF CNT < 6 THEN 140
200 PRINT
```

```
210 DATA 240, 500, 50, 320, 185, 169
220 END
```

6.
```
100 REM --  Noninteger values in ON...GO TO
110 PRINT "I can handle 4 alternatives: 4 will end the program."
120 INPUT "Enter a decimal value bigger than 1, less than 5"; X
130 ON X GO TO 150, 180, 210, 240
140 !
150 PRINT "This is the first alternative."
160 GO TO 120
170 !
180 PRINT "You have reached alternative 2."
190 GO TO 120
200 !
210 PRINT "You are now at alternative 3."
220 GO TO 120
230 !
240 PRINT "This is the end."
250 END
```

8.
```
100 REM --  Program using SELECT to compute employee bonuses.
110 PRINT
120 CNT = 0
130 READ NAME$, SALARY, YEARS%, RATING%
140 CNT = CNT + 1
150 SELECT RATING%

        CASE 3, 4
           BONUS = SALARY * 2
        CASE ELSE
           BONUS = SALARY

     END SELECT
160 !
170 SELECT YEARS%

        CASE >= 10
           BONUS = BONUS + 100.00
        CASE < 2
           BONUS = BONUS/2

     END SELECT
180 IF BONUS < 150 THEN BONUS = 150
190 PRINT "Employee "; NAME$; ", your bonus is $"; BONUS
200 PRINT
210 IF CNT < 10 THEN GO TO 120
220 !
230 DATA John Henry, 200.00, 6, 3
240 DATA Alice Smith, 350.00, 13, 1
250 DATA Jack B. Quick, 650.00, 1, 4
260 DATA Abe Lincoln, 300.00, 10, 2
270 DATA Mary Poppins, 2000.00, 11, 4
```

```
280 DATA Arnold Palmer, 300.00, 5, 1
290 DATA Hollie Collie, 1500.00, 1, 3
300 DATA Nancy Nice, 400.00, 8, 2
310 DATA Lotta Looks, 200.00, 1, 2
320 DATA Mike Hammer, 550.00, 1, 1
330 END
```

10.
```
100 !PROGRAM TO FIND COST OF TUITION ROOM AND BOARD AT A VIRGINIA SCHOOL
110 !AND NUMBER OF OUT OF AND IN STATE STUDENTS
120 !*************VARIABLES*********************
130 !T = TUITIION = $80/CREDIT FOR VA STUDENTS
140 !              $100/CREDIT FOR OUT OF STATE STUDENTS
150 !   MAXIMUM TUITION IS $1500
160 !RB = ROOM AND BOARD=2000 FOR MAIN HALL
170 !                   =2500 FOR RANDOLPH HALL
180 !N$ = NAME OF STUDENT
190 !S$ = STATE
200 !C  = NUMBER OF CREDITS
210 !D$ = DORM
220 !I  = TOTAL NUMBER OF IN STATE STUDENTS
230 !O  = TOTAL NUMBER OF OUT OF STATE STUDENTS
240 !TC = TOTAL COST (TUITION + ROOM AND BOARD)
250 !
260 !****************************************************
270      !PRINT HEADINGS
280 PRINT "NAME","STATE","CREDITS","ROOM/BOARD","TUITION","TOTAL COST"
290 PRINT "----","-----","-------","----------","-------","----------"
300      !READ DATA
310 READ N$,S$,C,D$
320 IF N$="NONAME" THEN 450                    !EOD FLAG
330      !FIND # OF IN AND OUT OF STATE STUDENTS
340 IF S$="VA" THEN N=80\ I=I+1                 !N IS MULTIPLIER TO FIND TUITION
    ELSE N=100\O=O+1
350      !FIND COST OF ROOM AND BOARD
360 IF D$="MAIN" THEN RB = 2000
    ELSE RB = 2500
370      !Find tuition
380 T = C*N
390 IF T> 1500 THEN T=1500
400      !FIND TOTAL COST (TUITION+ROOM AND BOARD)
410 TC=T+RB
420      !PRINT TABLE OF INFO
430 PRINT N$, S$, C, RB, T, TC
440 GOTO 310                                   !GOES TO READ
450      !PRINT LINE(-----)
460 FOR X=1 TO 80\PRINT "-";\NEXT X\PRINT
470 PRINT
480 PRINT "NUMBER OF IN STATE STUDENTS IS: ";I
490 PRINT "NUMBER OF OUT OF STATE STUDENTS IS:"; O
500 DATA "BEV STINSON",   "PA", 14, "RANDOLPH"
510 DATA "LACY SMITHERS", "CA", 18, "MAIN"
```

```
520 DATA "ANN WATSON",    "VA", 15, "RANDOLPH"
530 DATA "LISA SAUDERS",  "PA", 15, "MAIN"
540 DATA "CATHY MATHEWS", "VA", 15, "RANDOLPH"
550 DATA "JESSICA HALL",  "VA", 17, "RANDOLPH"
560 DATA "NONAME","NN",0,"NODORM"
570 END
```

CHAPTER 5

Exercises A

2.
```
100 REM --  Find largest and smallest number in a list of 10 numbers
110 READ L
120 S = L
130 !
140 FOR I = 2 TO 10
        READ N
        IF N > L THEN L = N
        ELSE
        IF N < S THEN S = N
150 NEXT I
160 !
170 PRINT "Largest number"; L
180 PRINT "Smallest number"; S
190 DATA 6, 4, 19, 17, 2, -4, -13, 0, 9, -6
200 END
```

4.
```
100 REM --  Calculate bank balance with 16% interest
110 B = 10000
120 FOR Y = 1 TO 10
        B = B + (.16) * B
        B = B - 2000
        PRINT "At the end of year"; Y; "your balance is $"; B
130 NEXT Y
140 END
```

6.
```
100 REM --  Determine test averages and grades
110 PRINT "Student name","Test average","Grade"
120 !
130 FOR STU = 1 TO 4
        READ N$
        TSCORE = 0
140     FOR S = 1 TO 5
            READ TS
            TSCORE = TSCORE + TS
150     NEXT S
        TAVG = TSCORE / 5
        IF TAVG >= 90 THEN G$ = "A"
        ELSE
```

```
            IF TAVG >= 80 THEN G$ = "B"
            ELSE
            IF TAVG >= 70 THEN G$ = "C"
            ELSE
            IF TAVG >= 60 THEN G$ = "D" ELSE G$ = "F"
    160     PRINT N$, TAVG, G$
    170 NEXT STU
    180 !
    190 DATA I. M. Grate, 92, 89, 97, 87, 94
    200 DATA U. R. Nott, 79, 81, 78, 83, 77
    210 DATA E. Z. Rider, 86, 67, 74, 89, 85
    220 DATA M. I. Wright, 45, 56, 38, 64, 61
    230 END
```

8.
```
    100 REM --  Count number of ways to make change for a dollar
    110 FOR HDOLLARS = 0 TO 2
    120   FOR QUARTERS = 0 TO 4 - HDOLLARS * 2
    130     FOR DIMES = 0 TO 10 - HDOLLARS * 5 - QUARTERS * 2.5
    140       FOR NICKELS = 0 TO 20 - HDOLLARS*10 - QUARTERS*5 - DIMES*2
    150         NUMB = NUMB + 1
    160       NEXT NICKELS
    170     NEXT DIMES
    180   NEXT QUARTERS
    190 NEXT HDOLLARS
    200 !
    210 PRINT "The number of different ways to make change for $1.00 is"; NUMB
    220 END
```

10.
```
    100 REM --  Find 3 integers such that X^3 + Y^3 + Z^3 = W^3
    110 FOR X = 1 TO 10
    120   FOR Y = 1 TO 10
    130     FOR Z = 1 TO 10
    140       FOR W = 1 TO 10
    150         IF X^3 + Y^3 + Z^3 = W^3 THEN
                  PRINT X;"^3 + "; Y;"^3 + "; Z;"^3 = "; W;"^3"
                  GO TO 200
                END IF
    160       NEXT W
    170     NEXT Z
    180   NEXT Y
    190 NEXT X
    200 END
```

12.
```
    100 REM --  Make change for a purchase < $20.00
    110 INPUT "Cost of purchase"; C
    120 INPUT "Amount given to clerk"; A
    130 PRINT "Amount of change: $"; A - C
    140 !
    150 CHG = 100 * (A - C)
    160 TEN = INT(CHG / 1000)
    170 CHG = CHG - 1000 * TEN
    180 FIV = INT(CHG / 500)
```

```
190 CHG = CHG - 500 * FIV
200 ONES = INT(CHG / 100)
210 CHG = CHG - 100 * ONES
220 HALF = INT(CHG / 50)
230 CHG = CHG - 50 * HALF
240 QT = INT(CHG / 25)
250 CHG = CHG - 25 * QT
260 DIME = INT(CHG / 10)
270 CHG = CHG - 10 * DIME
280 NICK = INT(CHG / 5)
290 CHG = CHG - 5 * NICK
300 PEN = INT(CHG)
310 !
320 PRINT "Denomination", "Quantity"
330 PRINT "    $10", TEN
340 PRINT "    $5";, FIV
350 PRINT "    $1";, ONES
360 PRINT "Half dollars", HALF
370 PRINT "Quarters", QT
380 PRINT "Dimes", DIME
390 PRINT "Nickels", NICK
400 PRINT "Pennies", PEN
410 END
```

14.
```
100 REM --  Compute student grades, class average, and 3-class average
110 SCHTOT = 0
120 FOR CLASS = 1 TO 3
130    CLTOT = 0
140    FOR STU = 1 TO 4
150       READ N$
160       STUTOT = 0
170       FOR TEST = 1 TO 5
180          READ TS
190          STUTOT = STUTOT + TS
200       NEXT TEST
210       STUAVG = STUTOT/5
220       IF STUAVG >= 90 THEN G$ = "A"
          ELSE IF STUAVG >= 80 THEN G$ = "B"
          ELSE IF STUAVG >= 70 THEN G$ = "C"
          ELSE IF STUAVG >= 60 THEN G$ = "D"
          ELSE G$ = "F"
          END IF
230       PRINT N$, STUAVG, G$
240       CLTOT = CLTOT + STUTOT
250    NEXT STU
260    PRINT "Average for class"; CLASS; "is"; CLTOT / (TEST * STU)
270    PRINT
280    SCHTOT = SCHTOT + CLTOT
290 NEXT CLASS
300 PRINT "Average for all classes is"; SCHTOT / (TEST * STU * CLASS)
310 !
```

```
320 DATA John Smith,    78, 89, 97, 98, 90
330 DATA Willy Simmons, 86, 67, 68, 96, 87
340 DATA Ann Gibbony,   77, 88, 69, 98, 99
350 DATA Beth Anders,   99, 98, 97, 96, 89
360 DATA Kim Stokes,    78, 76, 79, 80, 85
370 DATA Amy Lower,     86, 67, 69, 89, 78
380 DATA John Tota,     96, 85, 72, 61, 87
390 DATA Chris Kerns,   69, 70, 93, 82, 74
400 DATA Barb McHan,    68, 87, 89, 95, 74
410 DATA Ellen Dawson,  66, 87, 93, 84, 100
420 DATA Simon Temkin,  70, 94, 87, 68, 80
430 DATA Nathan Jones,  64, 87, 98, 80, 79
500 END
```

16.
```
100 REM --  Find largest score in a list and multiply it by each number
110 READ LRGSC
120 FOR I = 2 TO 10
        READ A
        IF A > LRGSC THEN LRGSC = A
130 NEXT I
140 PRINT "The largest score is"; LRGSC
150 RESTORE
160 REM --  Multiply largest score by every score
170 PRINT
180 PRINT "Product of each score and largest"
190 FOR I = 1 TO 10
        READ A
        A = A * LRGSC
        PRINT A
200 NEXT I
210 DATA 6, 5, 8, 7, 6, 9, 7, 8, 6, 7
220 END
```

Exercises B

2.
```
100 REM --  A formatted receipt
110 PRINT TAB(60); "November 30, 1982"
120 PRINT TAB(60); "-----------------"
130 PRINT TAB(30); "Barbara Jones"
140 PRINT "RECEIVED FROM"; TAB(30); "-------------"
150 PRINT TAB(38); "Amount  $30.68"
160 PRINT TAB(47); "-------"
170 PRINT TAB(40); "Signature"
180 PRINT TAB(50); "------------------------"
190 END
```

4.
```
100 PRINT TAB(-3); "This is TAB(-3)"
110 PRINT TAB(-70); "This is TAB(-70)"
120 PRINT TAB(85); "This is TAB(85)"
130 PRINT TAB(200); "This is TAB(200)"
140 END
```

Conclusions: For negative TAB arguments, VAX BASIC prints at the left margin. For TAB arguments which are larger than the number of columns, VAX BASIC continues to the next lines until the number of spaces specified is reached, and then prints.

6.
```
100 REM --  Print out the pay statement for four employees
110 FOR EMP = 1 to 4
120    READ NAME$, BCROSS$, RATE, HOURS
130    IF HOURS<= 40 THEN GROSS = HOURS * RATE
                 ELSE GROSS = 40 * RATE + (HOURS-40) * RATE * 2
140    SS = .07 * GROSS
150    IF BCROSS$ = "N" THEN BC = 0
                 ELSE IF BCROSS$ = "S" THEN BC = 9.5
                 ELSE BC = 24.75
160    ST = .03 * GROSS
170    PE = GROSS * 52
180    IF PE < 6000 THEN FT = 0
                 ELSE IF PE < 16000 THEN FT = GROSS * .08
                 ELSE IF PE < 24000 THEN FT = GROSS * .16
                 ELSE FT = GROSS * .24
190    NET = GROSS - SS - BC - FT - ST
200    PRINT
210    PRINT "NAME"; TAB(13); "RATE"; TAB(20); "HOURS"; TAB(27); "GROSS";
       PRINT TAB(36); "SS"; TAB(45); "BC"; TAB(52); "FT"; TAB(60); "ST";
       PRINT TAB(68); "NET PAY"
220       PRINT "-"; FOR I = 1 TO 76
230       PRINT
240       PRINT USING "'LLLLLLLLLL", NAME$;
250       PRINT TAB (12); \ PRINT USING "$$#.##", RATE;
260       PRINT TAB (19); \ PRINT USING "###", HOURS;
270       PRINT TAB (26); \ PRINT USING "$$###.##", GROSS;
280       PRINT TAB (35); \ PRINT USING "$$##.##", SS;
290       PRINT TAB (43); \ PRINT USING "$$##.##", BC;
300       PRINT TAB (51); \ PRINT USING "$$##.##", FT;
310       PRINT TAB (58); \ PRINT USING "$$##.##", ST;
320       PRINT TAB (67); \ PRINT USING "$$###.##", NET;
330       PRINT \ PRINT \ PRINT
340 NEXT EMP
350 !
360 DATA "Smith, J.", F, 3.75, 45
370 DATA "Jones, W.", S, 4.50, 38
380 DATA "Miller, R.", N, 6.25, 40
390 DATA "Reese, C.", F, 9.25, 42
400 END
```

CHAPTER 6

Exercises A

2.
```
100 REM --  Beginning with X = 9 replace X with X + SQR(X) until X > 100.
110 X = 9 \ PRINT X
120 C = 0
130 !
140 WHILE X <= 100
        X = X + SQR(X)
        PRINT X
        C = C + 1
150 NEXT
160 PRINT "The square root of X was added"; C; "times."
170 END
```

4.
```
100 REM --  Enter strings until a blank is entered.
              Count number of words and print words.
110 CNT = 0
120 PRINT "Enter one word at a time. To end, enter a blank for 'Word?'"
130 INPUT "Word"; WORD$
140 WHILE WORD$ <> " "
        CNT = CNT + 1
        PRINT WORD$
        INPUT "Word"; WORD$
    NEXT
150 PRINT \ PRINT "You entered"; CNT; "words."
160 PRINT
170 END
```

6.
```
100 REM --  Compute powers of two less than 5000.
110 X = 1
120 PRINT " X ", "2^X"
130 PRINT
140 WHILE 2^X < 5000
        PRINT X, 2^X
        X = X + 1
    NEXT
150 PRINT
160 END
```

8.
```
100 REM --  Determine test averages and grades
110 PRINT "STUDENT NAME","TEST AVERAGE","GRADE"
120 READ N$
130 WHILE N$ <> "STOP"
        TSCORE = 0
        FOR S = 1 TO 5
            READ TS
            TSCORE = TSCORE + TS
        NEXT S
        TAVG = TSCORE / 5
```

```
          IF TAVG >= 90 THEN G$ = "A"
           ELSE
          IF TAVG >= 80 THEN G$ = "B"
           ELSE
          IF TAVG >= 70 THEN G$ = "C"
           ELSE
          IF TAVG >= 60 THEN G$ = "D" ELSE G$ = "F"

160    PRINT N$, TAVG, G$
       READ N$
170 NEXT
180 !
190 DATA I. M. GRATE,   92, 89, 97, 87, 94
200 DATA U. R. NOTT,    79, 81, 78, 83, 77
210 DATA E. Z. RIDER,   86, 67, 74, 89, 85
220 DATA M. I. WRIGHT,  45, 56, 38, 64, 61
225 DATA STOP, 0
230 END
```

Exercises B

```
2. 100 REM --  Use WHILE modifier to calculate sum for INPUT numbers
   110 PRINT "Enter one number at a time. To stop the program, enter"
       PRINT "a number which is less than 8."
   120 PRINT \ INPUT "Number"; NUMBER
   130 TOT = 0
   140 FOR X = 0 WHILE NUMBER >= 8
           TOT = TOT + NUMBER
           INPUT "Number"; NUMBER
       NEXT X
   150 PRINT "The sum of the numbers is"; TOT
   160 PRINT
   170 END

4. 100 REM --  Read list of words and print all words which begin with
                a letter after R in the alphabet.
   110 READ WORD$
   120 FOR X = 0 UNTIL WORD$ = "END"
           IF WORD$ > "R" THEN
               PRINT WORD$
           END IF
           READ WORD$
       NEXT X
   130 !
   140 DATA TONY, BERT, VIVIAN, WALLY, ELLEN, JANE
   150 DATA HARRY, SALLY, MARTHA, LISA, END
   160 END

6. 100 REM --  Read and average test scores
   110 READ TEST
   120 TOT, AVG = 0
```

```
130 FOR X = 0 WHILE TEST > 0
        TOT = TOT + TEST
        READ TEST
    NEXT X
140 AVG = TOT / X
150 PRINT "The average of all test grades is"; AVG
160 PRINT
170 DATA 65, 79, 90, 89, 78, 69, 100, 98, 45, 99, 87, -1
180 END
```

8.
```
100 REM --  Print pay statements for four employees
110 FOR J = 1 TO 4
120     READ NAME$, BCROSS$, RATE, HOURS
130     GOSUB 300      ! Gross pay
140     GOSUB 350      ! Blue Cross
150     GOSUB 400      ! Federal tax
160     SS = .07 * GROSS
170     ST = .03 * GROSS
180     PE = GROSS * 52
190     NET = GROSS - SS - BC - FT - ST
200     PRINT
        PRINT "NAME"; TAB(13); "RATE"; TAB(20); "HOURS"; TAB(27); "GROSS";
        PRINT TAB(36); "SS"; TAB(45); "BC"; TAB(52); "FT"; TAB(60); "ST";
        PRINT TAB(68); "NET PAY"
        PRINT "-"; FOR I = 1 TO 76
        PRINT
210     RATE = INT(RATE * 10^2 + .5) / 10^2
        HOURS = INT(HOURS * 10^2 + .5) / 10^2
        GROSS = INT(GROSS * 10^2 + .5) / 10^2
        SS = INT(SS * 10^2 + .5) / 10^2
        BC = INT(BC * 10^2 + .5) / 10^2
        FT = INT(FT * 10^2 + .5) / 10^2
        ST = INT(ST * 10^2 + .5) / 10^2
        NET = INT(NET * 10^2 + .5) / 10^2

220     PRINT NAME$;
        PRINT TAB (12); RATE;
        PRINT TAB (19); HOURS;
        PRINT TAB (26); GROSS;
        PRINT TAB (35); SS;
        PRINT TAB (43); BC;
        PRINT TAB (51); FT;
        PRINT TAB (58); ST;
        PRINT TAB (67); NET;
        PRINT \ PRINT \ PRINT
230 NEXT J
240 !
250 DATA "Smith, J.", F, 3.75, 45
260 DATA "Jones, W.", S, 4.50, 38
270 DATA "Miller, R.", N, 6.25, 40
280 DATA "Reese, C.", F, 9.25, 42
```

```
290 GO TO 450
300 !!!!!!!!!!!!!!!!!!!!!!!!!!!!!!!!!!!!!!!!!!!!!!!!!!!!!!!!!!!!!!!!!!!!!!!!
310 !          Subroutine to calculate gross pay                         !
320 !!!!!!!!!!!!!!!!!!!!!!!!!!!!!!!!!!!!!!!!!!!!!!!!!!!!!!!!!!!!!!!!!!!!!!!!
330 IF HOURS<= 40 THEN GROSS = HOURS * RATE
    ELSE GROSS = 40 * RATE + (HOURS-40) * RATE * 2
340 RETURN
350 !!!!!!!!!!!!!!!!!!!!!!!!!!!!!!!!!!!!!!!!!!!!!!!!!!!!!!!!!!!!!!!!!!!!!!!!
360 !          Subroutine to calculate Blue Cross                        !
370 !!!!!!!!!!!!!!!!!!!!!!!!!!!!!!!!!!!!!!!!!!!!!!!!!!!!!!!!!!!!!!!!!!!!!!!!
380 IF BCROSS$ = "N" THEN BC = 0
    ELSE IF BCROSS$ = "S" THEN BC = 9.5
    ELSE BC = 24.75
390 RETURN
400 !!!!!!!!!!!!!!!!!!!!!!!!!!!!!!!!!!!!!!!!!!!!!!!!!!!!!!!!!!!!!!!!!!!!!!!!
410 !          Subroutine to calculate federal tax                       !
420 !!!!!!!!!!!!!!!!!!!!!!!!!!!!!!!!!!!!!!!!!!!!!!!!!!!!!!!!!!!!!!!!!!!!!!!!
430 IF PE < 6000 THEN FT = 0
    ELSE IF PE < 16000 THEN FT = GROSS * .08
    ELSE IF PE < 24000 THEN FT = GROSS * .16
    ELSE FT = GROSS * .24
440 RETURN
450 END
```

CHAPTER 7

Exercises A

```
2. 100 REM --  Sort a list of up to 200 names
   110 DIM N$(200)
   120 READ N              ! N is the number of values to be sorted
   130 READ N$(I) FOR I = 1 TO N
   140 PRINT "The names in alphabetical order are:"
   150 !
   160 FOR STP = 1 TO N - 1
   170    FOR J = STP + 1 TO N
   180            IF N$(J) < N$(STP) THEN
                  T$ = N$(J)
                  N$(J) = N$(STP)
                  N$(STP) = T$
               END IF
   190    NEXT J
   200 NEXT STP
   210 PRINT N$(I) FOR I = 1 TO N
   220 !
   230 DATA 5
   240 DATA "SMITH, JOE", "WITT, DON", "LOWER, BETH"
   250 DATA "BRATTEN, ANN", "TAYLOR, GEORGE"
   300 END
```

```
 4. 100 REM --  Sort and print a list of numbers without duplicates
    110 DIM X(200)
    120 READ N            ! N is the number of values to be sorted
    130 READ X(I) FOR I = 1 TO N
    140 PRINT "The values in ascending order (without duplicates) are:"
    150 !
    160 FOR STP = 1 TO N - 1
    170    FOR J = STP + 1 TO N
    180       IF X(J) < X(STP) THEN
                 T = X(J)
                 X(J) = X(STP)
                 X(STP) = T
              END IF
    190    NEXT J
    200 NEXT STP
    210 !
    220 I = 1
    230 WHILE I <=  N - 1
    240       IF X(I) <> X(I + 1) THEN PRINT X(I);
    250       I = I + 1
    260 NEXT
    270 PRINT X(N)
    280 !
    290 DATA 13
    300 DATA 6, 8, 7, 3, 6, 5, 6, 9, 6, 7, 5, 6, 8
    310 END

 6. 100 REM --  Count occurrences of digits 0, 1, 2,..., 9 in an input list
    110 PRINT "Enter a negative number to indicate end of input."
    120 PRINT
    130 INPUT "Enter a digit 0, 1, 2,..., 9"; X
    140 WHILE X >= 0 AND X <= 9
    150    ! C(X) (for X = 0 TO 9) are the counters for the various digits
    160       C(X) = C(X) + 1
    170       INPUT "Enter a digit 0, 1, 2,..., 9"; X
    180 NEXT
    190 !
    200 PRINT "DIGIT    OCCURRENCES"
    210 PRINT X, C(X) FOR X = 0 TO 9
    220 END

 8. 100 REM --  Find median of list of numbers in data
    110 DIM N(100)
    120 READ I     ! I is the number of items in the list
    130 READ N(J) FOR J = 1 TO I
    140 !
    150 FOR J = 1 TO I - 1
    160    FOR STP = J + 1 TO I
    170       IF N(J) > N(STP) THEN
                 T      = N(J)
                 N(J)   = N(STP)
```

```
                    N(STP) = T
                END IF
180     NEXT STP
190 NEXT J
200 !
210 PRINT "The numbers in your list in increasing order are:"
220 PRINT TAB(36); N(J) FOR J = 1 TO I
230 !            Calculate median
240 IF I / 2 <> INT(I / 2) THEN
        M = N(INT(I / 2) + 1)
    ELSE
        M = (N(I / 2) + N((I / 2) + 1)) / 2
    END IF
250 PRINT "The median of your list is "; M
260 DATA 10
270 DATA 3, 5, 4, 7, 6, 8, 1, 11, 14, 9
280 END
```

10a.
```
100   REM -- Tic-Tac-Toe game
110   FOR I = 1 TO 9
          BOARD$(I) = STR$(I)
120   NEXT I
130 !
140   GOSUB 610
150   FOR I = 1 TO 9 ! Loop to clear board
160       BOARD$(I) = " "
170   NEXT I
180 !
190 MOVE$ = "PLAYER"
200 GOSUB 610
210 !
220         ! Subroutine - player's move
230 INPUT "Give me a number between 1 and 9"; PL
240 WHILE PL < 1 OR PL > 9
          PRINT "Try again!"
          INPUT "Give me a number between 1 and 9"; PL
250 NEXT
260 !
270 WHILE BOARD$(PL) <> " "
          PRINT "That square is taken."
          INPUT "Give me a number between 1 and 9"; PL
280 NEXT
290 !
300 BOARD$(PL) = "X"
310 GOSUB 610
320 GOSUB 550
330 GOSUB 470
340 !
350         ! Subroutine - computer's move
360 MV$ = "0"
370 NXTPL = 0
```

```
380 FOR I = 1 TO 9
390     IF BOARD$(I) = " " THEN NXTPL = I \ GO TO 410
400 NEXT I
410 IF NXTPL = 0 THEN 510 ELSE BOARD$(I) = "0"
420 GOSUB 610
430 GOSUB 550
440 GOSUB 470
450 MOVE$ = "PLAYER" \ GO TO 220
460 !
470          ! CHECK FOR TIE GAME
480 FOR I = 1 TO 9
490     IF BOARD$(I) = " " THEN TIE$ = "NO" \ GO TO 520
500 NEXT I
510 PRINT "TIE GAME"\ GO TO 710
520 RETURN
530 !
540 !  Subroutine to check for victory
550 IF BOARD$(1) + BOARD$(2) + BOARD$(3) = "XXX" OR &
       BOARD$(4) + BOARD$(5) + BOARD$(6) = "XXX" OR &
       BOARD$(7) + BOARD$(8) + BOARD$(9) = "XXX" OR &
       BOARD$(1) + BOARD$(4) + BOARD$(7) = "XXX" OR &
       BOARD$(2) + BOARD$(5) + BOARD$(8) = "XXX" OR &
       BOARD$(3) + BOARD$(6) + BOARD$(9) = "XXX" OR &
       BOARD$(1) + BOARD$(5) + BOARD$(9) = "XXX" OR &
       BOARD$(3) + BOARD$(5) + BOARD$(7) = "XXX" THEN
            WINNER$ = "PLAYER"
     ELSE IF                                      &
       BOARD$(3) + BOARD$(5) + BOARD$(7) = "000" OR &
       BOARD$(1) + BOARD$(2) + BOARD$(3) = "000" OR &
       BOARD$(4) + BOARD$(5) + BOARD$(6) = "000" OR &
       BOARD$(7) + BOARD$(8) + BOARD$(9) = "000" OR &
       BOARD$(1) + BOARD$(4) + BOARD$(7) = "000" OR &
       BOARD$(2) + BOARD$(5) + BOARD$(8) = "000" OR &
       BOARD$(3) + BOARD$(6) + BOARD$(9) = "000" OR &
       BOARD$(1) + BOARD$(5) + BOARD$(9) = "000" THEN
            WINNER$ = "COMPUTER"
     END IF
560 !
570 IF WINNER$ = "COMPUTER" THEN
       PRINT "The computer has won" \ GO TO 710
     ELSE IF WINNER$ = "PLAYER" THEN
        PRINT "You win!" \ GO TO 710
     END IF
580 RETURN
590 !
600          !  Subroutine to print board
610 PRINT TAB(16); "*"; TAB(20); "*"
620 PRINT TAB (14); BOARD$(1); TAB(16); "*"; TAB(18); BOARD$(2);
    PRINT TAB(20); "*"; TAB(22); BOARD$(3)
630 PRINT TAB(13); "***********"
```

```
640 PRINT TAB(16); "*" ; TAB(20); "*"
650 PRINT TAB (14); BOARD$(4); TAB(16); "*"; TAB(18); BOARD$(5);
    PRINT TAB(20); "*"; TAB(22); BOARD$(6)
660 PRINT TAB(13); "**********"
670 PRINT TAB(16); "*" ; TAB(20); "*"
680 PRINT TAB(14); BOARD$(7); TAB(16); "*"; TAB(18); BOARD$(8);
    PRINT TAB(20); "*"; TAB(22); BOARD$(9)
690 PRINT
700 RETURN
710 END
```

10b.
```
100  REM -- Tic-Tac-Toe game that keeps score
110  CW, PW, T = 0
120  FOR I = 1 TO 9
           BOARD$(I) = STR$(I)
130  NEXT I
140  !
150   GOSUB 650
160  WINNER$ = "NOBODY"
170  A$ = "YES"
180  WHILE WINNER$ = "NOBODY" AND A$ = "YES"
190   FOR I = 1 TO 9  ! Loop to clear board
200       BOARD$(I) = " "
210   NEXT I
220  !
230  MOVE$ = "PLAYER"
240  GOSUB 650
250  !
260        ! Subroutine - player's move
270  INPUT "Give me a number between 1 and 9"; PL
280  WHILE PL < 1 OR PL > 9
           PRINT "Try again!"
           INPUT "Give me a number between 1 and 9"; PL
290  NEXT
300  !
310  WHILE BOARD$(PL) <> " "
           PRINT "That square is taken."
           INPUT "Give me a number between 1 and 9"; PL
320  NEXT
330  !
340  BOARD$(PL) = "X"
350  GOSUB 650
360  GOSUB 590
370  GOSUB 510
380  !
390        ! Subroutine - computer's move
400  MV$ = "O"
410  NXTPL = 0
420  FOR I = 1 TO 9
430     IF BOARD$(I) = " " THEN NXTPL = I \ GO TO 450
440  NEXT I
```

```
450 IF NXTPL = 0 THEN 550 ELSE BOARD$(I) = "0"
460 GOSUB 650
470 GOSUB 590
480 GOSUB 510
490 MOVE$ = "PLAYER" \ GO TO 260
500 !
510          ! Check for tie game
520 FOR I = 1 TO 9
530    IF BOARD$(I) = " " THEN TIE$ = "NO" \ GO TO 560
540 NEXT I
550 PRINT "TIE GAME"\ T = T + 1 \ GO TO 800
560 RETURN
570 !
580 ! Subroutine to check for victory
590 IF BOARD$(1) + BOARD$(2) + BOARD$(3) = "XXX" OR &
       BOARD$(4) + BOARD$(5) + BOARD$(6) = "XXX" OR &
       BOARD$(7) + BOARD$(8) + BOARD$(9) = "XXX" OR &
       BOARD$(1) + BOARD$(4) + BOARD$(7) = "XXX" OR &
       BOARD$(2) + BOARD$(5) + BOARD$(8) = "XXX" OR &
       BOARD$(3) + BOARD$(6) + BOARD$(9) = "XXX" OR &
       BOARD$(1) + BOARD$(5) + BOARD$(9) = "XXX" OR &
       BOARD$(3) + BOARD$(5) + BOARD$(7) = "XXX" THEN
            WINNER$ = "PLAYER" \ PW = PW + 1
    ELSE IF                                        &
       BOARD$(3) + BOARD$(5) + BOARD$(7) = "000" OR &
       BOARD$(1) + BOARD$(2) + BOARD$(3) = "000" OR &
       BOARD$(4) + BOARD$(5) + BOARD$(6) = "000" OR &
       BOARD$(7) + BOARD$(8) + BOARD$(9) = "000" OR &
       BOARD$(1) + BOARD$(4) + BOARD$(7) = "000" OR &
       BOARD$(2) + BOARD$(5) + BOARD$(8) = "000" OR &
       BOARD$(3) + BOARD$(6) + BOARD$(9) = "000" OR &
       BOARD$(1) + BOARD$(5) + BOARD$(9) = "000" THEN
            WINNER$ = "COMPUTER" \ CW = CW + 1
    END IF
600 !
610 IF WINNER$ = "COMPUTER" THEN
       PRINT "The computer has won" \ GO TO 750
    ELSE IF WINNER$ = "PLAYER" THEN
       PRINT "You win!" \ GO TO 750
    END IF
620 RETURN
630 !
640          ! Subroutine to print board
650 PRINT TAB(16); "*"; TAB(20); "*"
660 PRINT TAB(14); BOARD$(1); TAB(16); "*"; TAB(18); BOARD$(2);
    PRINT TAB(20); "*"; TAB(22); BOARD$(3)
670 PRINT TAB(13); "***********"
680 PRINT TAB(16); "*" ; TAB(20); "*"
690 PRINT TAB(14); BOARD$(4); TAB(16); "*"; TAB(18); BOARD$(5);
    PRINT TAB(20); "*"; TAB(22); BOARD$(6)
```

```
700 PRINT TAB(13); "**********"
710 PRINT TAB(16); "*" ; TAB(20); "*"
720 PRINT TAB(14); BOARD$(7); TAB(16); "*"; TAB(18); BOARD$(8);
    PRINT TAB(20); "*"; TAB(22); BOARD$(9)
730 PRINT
740 RETURN
750 PRINT "SCORE:"
760 PRINT "Computer wins:"; CW, "Player wins:"; PW, "Ties:"; T
770 INPUT "Would you like to play again (YES OR NO)"; A$
780 WINNER$ = "NOBODY"
790 NEXT
800 END
```

12.
```
100 REM --  Find smallest ratio with positive denominator
110 READ A(I) FOR I = 1 TO 10
120 READ B(I) FOR I = 1 TO 10
130 !
140 DATA 3, 7, 5, 9, 45, 68, 1, 54, 60, 22
150 DATA 5, -8, 0, -66, -43, 65, 1000, -4, 9, 11
160 I = 1
170 WHILE B(I) <= 0
180     IF B(I) > 0 THEN SMRAT = A(I) / B(I)
190 NEXT
200 !
210 FOR J = I + 1 TO 10
220     IF B(J) > 0 THEN
            IF A(J) / B(J) < SMRAT THEN SMRAT = A(J) / B(J) \ GO TO 240
230 NEXT J
240 PRINT "The smallest ratio is"; SMRAT
250 END
```

14.
```
100 REM --  Sort inventory into alphabetical order
110 READ ITEM$(I), Q(I), P(I) FOR I = 1 TO 5
120 !
130 FOR I = 1 TO 4
140     FOR J = I + 1 TO 5
150             IF ITEM$(I) >= ITEM$(J) THEN
                    T$       = ITEM$(I)
                    ITEM$(I) = ITEM$(J)
                    ITEM$(J) = T$
                    T    = Q(I)
                    Q(I) = Q(J)
                    Q(J) = T
                    T    = P(I)
                    P(I) = P(J)
                    P(J) = T
                END IF
160     NEXT J
170 NEXT I
180 !
190 PRINT "ITEM", "QUANTITY", "PRICE"
```

```
200 PRINT ITEM$(I), Q(I), P(I) FOR I = 1 TO 5
210 !
220 DATA PEN, 3, 1.98, PENCIL, 8, .15, ERASER, 6, .06
230 DATA NOTEBOOK, 5, .75, RULER, 7, .5
240 END
```

Exercises B

2.
```
100 REM --  Base 10 to base 2 conversion for positive integers
120 INPUT "Positive integer"; X
130 BIGPOWER = INT( LOG(X)/LOG(2) )
140 PRINT "1";
150 SUBTOTAL = 2**BIGPOWER
160 FOR I = BIGPOWER - 1 TO 0 STEP -1
        IF SUBTOTAL + 2**I > X THEN
            PRINT "0";
        ELSE
            PRINT "1";
            SUBTOTAL = SUBTOTAL + 2**I
        END IF
170 NEXT I
180 PRINT
190 PRINT "is the binary representation for"; X
200 END
```

4.
```
100 REM --  Read, print and correct errors in a list of numbers
110 REM --  Error handling is done in a subroutine
120 DIM A(100)
130 PRINT "Enter list of numbers and end with -9999"
140 X = 1
150 INPUT A(X)
160 WHILE A(X) <> -9999
        X = X + 1
        INPUT A(X)
170 NEXT
180 !
190 HOLD = X - 1
200 GOSUB 270       ! Print the list
210 INPUT "Do you wish to make any changes (YES or NO)"; ANS$
220 WHILE ANS$ = "YES"
        INPUT "Which place needs to be corrected"; X
        PRINT "The present value of place "; X;" is "; A(X)
        INPUT "What is the new value"; A(X)
        INPUT "More changes (YES or NO)"; ANS$
230 NEXT
240 GOSUB 270       ! Print the list
250 GO TO 350
260 !!!!!!!!!!!!!!!!!!!!!!!!!!!!!!!!!!!!!!!!!!!!!!!!!!!!!!!!
270 ! Subroutine to print the list
280 PRINT "The list is as follows:"
290 PRINT "PLACE", "VALUE"
```

```
300    FOR J = 1 TO HOLD
310       PRINT J, A(J)
320    NEXT J
330 RETURN
340 !!!!!!!!!!!!!!!!!!!!!!!!!!!!!!!!!!!!!!!!!!!!!!!!!!!!!!!!!!!!!
350 END
```

6.
```
100 REM --  Tic-Tac-Toe
110             ! Player has X
120             ! Computer has 0
130             ! BOARD$  -- the board
140             ! NXTPL$  -- the next play
150             ! WINNER$ -- the winner, or nobody
160             ! MV$     -- X or 0
170             ! MOVE$   -- a move
180             ! RM      -- a random move
190   ! Print board with boxes labeled
200   FOR I = 1 TO 9
210     BOARD$(I) = STR$(I)
220   NEXT I
230 GOSUB 910
240 !
250 ! Clear board
260   FOR I = 1 TO 9
270       BOARD$(I) = " "
280   NEXT I
290             ! Who goes first
300 RANDOMIZE
310     IF RND < .5 THEN MOVE$ = "PLAYER" ELSE MOVE$ = "COMPUTER"
320     PRINT "First move is "; MOVE$
330 !
340 GOSUB 910
350 WINNER$ = " "
360 WHILE WINNER$ = " "
370 !
380 WHILE MOVE$ = "PLAYER"
390             ! Start subroutine - Player goes first
400         INPUT "Give me a number between 1 and 9"; PL
410         WHILE PL < 0 OR PL > 9
               PRINT "Try again!"
               INPUT "Give me a number between 1 and 9"; PL
420         NEXT
430 !
440         WHILE BOARD$(PL) <> " "
               PRINT "That square is taken"
               INPUT "Give me a number between 1 and 9"; PL
450         NEXT
460 !
470         BOARD$(PL) = "X"
480 GOSUB 910
490 GOSUB 850
```

```
500 GOSUB 700
510 MOVE$ = "COMPUTER"
520 NEXT
530 !
540          ! Subroutine - computer goes first
550 MV$ = "O"
560 GOSUB 790
570 IF NXTPL > 0 THEN RM = NXTPL \ GO TO 620
580 MV$ = "X"
590 GOSUB 790
600 IF NXTPL > 0 THEN RM = NXTPL \ GO TO 620
610 RM = INT(RND * 9) + 1
620     IF BOARD$(RM) <> " " THEN GO TO 610
630        BOARD$(RM) = "O"
640 GOSUB 910
650 GOSUB 850
660 GOSUB 700
670   MOVE$ = "PLAYER"
680 NEXT
690 !
700             ! Check for tie game
710 CNT = 0
720 FOR I = 1 TO 9
730   IF BOARD$(I) <> " " THEN CNT = CNT + 1
740 NEXT I
750 IF CNT = 9 THEN PRINT "Tie game" \ WINNER$ = "NOBODY" \ GO TO 1020
760 RETURN
770 !
780             ! Look for next play
790 NXTPL = 0
800     IF BOARD$(1) + BOARD$(2) = MV$ + MV$ THEN NXTPL = 3
    ELSE IF BOARD$(2) + BOARD$(3) = MV$ + MV$ THEN NXTPL = 1
    ELSE IF BOARD$(1) + BOARD$(3) = MV$ + MV$ THEN NXTPL = 2
    ELSE IF BOARD$(4) + BOARD$(5) = MV$ + MV$ THEN NXTPL = 6
    ELSE IF BOARD$(5) + BOARD$(6) = MV$ + MV$ THEN NXTPL = 4
    ELSE IF BOARD$(4) + BOARD$(6) = MV$ + MV$ THEN NXTPL = 5
    ELSE IF BOARD$(7) + BOARD$(8) = MV$ + MV$ THEN NXTPL = 9
    ELSE IF BOARD$(8) + BOARD$(9) = MV$ + MV$ THEN NXTPL = 7
    ELSE IF BOARD$(7) + BOARD$(9) = MV$ + MV$ THEN NXTPL = 8
    ELSE IF BOARD$(1) + BOARD$(4) = MV$ + MV$ THEN NXTPL = 7
    ELSE IF BOARD$(1) + BOARD$(7) = MV$ + MV$ THEN NXTPL = 4
    ELSE IF BOARD$(4) + BOARD$(7) = MV$ + MV$ THEN NXTPL = 1
    ELSE IF BOARD$(2) + BOARD$(5) = MV$ + MV$ THEN NXTPL = 8
    ELSE IF BOARD$(2) + BOARD$(8) = MV$ + MV$ THEN NXTPL = 5
    ELSE IF BOARD$(5) + BOARD$(8) = MV$ + MV$ THEN NXTPL = 2
    ELSE IF BOARD$(3) + BOARD$(6) = MV$ + MV$ THEN NXTPL = 9
    ELSE IF BOARD$(3) + BOARD$(9) = MV$ + MV$ THEN NXTPL = 6
    ELSE IF BOARD$(6) + BOARD$(9) = MV$ + MV$ THEN NXTPL = 3
    ELSE IF BOARD$(1) + BOARD$(5) = MV$ + MV$ THEN NXTPL = 9
    ELSE IF BOARD$(1) + BOARD$(9) = MV$ + MV$ THEN NXTPL = 5
```

```
        ELSE IF BOARD$(5) + BOARD$(9) = MV$ + MV$ THEN NXTPL = 1
        ELSE IF BOARD$(3) + BOARD$(5) = MV$ + MV$ THEN NXTPL = 7
        ELSE IF BOARD$(3) + BOARD$(7) = MV$ + MV$ THEN NXTPL = 5
        ELSE IF BOARD$(5) + BOARD$(7) = MV$ + MV$ THEN NXTPL = 3

      END IF
810 !
820 RETURN
830 !

840 !      Subroutine to check for victory
850 IF BOARD$(1) + BOARD$(2) + BOARD$(3) = "XXX" OR &
      BOARD$(4) + BOARD$(5) + BOARD$(6) = "XXX" OR &
      BOARD$(7) + BOARD$(8) + BOARD$(9) = "XXX" OR &
      BOARD$(1) + BOARD$(4) + BOARD$(7) = "XXX" OR &
      BOARD$(2) + BOARD$(5) + BOARD$(8) = "XXX" OR &
      BOARD$(3) + BOARD$(6) + BOARD$(9) = "XXX" OR &
      BOARD$(1) + BOARD$(5) + BOARD$(9) = "XXX" OR &
      BOARD$(3) + BOARD$(5) + BOARD$(7) = "XXX" THEN
          WINNER$ = "PLAYER"
    ELSE IF                                          &
      BOARD$(3) + BOARD$(5) + BOARD$(7) = "000" OR &
      BOARD$(1) + BOARD$(2) + BOARD$(3) = "000" OR &
      BOARD$(4) + BOARD$(5) + BOARD$(6) = "000" OR &
      BOARD$(7) + BOARD$(8) + BOARD$(9) = "000" OR &
      BOARD$(1) + BOARD$(4) + BOARD$(7) = "000" OR &
      BOARD$(2) + BOARD$(5) + BOARD$(8) = "000" OR &
      BOARD$(3) + BOARD$(6) + BOARD$(9) = "000" OR &
      BOARD$(1) + BOARD$(5) + BOARD$(9) = "000" THEN
          WINNER$ = "COMPUTER"
    END IF
860 !
870 IF WINNER$ = "COMPUTER" THEN
      PRINT "The computer has won" \ GO TO 1020
    ELSE IF WINNER$ = "PLAYER" THEN
      PRINT "You win!" \ GO TO 1020
    END IF
880 RETURN
890 !

900         ! Subroutine to print board
910 PRINT TAB(16); "*"; TAB(20); "*"
920 PRINT TAB (14); BOARD$(1); TAB(16); "*"; TAB(18); BOARD$(2);
    PRINT TAB(20); "*"; TAB(22); BOARD$(3)
930 PRINT TAB(13); "***********"
940 PRINT TAB(16); "*" ; TAB(20); "*"
950 PRINT TAB (14); BOARD$(4); TAB(16); "*"; TAB(18); BOARD$(5);
    PRINT TAB(20); "*"; TAB(22); BOARD$(6)
960 PRINT TAB(13); "***********"
970 PRINT TAB(16); "*" ; TAB(20); "*"
```

```
980 PRINT TAB(14); BOARD$(7); TAB(16); "*"; TAB(18); BOARD$(8);
    PRINT TAB(20); "*"; TAB(22); BOARD$(9)
990 PRINT
1000 PRINT
1010 RETURN
1020 END
```

8a.
```
100 REM -- - Use subroutine to convert integers to old Roman numeral
110 REM -- - form and write sum and product in the same form.
120 !
130 INPUT "Type in two positive integers", NO1, NO2
140 REM --  Go to subroutine to convert the numbers to Roman numerals
150 A = NO1
160    PRINT "The number ";A;" in Roman numeral form is ";
170 GOSUB 340
180 !
190 A = NO2
200    PRINT "The number ";A;" in Roman numeral form is ";
210 GOSUB 340
220 !
230 A = NO1 + NO2
240   PRINT "The sum is "; A
250   PRINT "The sum in Roman numeral form is ";
260 GOSUB 340
270 !
280 A = NO1 * NO2
290   PRINT "The product is ";A
300   PRINT "The product in Roman numeral form is ";
310 GOSUB 340
320 GO TO 450
330 !!!!!!!!!!!!!!!!!!!!!!!!!!!!!!!!!!!!!!!!!!!!!!!!!!!!!!!!!!!!!!!!!
340 !   Subroutine to convert integers to Roman numerals
350 DATA 1000, "M", 500, "D", 100, "C", 50, "L"
360 DATA 10, "X", 5, "V", 1, "I"
370 FOR B = 1 TO 7
380    READ X, X$
390    C = INT(A / X)
400    IF C <> 0 THEN
                FOR Z = 1 TO C
                   PRINT X$;
                NEXT Z
                A = A - (C * X)
           END IF
410 NEXT B
420 PRINT
430 RESTORE
440 RETURN
450 END
```

8b.
```
100 REM -- - Use subroutine to convert integers to Roman numerals
110 REM -- - and write sum and product in Roman numeral form.
```

```
120 !
130 INPUT "Type in two positive integers", NO1%, NO2%
140 REM --  Go to subroutine to convert the numbers to Roman numerals
150 A% = NO1%
160    PRINT "The number ";A%;" in Roman numeral form is ";
170 GOSUB 340
180 !
190 A% = NO2%
200    PRINT "The number ";A%;" in Roman numeral form is ";
210 GOSUB 340
220 !
230 A% = NO1% + NO2%
240   PRINT "The sum is "; A%
250   PRINT "The sum in Roman numeral form is ";
260 GOSUB 340
270 !
280 A% = NO1% * NO2%
290   PRINT "The product is ";A%
300   PRINT "The product in Roman numeral form is ";
310 GOSUB 340
320 GO TO 450
330 !!!!!!!!!!!!!!!!!!!!!!!!!!!!!!!!!!!!!!!!!!!!!!!!!!!!!!!!!!!!!!!!!!!!!
340 !   Subroutine to convert integers to Roman numerals
350 DATA 1000, "M", 500, "D", 100, "C", 50, "L"
360 DATA 10, "X", 5, "V", 1, "I"
370 FOR B = 1 TO 7
380    READ X%, X$
390    C% = INT(A% / X%)
400    IF A% >= 900% AND A% < 1000% THEN
             PRINT "CM";
             A% = A% - 900%
         ELSE IF A% >= 90% AND A% < 100% THEN
             PRINT "XC";
             A% = A% - 90%
         ELSE IF A% >= 40% AND A% < 50% THEN
             PRINT "XL";
             A% = A% - 40%
         ELSE IF A% = 9% THEN
             PRINT "IX";
             A% = 0%
         ELSE IF A% = 4% THEN
             PRINT "IV";
             A% = 0%
         ELSE IF C% > 0% THEN
             FOR Z% = 1% TO C%
                 PRINT X$;
             NEXT Z%
             A% = A% - (C% * X%)
         END IF
410 NEXT B
```

```
420 PRINT
430 RESTORE
440 RETURN
450 END
```

CHAPTER 8

Exercises A

2a.
```
100 REM --  To create a terminal format file with list of
110 REM --   prime numbers from 2 to 100.
120 OPEN "PRIME.DAT" FOR OUTPUT AS #2
130 FOR I = 2 TO 100
       IF I/2 <> INT(I/2) OR I = 2 THEN
          IF I/3 <> INT(I/3) OR I = 3 THEN
             IF I/5 <> INT(I/5) OR I = 5 THEN
                IF I/7 <> INT(I/7) OR I = 7 THEN
                   PRINT #2, I
                END IF
             END IF
          END IF
       END IF
     NEXT I
140 PRINT #2, -9999
150 !
160 CLOSE #2
170 END
```

2b.
```
100 REM --  Read the file PRIME.DAT containing prime numbers between
110 REM --   2 and 100 and count the number of records in the file.
120 OPEN "PRIME.DAT" FOR INPUT AS #2
130 !
140 CNT = 0
150 INPUT #2, LINE$
160 WHILE LINE$ <> "-9999"
       CNT = CNT + 1
       INPUT #2, LINE$
     NEXT
170 !
180 PRINT "There are "; CNT; " prime numbers between 2 and 100."
190 PRINT
200 CLOSE #2
210 END
```

4a.
```
100 REM --  Create a file with records containing
110 REM --   three real numbers separated by commas.
120 OPEN "REALNUM.DAT" FOR OUTPUT AS #1
130 !
140 PRINT "Enter three real numbers, separated by commas"
150 PRINT "Enter -9999 for first number to end program"
```

```
      160 PRINT
      170 INPUT R1, R2, R3
      180 WHILE R1 <> -9999
      190    PRINT #1, R1; ","; R2; ","; R3
      200    PRINT "Enter three real numbers, separated by commas."
      210    PRINT "To end program, enter -9999 for first number."
      220    INPUT R1, R2, R3
      230 NEXT
      240 !
      250 CLOSE #1
      260 END
```

4b.
```
      100 REM --  Read real numbers from REAL.DAT and
      110 REM --  use ON ERROR GO TO to find end of file.
      120 REM --  Program also indicates smallest and largest numbers.
      130 OPEN "REALNUM.DAT" FOR INPUT AS #5
      140 DIM X(1000)
      150 !
      160 ON ERROR GO TO 900
      170 CNT = 0
      180 INPUT #5, R1, R2, R3
      190 LARGETOT = R1
      200 SMALLTOT = R2
      210 WHILE 1%
      220    CNT = CNT + 1
      230 !
      240    LARGE = R1
      250    IF LARGE < R2 THEN LARGE = R2
      260    IF LARGE < R3 THEN LARGE = R3
      270 !
      280    SMALL = R1
      290    IF SMALL > R2 THEN SMALL = R2
      300    IF SMALL > R3 THEN SMALL = R3
      310 !
      320    PRINT
      330    PRINT "The largest number in record #"; CNT; " is "; LARGE
      340    PRINT "The smallest number in record #"; CNT; " is "; SMALL
      350    PRINT
      360 !
      370    IF LARGETOT < LARGE THEN LARGETOT = LARGE
      380    IF SMALLTOT > SMALL THEN SMALLTOT = SMALL
      390 !
      400    INPUT #5, R1, R2, R3
      410 !
      420 NEXT
      430 !
      440 PRINT
      450 PRINT "The largest number in the file is "; LARGETOT
      460 PRINT "The smallest number in the file is "; SMALLTOT
      470 PRINT
      480 GO TO 999
```

```
490 !
900 !!!!!!!!!!!!!!!!!!!!!!!!!!!!!!!!!!!!!!!!!!!!!!!!!!!!!!!!!!!!!!!!!!!!!!!!!
910 !                 Error handler; End of file ERR is 11.
920 IF ERR = 11% THEN
        PRINT "End of file"
        PRINT
        RESUME 440
     ELSE ON ERROR GO TO 0
999 END
```

6.
```
100 REM --  Read file INVEN.DAT and print all records
110 REM --   where quantity on hand is less than or equal to reorder
120 REM --   level, plus all records where quantity on hand is greater
130 REM --   than reorder level. ( Using RESTORE # statement)
140 OPEN "INVEN.DAT" FOR INPUT AS FILE #1
150 !
160 DIM LINE$(2)
170 PRINT
180 PRINT "Records in which reorder level > or = quantity on hand: "
190 PRINT
200 INPUT #1, LINE$(I) FOR I = 1 TO 2
210 PRINT LINE$(I) FOR I = 1 TO 2
220 !
230 INPUT #1, PARTNO, NAME$, QUAN, REORDER, REORQUAN
240 WHILE PARTNO <> 0
        IF QUAN <= REORDER THEN
           PRINT PARTNO, NAME$, QUAN, REORDER, REORQUAN
        END IF
        INPUT #1, PARTNO, NAME$, QUAN, REORDER, REORQUAN
     NEXT
250 PRINT
260 !
270 RESTORE #1
280 PRINT "Records in which quantity on hand > reorder level: "
290 PRINT
300 INPUT #1, LINE$(I) FOR I = 1 TO 2
310 PRINT LINE$(I) FOR I = 1 TO 2
320 !
330 INPUT #1, PARTNO, NAME$, QUAN, REORDER, REORQUAN
340 WHILE PARTNO <> 0
        IF QUAN > REORDER THEN
           PRINT PARTNO, NAME$, QUAN, REORDER, REORQUAN
        END IF
        INPUT #1, PARTNO, NAME$, QUAN, REORDER, REORQUAN
     NEXT
350 PRINT
360 !
370 CLOSE #1
380 END
```

CHAPTER 9

Exercises A

2.
```
100 REM --  Ask for two numbers, print out the larger number
110 PRINT \ INPUT "Give me two numbers"; A, B
120 LARGER = (A + B + ABS(A - B)) / 2
130 PRINT "The larger number is"; LARGER
140 END
```

4.
```
100 REM -- Principal values of arccosine (.866) and arcsine (.9)
110 REM -- Both angles are in first quadrant
120 SINE = SQR(1 - .866^2)
130 RANGLE = ATN(SINE / .866)
140   PRINT "Arccosine(.866) is"; RANGLE ; "radians or";
      PRINT  180 * RANGLE/PI ; "DEGREES"
150 SINE = .9
160 COSINE = SQR(1 - .9^2)
170 RANGLE = ATN(.9 / COSINE)
180   PRINT "Arcsine(.9) is"; RANGLE ; "radians or";
      PRINT  180 * RANGLE/PI ; "DEGREES"
190 END
```

6.
```
100 REM --  Accept the length of 3 sides of a triangle and calculate
110 REM --  the angles using the law of cosines
120 INPUT "Type in the lengths of the three sides"; SA, SB, SC
130 !
140 COSA = (SB^2 + SC^2 - SA^2) / (2 * SB * SC)
150 COSB = (SA^2 + SC^2 - SB^2) / (2 * SA * SC)
160 !
170 REM -- Calculate angle B
180 IF COSB <> 0 AND COSA <> 0 THEN
        BRAD = ATN (SQR(1 - COSB^2) / COSB)
        IF BRAD < 0 THEN
           BRAD = BRAD + PI
        END IF
        B= (BRAD * 180) / PI
      ! Calculate angle A
        ARAD = ATN (SQR(1 - COSA^2) / COSA)
        IF ARAD < 0 THEN
           ARAD = ARAD + PI
        END IF
        A = (ARAD * 180) / PI
     ELSE IF COSB = 0 THEN
        B = 90
     ELSE
        A = 90
     END IF
280 C = 180 - A - B
290 !
300   PRINT "SIDE          SIDE          ANGLE(DEGREES)"
```

```
310    PRINT "A", SA, A
320    PRINT "B", SB, B
330    PRINT "C", SC, C
340 END
```

8.
```
100 REM --  Find the value of 80! and 100! and print them in E notation
110 LOGFAC = 0
120 FOR I = 1 TO 80
    LOGFAC = LOGFAC + LOG10(I)
130 NEXT I
140 INTEG = INT(LOGFAC)
150 DECIM = LOGFAC - INTEG
160 PRINT "Value of 80! in E-notation is"; 10 ** DECIM; "E+"; INTEG
170 FOR I = 81 to 100
180    LOGFAC = LOGFAC + LOG10(I)
190 NEXT I
200 INTEG = INT(LOGFAC)
210 DECIM = LOGFAC - INTEG
220 PRINT "Value of 100! in E-notation is"; 10 ** DECIM; "E+"; INTEG
230 END
```

10.
```
100 REM --  Print the value of EXP(100) = 10 ** 100LOG10(e)
110 INTEG = INT(100*LOG10(2.718282))
120 DECIM = 100*LOG10(2.718282) - INTEG
130 PRINT "EXP(100) is"; 10 ** DECIM; "E+"; INTEG
140 END
```

12.
```
100 PRINT "INVENTORY NUMBER","PRICE"
110 FOR X = 1 TO 6
120    READ CODE$
130    L = LEN(CODE$)
140    DEPT$ = SEG$(CODE$,L,L)
150    IF DEPT$ = "2" THEN
           P1 = POS(CODE$,"-",1)
           NUMB$ = SEG$(CODE$,1,P1-1)
           P2 = POS(CODE$,"-",P1+1)
           PRICE$ = SEG$(CODE$,P1+1,P2-1)
           PRINT "      ";NUMB$,"                 ";PRICE$
160 NEXT X
170 DATA 163-4.30-2
180 DATA 51-8.00-1
190 DATA 916-9.50-2
200 DATA 811-10.45-2
210 DATA 6813-5.33-1
220 DATA 333-.45-2
230 END
```

Exercises B

2.
```
100 REM --  Define and use different user-defined functions
110 REM --  FNMAX(X, Y) gives larger of two values
120    DEF FNMAX(X, Y)
```

```
130      IF X > Y THEN FNMAX = X ELSE FNMAX = Y
140    FNEND
150 INPUT "Type in 2 numbers", X1, Y1
160    PRINT "The larger is"; FNMAX( X1, Y1)
170 !
180 REM --  FNDELTA(A, B) = A + B - 2 * A * B
190    DEF FNDELTA(A, B) = A + B - 2 * A * B
200 INPUT "Type in 2 numbers"; A1, B1
210   PRINT "The value of FNDELTA is "; FNDELTA(A1, B1)
220 REM --  FNSINH(X) = (EXP(X) - EXP(-X)) / 2 (Hyperbolic sine of X)
230    DEF FNSINH(X) = (EXP(X) - EXP(-X)) / 2
240 !
250 INPUT "Enter a value for X"; X1
260   PRINT "The hyperbolic sine of "; X1; " is "; FNSINH(X1)
270 REM --  FNMEDIAN(A, B, C) gives the median of A, B, C
280    DEF FNMEDIAN(A, B, C)
290      IF (A < B AND B < C) OR (C < B AND B < A) THEN FNMEDIAN = B
300      IF (B < A AND A < C) OR (C < A AND A < B) THEN FNMEDIAN = A
310      IF (B < C AND C < A) OR (A < C AND C < B) THEN FNMEDIAN = C
320    FNEND
330 !
340    INPUT "Please type in three numbers"; A1, B1, C1
350    DIM N(3)
360    N(1) = A1 \ N(2) = B1 \ N(3) = C1
370 !
380      FOR I = 1 TO 2
390        FOR J = 2 TO 3
400          IF N(I) < N(J) THEN 420
410          TEMP = N(I) \ N(I) = N(J) \ N(J) = TEMP
420        NEXT J
430      NEXT I
440 !
450    PRINT N(1), N(2), N(3)
460    A1 = N(1)\ B1 = N(2)\ C1 = N(3)
470    PRINT "The median of"; A1; B1; C1; "is"; FNMEDIAN(A1, B1, C1)
480 !
490 REM --  FNMOD(M, N) gives the remainder from M / N
500    DEF FNMOD(M, N)
510       NUMB = M / N
520       WHOLE = INT(NUMB)
530       NUMB = NUMB - WHOLE
540       NUMB = NUMB * N
550       FNMOD = NUMB
560    FNEND
570 !
580 INPUT "Enter two numbers to divide"; M1, N1
590   PRINT "The remainder of "; M1; "divided by "; N1; "is"; FNMOD(M1,N1)
600 END
```

CHAPTER 10

Exercises A

2.
```
100 REM --  Read a string and print it in reverse
110 PRINT \ INPUT "Type a line"; LINE$
120 LENGTH = LEN(LINE$)
122 NEWLINE$ = ""
130 FOR I = 1 TO LENGTH
        A$ = SEG$(LINE$, LENGTH - (I - 1), LENGTH - (I - 1))
        NEWLINE$ = NEWLINE$ + A$
    NEXT I
140 PRINT \ PRINT "Here is the line printed backwards: "
150 PRINT NEWLINE$
160 PRINT
170 END
```

4.
```
100 REM --  Edit program to change several occurrences of the same mistake
110 DIM P(20)
120 INPUT "Type in a line"; LINE$
130 INPUT "What needs to be deleted"; DEL$
140 INPUT "What replaces it"; ADD$
150 !
160 I = 1
170 P(I) = 0
180 P(I) = POS(LINE$, DEL$, P(I - 1) + 1)
190 IF P(I) <> 0 THEN
        I = I + 1
        GO TO 170
    END IF
200 IF P(1) = 0 THEN
        PRINT "Can't find error"
        GO TO 300
    END IF
210 !
220 LDEL = LEN(DEL$)
230 FOR J = I - 1 TO 1 STEP -1
240    LLIN = LEN(LINE$)
250    LINE$ = SEG$(LINE$, 1, P(J) - 1) + ADD$ +    &
               SEG$(LINE$, P(J) + LDEL, LLIN)
260 NEXT J
270 !
280 PRINT "The corrected line is:"
290 PRINT LINE$
300 END
```

6.
```
100 REM --  Transposition code
110 INPUT "What is the message that you want to code"; M$
120 DIM B(80)
130 CHANGE M$ TO B
140 !
```

```
150 FOR I = 1 TO B(0)
160    B(I) = B(I) + 5
170    IF B(I) > 90 THEN B(I) = B(I) - 26
180 NEXT I
190 CHANGE B TO CODEDM$
200 PRINT "The coded message is:" \ PRINT CODEDM$
210 END
```

8.
```
100 REM --  Switch 2 strings in a paragraph
102 PARA$ = ""
103 SP$ = " "
104 PRINT "You may type in a paragraph."
106 PRINT "When you've finished, type STOP for the last line."
110 INPUT "Type in a line of text"; L$
112 WHILE L$ <> "STOP"
        PARA$ = PARA$ + SP$ + L$
        INPUT "Type in another line"; L$
    NEXT
120 PRINT "Enter the two strings that you want to switch, separated"
130 PRINT "by a comma.  Please enter these strings in the order they"
140 PRINT "occur in the text"
150 INPUT S1$, S2$
160 P1 = POS(PARA$, S1$, 1)
170 P2 = POS(PARA$, S2$, 1)
180 L1 = LEN(S1$)   \ L2 = LEN(S2$)
190 L3 = LEN(PARA$)
200 PARA$ = SEG$(PARA$, 1, P2 - 1) + S1$ + SEG$(PARA$, P2 + L2, L3)
210 PARA$ = SEG$(PARA$, 1, P1 - 1) + S2$ + SEG$(PARA$, P1 + L1,
    LEN(PARA$))
220 !
230 PRINT PARA$
240 END
```

Exercises B

2.
```
100    REM --  Create a business memo
110    A$ = "'" + STRING$(79, 67)   ! ASCII 67 is C
120    PRINT "TO:  President Jones"
130    PRINT
140    PRINT "FROM:   Allison Dalton"\ PRINT
150    PRINT "DATE:   "; DATE$(0)
170    PRINT "TIME:   "; TIME$(0)
180    PRINT
190    PRINT USING A$, "SUBJECT: Purchase of new store"
200    PRINT \ PRINT \ PRINT
210    PRINT USING A$, "Contents of memo"
220 END
```

4.
```
100 REM --  Determine whether input string is a palindrome.
110 DIM LETTER$(100)
120 PRINT \ LINPUT "Type a line"; LINE$
```

```
130 LINE$ = EDIT$(LINE$, 2)
140 LINE$ = EDIT$(LINE$, 32)
150 !
160 LENGTH = LEN(LINE$)
170 NEWLINE$ = ""
180 FOR I = 1 TO LENGTH
        LETTER$(I) = SEG$(LINE$, I, I)
        IF ASCII(LETTER$(I)) < 65 OR ASCII(LETTER$(I)) > 122 THEN
           LETTER$(I) = ""
        END IF
        NEWLINE$ = NEWLINE$ + LETTER$(I)
    NEXT I
190 !
200 NEWLINE2$ = ""
210 LENGTH = LEN(NEWLINE$)
220 FOR I = 1 TO LENGTH
        LETTER$(I) = SEG$(NEWLINE$, I, I)
        LETTER2$ = SEG$(NEWLINE$, LENGTH - (I - 1), LENGTH - (I - 1))
        IF LETTER$(I) = LETTER2$ THEN
           NEWLINE2$ = NEWLINE2$ + LETTER$(I)
        END IF
    NEXT I
230 PRINT
240 IF NEWLINE2$ = NEWLINE$ THEN
        PRINT "This is a palindrome"
    ELSE
        PRINT "This is not a palindrome"
    END IF
250 PRINT
260 END
```

```
6. 100 REM --  Find longest word in five lines
   110 DIM WL(100)     ! Stores the length of each word
   120 PRINT "Type in 5 lines of text (one line for each question mark)."
   130 PRINT "I'll type out the longest word in the text"
   140 INPUT L$(I) FOR I = 1 TO 5
   150 !
   160 I = 1
   170 FOR LI = 1 TO 5            ! LI is the line number
   180    L = LEN(L$(LI)) \ L$ = L$(LI)
   190    FOR J = 1 TO L
   200        C$ = SEG$(L$, J, J)
   210        IF C$ <> " " AND C$ <> "," AND C$ <> "." AND C$ <> "?" THEN
                 WL(I) = WL(I) + 1 \ W$ = W$ + C$
              ELSE
                 I = I + 1
                 GO TO 240
              END IF
   220        IF J = L THEN
                 I = I + 1
                 ELSE 260
```

```
230        ! LWL is longest word length.  LW$ stores the longest word.
240        IF WL(I - 1) > LWL THEN
              LWL = WL(I - 1)
              LW$ = W$
           END IF
250        W$ = ""
260    NEXT J
270 NEXT LI
280 PRINT "The longest word is "; LW$
290 END
```

Exercises C

2.
```
100 REM --  Create a business memo
110 A$ = "'" + STRING$(79, 67)   ! ASCII 67 is C
120   PRINT "TO:  President Jones"
130   PRINT
140   PRINT "FROM:   Allison Dalton" \ PRINT
150   PRINT USING A$, "SUBJECT: Purchase of new store"
160   PRINT \ PRINT \ PRINT
170   PRINT USING A$, "Contents of memo"
180 END
```

4.
```
100 REM --  Use of PRINT USING to align columns
110 FOR I = 1 TO 4
        READ N$, ACTN, AMT, STAT$
        PRINT USING "Name: 'LLLLLLLLLL   Account: #####"; N$, ACTN
        PRINT USING "Amount: $$###.##-   STATUS: 'RRRRRR"; AMT, STAT$
120 NEXT I
130 !
140 DATA "Smith, John",  13654, 1335.32, DUE
150 DATA "Jones, Betty", 63581, -321.05, OVERDUE
160 DATA "Dickey, Jack", 89765, 1987.36, PAID
170 DATA "Abbott, Mary", 24689,  785.63, DUE
200 END
```

6.
```
100 REM --  Generate a receipt
110 A$ = "'" + STRING$(79, 67) ! ASCII 67 is C
120 PRINT USING A$; "PEANUT BUTTER AND BANANAS"
130 PRINT USING A$; "123 MARKET STREET"
140 PRINT USING A$; "TOWN, VA. 01234"
150 PRINT \ PRINT
160 PRINT TAB(42); "DEC. 8, 1987"
170 PRINT \ PRINT
180 TP = 0
190 B$ = SPACE$(20) + "'LLLLLLLLLLLLLLL" + SPACE$(10) + "$$###.##"
200 FOR I = 1 TO 6
        READ ITEM$, PR
        TP = TP + PR
        PRINT USING B$; ITEM$, PR
220 NEXT I
```

```
230 PRINT SPACE$(20)+STRING$(34, ASCII("_"))
240 PRINT USING SPACE$(46) + "$$###.##"; TP
250 PRINT USING B$; "TAX", .04 * TP
260 DATA 1 SHIRT, 25, 2 BLOUSES, 12.5, " ", 17.5
270 DATA 1 JACKET, 45, 1 PURSE, 18, 3 PAIR OF SOCKS, 8
280 FC = TP + .04 * TP
290 PRINT USING B$; "TOTAL COST", FC
300 END
```

CHAPTER 11

Exercises A

```
2. 100 PRINT "Program to create an inventory file" \ PRINT
   110 MAP (INVEN) INV.NO, DESC$ = 20%, PR, N.ON.HAND, N.ON.ORD
   120 OPEN "INVENTORY.DAT" AS FILE #1%,    &
           ORGANIZATION SEQUENTIAL,         &
           MAP INVEN
   130 !
   140 PRINT "If you make a typing error, type 'NO' after 'OK?'"
   150 PRINT "To stop, type '0' after the inventory number"
   160 ANS$ = "NO"
   170 INPUT "Inventory number"; INV.NO
   180 WHILE ANS$ = "NO"
   190 WHILE INV.NO <> 0
   200    INPUT "Description"; DESC$
   210    INPUT "Price"; PR
   220    INPUT "Number on hand"; N.ON.HAND
   230    INPUT "Number on order"; N.ON.ORD
   240    INPUT "OK"; ANS$
   250    IF ANS$ = "NO" THEN
              PRINT "Reenter information"
           ELSE
              PUT #1%
   260    INPUT "Inventory number"; INV.NO
   270 NEXT
   280 NEXT
   290 !
   300 PUT #1%
   310 CLOSE #1%
   320 END
```

Exercises B

```
2. 100 REM -- Program to read student data and compute class averages
   110 ON ERROR GO TO 19000
   120 MAP (STU) NAME$ = 20%, CL, AVER, MAJOR$
   130 OPEN "STUDENT.DAT" AS FILE #1%,     &
           ORGANIZATION SEQUENTIAL,        &
           MAP STU
```

```
140 !
150 READ CLASS$(I) FOR I = 1 TO 4
160 DATA Freshman, Sophomore, Junior, Senior
170 GET #1%
180 WHILE NAME$ <> "DONE"
190    PRINT NAME$; TAB(25); CLASS$(CL); TAB(35); AVER; TAB(45); MAJOR$
200    NO(CL) = NO(CL) + 1
210    TOT(CL) = TOT(CL) + AVER
220    GET #1%
230 NEXT
240 !
250 FOR CL = 1 TO 4
260    IF NO(CL) <> 0 THEN AVER(CL) = TOT(CL) / NO(CL)
270 NEXT CL
280 !
290 PRINT \ PRINT TAB(20); "Class averages" \ PRINT
300 PRINT TAB(9); "Freshman"; TAB(19);"Sophomore"; TAB(29);"Junior";
    PRINT TAB(39); "Senior"
    PRINT
310 PRINT TAB(10*CL); AVER(CL); FOR CL = 1 TO 4
320 CLOSE #1%
330 GO TO 20000
340 !
19000 IF ERR = 11 THEN RESUME 240 ELSE ON ERROR GO TO 0
20000 END
```

4.
```
100 REM --  Find and delete a record from STUDENTS.DAT.
              Create new file, NEWSTUD.DAT, and copy all
              but the deleted record into it.
110 MAP(GRADE) NAME$ = 20%, CL, AVER, MAJOR$
120 OPEN "STUDENT.DAT" AS FILE #1,                    &
            ORGANIZATION SEQUENTIAL,                  &
            MAP GRADE
130 OPEN "NEWSTUD.DAT" AS FILE #5%,                   &
            ORGANIZATION SEQUENTIAL,                  &
            MAP GRADE
140 PRINT "This program will allow you to find and"
    PRINT "delete a record from the file STUDENT.DAT."
    PRINT
    INPUT "What is the student name of the record to be deleted"; ASKN$
    PRINT
150 FLAG = 0
160 GET #1%
170 WHILE NAME$ <> "DONE" AND NAME$ <> ASKN$
        PUT #5%
        GET #1%
    NEXT
180 !
190 IF NAME$ = "DONE" THEN
        PRINT "That name is not in the file"
```

```
        ELSE
          PRINT "Record deleted."
          WHILE NAME$ <> "DONE"
             GET #1%
             PUT #5%
          NEXT
        END IF
200 PRINT "Finished"
210 CLOSE #1%
220 CLOSE #5%
230 END
```

Exercises C

```
2. 100 REM --  Update INVENTORY.DAT file
   110 MAP (INVEN) INV.NO, DESC$=20%, PR, N.ON.HAND, N.ON.ORD
   120 OPEN "INVENTORY.DAT" AS FILE #1%,        &
            ORGANIZATION SEQUENTIAL,            &
            ACCESS MODIFY,                      &
            MAP INVEN
   130 !
   140 PRINT "To stop, type 'QUIT' when asked if you want to update."
       PRINT
   150 GET #1%
   160 WHILE INV.NO <> 0
   170     PRINT "Inv No", "Description"; TAB(36); "Price";
           PRINT TAB(48); "No. on hand"; TAB(63); "No. on order"
   180     PRINT
   190     PRINT INV.NO, DESC$; TAB(35); "$"; PR; TAB(50); N.ON.HAND;
           PRINT TAB(66); N.ON.ORD
   200     A$ = " "
   210     WHILE A$ <> "Y" AND A$ <> "N" AND A$ <> "Q"
              PRINT
   220        INPUT "Would you like to update this information"; ANS$
   230        A$ = SEG$(ANS$, 1, 1)
   240        IF A$ = "Q" THEN 480
              ELSE IF A$ <> "Y" AND A$ <> "N" THEN
                 PRINT "Please type YES, NO, or QUIT"
   250     NEXT
   260     WHILE A$ = "Y"
   270        PRINT \ PRINT "Select a column to update"
   280        PRINT \ PRINT TAB(10); "Price  (type P)"
   290        PRINT TAB(10); "Number on order  (type N)"
   300        !
   310        X$ = "X"
   320        WHILE X$ <> "P" AND X$ <> "N" AND INV.NO <> 0
   330           INPUT X$
   340           IF X$ = "P" THEN
                    PRINT \ INPUT "Price"; PR
```

```
                ELSE IF X$ = "N" THEN
                   PRINT \ INPUT "Number on order"; N.ON.ORD
                ELSE
                   PRINT "Answer P or N"
350       NEXT
360       !
370       A$ = " "
380       WHILE A$ <> "Y" AND A$ <> "N" AND INV.NO <> 0
                PRINT
390             INPUT "Do you want to update another column"; ANS$
400             A$ = SEG$(ANS$, 1, 1)
410             IF A$ <> "N" AND A$ <> "Y" THEN
                     PRINT "Answer YES or NO"
                END IF
420       NEXT
430    NEXT
440    UPDATE #1%
450    GET #1%
460    NEXT
470 PRINT \ PRINT "End of inventory" \ PRINT
480 !
490 CLOSE #1%
500 END
```

Exercises D

```
2. 100 REM --  Create relative charge account file
   110 MAP (CRGACT) ACCT.NO, CUR.CHG, CRG.LIM
   120 OPEN  "BANK.DAT" AS FILE #1%,        &
            ORGANIZATION RELATIVE,         &
            MAP CRGACT
   130 !
   140 PRINT "To end the program, type 0 for the account number"
   150 PRINT "For each account enter the account number, the current"
   160 PRINT "amount charged and the charge limit."
   170 !
   180 PRINT \ INPUT "Charge account number"; ACCT.NO
   190 WHILE ACCT.NO <> 0
   200    INPUT "Current amount charged"; CUR.CHG
   210    INPUT "Charge limit"; CRG.LIM
   220    A$ = "0"
   230    WHILE A$ <> "Y" AND A$ <> "N"
   240         INPUT "Is all information OK"; A$
   250         A$ = SEG$(A$, 1, 1)
   260         IF A$ = "N" THEN
                    PRINT "Reenter information:" \ PRINT
                ELSE IF A$ = "Y" THEN
                   PUT #1%, RECORD ACCT.NO
                ELSE IF A$ <> "Y" THEN
                   PRINT "Type YES or NO"
```

```
270    NEXT
280    PRINT
290    INPUT "Charge account number"; ACCT.NO
300 NEXT
310 !
320 CLOSE #1%
330 END
```

4.
```
100 REM --  Add a record to file BANK.DAT. Use error handler if
              record already exists.
110 ON ERROR GO TO 900
120 MAP (CRGACT) ACCT.NO, CUR.CHG, CRG.LIM
130 OPEN "BANK.DAT" AS FILE #1%,                &
    ORGANIZATION RELATIVE,                      &
    MAP CRGACT
140 !
150 PRINT "This program will allow you to add a new record to"
160 PRINT "the file BANK.DAT. Enter the information as requested."
170 PRINT
180 INPUT "Account number"; ACCT.NO
190 INPUT "Amount charged"; CUR.CHG
200 INPUT "Charge limit  "; CRG.LIM
210 INPUT "What record number"; R%
220 PUT #1%, RECORD R%
230 PRINT
240 PRINT "The record has been added."
250 PRINT
260 GO TO 950
900 !!!!!!!!!!!!!!!!!!!!!!!!!!!!!!!!!!!!!!!!!!!!!!!!!!!!!!!!!!!!!!!!!!!!!!!!
910 !          Error handler; ERR is 153 for duplicate record          !
920 !!!!!!!!!!!!!!!!!!!!!!!!!!!!!!!!!!!!!!!!!!!!!!!!!!!!!!!!!!!!!!!!!!!!!!!!
930 IF ERR = 153 THEN
        PRINT
        PRINT "That record already exists."
        INPUT "Would you like to add another record"; ANS$
        A$ = SEG$(ANS$, 1, 1)
           IF A$ = "Y" THEN
             RESUME 170
           ELSE
             RESUME 950
           END IF
     ELSE
        ON ERROR GO TO 0
     END IF
950 CLOSE #1
999 END
```

CHAPTER 12

Exercises A

2.
```
100 REM --  Open the file BOOK.DAT, ask the user which key to use,
              ask for the desired key value. Print corresponding
              record or inform user if record does not exist.
110 ON ERROR GO TO 900
120 GOSUB 300          ! Define records and open file
130 GOSUB 400          ! Print instructions
140 GOSUB 500          ! Get key choice, ask for value, print record
150 CLOSE #1
160 GO TO 999
300 !!!!!!!!!!!!!!!!!!!!!!!!!!!!!!!!!!!!!!!!!!!!!!!!!!!!!!!!!!!!!!!!!!!!
310 ! Subroutine; Define records and open file
320 MAP (BOOKS) TITLE$ = 25%, AUTHORLAST$ = 20%,          &
                AUTHORFIRST$ = 10%, YEAR$ = 4%
330 OPEN "BOOK.DAT" AS FILE #1,                           &
            ORGANIZATION INDEXED FIXED,                   &
            MAP BOOKS, PRIMARY KEY TITLE$,                &
            ALTERNATE KEY AUTHORLAST$  DUPLICATES,        &
            ALTERNATE KEY YEAR$  DUPLICATES
340 RETURN
400 !!!!!!!!!!!!!!!!!!!!!!!!!!!!!!!!!!!!!!!!!!!!!!!!!!!!!!!!!!!!!!!!!!!!
410 ! Subroutine; Print instructions
420 PRINT
    PRINT "This program will allow you to access a record from"
    PRINT "the data file BOOK.DAT using any of the three possible"
    PRINT "keys. It will then print out the specified record."
    PRINT
430 RETURN
500 !!!!!!!!!!!!!!!!!!!!!!!!!!!!!!!!!!!!!!!!!!!!!!!!!!!!!!!!!!!!!!!!!!!!
510 ! Subroutine; Get key choice, ask for value, print record
520 ANS$ = "Y"
530 WHILE ANS$ = "Y"
        PRINT "Which key would you like to use for the file BOOK.DAT ?"
        PRINT
        PRINT "1. Book title"
        PRINT "2. Author's last name"
        PRINT "3. Year of publication"
        PRINT
        INPUT "Please choose 1, 2 or 3"; CHOICE%

540     IF CHOICE% = 1% THEN
            PRINT
            INPUT "Enter title"; ASKTITLE$
            GET #1, KEY #0 EQ ASKTITLE$
```

```
           ELSE IF CHOICE% = 2% THEN
               PRINT
               INPUT "Enter author's last name"; ASKAUTHORLAST$
               GET #1, KEY #1 EQ ASKAUTHORLAST$

           ELSE IF CHOICE% = 3% THEN
               PRINT
               INPUT "Enter year"; ASKYEAR$
               GET #1, KEY #2 EQ ASKYEAR$

           END IF

550        PRINT
           PRINT TAB(5); "Title"; TAB(25); "Author"; TAB(55); "Year"
           PRINT STRING$(60%, 45%)
           PRINT TITLE$; TRM$(AUTHORLAST$); ", ";
           PRINT AUTHORFIRST$; TAB(55); YEAR$

560        PRINT
           INPUT "Would you like to run this program again"; ANS$
           ANS$ = SEG$(ANS$, 1, 1)
           PRINT

570 NEXT
580 RETURN
900 !!!!!!!!!!!!!!!!!!!!!!!!!!!!!!!!!!!!!!!!!!!!!!!!!!!!!!!!!!!!!!!!!!!!
910 !   Error handler - ERR number for nonexistent record is 155  !
920 !!!!!!!!!!!!!!!!!!!!!!!!!!!!!!!!!!!!!!!!!!!!!!!!!!!!!!!!!!!!!!!!!!!!
930 IF ERR = 155% THEN
        PRINT "There is no such record."
        RESUME 560
    ELSE
        ON ERROR GO TO 0
    END IF
999 END

4. 100 REM --  Read the file BOOK.DAT and ask the user for a record
                to delete. Print the record, verify and delete record.
   110 ON ERROR GO TO 900
   120 GOSUB 300      ! Define records and open file
   130 GOSUB 400      ! Print instructions
   140 GOSUB 500      ! Main loop
   150 CLOSE #1
   160 GO TO 999
   300 !!!!!!!!!!!!!!!!!!!!!!!!!!!!!!!!!!!!!!!!!!!!!!!!!!!!!!!!!!!!!!!!!!
   310 ! Subroutine; define records and open file
   320 MAP (BOOKS) TITLE$ = 25%, AUTHORLAST$ = 20%,            &
                   AUTHORFIRST$ = 10%, YEAR$ = 4%
```

```
330 OPEN 'BOOK.DAT' AS FILE #1,                            &
        ORGANIZATION INDEXED FIXED,                        &
        MAP BOOKS, PRIMARY KEY TITLE$,                     &
        ALTERNATE KEY AUTHORLAST$  DUPLICATES,             &
        ALTERNATE KEY YEAR$  DUPLICATES
340 RETURN
400 !!!!!!!!!!!!!!!!!!!!!!!!!!!!!!!!!!!!!!!!!!!!!!!!!!!!!!!!!!!!!!!!!!!
410 ! Subroutine; Print instructions
420 PRINT
    PRINT "This program will read the data file BOOK.DAT and will ask"
    PRINT "you for a record to delete. After verification, it will then"
    PRINT "delete the record."
    PRINT
430 RETURN
500 !!!!!!!!!!!!!!!!!!!!!!!!!!!!!!!!!!!!!!!!!!!!!!!!!!!!!!!!!!!!!!!!!!!
510 ! Subroutine; Main loop - continue until user enters NO        !
520 !!!!!!!!!!!!!!!!!!!!!!!!!!!!!!!!!!!!!!!!!!!!!!!!!!!!!!!!!!!!!!!!!!!
530 ANS$ = "Y"
540 WHILE ANS$ = "Y"
        PRINT "Enter the title of the book for the record you would "
        INPUT "like to delete"; ASKTITLE$
        GET #1, KEY #0 EQ ASKTITLE$

        PRINT
        PRINT TAB(5); "Title"; TAB(25); "Author"; TAB(55); "Year"
        PRINT STRING$(60%, 45%)
        PRINT TITLE$; TRM$(AUTHORLAST$); ", "; AUTHORFIRST$;
        PRINT TAB(55); YEAR$
        PRINT

        INPUT "Is this the record you wish to delete"; A$
        A$ = SEG$(A$, 1, 1)
        IF A$ = "Y" OR A$ = "y" THEN
           DELETE #1
           PRINT "That record has been deleted."
           PRINT

550     INPUT "Would you like to delete another record"; ANS$
        ANS$ = SEG$(ANS$, 1, 1)
        PRINT
    NEXT
560 RETURN
900 !!!!!!!!!!!!!!!!!!!!!!!!!!!!!!!!!!!!!!!!!!!!!!!!!!!!!!!!!!!!!!!!!!!!!
910 ! Error handler - check for nonexistent record              !
920 !!!!!!!!!!!!!!!!!!!!!!!!!!!!!!!!!!!!!!!!!!!!!!!!!!!!!!!!!!!!!!!!!!!!!
930 IF ERR = 155% THEN
        PRINT
        PRINT "There is no such record."
        PRINT
        RESUME 550
```

```
          ELSE
             ON ERROR GO TO 0
     999 END

  6. 100 REM --  Read indexed file PERSONNEL.DAT and sequential file
                 WEEKLY.DAT. Match records from WEEKLY.DAT to records
                 of PERSONNEL.DAT, calculate payroll data for each
                 employee.
     110 ON ERROR GO TO 900
     120 MAP (EMPLOY) NAME$ = 20%, SSN$ = 11%, RATE, BCSTAT$ = 6
     130 OPEN 'PERSONNEL.DAT' AS FILE #1,                        &
             ORGANIZATION INDEXED FIXED,                         &
             MAP EMPLOY, PRIMARY KEY SSN$
     140 MAP (TRANS) SSNUM$ = 11%, HOURS%
     150 OPEN 'WEEKLY.DAT' AS FILE #2,                           &
             ORGANIZATION SEQUENTIAL,                            &
             MAP TRANS
     160 GOSUB 300      ! Read sequential file, match records
     170 GOSUB 400      ! Calculate payroll data, print
     180 CLOSE #1
     190 CLOSE #2
     200 GO TO 999
     300 !!!!!!!!!!!!!!!!!!!!!!!!!!!!!!!!!!!!!!!!!!!!!!!!!!!!!!!!!!!!!!!!!!!
     310 !      Subroutine; read sequential file, match records        !
     320 WHILE 1%
             GET #2
             GET #1, KEY #0 EQ SSNUM$
             WEEKHOURS% = HOURS%
             DELETE #1
             PUT #1
     330 NEXT
     340 RETURN
     400 !!!!!!!!!!!!!!!!!!!!!!!!!!!!!!!!!!!!!!!!!!!!!!!!!!!!!!!!!!!!!!!!!!!
     410 !      Subroutine; Calculate payroll data                     !
     420 PRINT ; "Employee"; TAB(21); "Gross"; TAB(32); "Federal";
         PRINT TAB(40); " Social"; TAB(49); "State"; TAB(56); "Blue";
         PRINT TAB(66); "Net"

         PRINT ; " Name  "; TAB(21); " Pay "; TAB(32); " Tax  ";
         PRINT TAB(40); "Security"; TAB(49); " Tax "; TAB(56); "Cross";
         PRINT TAB(66); "Pay"

         PRINT STRING$(71%, 45%)

         RESTORE #1
     430 WHILE 1%
             GET #1
             GROSS = WEEKHOURS% * RATE

             IF GROSS < 150 THEN
                 FEDTAX = 0
```

```
            ELSE IF GROSS < 250 THEN
                FEDTAX = GROSS * 0.07
            ELSE IF GROSS < 300 THEN
                FEDTAX = GROSS * 0.11
            ELSE IF GROSS < 350 THEN
                FEDTAX = GROSS * 0.15
            ELSE IF GROSS < 400 THEN
                FEDTAX = GROSS * 0.18
            ELSE IF GROSS < 450 THEN
                FEDTAX = GROSS * 0.21
            ELSE IF GROSS < 500 THEN
                FEDTAX = GROSS * 0.24
            ELSE
                FEDTAX = GROSS * 0.27
            END IF

  440     SOCSEC = GROSS * 0.175

  450     IF GROSS < 150 THEN STATETAX = 0
          ELSE IF GROSS >= 150 AND GROSS < 300 THEN
              STATETAX = GROSS * 0.02
          ELSE IF GROSS >= 300 THEN
              STATETAX = GROSS * 0.04
          END IF

  460     IF BCSTAT$ = "FAMILY" THEN BC = 37.5
          ELSE IF BCSTAT$ = "SINGLE" THEN BC = 13.5
          ELSE BC = 0
          END IF

  470     NET = GROSS - FEDTAX - STATETAX - BC - SOCSEC

  480     PRINT NAMES$; TAB(19);
          PRINT USING "####.##"; GROSS;
          PRINT TAB(32);
          PRINT USING "##.##"; FEDTAX;
          PRINT TAB(41);
          PRINT USING "##.##"; SOCSEC;
          PRINT TAB(49);
          PRINT USING "##.##"; STATETAX;
          PRINT TAB(56);
          PRINT USING "##.##"; BC;
          PRINT TAB(65);
          PRINT USING "###.##"; NET

      NEXT
  490 PRINT
  500 RETURN
  900 !!!!!!!!!!!!!!!!!!!!!!!!!!!!!!!!!!!!!!!!!!!!!!!!!!!!!!!!!!!!!!!!!!!!!!!!!!!!
  910 ! Error handler - end-of-file error or nonexistent record      !
```

```
920 !!!!!!!!!!!!!!!!!!!!!!!!!!!!!!!!!!!!!!!!!!!!!!!!!!!!!!!!!!!!!!!!!!!!!!!!!
930 IF ERR = 11% AND ERL = 320% THEN
        RESUME 170
     ELSE IF ERR = 11% AND ERL = 430% THEN
        RESUME 180
     ELSE IF ERR = 155% THEN
        RESUME 320
     ELSE
        ON ERROR GO TO 0
     END IF
999 END
```

CHAPTER 13

Exercises

2.
```
100 REM --  Read size of matrix and values;  Find largest entry
110 DIM A(10, 10)
120 READ R, C
130 MAT READ A(R, C)
140 L = A(1, 1)
150 !
160 FOR I = 1 TO R
170     FOR J = 1 TO C
180         IF L < A(I, J) THEN L = A(I, J)
190     NEXT J
200 NEXT I
210 MAT PRINT A,
220 PRINT "The largest element in the matrix is "; L
230 !
240 DATA 3, 5
250 DATA 1, -2, 3, -4, 5, 2, 4, 6, 8, 20, 3, 6, 9, 12, 15
260 END
```

4.
```
100 REM --  Find total value of shirt inventory
110 DIM SHIRT(4, 3), PRICE(1, 4)
120 MAT READ SHIRT
130 MAT READ PRICE
140 MAT VALU = PRICE * SHIRT
150 SUM = 0
160 ROW = 1
170 !
180 FOR COL = 1 TO 3
190     SUM = SUM + VALU(ROW, COL)
200 NEXT COL
210 PRINT "Total value of inventory is $"; SUM
220 !
230 DATA 22, 12, 18,  28, 17, 19,  24, 14, 20,  12, 10, 13
240 DATA 10, 10.5, 11, 11.5
250 END
```

```
6. 100 DIM B$(3, 3)
   110 CW, PW, T = 0
   120 REM --  Tic-Tac-Toe game
   125 A$ = "YES"
   126 WHILE A$ = "YES"
   130 WINNER$ = " "
   140 !
   150 MAT READ B$
   160 DATA "(1,1)", "(1,2)", "(1,3)", "(2,1)", "(2,2)", "(2,3)"
   170 DATA "(3,1)", "(3,2)", "(3,3)"
   170 GOSUB 790
   180 !
   190  FOR R = 1 TO 3   ! Loop to clear board
   200       FOR C = 1 TO 3
   210            B$(R, C) = " "
   220       NEXT C
   230 NEXT R
   240 MOVE$ = "PLAYER"
   250 GOSUB 790
   255 WHILE WINNER$ = " "
   260 !
   270 !  Start subroutine - player
   280       INPUT "Give me 2 numbers between 1 and 3 (ROW, COL)"; R, C
   290       WHILE R < 1 OR R > 3 OR C < 1 OR C > 3
                 PRINT "Try again!"
                 INPUT "Give me 2 numbers between 1 and 3 (ROW, COL)"; R, C
   300       NEXT
   310 !
   320      WHILE B$(R, C) <> " "
                 PRINT "That square is taken"
                 INPUT "Give me 2 numbers between 1 and 3 (ROW, COL)"; R, C
   330      NEXT
   340 !
   350      B$(R, C) = " X"
   360 GOSUB 790
   370 GOSUB 740
   380 GOSUB 570
   390 !
   400 !  Start subroutine - computer
   410 MV$ = " O"
   420 GOSUB 680
   430 IF R > 0 THEN GO TO 490
   440 MV$ = " X"
   450 GOSUB 680
   460 IF R > 0 THEN GO TO 490
   470 !
   480 R = INT(RND * 3) + 1 \ C = INT(RND * 3) + 1
   490 IF B$(R, C) <> " " THEN GO TO 480
   500 B$(R, C) = " O"
   510 GOSUB 790
   520 GOSUB 740
```

```
530 GOSUB 570
540 !
550 MOVE$ = "PLAYER"
555 NEXT
560 !
570            ! Check for tie game
575 CNT = 0
580 FOR R = 1 TO 3
590    FOR C = 1 TO 3
600       IF B$(R, C) <> " " THEN CNT = CNT + 1
610    NEXT C
620 NEXT R
630 !
640 IF CNT = 9 THEN PRINT "Tie game"\ WINNER$ = "NOBODY"\ T = T + 1\ GO TO 930
650 RETURN
660 !
670            ! Look for next play
680 R = 0 \ C = 0
690       IF B$(1, 1) + B$(1, 2) = MV$ + MV$ THEN R = 1\ C = 3
    ELSE IF B$(1, 2) + B$(1, 3) = MV$ + MV$ THEN R = 1\ C = 1
    ELSE IF B$(1, 1) + B$(1, 3) = MV$ + MV$ THEN R = 1\ C = 2
    ELSE IF B$(2, 1) + B$(2, 2) = MV$ + MV$ THEN R = 2\ C = 3
    ELSE IF B$(2, 2) + B$(2, 3) = MV$ + MV$ THEN R = 2\ C = 1
    ELSE IF B$(2, 1) + B$(2, 3) = MV$ + MV$ THEN R = 2\ C = 2
    ELSE IF B$(3, 1) + B$(3, 2) = MV$ + MV$ THEN R = 3\ C = 3
    ELSE IF B$(3, 2) + B$(3, 3) = MV$ + MV$ THEN R = 3\ C = 1
    ELSE IF B$(3, 1) + B$(3, 3) = MV$ + MV$ THEN R = 3\ C = 2
    ELSE IF B$(1, 1) + B$(2, 1) = MV$ + MV$ THEN R = 3\ C = 1
    ELSE IF B$(1, 1) + B$(3, 1) = MV$ + MV$ THEN R = 2\ C = 1
    ELSE IF B$(2, 1) + B$(3, 1) = MV$ + MV$ THEN R = 1\ C = 1
    ELSE IF B$(1, 2) + B$(2, 2) = MV$ + MV$ THEN R = 3\ C = 2
    ELSE IF B$(1, 2) + B$(3, 2) = MV$ + MV$ THEN R = 2\ C = 2
    ELSE IF B$(2, 2) + B$(3, 2) = MV$ + MV$ THEN R = 1\ C = 2
    ELSE IF B$(1, 3) + B$(2, 3) = MV$ + MV$ THEN R = 3\ C = 3
    ELSE IF B$(1, 3) + B$(3, 3) = MV$ + MV$ THEN R = 2\ C = 3
    ELSE IF B$(2, 3) + B$(3, 3) = MV$ + MV$ THEN R = 1\ C = 3
    ELSE IF B$(1, 1) + B$(2, 2) = MV$ + MV$ THEN R = 3\ C = 3
    ELSE IF B$(1, 1) + B$(3, 3) = MV$ + MV$ THEN R = 2\ C = 2
    ELSE IF B$(2, 2) + B$(3, 3) = MV$ + MV$ THEN R = 1\ C = 1
    ELSE IF B$(1, 3) + B$(2, 2) = MV$ + MV$ THEN R = 3\ C = 1
    ELSE IF B$(1, 3) + B$(3, 1) = MV$ + MV$ THEN R = 2\ C = 2
    ELSE IF B$(2, 2) + B$(3, 1) = MV$ + MV$ THEN R = 1\ C = 3

    END IF
700 !
710 RETURN
720 !
730            ! Check for victory
740 IF B$(1, 1) + B$(1, 2) + B$(1, 3) = " X X X" OR &
       B$(2, 1) + B$(2, 2) + B$(2, 3) = " X X X" OR &
       B$(3, 1) + B$(3, 2) + B$(3, 3) = " X X X" OR &
```

```
            B$(1, 1) + B$(2, 1) + B$(3, 1) = " X X X" OR &
            B$(1, 2) + B$(2, 2) + B$(3, 2) = " X X X" OR &
            B$(1, 3) + B$(2, 3) + B$(3, 3) = " X X X" OR &
            B$(1, 1) + B$(2, 2) + B$(3, 3) = " X X X" OR &
            B$(1, 3) + B$(2, 2) + B$(3, 1) = " X X X" THEN
                WINNER$ = "PLAYER" \ PW = PW + 1

        ELSE IF                                      &
            B$(1, 3) + B$(2, 2) + B$(3, 1) = " 0 0 0" OR &
            B$(1, 1) + B$(1, 2) + B$(1, 3) = " 0 0 0" OR &
            B$(2, 1) + B$(2, 2) + B$(2, 3) = " 0 0 0" OR &
            B$(3, 1) + B$(3, 2) + B$(3, 3) = " 0 0 0" OR &
            B$(1, 1) + B$(2, 1) + B$(3, 1) = " 0 0 0" OR &
            B$(1, 2) + B$(2, 2) + B$(3, 2) = " 0 0 0" OR &
            B$(1, 3) + B$(2, 3) + B$(3, 3) = " 0 0 0" OR &
            B$(1, 1) + B$(2, 2) + B$(3, 3) = " 0 0 0" THEN
                WINNER$ = "COMPUTER" \ CW = CW + 1
        END IF
750 IF WINNER$ = "PLAYER" THEN
        PRINT "You win!"
        GO TO 930
    ELSE IF WINNER$ = "COMPUTER" THEN
        PRINT "The computer wins"
        GO TO 930
    END IF
760 RETURN
770 !
780 !  Subroutine to print board
790 PRINT TAB(15); "*"; TAB(23); "*"
800 PRINT TAB (9); B$(1,1); TAB(15); "*"; TAB(17); B$(1,2);
    PRINT TAB(23); "*"; TAB(25); B$(1,3)
810 PRINT TAB(15); "*"; TAB(23); "*"
820 PRINT TAB(8); "***********************"
830 PRINT TAB(15); "*" ; TAB(23); "*"
840 PRINT TAB (9); B$(2,1); TAB(15); "*"; TAB(17); B$(2,2);
    PRINT TAB(23); "*"; TAB(25); B$(2,3)
850 PRINT TAB(15); "*"; TAB(23); "*"
860 PRINT TAB(8); "***********************"
870 PRINT TAB(15); "*" ; TAB(23); "*"
880 PRINT TAB(9); B$(3,1); TAB(15); "*"; TAB(17); B$(3,2);
    PRINT TAB(23); "*"; TAB(25); B$(3,3)
890 PRINT TAB(15); "*"; TAB(23); "*"
900 PRINT
910 RETURN
920 !
930 PRINT "SCORE:"
940 PRINT "Computer wins:"; CW, "Player wins:"; PW, "Ties:"; T
950 !
960 INPUT "Play again? (YES OR NO)"; A$
970 IF A$ = "YES" THEN RESTORE
975 NEXT
980 END
```

8.
```
100 REM --  Find determinant of 2x2 and 3x3 matrix
110 DIM A(2, 2), B(3, 3)
120 MAT READ A, B
130 !
140 DATA 2, 3, 4, 5, 6, 7, 1, 2, 3, 4, 5, 3, 2, 1
150 MAT PRINT A;
160 PRINT \ MAT PRINT B;
170 DETA = A(1, 1) * A(2, 2) - (A(2, 1) * A(1, 2))
180 PRINT
190 PRINT "DET A ="; DETA
200 !
210 D1 = B(1,1)*B(2,2)*B(3,3)+B(1,2)*B(2,3)*B(3,1)+B(1,3)*B(2,1)*B(3, 2)
220 D2 = B(3,1)*B(2,2)*B(1,3)+B(3,2)*B(2,3)*B(1,1)+B(3,3)*B(2,1)*B(1, 2)
230 DETB = D1 - D2
240 PRINT "DET B ="; DETB
250 END
```

10.
```
100 REM --  Matrix game
110 DIM M(10, 10)
120 READ ROW, COL
130 MAT READ M(ROW, COL)
140 !
150 FOR R = 1 TO ROW
160     LRGEL(R) = M(R, 1)
170     FOR C = 2 TO COL
180         IF M(R, C) > LRGEL(R) THEN LRGEL(R) = M(R, C)
190     NEXT C
200     PRINT "The largest number in row"; R; "is"; LRGEL(R)
210 NEXT R
220 SMMAX = LRGEL(1)
230 ROWNO = 1
240 !
250 FOR R = 2 TO ROW
260     IF LRGEL(R) < SMMAX THEN SMMAX = LRGEL(R) \ ROWNO = R
270 NEXT R
280 PRINT "Row"; ROWNO, "has the smallest maximum: "; SMMAX
290 !
300 DATA 4, 4
310 DATA 2, 3, 4, -8,   -5, -7, 10, 4,  6, -6, -2, 9,  5, 7, -2, 1
320 END
```

12.
```
100 REM --  Tabulate questionnaire
110 SEX$(1) = "MALE" \ SEX$(2) = "FEMALE"
120 DIM M(2, 3)
130 MAT M = ZER
140 PRINT TAB(10); "YES"; TAB(20); "NO"; TAB(30); "DON'T KNOW"
150 PRINT
160 !
170 FOR I = 1 TO 30
180     READ S, A              ! Sex, answer
190     M(S, A) = M(S, A) + 1
200 NEXT I
```

```
210 !
220 FOR R = 1 TO 2
230     PRINT SEX$(R); TAB(10);
240     FOR C = 1 TO 3
250         PRINT TAB(10 * C); M(R, C);
260     NEXT C
270     PRINT \ PRINT
280 NEXT R
290 !
300 DATA 2, 3, 2, 3, 2, 2, 2, 1, 1, 2, 1, 1, 1, 3, 1, 2, 1, 3, 2, 3, 2
310 DATA 1, 2, 3, 2, 2, 2, 2, 2, 1, 1, 2, 1, 2, 1, 1, 1, 1, 2, 1, 2, 1
320 DATA 2, 3, 2, 3, 2, 2, 2, 2, 2, 2, 2, 1, 1, 2, 1, 3, 1, 2
330 END
```

CHAPTER 14

Exercises A

2.
```
100 REM --  Select specified number of random numbers from selected range
110 RANDOMIZE
120 INPUT "How many numbers do you want to select"; N
130 INPUT "What are the lower and upper limits of the range"; LL, UL
140 !
150 DIM RANGE(500)
160 RANGE(I) = I FOR I = LL TO UL
170 !
180 FOR STP = 1 TO N
190     R = INT((UL - LL - STP + 1) * RND) + LL + STP
200     T = RANGE(R)
210     RANGE(R) = RANGE(STP + LL - 1)
220     RANGE(STP) = T
230 NEXT STP
240 !
250 PRINT "The"; N; "numbers are"
260 PRINT TAB(5 * (I - 1)); RANGE(I); FOR I = 1 TO N
270 END
```

4.
```
100 PRINT "Program to generate 50 random integers from 1 through 100 and"
110 PRINT "print them in increasing order"
120 !
130 RANDOMIZE
140 DIM N(100)
150 REM --  Lines 40 to 70 fill 50 elements of array N with a 1
160 !
170 FOR I = 1 TO 50
180         R = INT(100 * RND + 1)
190 !  If R has been previously generated, get a new R
200         IF N(R) = 0 THEN N(R) = 1 ELSE 180
210 NEXT I
```

```
220 !   Print the numbers in increasing order
230 FOR I = 1 TO 100
240        IF N(I) = 1 THEN PRINT I;
250 NEXT I
260 END
```

Exercises B

2.
```
100 REM --  Simulate tossing of 2 dice and record totals
110 DIM C(12)
120 RANDOMIZE
130 !
140 FOR I = 1 TO 1000
150    R1 = INT(6 * RND + 1)
160    R2 = INT(6 * RND + 1)
170    N = R1 + R2
180    PRINT TAB(4 * (I - 1)); N;
190    C(N) = C(N) + 1
200 NEXT I
210 !
220 PRINT \ PRINT "TOTAL", "OCCURRENCES"
230 PRINT N, C(N) FOR N = 2 TO 12
240 END
```

4.
```
100 REM --  Simulate a tennis game
110 INPUT "Enter two players"; PLAYER$(1), PLAYER$(2)
120 RANDOMIZE
130 WINNER$ = "NO"
140 !
150 IF RND < .5 THEN
       SERVER = 1
       RECEIVER = 2
     ELSE
       SERVER = 2
       RECEIVER = 1
     END IF
160 PRINT PLAYER$(SERVER); ", you serve" \ PRINT
170 WHILE WINNER$ = "NO"
180 !
190 IF RND < .55 THEN
       POINT = SERVER
     ELSE
       POINT = RECEIVER
     END IF
200 SCORE(POINT) = SCORE(POINT) + 1
210 IF SCORE(1) > SCORE(2) THEN
       LEADER = 1
       TRAILER = 2
     ELSE
       LEADER = 2
       TRAILER = 1
     END IF
```

```
220 !
230 IF SCORE(LEADER) >= 4 AND SCORE(LEADER) - SCORE(TRAILER) >= 2 THEN
        PRINT "Congratulations " ; PLAYER$(LEADER) ; " you won!"
        PRINT "Final score: "; SCORE(LEADER); "-"; SCORE(TRAILER)
        WINNER$ = PLAYER$(LEADER)
    ELSE IF SCORE(LEADER) = SCORE(TRAILER) THEN
        PRINT "The score is"; SCORE(LEADER); "all"
    ELSE IF SCORE(LEADER) >= 4 THEN
        PRINT "Advantage to "; PLAYER$(LEADER)
    ELSE
        PRINT PLAYER$(LEADER); " is ahead.  ";
        PRINT "The score is"; SCORE(LEADER); "-"; SCORE(TRAILER)
    END IF
240 PRINT
250 NEXT
260 !
270 PRINT \ PRINT
280 END
```

6.
```
100 REM -- Blackjack
110 DIM S$(17), CS$(52), D(15), P(15), V(52)
120 RANDOMIZE
130 !
140 READ S$(I) FOR I = 1 TO 17
150 DATA "Ace", "2", "3", "4", "5", "6", "7", "8", "9", "10", "Jack"
160 DATA "Queen", "King"
170 DATA " of spades", " of hearts", " of clubs", " of diamonds"
180 !
190 FOR I = 0 TO 51
200     C = INT(13 * RND + 1)      ! Denomination of card
210     S = INT(4 * RND + 14)      ! Suit
220     CS$(I) = S$(C) + S$(S)
230     FOR J = 1 TO I - 1
240         IF CS$(I) = CS$(J) THEN 200
250     NEXT J
260     IF C < 11 THEN
            V(I) = C
        ELSE
            V(I) = 10
270 NEXT I
280 !
290 SWP, SWD = 1   ! Switches = 1 if players are still drawing cards
300 P$(1) = CS$(1) \ D$(1) =CS$(2) \ P$(2) = CS$(3) \ D$(2) = CS$(4)
310 PV(1) = V(1) \ DV(1) = V(2) \ PV(2) = V(3) \ DV(2) = V(4)
320 !
330 DC, PC = 2     ! Number of cards dealt to dealer and player so far
340 PRINT "The dealer has a "; D$(2); " showing"
350 PRINT "Your cards are a "; P$(2);"  showing and a "; P$(1); " down"
360 IF DV(1) = 1 AND DV(2) = 10 OR DV(1) = 10 AND DV(2) = 1 THEN
        PRINT "BLACKJACK!!! The dealer has exactly 21!"
        PRINT "The dealer wins" \ PRINT
        GO TO 600
```

```
370 IF PV(1) = 1 AND PV(2) = 10 OR PV(1) = 10 AND PV(2) = 1 THEN
        PRINT "BLACKJACK!!! You have exactly 21! You win!" \ PRINT
        GO TO 600
380 WHILE SWD = 1 OR SWP = 1
390 WHILE A$ <> "H"
400 INPUT "Do you want to take another card or hold? (Type C OR H)"; A$
410 IF A$ = "C" THEN
        PC = PC + 1
        P$(PC) = CS$(PC + DC)
        PV(PC) = V(PC + DC)
        VPH = VPH + PV(PC)
        PRINT "Your next card is a "; CS$(PC + DC)
        IF VPH > 21 THEN
           PRINT "BUST!!! You went over 21! The dealer wins" \ PRINT
           GO TO 600
        END IF
    ELSE              ! Evaluate player's hand when he decides to hold
        SWP = 0       ! Indicates player wants to hold
        VPH = 0
        VPH = VPH + PV(I) FOR I = 1 TO PC
        CACE = 0      ! Counts aces in hand
        FOR I = 1 TO PC
           IF PV(I) = 1 THEN
           CACE = CACE + 1
           END IF
        NEXT I
        PRINT "The value of your hand is:";
           IF CACE = 0 THEN
              PRINT VPH
           ELSE
              PRINT VPH; " OR "; VPH + 10
              IF VPH + 10 < 22 THEN VPH = VPH + 10
           END IF
    END IF
420 !
430 NEXT
440 ! Dealer's turn
450 ! Evaluate dealer's hand
460 VDH, VDH1 = 0
470 !
480 VDH = VDH + DV(I) FOR I = 1 TO DC
490 !
500 CACE = 0
510 IF DV(I) = 1 THEN
        CACE = CACE + 1 FOR I = 1 TO DC
520 IF CACE <> 0 THEN VDH1 = VDH + 10
530 IF VDH > 15 OR VDH1 > 15 AND VDH1 < 22 THEN
        SWD = 0
        IF VDH1 > 15 AND VDH1 < 22 THEN
           VDH = VDH1
```

```
          END IF
          PRINT "The dealer will hold"
       ELSE
          PRINT "The dealer took another card"
          DC = DC + 1
          D$(DC) = CS$(DC + PC)
          DV(DC) = V(DC + PC)
          VDH = VDH + DV(DC)
          IF VDH > 21 THEN
             PRINT "BUST!!! The dealer went over 21. You win!" \ PRINT
             GO TO 600
          END IF
       END IF
540 NEXT
550 !
560 PRINT "Score:    Dealer:"; VDH, "Player:"; VPH
570 PRINT
580 IF VPH > VDH THEN
       PRINT "You win!"
    ELSE
       PRINT "The dealer has won"
590 PRINT
600 END
```

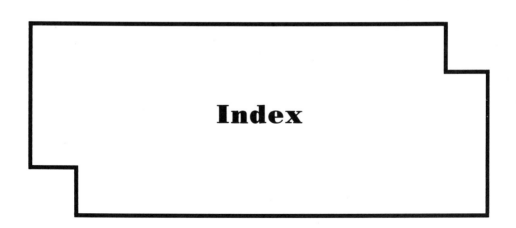

Index